EXPLORING RUSSIA'S PAST

NARRATIVE, SOURCES, IMAGES

VOLUME 1:

FROM PREHISTORY TO 1856

David G. Rowley

University of Wisconsin–Platteville

PEARSON

Prentice
Hall

Upper Saddle River, New Jersey 07458

Library of Congress Cataloging-in-Publication Data

Rowley, David G. (date)
   Exploring Russia's past : narrative, sources, images / David G. Rowley.— 1st ed.
      p. cm.
   ISBN 0-13-065363-2
   1. Russia--History. 2.   Kievan Rus--History. 3.   Soviet Union--History.
   4. Russia (Federation)—History.   I. Title.
   DK40.R678 2005
   947--dc22

                                                                2005005036

VP/Editorial Director: Charlyce Jones Owen
Executive Editor: Charles Cavaliere
Editorial Assistant: Shannon Corliss
Marketing Manager: Heather Shelstad
Marketing Assistant: Cherron Gardner
Production Liaison: Marianne Peters-Riordan
Manufacturing Buyer: Ben Smith
Art Director: Jayne Conte
Cover Design: Bruce Kenselaar
Cover Photo: Courtesy of the Library of Congress, Prints and Photographs Division,
"Parade of Tsarina's Meadow." Vsesoiuznyi Muzei A.S. Pushkina.
Director, Image Resource Center: Melinda Reo
Manager, Rights and Permissions: Zina Arabia
Manager, Visual Research: Beth Brenzel
Manager, Cover Visual Research & Permissions: Karen Sanatar
Image Permission Coordinator: Cynthia Vincenti
Composition/Full-Service Project Management: Mike Remillard/Pine Tree Composition, Inc.
Printer/Binder: Courier/Stoughton
Cover Printer: Phoenix Color Corp.

Pearson Education LTD
Pearson Education Singapore, Pte. Ltd
Pearson Education, Canada, Ltd
Pearson Education—Japan
Pearson Education Australia PTY, Limited

Pearson Education North Asia Ltd
Pearson Educación de Mexico, S.A. de C.V.
Pearson Education Malaysia, Pte. Ltd
Pearson Education, Upper Saddle River, New Jersey

10 9 8 7 6 5 4 3 2 1

ISBN 0-13-065363-2

**To my students,
past, present, and future**

CONTENTS

CHAPTER FIVE

THE RISE OF MOSCOW, 1360–1460

CHAPTER SIX

THE MAKING OF THE MUSCOVITE STATE, 1460–1560

CHAPTER SEVEN

THE COLLAPSE AND RECOVERY OF MUSCOVY, 1560–1620   127

CHAPTER EIGHT

MUSCOVITE IMPERIAL EXPANSION, 1620–1700   148

Chapter Eleven

Russia in the Age of Conservatism, 1815–1856

Appendix A: Timeline

Appendix B: Guide to Transliteration and Pronunciation of the Russian Alphabet

Appendix C: Dynastic Succession from Kiev Rus to the Russian Empire

Glossary

Index

PREFACE

Exploring Russia's Past is a comprehensive but concise survey of Russian history written for college and university undergraduates. Each chapter begins with a brief narrative presenting the key developments in political, social, economic, and cultural history. The narrative is followed by a number of primary text documents and primary visual documents that exemplify key themes and provide students the opportunity to make their own analysis of Russian history.

Exploring Russia's Past looks at Russia from three vantage points. First, it considers Russia as a unique nation and civilization. Beginning with the appearance of the Eastern Slavs in the Dnieper River valley and their conversion to Christianity, it follows one branch of the Slavs (that later became known as "Russian") as it took on the characteristics of a nation in the upper reaches of the Volga River and gradually evolved into a major civilization and state. Second, it considers Russia as an empire. The text examines Russia's relation with other peoples of north central Eurasia as it expanded to become a multinational empire and then as it has recently contracted somewhat (after 1991). Third, it considers Russia in the context of world history. Before 1700, Russia's interaction with the nomadic empires of the steppes was typical of the interchange between the nomadic societies of Inner Eurasia and the sedentary civilizations of Outer Eurasia. After 1700, however, the Russian experience was typical of the relationship between the imperialist nations of Europe and the traditional civilizations of Asia.

Exploring Russia's Past considers Russian society in the broadest context; it examines government and politics, foreign affairs, religion and culture, the status and roles of women, social relations, and economic developments. Primary text documents and visual images have been chosen to shed light on many aspects of Russian society and civilization. Most chapters also contain a map to better situate Russian history in a geographical context.

Exploring Russia's Past is comprehensive as well in regard to its approach to student learning. As the title suggests, it attempts actively to involve students in understanding Russian history. Each chapter begins with a survey of developments in Eurasia that both situates Russia in the context of world trends and provides key information regarding Russia's neighbors that is essential for understanding Russia's relation with them. The narrative provides essential information with which all students of Russian history must be familiar (and prepares the reader to analyze the primary documents). The documents include several brief readings (generally about 800 words each) and pictures or other visual images that come from the time period covered by the chapter. The reader is not told how to read or interpret the readings or images but is asked questions that encourage original and critical thinking. Text and visual documents are chosen to enable students to follow particular themes (art, architecture, social relations, law, role of women, etc.) over the entire course of Russian history.

Chapters have a common structure. An introductory paragraph presents the key theme of the chapter or an important development that sets the stage for the chapter. "Eurasian Context" is a concise summary of world trends and a thumbnail sketch of each of the major civilizations of Eurasia and of the countries on Russia's borders. This is followed by sections on government and foreign affairs, church and culture, roles and status of women, and social and economic trends. The narrative concludes with a consideration of the non-Russian peoples of the empire (or Soviet Union). A brief conclusion summarizes key developments or anticipates the next period in Russian history.

The narrative is followed by (on average) eight primary documents; four text and four visual. These documents are chosen to provide as wide as possible an insight into political, legal, cultural, social, gender, and economic aspects of Russian history. In almost all chapters, at least one text document and one image is directly related to the experience of women, and at least one text document and one image is directly related to a non-Russian region or ethnic group. A hemispheric map showing key developments across Eurasia follows the documents. A brief list of books recommended for further reading concludes each chapter. A systematic bibliography is impossible in a work of this scope, and the lists are very eclectic, including some classics as well as some of the most recent works, and attempt to represent a wide variety of topics.

The text is divided into twenty-two chapters, but more attention is paid to recent events than to early ones. The first two chapters cover several thousand years. Kiev Rus (1000–1240) is covered in Chapter Three. Muscovite Russia is covered by four chapters, which include about a century each. The eighteenth and nineteenth centuries are covered by five chapters, which average fifty years in length. The nine chapters that cover the twentieth century average a little more than one decade each. Continuity is far more usual in history than discontinuity, and beginning and ending points of chapters are chosen more for considerations of length than for any other reason. Chapters begin or end with the death of a tsar or a Soviet leader only when these dates indicate significant breaks or turning points in Russian history.

It is the intention of this text to present the data of Russian history in as straightforward and dispassionate a manner as possible. I follow scholarly consensus where it exists, take note of historical controversy, and try to present the facts in such a way that the reader can make his or her own judgment. It is, of course, impossible to avoid interpretive bias, and the reader should be aware of the following viewpoints that I hold.

First, I absolutely disagree with Winston Churchill's judgment that "Russia is a riddle wrapped in a mystery inside an enigma." The Russians are normal human beings who act in quite understandable ways. Their wealthy elites have been neither more nor less selfish, arrogant, or brutal than other elites in world history, and ordinary Russians have been neither unusually passive nor unusually aggressive in responding to injustice. The behavior of Russians of all classes is completely understandable when considered in its historical context.

Second, I treat Russia as a European civilization, by virtue of its Christian religion, Slavic culture and society, Indo-European language, and, for that matter, its geographical location. Europe has great social and political diversity, and there is no "typical" European nation. Russia is surely no further from the European "norm" (whatever that might be) than are England, Sweden, Spain, or Greece.

Because the Russian (Cyrillic) alphabet is different from the Latin alphabet used in English, transliteration of Russian names and terms creates difficulties for those who write about Russia in English. It is not that no good system of transliteration exists; the Library of Congress has developed a quite satisfactory system (and one that is used, with minor modifications and many exceptions as described below). The problem is that past attempts at transliteration/translation have produced words that have become standard in English. "Moscow" must be used instead of "Moskva," "Catherine the Great" instead of "Ekaterina," and "Yeltsin" rather than "El'tsin." Any consistent and systematic application of a transliteration system would be confusing and counterproductive. The multi-ethnic character of the Russian empire adds another difficulty: Should terms relevant to Ukraine, Georgia, or Uzbekistan, for example, be transliterated from the national language or from the Russian version of the term?

Since this text is intended for university undergraduates studying Russian history, its first priority is to facilitate further study and research in history, not to provide a consistent guide to Russian orthography. Therefore, all names appear in the form given in the twenty-sixth edition of the *Library of Congress Subject Headings* (2003). In addition, all geographical terms are spelled as they appear in primary entry of *The Columbia Gazetteer of the World* (1998). All other names and terms will be transliterated from Russian according to the Library of Congress transliteration system without diacritical marks, the hard sign, and only one capital letter per word (not IAroslav, but Iaroslav). The soft sign will be also omitted, and "-ie" will replace "-'e" where it will help English speakers to pronounce Russian words. Thus *Riazan'* will appear as *Riazan,* and *pomestie* will be used instead of *pomest'e.* Plurals of Russian terms will be formed by simply adding "-s" as in English. The only exceptions are *streltsy* and *Rurikovichi,* which are already familiar in English. Names and terms in the documents will be spelled the same as they appear in the narrative, and in the index names and terms will be followed by their exact Library of Congress transliteration with hard and soft signs (but without diacritical marks).

ACKNOWLEDGMENTS

Charles Cavaliere, Executive Editor at Prentice Hall, deserves the credit for conceiving of this textbook in its current form. The book I originally proposed was quite different, and it was Charles who suggested this format. I took enthusiastic ownership of his concept and have done my best to realize it. I thank Charles, as well, for his help, advice, and patience while I have been at work on this project.

I am indebted a number of reviewers for their invaluable advice, including Eve Levin, University of Kansas; Rex Wade, George Mason University; Donald Raleigh, University of North Carolina; Roshanna Sylvester, DePaul University; Hugh Hudson, Georgia State University; Jonathan Grant, Florida State University; William Benton Whisenhunt, College of DuPage; and one reviewer who wished to remain anonymous. I also thank my former Russian history students at the University of Wisconsin–Platteville whose discussion of many documents (both text and visual) has helped me make the choices for this book. Last, but not least, I owe a huge debt of gratitude to my dear life partner, A. E. Bothwell, for her help in writing this book. Lee read the entire manuscript with great care and gave me excellent advice.

Any deficiencies in this work are due solely to the author's willful refusal to fully implement the ideas and suggestions offered by his editor, reviewers, and partner.

About the Author

David Rowley graduated from the University of Michigan with the individualized major of Sino-Soviet Studies and then earned the M.A. from the University of Chicago and PhD from the University of Michigan in Russian history. As a teacher, David has been a Eurasian-ist from the beginning of his career; he has taught Chinese, Japanese, Middle Eastern, and World history, as well as the histories of Russia, England, and Europe. He has taught at Northwestern Michigan College, William Penn University, the University of North Dakota, and, since 1999, at the University of Wisconsin–Platteville.

David's dissertion, *Millenarian Bolshevism, 1900–1921,* was published in 1987, and he has published articles on Russian Marxism and Russian nationalism in a number of journals, in-cluding the *American Historical Review, Journal of Contemporary History, Kritika,* and *Nations and Nationalism.*

INTRODUCTION: EURASIA, INNER EURASIA, AND RUSSIA

This book is about the history of Russia in Eurasia, and the story it tells can be summarized as follows: In the tenth century C.E., an East Slavic civilization arose in a state centered on the city of Kiev on the Dnieper River in what is now Ukraine. Their Greek neighbors knew its ruling elite as the Rhos. Following the defeat and occupation of this state by the Mongols in the thirteenth century, Kiev declined and other Slavic cities increased in importance. Moscow, a city to the northeast of Kiev, became the center of a new state which aspired to reunite the East Slavs under its rule and to absorb Mongol territories as well. This state, known at first to western Europeans as Muscovy, ultimately adopted the name Rossiia (the Slavic form of the Greek Rhosia) which is written in English as "Russia." Russia's expansion did not stop until it had become an empire that, by the nineteenth century, ruled the length and breadth of Northern Eurasia (and, until 1867, part of North America). In the twentieth century the Russian empire, reconstituted as the Union of Soviet Socialist Republics (U.S.S.R.), expanded its influence further into Europe and competed with the United States, its only rival, for world hegemony. At the end of the twentieth century, the U.S.S.R. abruptly collapsed leaving the core Russian state reduced in territory and world influence, but still the largest country in Eurasia (and the world). This text will examine these developments in the context of world history and consider how Russia has been interconnected socially, economically, politically, and culturally with its Eurasian neighbors.

It will also deal with perceptions of Russia's nature and place in the world, both from its own point of view and in the view of outside observers. In fact, that discussion must begin immediately, since three terms—Eurasia, Inner Eurasia, and Russia—have already used that bring with them problematic connotations.

The term "Eurasia" will be used to refer to the largest of the world's continents—that part of the earth that is bordered by the Atlantic, Arctic, Pacific, and Indian Oceans, and the Red and Mediterranean Seas. No geographical features on this continent have served as impermeable barriers to human travel and trade, and, from the beginning of human habitation, Eurasia has been the scene of continual intercultural exchange (and conflict). The perceptual difficulty arises from a tradition that treats Europe as a separate continent from Asia.

Europe is a cultural rather than a geographical continent. It has been treated as a continent in its own right only because a major civilization appeared there that wanted to mark itself off as different from the "Orient," or the East. This civilization, known as Western Civilization because of its location on the western edge of Eurasia, has had the cultural power to make the notion of a European "continent" relatively uncontested. That the notion of Europe is indeed cultural is illustrated by an ongoing argument about where the eastern boundary of Europe lies. Those who look for physical boundaries use the Ural Mountains, but some of those who focus on civilizations would draw an imaginary line from the Baltic to the Black Seas or maybe even further west.

The uncertainty of the dividing line between Europe and Asia directly depends on definitions of Russia's essential nature. Is Russia European or Asian? Those who define Western civilization in terms that exclude Russia try to draw the boundary further to the west. Those who see Russia as fundamentally European accept the Urals as the eastern boundary of Europe and speak of "European Russia" and "Russia in Asia." In order to avoid any definitions that carry unnecessary preconceptions, Russia will be considered to have arisen in the middle of one continent: Eurasia.

The term Eurasia has been loaded with a set of preconceptions of its own. A school of thought known as Eurasianism, that was especially popular among Russian émigrés after the Revolution of 1917, defines Eurasia as a specific ecological unit: a more or less uninterrupted, unforested plain extending from the Carpathian Mountains to the Pacific Ocean. The Eurasianists called this the "steppe system," and they argued that it naturally predisposes those who live in it (if they can marshal the power) to build an empire and rule it in its entirety. This was precisely the territory that the Russian empire encompassed at its greatest extent, and the Eurasianists held that Russia is neither European nor Asia but "Eurasian" a synthesis of the geopolitical vision of Genghis Khan with the spiritual worldview of Eastern Christianity.

As used in this book, however, the term Eurasia is intended to refer to the entire continent and should not be taken as implying adherence to the tenets of the "Eurasian school." I do not believe that the Eurasian steppe infects its inhabitants with dreams of empire. To describe the part of Eurasia that the Russian empire expanded to fill this text will borrow the more inclusive term "Inner Eurasia" from the Russian and world historian David Christian.[1] In his usage, Inner Eurasia refers to the subregion of northern Eurasia bounded in the west by the Carpathian Mountains and the Pripet Marshes and bounded in the south by the Black Sea, the Caucasus Mountains, the Caspian Sea, and the series of complex mountain ranges that extend eastward to the Pacific Ocean. That Russia expanded only to those borders and no farther is explained more by the relation of the Russian state to its neighbors than by geography. The mountains that marked the boundaries of Russia's expansion were not, after all, barriers to Genghis Khan.

Finally, what is "Russian Civilization," and when did it originate? These questions, too, are controversial. Three current nations—Belarus, Russia, and Ukraine—can claim to have descended from the East Slavic civilization that originated in the Dnieper River valley in the late first millennium C.E. To call that original civilization "Russian" would suggest that Russia was its natural and direct descendant, and Belarus and Ukraine are lesser variants. This book does not ignore Belarus or Ukraine, and it does not wish to imply that Russia was the only authentic descendent of the original state of Rhosia. Nevertheless, its primary focus is Russia, the state that grew to be a world political and cultural power, and a descendent of that first East Slavic state and civilization.

[1]David Christian, *A History of Russia, Central Asia and Mongolia, Volume I, Inner Eurasia from Prehistory to the Mongol Empire* (Oxford: Blackwell, 1998).

CHAPTER ONE

INNER EURASIA BEFORE THE SLAVIC ERA, PREHISTORY TO 500 C.E.

THE OUTER EURASIAN CONTEXT

Human beings, having originated in Africa, began to migrate to Eurasia more than a million years ago. They hunted animals, using their flesh for food and skins for clothing, and they foraged for vegetable food. Early humans gradually expanded to fill the continent until, no later than 35,000 B.C.E., even the cold and inhospitable north was populated. The human population remained relatively constant for thousands of years more, since it depended on the natural production of animal and plant life.

Soon after 8,000 B.C.E., as the last ice age was ending, human beings made momentous discoveries: that seeds of edible plants could be planted and harvested, and that certain animals could be bred in captivity. The invention of agriculture, in turn, had major consequences for human society. First, farmers could no longer move about; they had to settle permanently to tend (and protect) their fields and corrals. (Nomadic herding arose only later, as will be discussed below.) Second, growing crops and raising livestock was vastly more productive than hunting or foraging; a family could produce considerably more food than it needed to survive. This meant that there were no longer natural controls on human populations; the more productive agriculture became, the greater the number of people it could support. It also meant that durable wealth could be amassed. Some people were able to spend their time in other pursuits, making material goods to trade with farmers for their surplus food.

These developments made possible the rise of civilization. Civilization means the culture associated with cities, and it is characterized by monumental buildings of stone and brick, written languages, and specialized professions, including administrators, priests, soldiers,

Turn to page 18 for a map showing key geographic locations and features for this time period.

artisans, and artists. These specialists do not grow their own food, of course, and depend on the willingness of farmers to give up some of their surplus. One may think of this process in a benign way, imagining that farmers willingly pay taxes so the rulers of cities can hire armies to defend them from invasion, priests to perform rituals to obtain sun and rain in the right proportion, and artisans to build useful or beautiful things. One may be less charitable and conceive of taxation as theft, and civilization as parasitic upon agriculture. Either way, the prosperity of a civilization is directly related to the productivity of its farmers.

Mesopotamia, the land between the Tigris and Euphrates Rivers in what is now Iraq, produced the first civilization in Eurasia (and, in fact, the world) around 3500 B.C.E., and it provided the model for the civilization of the entire Middle East. The first monumental architecture was built there; its engineers invented arithmetic and geometry, and its artisans invented the arch and the dome. Mesopotamian astronomers charted the heavens and made the first calendar. The state—an institution in which the provision of law and order is formally separated from other social functions—was invented there, as was the empire—a state that rules two or more subordinate states. The greatest of these empires were a series of Persian dynasties in what is now Iran: the Achaemenids (558–330 B.C.E.), Seleucids (323–83 B.C.E.), Parthians (247 B.C.E.–224 C.E.), and the Sasanids (224–651 C.E.) Yet another contribution of the Middle East to the world was ethical monotheism—the idea that the universe was created by one, all-powerful god who is the source of moral law and who rewards goodness and punishes evil. The Middle East produced Zarathustra, Moses, Jesus, and Muhammad.

Sedentary agriculture and civilization appeared on the Indus River only slightly later than in Mesopotamia. Indian society was centered on family, village, and caste. The Indian subcontinent has rarely been unified under one government before modern times, and when this has occurred, it has usually resulted from foreign invasion. Indian armies never aggressively expanded beyond the subcontinent's natural boundaries, the Himalayas and Hindukush mountain ranges. Nor was its major and enduring religion, Hinduism, imported by other peoples. Buddhism, a variant of Hinduism, spread to East and Southeast Asia and influenced nomads of Inner Eurasia. Otherwise, India's role in Inner Eurasian history was to provide goods for trade on its northern border.

In East Asia, agriculture was independently invented by farmers living on the loess plain north of the Yellow River in the fifth millennium B.C.E., and cities were first built there around 2500 B.C.E. The style of government that evolved in China was imperial; it was headed by an emperor, thought to be the intermediary between heaven and earth, who ruled through a bureaucracy of salaried professionals chosen and promoted on the basis of written examinations. Ruling dynasties repeatedly rose and fell. Some lasted hundreds of years, some only a couple of generations; some ruled all of continental East Asia, some only a small part. These dynastic cycles were a regular feature of Chinese political history, while the basic state structure remained.

Historically, China was most remarkable for its high level of material culture. Until modern times, China had consistently been the most technologically advanced and one of the most artistically sophisticated civilizations in the world, and its goods attracted Eurasian traders from the earliest times. Porcelain, for example, is called "china," since Chinese artisans made the best in the world. The Chinese learned to make a drink from tea, and merchants found a Eurasian market for it. The most important item of international trade from China was silk, a textile made from fibers from the cocoons of a caterpillar indigenous to China. Silk is strong, lustrous, and holds dye exceptionally well. Silk is very light and can be packaged compactly, and it is therefore ideal for overland trade. As early as the second millennium B.C.E., silk was being carried from China to Bactria (present-day Afghanistan).

During the Han Dynasty (202 B.C.E.–220 C.E.), China achieved unprecedented unity, dynastic continuity, and territorial expanse. It expanded to the border of Central Asia and established trade contacts, via the Silk Road, with the Roman Empire, then at its height. China was weak and fragmented during the "Six Dynasties" period (220–581), but its goods continued to attract Eurasian merchants.

The most recent of the ancient civilizations of Eurasia were those of Greece and Rome (often spoken of as a single "classical" civilization). As early as the sixth century B.C.E., Greeks were colonizing the northern shore of the Black Sea and sharing their culture—mythology and art—with the peoples of Inner Eurasia. From the second century B.C.E. until the fifth century C.E., the Roman Empire ruled the Mediterranean world and Europe south of the Danube and west of the Elbe. Greek civilization is best known for its secularism (focus on this world rather than the afterlife), humanism (celebration of the human potential for great achievement), and rationalism (the idea that humans can know the world—and make it better—by the use of reason). The Romans are most famous for their conception of empire. They thought of their empire as cosmopolitan and universal and their emperor as the source of justice arrived at by applying reason to the principles of natural law.

The classical world also played a key role in transforming Christianity—one of the varieties of Middle Eastern ethical monotheism—into a universal religion. The theology of the Christian religion was created by interpreting the teachings and actions of a Jewish religious figure, Jesus of Nazareth, in terms of Greek philosophy, especially Platonism. In addition, the Roman Empire gave the Christian Church an institutional structure and promoted the standardization of theology and rituals. Emperor Constantine (275–337), a convert to Christianity, made financial contributions to the church and took an interest in church administration and doctrine. It was he who called the Council of Nicea in 325 in order to resolve doctrinal uncertainties and to create a single "orthodoxy" (correct belief). Constantine asserted that the Church needed the protection and guidance of an emperor and that Church and empire should work together to provide for the spiritual and physical well-being of its Christian population.

The emperor Theodosius (379–395) made Christianity the official religion of the Empire in 391–392, and, as a result, the church developed an institutional structure that paralleled that of the empire. The basic unit of Roman government was the diocese, and just as each diocese was given a magistrate to represent Roman law, so each received a bishop to care for the spiritual needs of the population. At first Christian bishops were autonomous and equal, but the hierarchical structure of the Roman Empire suggested that the church should have a similar structure. The bishop of the capital city in a province of the Empire became known as a metropolitan, and he supervised the bishops within the province. If the church were to be an exact parallel of the Roman Empire, it would need a single head to parallel the office of emperor, but such an institution did not develop while emperors ruled in Rome.

GEOGRAPHY AND ENVIRONMENT OF INNER EURASIA

Inner Eurasia, following the usage of David Christian,[1] refers to the subregion of northern Eurasia bounded in the west by the Carpathian Mountains and the Pripet Marshes and in the south by the Black Sea, the Caucasus Mountains, the Caspian Sea, and a series of mountain ranges that extend eastward to the Pacific Ocean. Inner Eurasia is divided into a series of parallel ecological bands running East and West. The most northern band is the tundra, a cold flat land lying along the Arctic coast. It is three hundred miles wide in the center of the continent but narrows at its eastern and western ends. The extreme cold (summer temperatures are rarely higher than 40° F, winter temperatures rarely higher than −25° F) and low rainfall (an average of fifteen inches a year) permits only a very simple food web. Vegetation is sparse and predominantly composed of mosses, lichens, grasses, and low shrubs. Lemmings, hares, ptarmigan, migratory geese, and reindeer live off the vegetation, and they, in turn, are preyed upon by foxes, wolves, and snowy owls.

South of the tundra and extending from Scandinavia to the shores of the Bering Sea lies the largest continuous forest in the world. The greatest part of this forest is the taiga which consists primarily of evergreen conifers but with some stands of birch and alder and occasional swamps and peat bogs. Located north of the 56th parallel (at approximately the same longitude as the south coast of Hudson's Bay in Canada), the taiga is hardly more hospitable than the tundra. West of the Yenisei River the climate is somewhat less extreme, but East of the Yenisei, in Siberia, temperatures are lower even than those of the North Pole. A temperature of −96° F has been recorded near the Siberian city of Verkhoyansk. The taiga is home to a variety of small fur-bearing animals (including sable, squirrel, marten, and fox) and to elk, bear, muskrat, and wolf. The soils of the taiga are thin, acidic, and not conducive to agriculture.

In both the Southwest (now European Russia) and Southeast (now northern China), the taiga blends into a belt of mixed (coniferous and deciduous) forest, which, in turn, becomes a forest of oak, aspen, birch, elm, and maple. Squirrel, deer, fox, and wolf are the predominant fauna. Though its climate is somewhat more moderate than that of the taiga, even the deciduous forests lie above the 50th parallel. (For comparison, the 49th parallel defines the United States–Canadian border west of the Great Lakes). Inhabitants experience cold winters and typically enjoy ninety days (or fewer) of frost-free weather in the summer. The further south one goes, the more fertile and suitable for agriculture the soil becomes.

Below the forest lies the steppe (the transitional edge of which is called the wooded steppe, in which grassland is interspersed with groves of oak, birch, and aspen), a rolling grassland approximately three hundred miles wide, which begins just East of the Carpathian Mountains in what is now Moldova and extends westward to the Altai Mountains on the eastern border of what is now Mongolia. The steppe proper is unbroken grassland with no natural shelter for animals, and the predominant mammals are burrowing rodents, skunks, foxes, wolves, and antelopes. Native birds include eagles, larks, bustards, and quail. The steppe was the original home of the horse, the two-humped camel, and European cattle. As is typical of grasslands in temperate climates, humus built up over the millennia until steppe topsoil reached a depth of more than four feet. This soil, called chernozem or black earth, makes the steppe one of the most fertile farmlands in the world, although modern industrial agriculture has greatly depleted it.

Between the steppe and the mountain ranges that separate Inner from Outer Eurasia, the land becomes semi-desert and desert. Rainfall is so light (only six to eight inches per year) that vegetation (desert sedge and grasses) becomes minimal and the soil has little humus. Wild sheep and goats live in the mountains and plateaus bordering the deserts; rodents, antelopes, foxes, and lynxes live in the deserts. Oases, lakes, and rivers that appear within this desert band provide limited ecologies for vegetation, migratory birds, and mammals.

WAYS OF LIFE IN INNER EURASIA

Tundra and Taiga

Because of the cold climate and infertile soil, the two northernmost ecological bands support only sparse populations of humans. On the tundra, people must depend upon a mainly carnivorous diet and so have had to compete with other predators. The peoples of the forest, until quite recent times, have been semi-nomadic hunter-gatherers who herd reindeer in the northern taiga and who raise cattle and grain in the southern forests. The timber of the taiga was too remote to be exploited before the building of railroads, and its vast deposits of minerals and oil had no value before the Industrial Revolution. Consequently, before the intrusion of Slavic explorers and settlers in relatively recent times, the peoples of northern Inner Eurasia pursued their traditional economic, social, and religious practices with no interference or encroachment from the larger and more organized and specialized societies to their south.

The peoples of the forests and tundra have never recorded their histories. They lived in small, self-sufficient, face-to-face kinship communities with no written languages. They believed in animistic religions in which shamans mediated between the human and spirit worlds. To the extent that conflict occurred among them, they typically practiced ritualistic warfare. Tundra nomads initiated no contacts with the outside world, and trade was practically non-existent. Forest-dwellers traded furs for metal goods produced by the peoples of the steppe, but there was little cultural interaction between them, although it has been argued that reindeer herding was learned from horse-herding peoples in the second or first century B.C.E., and that shamanism may have been influenced by Buddhism at roughly the same time. Change in the societies of the taiga and tundra has been extremely slow.

The Steppe

While societies in the northern forests adopted agriculture quite late and never completely gave up nomadic practices, peoples on the steppe settled down to farming quite early in human history. By the seventh millennium B.C.E., people known as the Jeitun were practicing sedentary agriculture by the lakes, rivers, and oases between the Caspian Sea and the Amu Darya River. An outgrowth of Mesopotamian culture, they grew the same grains (barley and wheat), raised the same animals (sheep, goats, and cattle), and used the same methods of irrigation as the peoples of the Tigris-Euphrates River valley. The Jeitun also manifested Mesopotamian influences in their art and material culture. In the sixth millennium B.C.E., a people known by the name given to their culture, "Linear Pottery," began to practice agriculture on the semi-wooded steppe north of the Black Sea. Farming rain-watered land, the Linear Pottery people grew barley, wheat, and flax, and raised cattle and pigs. They seem to have been an Indo-European people who migrated from the Mediterranean cultural area.

At the earliest stage of their development, these sedentary agricultural communities were small-scale and peaceful. Jeitun communities typically contained thirty dwellings and two hundred people, while Linear Pottery settlements were even smaller. Their villages were not protected by walls, suggesting either that they had not accumulated enough wealth to attract raiders or that population density was low and resources were abundant. Moreover, these villages do not seem to have violently displaced the original stone-age hunter-gatherers. Instead, they lived in harmony and traded with one another.

As this is a history of Russia in Inner Eurasia and not a history of Inner Eurasia per se, there is no need to follow the sequence of sedentary, agricultural societies from the Jeitun to the Eastern Slavs. We need only note two things. First, sedentary agriculture has been practiced continuously along the river valleys of what is now Ukraine and Western Russia ever since such agriculture first began. Second, whereas agriculture in the Outer Eurasian river valleys of Egypt, Mesopotamia, India, and China created the basis for the rise of major civilizations, agriculture in Inner Eurasia did not. The climate was too cold, the amount of arable land too limited, and the rainfall too light. Cities and sedentary agriculture on the southern edge of Inner Eurasia were not native developments but were extensions of Outer Eurasian civilizations.

There was, as we have already seen, a vast amount of fertile steppeland running across Inner Eurasia, but, because ancient cultures did not possess plows capable of cutting and turning over the heavy sod, humans could not take advantage of its fertility by raising crops. Instead, they harvested the wealth of the grass that grew there naturally by herding animals that ate it. Nomadic pastoralism, the herding of flocks of grass-eating animals, was invented in the fourth millennium B.C.E. in the region between the Dnieper and Don Rivers.

Cattle had been domesticated much earlier, but two developments were necessary before it was possible to live off cattle-herding alone. First, people had to be able to travel further and faster than the animals they herded. This was accomplished by learning to ride horses. Originally horses were domesticated by farmers for their meat, but sometime during the fourth millennium, farmers on the western steppe bred horses large enough for humans to ride. Second, cattle had to be made useful over their entire lives, instead of only when they were slaughtered for their meat and hides. Once humans discovered how to use the milk (as food) and the hair of sheep, goats, and horses (to make felt), living primarily on animal products became possible.

Nomadic pastoralists did not become completely self-sufficient, however. They maintained an economic relationship with the agriculturalists who had first provided them with horses. Nomads supplement their animal diet with grain when possible, as farmers supplement their diet with meat. Farmers exchanged woodland products for hides and felt, as well. Thus, the normal relationship between the herder (who produces cattle, horses, felt, and hides) and the farmer (who grows grain and weaves cloth) is one of peaceful coexistence. Each trading partner gives what it can produce in exchange for what it cannot.

However, the relationship was not always one of mutually beneficial cooperation. The appearance of walls around agricultural settlements after the invention of pastoralism suggests that nomads were not always content to make their livelihoods by trade. They must sometimes have given in to the common human temptation to take what they had neither earned nor paid for. In the absence of a superior law and order, the time-honored custom of traders is to exchange goods when strength on both sides is equal and to seize them by force when the other side is weak.

Piracy probably came naturally to nomads simply because the skills of the steppe herding, horseback riding, and hunting are also the skills of warfare. A Chinese historian made this observation of northern pastoralists at the end of the first millennium B.C.E., but it probably describes pastoral traditions from the very beginning: "The little boys start out by learning to ride sheep and shoot birds and rats with a bow and arrow, and when they get a little older they shoot foxes and hares, which are used for food. Thus all the young men are able to use a bow and act as armed cavalry in time of war. It is their custom to herd their flocks in times of peace and make their living by hunting, but in periods of crisis they take up arms and go off on plundering and marauding expeditions."[2]

Thus the pastoral way of life on the great plain of Inner Eurasia went in a direction far different from that of the societies in Outer Eurasia. The great river-valley civilizations, based as they were upon sedentary agriculture, were notable for accumulation of wealth, specialization of function, creation of class hierarchies, and development of sharp gender distinctions. They were remarkably stable. Chinese and Indian civilizations have been essentially continuous from their origins until the present, and, although civilizations have risen and fallen in the Middle East, the basic structural characteristics of the successive societies have remained constant.

The lifestyle of nomadic pastoralists was much less static and hierarchical. Since they moved their camps according to the season and could only possess what their animals could carry, accumulation of great wealth was impossible and social hierarchies were not extreme. Sex segregation was less evident, and sex roles tended to be mutable. Women typically learned the same skills as men including the use of weapons of war.

In normal times, nomadic pastoralists lived in camping groups or primary kin groups of no more than several dozen members who herded their flocks from one seasonal pasture to another. However, nomadic pastoralists were subject to rapid increases in population, and, when the climate reduced forage for cattle, overpopulation could produce competition with other groups for the same pastureland. It sometimes occurred, too, that neighboring agricultural civilizations attempted to appropriate land from or levy taxes on pastoralists. Under such circumstances, much more complex organizations, on the basis of kinship or supposed kinship, could arise. They could take the forms of tribal unification, inter-tribal federations, or even states.

Deserts and Oases

The borderland between Inner and Outer Eurasia is a band of desert and semi-desert, dotted with oases, lakes, and rivers that extends from the Caspian Sea through the Mongolian highlands. It was predominantly in this region that sedentary and pastoral peoples came in contact with one another. Peoples to the south of the boundary (China in the East and a variety Middle Eastern empires in Central Asia) were fated by the productivity of their agriculture to build sedentary civilizations. In times of prosperity, their growing populations put pressure on their northern borders as agriculturalists sought new land to till. The wealth of these civilizations at their cyclic apogees permitted them either to hire (or bribe) pastoral nomads or to conquer and subordinate them.

This borderland was also a trade nexus for the cultural and economic systems of Eurasia connecting China, India, and Mesopotamia with the farmers and pastoralists of Inner Asia. In the era of land transportation by pack animal, long-distance trade was limited to goods that were easy to carry and valuable. Chief among the goods traded was silk, a product that meets those criteria admirably. This borderland has been known ever since as the Silk Road.

Mountain Peoples

The final ecological band of Inner Eurasia is the chain of mountains that divide Inner from Outer Eurasia. Mountains are not impermeable to determined travelers, traders, or armies, and they serve as barriers only when powerful defenders live on the other side of them. The Caucasus Mountains were no barrier to the neolithic farmers from Mesopotamia in their travels north, and they did not stop Indo-European ("Caucasian") warriors from later invading Mesopotamia. In later centuries, Scythians, Khazars, and Mongols all sent armies south of the Caucasus. Similarly, the Hindukush Mountains between Afghanistan and India could not keep out Aryan, Hun, or Mughul armies, to name only three.

Mountains exhibit the same ecological zones as Inner Eurasia. They have meadows at their base followed first by mixed forest, then taiga, and they are capped with tundra at their peaks. Just as in Inner Eurasia, each successive ecological band is less productive of food and more sparsely populated. Peoples who have passed through the Caucasus over the millennia have had no more interest in mountain taiga than steppe nomads had in the northern forests of Inner Eurasia. Consequently, peoples who wanted to avoid invaders had only to seek refuge in ravines that led nowhere or on heights that invaders would find no profit in scaling. The Caucasus, therefore, contains one of the most diverse collection of ethnic groups in the world. More than fifty languages are spoken there. The Caucasus has allowed some very ancient peoples to retain their ethnic identity over the course of millennia. The most numerous of these are the Georgian, Armenian, and Azerbaijani peoples.

Georgian culture has historically been centered on the lowlands on the Black Sea shore. The Georgian people speak a Caucasian language, and it is believed that they are descended from the original paleolithic inhabitants. The Azerbaijanis, too, descended in part from an indigenous population. The Armenians are an Indo-European people who first appeared in the region in the seventh century B.C.E. when they established a large kingdom extending from the southern Caucasus into northern Mesopotamia. A wealthy and powerful state based upon agriculture, Armenia played a significant role in Mesopotamia. Though it often lost its independence, Armenia maintained its ethnic identity and political coherence and served alternately as a vassal of or a buffer state between the great Middle Eastern and Mediterranean empires of the ancient world. In the early fourth century C.E., while a vassal of the Roman Empire, Armenia adopted Christianity.

Georgia and Azerbaijan, more shielded by the mountains, were not players in the game of Mesopotamian power politics, but they were influenced by their imperial neighbors. Georgia was ruled at different times by the Scythians and the Persians, and Greece established cities on the eastern Black Sea coast. Georgia was then incorporated into the Roman empire, and it was while a Roman province in 330 C.E. that Georgia became Christian. The inhabitants of what is now Azerbaijan fell under the influence of Persia, rather than Rome. Around 500 C.E., when the Slavic era was beginning, Georgia was temporarily independent of Byzantium, half of Armenia was ruled by Byzantium and half was temporarily independent, and Azerbaijan was ruled by the Persian Sasanid dynasty.

NOMADIC EMPIRES OF THE STEPPE

Shortly after 1000 B.C.E., a new pattern began to appear among the pastoralists who inhabited the Inner Eurasia grasslands: Nomad armies of tens of thousands or even hundreds of thousands of warriors created empires that conquered the border regions of Inner Eurasia. There were two likely precipitating factors. The first was the invention of the compound (double-curved) bow, an extremely powerful weapon small enough to be used on horseback. The second was an apparent increase in competition among pastoralists for grazing lands, caused by natural population increase and by the increased demand for horses by Outer Eurasian civilizations. At some point, tribal leaders must have realized that by allying instead of fighting among themselves for pasture land, they could create armies large enough to stage wars of conquest in Inner Eurasia. They could become wealthy not by raising cattle but by levying tribute on conquered cities.

The name Scythian was given by the ancient Greeks to the first major empire-building nomads of the steppes. The Scythians seem to have originated on the steppe north of the Aral Sea in the early first millennium B.C.E. They spread both east and west across the steppe, creating empires that infringed on China in the east and Mesopotamia in the west. In the west, they became involved in the wars between the Medes and the Assyrians in the seventh century B.C.E. and raided as far south as Egypt.

In the sixth century B.C.E., the Scythians were pushed by the Persians permanently north of the Caucasus Mountains, and by the fifth century B.C.E., they had established a less warlike, more settled society on the steppe north of the Black Sea (in what is now southern Ukraine and Russia). While perhaps most of the Scythians preserved their pastoral way of life, many also became sedentary agriculturalists, no doubt intermarrying with the native farmers. Simultaneously Greek city-states began to establish colonies on the coast of the Black Sea for the purpose of manufacturing pottery and iron goods for trade with the farmers of the river valley and forest and the pastoralists of the steppe.

The Scythian empire largely disintegrated by the end of the third century B.C.E. Nomadic empires of the steppes are relatively short-lived compared with sedentary civilizations. The wealth their elites acquire does not derive from economic productivity, but from their ability to organize their peoples and to motivate them to turn their hunting skills to piracy and conquest. Nomad coalitions are formed by charismatic leaders, and armies are rewarded with pillage. However, charisma is not a regularly inheritable characteristic, and when the period of conquest is over, and the elites settle down to rule, they must be content with tax-gathering. Thus succeeding generations of nomad leaders lose both the personal loyalty of their armies and the ability to reward them. It typically takes only a few generations for elites to lose their cohesiveness and to become alienated from their armies, or, if they have invaded sedentary states, to be assimilated into the civilization they have conquered. As kinship alliances break down, the nomadic tribes look for other coalition-builders or fall back upon their traditional pastoral way of life.

The Scythians were followed by a series of nomadic empires of the steppes that formed on the Mongolian plateau to the north of China and waxed in power as the current Chinese ruling dynasty waned. In the cyclic rhythm typical of sedentary-nomad relations, China would revive, reassert its power in the north, and the tribal federations that had once composed the nomad empire would separate and travel westward looking for new opportunities.

Such, for example, was the case of the Xiongnu, who built an empire on the northern Chinese borderlands in the second century B.C.E. Their empire lasted little more than a century, before it was broken up by the rising Han Dynasty. From the first century B.C.E. through the second century C.E., the Han joined three other empires—the Kushan centered in Bactria, the Parthian in the Middle East, and the Roman Empire in the Mediterranean world—to form one contiguous band of sedentary civilizations. They established the Silk Road, for the first time, as a peaceful, stable, and continuous trade route from China all the way to the Mediterranean.

After the breakup of the Xiongnu Confederation, successor states spread across Inner Eurasia, ready to take advantage of any decline in vitality of one of the sedentary civilizations. The Han Dynasty fell in 220 C.E., and China experienced regionalism and turmoil for three and a half centuries. The power vacuum in the East allowed the Turk Empire to rule the Inner Eurasian borderlands from northern China to Bactria. The Huns appeared on the western steppe in the fourth century and invaded both India and Rome in the fifth. The Huns thus played a role in the decline and fall of the Kushan dynasty in Bactria, the Gupta dynasty in India, and the Western Roman Empire. By 500 C.E., Outer Eurasia was in turmoil.

NOTES

1. David Christian, *A History of Russia, Central Asia and Mongolia, Volume I, Inner Eurasia from Prehistory to the Mongol Empire* (Oxford: Blackwell, 1998), 3–4.
2. Sima Qian, quoted in Christian, *A History of Russia*, 87.

_____ TEXT DOCUMENTS _____

Herodotus on Scythia

Herodotus (c. 484–c. 425 B.C.E.) the Greek "Father of History" was a contemporary of the Scythians when they were at the height of their power. Herodotus's account of the Scythians has been largely substantiated by recent archaeology.

- How would you define the "warrior style" of nomadic peoples? How does it compare with the fighting styles of settled civilizations? How can this be explained?

[The wisdom of the Scythians consists in the fact that their lifestyle makes] . . . it impossible for the enemy who invades them to escape destruction, while they themselves are entirely out of his reach, unless it please them to engage with him. Having neither cities nor forts, and carrying their dwellings with them wherever they go; accustomed, moreover, one and all of them, to shoot from horseback; and living not by husbandry but on their cattle, their wagons the only houses that they possess, how can they fail of being unconquerable, and unassailable, even?

In what concerns war, their customs are the following. The Scythian soldier drinks the blood of the first man he overthrows in battle. Whatever number he slays, he cuts off all their heads, and carries them to the king; since he is thus entitled to a share of the booty, whereto he forfeits all claim if he does not produce a head.

The skulls of their enemies, not indeed of all, but of those whom they most detest, they treat as follows. Having sawn off the portion below the eyebrows, and cleaned out the inside, they cover the outside with leather. When a man is poor, this is all that he does; but if he is rich, he also lines the inside with gold: in either case the skull is used as a drinking-cup.

[When Darius, Emperor of Persia, invaded the land of the Scythians] . . . the Scythians who remained behind resolved no longer to lead the Persians hither and thither about their country, but to fall upon them whenever they should be at their meals. . . . In these combats, the Scythian [cavalry] always put to flight the [cavalry] of the enemy; these last, however, when routed, fell back upon their [infantry], who never failed to afford them support; while the Scythians, on their side, as soon as they had driven the [cavalry] in, retired again, for fear of the [infantry]. By night, too, the Scythians made many similar attacks.

- What does the following account add to your understanding of the Scythian lifestyle?

. . . In order to cleanse their bodies, they act as follows: they make a booth by fixing in the ground three sticks inclined towards one another, and stretching around them woolen felts, which they arrange so as to fit as close as possible: inside the booth a dish is placed upon the ground, into which they put a number of red-hot stones, and then add some hemp-seed.

_____

Source: Herodotus. *The Text of Canon Rawlinson's Translation with the Notes Abridged.* London: John Murray, 1897: 355, 363, 364, 369–70, 386–7, 389–90, 395.

Hemp grows in Scythia: it is very like flax; only that it is a much coarser and taller plant: some grows wild about the country, some is produced by cultivation: the Thracians make garments of it which closely resemble linen; so much so, indeed, that if a person has never seen hemp he is sure to think they are linen, and if he has, unless he is very experienced in such matters, he will not know of which material they are.

The Scythians, as I said, take some of this hemp seed, and, creeping under the felt coverings, throw it upon the red-hot stones; immediately it smokes, and gives out such a vapor as no Grecian vapor-bath can exceed; the Scyths, delighted, shout for joy, and this vapor serves them instead of a water-bath; for they never by any chance wash their bodies with water. Their women make a mixture of cypress, cedar, and frankincense wood, which they pound into a paste upon a rough piece of stone, adding a little water to it. With this substance, which is of a thick consistency, they plaster their faces all over, and indeed their whole bodies. A sweet odor is thereby imparted to them, and when they take off the plaster on the day following, their skin is clean and glossy.

In the following passages Herodotus describes several of the neighbors of the Scythians (who ally with them against Darius), the Budini, the Geloni, and the Sauromatae. He also mentions the Amazons.

- How do you understand the possible origins of this story?
- As Herodotus portrays them, how "immutable" do gender roles and ethnic identities on the steppe seem to be?
- What connections can you see between geography and ways of life?
- What factors seem to influence gender roles and ethnic identities?

The Budini are a large and powerful nation: they have all deep blue eyes, and bright red hair. [But] there is a city in their territory, called Gelonus, which is surrounded with a lofty wall, thirty furlongs each way, built entirely of wood. All the houses in the place and all the temples are of the same material. Here are temples built in honor of the Grecian gods, and adorned after the Greek fashion with images, altars, and shrines, all in wood. . . . For the fact is that the Geloni were anciently Greeks, who, being driven out of the factories along the coast, fled to the Budini and took up their abode with them. They still speak a language half Greek, half Scythian.

The Budini, however, do not speak the same language as the Geloni, nor is their mode of life the same. They are the aboriginal people of the country, and are nomads . . . The Geloni, on the contrary, are tillers of the soil, eat bread, have gardens, and both in shape and complexion are quite different from the Budini.

[In describing the people known as Sauromatae Herodotus says that they originated with the intermarriage of Scythians and Amazons. The Amazons, an army of female warriors, were defeated and captured by the Greeks but escaped into Scythia. At first the Scythians fought against them, but, after discovering that they were women, wanted to ally with them "on account of their strong desire to obtain children from so notable a race." The Scythians sent a group of young men to camp near the Amazons. The two camps soon joined, "the Scythians living with the Amazons as their wives," and the men asked the women to move back home with them.]

But the Amazons said "We could not live with your women our customs are quite different from theirs. To draw the bow, to hurl the javelin, to bestride the horse, these are our arts of womanly employments we know nothing. Your women, on the contrary, do none of these things; but stay at home in their wagons, engaged in womanish tasks, and never go out to hunt, or to do anything. We should never agree together."

[Therefore the men agreed to move to a new territory.]

Crossing the Don they journeyed eastward a distance of three day's march from that stream, and again northward a distance of three days' march from the Black Sea. Here they came to the country where they now live, and took up their abode in it. The women of the Sauromatae have continued from that day to the present to observe their ancient customs, frequently hunting on horseback with their husbands, sometimes even unaccompanied; in war taking the field; and wearing the very same dress as the men.

Strabo on Iberia (Western Georgia)

Strabo (c. 64 b.c.e.–23 c.e.) was a Greek geographer and historian. Strabo did not visit the Caucasus Mountains, and his account of the Caucasus was based upon the works of earlier travelers.

- What elements of nomad and sedentary civilizations seem to be present in the Caucasus?
- How does ethnicity and lifestyle seem to be related to geography?
- What concepts in the narrative for Chapter One does this passage exemplify?

. . . The greater part of Georgia is so well built up in respect to cities and farmsteads that their roofs are tiled, and their houses as well as their market-places and other public buildings are constructed with architectural skill.

Parts of the country are surrounded by the Caucasian Mountains; for branches of these mountains, as I said before, project towards the south; they are fruitful, comprise the whole of Iberia, and border on both Armenia and Colchis. In the middle is a plain intersected by rivers, the largest being the Cyrus.

Now the plain of the Georgians is inhabited by people who are rather inclined to farming and to peace, and they dress after both the Armenian and the Median fashion; but the major, or warlike, portion occupy the mountainous territory, living like the Scythians and the Sarmatians, of whom they are both neighbors and kinsmen; however, they engage also in farming. And they assemble many tens of thousands, both from their own people and from the Scythians and Sarmatians, whenever anything alarming occurs.

From the country of the nomads on the north there is a difficult ascent into Iberia requiring three days' travel; and after this ascent comes a narrow valley on the Aragus River, with a single-file road requiring a four days' journey. The end of the road is guarded by a fortress

Source: Strabo, *The Geography of Strabo.* (New York: G. P. Putnam's Sons, 1917), 217, 218, 221. [Modern names have substituted for the archaic ethnic terms used by the translator.]

which is hard to capture. The pass leading from Albania into Iberia is at first hewn through rock, and then leads through a marsh formed by the River Alazonius, which falls from the Caucasus. The passes from Armenia into Georgia are the defiles on the Cyrus and those on the Aragus. . . .

There are also four castes among the inhabitants of Iberia. One, and the first of all, is that from which they appoint their kings, the appointee being both the nearest of kin to his predecessor and the eldest, whereas the second in line administers justice and commands the army. The second caste is that of the priests, who among other things attend to all matters of controversy with the neighboring peoples. The third is that of the soldiers and the farmers. And the fourth is that of the common people, who are slaves of the king and perform all the services that pertain to human livelihood. Their possessions are held in common by them according to families, although the eldest is ruler and steward of each estate . . .

Sima Qian on Central Asia

Sima Qian (c.145–86 B.C.E.*) served as the Grand Historiographer of China in the early Han Dynasty. His* Historical Records *was a massive work that covered the history of China from its origins until Sima Qian's own time. The selections presented here give the Chinese perspective on the peoples of Central Asia and the Inner Eurasian steppe. "Great Scythia" refers to the steppe to the north of the Caspian and Black Seas.*

- Compare and contrast the various peoples discussed by Sima Qian with one another and with the peoples already described by Herodotus and Strabo.
- Are there any variations in the nomadic versus sedentary patterns of gender, ethnicity, and ways of life?
- What does this reveal about international contacts at that time and about the creation of the Great Silk Road?

Zhang Qian was the first person to bring back a clear account of Fergana. He was a native of Hanzhong and served as a palace attendant [from 140-135 B.C.E.]. At this time the emperor questioned various Xiongnu who had surrendered to the Han and they all reported that the Xiongnu had defeated the king of the Scythians and made his skull into a drinking vessel. As a result the Scythians had fled and bore a constant grudge against the Xiongnu though as yet they had been unable to find anyone to join them in an attack on their enemy.

Source: *Records of the Grand Historian of China, vol 2, The Age of Emperor Wu, 140 to circa 100* B.C., by Ssu-Ma Ch'ien, translated by Burton Watson, © 1961, Columbia University Press, 264, 265, 266, 267, 269–70. Western terms have been substituted for the Chinese ethnic and geographical terms. Chinese words have been transliterated into Pinyin.

The Han at this time was engaged in a concerted effort to destroy the Xiongnu and therefore, when the emperor heard this, he decided to try to send an envoy to establish relations
with the Scythians . . .

Since the king of the Great Scythians had been killed by the Xiongnu, his son had succeeded him as ruler and had forced the kingdom of Bactria to recognize his sovereignty. The
region he ruled was rich and fertile and seldom troubled by invaders, and the king thought
only of his own enjoyment. He considered the Han too far away to bother with and had no
particular intention of avenging his father's death by attacking the Xiongnu.

Zhang Qian in person visited the lands of Fergana, the Great Scythia, Bactria, and Transoxiana, and in addition he gathered reports on five or six other large states in the neighbor-
hood. All of this information he related to the emperor on his return. The substance of his
report was as follows:

Fergana lies southwest of the territory of the Xiongnu, some ten thousand *li* directly west
of China. The people are settled on the land, plowing the fields and growing rice and wheat.
They also make wine out of grapes. The region has many fine horses . . . ; their forebears are
supposed to have been foaled from heavenly horses. The people live in houses in fortified
cities, there being some seventy or more cities of various sizes in the region. The population
numbers several hundred thousand. The people fight with bows and spears and can shoot
from horseback.

The Great Scythians live some two or three thousand *li* west of Fergana, north of the
Amu Darya River. They are bordered on the south by Bactria, on the west by Parthia, and
on the north by Transoxiana. They are a nation of nomads, moving from place to place with
their herds, and their customs are like those of the Xiongnu. They have some one or two
hundred thousand archer warriors. Formerly they were very powerful and despised the
Xiongnu, but later, when Modun became leader of the Xiongnu nation, he attacked and defeated the Scythians.

Parthia is situated several thousand *li* west of the region of the Great Scythians. The people are settled on the land, cultivating the fields and growing rice and wheat. They also
make wine out of grapes. They have walled cities like the people of Fergana, the region containing several hundred cities of various sizes. The kingdom, which borders the Syr Darya
River, is very large, measuring several thousand *li* square. Some of the inhabitants are merchants to travel by carts or boats to neighboring countries, sometimes journeying several
thousand *li*. The coins of the country are made of silver and bear the face of the king.

Transoxiana is situated over two thousand *li* southwest of Fergana, south of the Syr Darya.
Its people cultivate the land and have cities and houses. Their customs are like those of Fergana. It has no great ruler but only a number of petty chiefs ruling the various cities. The
people are poor in the use of arms and afraid of battle, but they are clever at commerce. . . .

Southeast of Bactria is the kingdom of India. "When I was in Bactria," Zhang Qian reported, "I saw bamboo canes from Qiong and cloth made in the province of Shu. when I
asked the people how they had gotten such articles, they replied, "Our merchants go to buy
them in the markets of India." India lies several thousand *li* southeast of Bactria. The region
is said to be hot and damp. The inhabitants ride elephants when they go into battle. The
kingdom is situated on a great river.

Thus the emperor learned of Fergana, Bactria, Parthia, and the others, all great states rich
in unusual products whose people cultivated the land and made their living in much the
same way as the Chinese. All these states, he was told, were militarily weak and prized Han
goods and wealth. He also learned that to the north of them lived the Scythian and Tansoxi-
anan people who were strong in arms but who could be persuaded by gifts and the prospect
of gain to acknowledge allegiance to the Han court. If it were only possible to win over these

states by peaceful means, the emperor thought, he could then extend his domain ten thousand *li*, attract to his court men of strange customs . . . , and his might would become known to all the lands within the four seas.

Earlier the Han had tried to establish relations with the barbarians of the southwest, but the expense proved too great and no road could be found through the region and so the project was abandoned. After Zhang Qian reported that it was possible to reach Bactria by traveling through the region of the southwestern barbarians, the Han once more began efforts to establish relations with the tribes in the area.

VISUAL DOCUMENTS

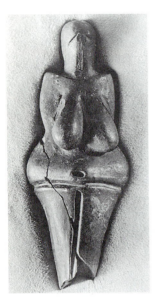

Figure 1-1 Female Figurine
This is the "Vestonice Venus," an Old Stone Age statuette discovered in the southern Czech Republic. It is about five inches long, made of baked clay, and is dated at approximately 23,000 B.C.E.
- What is the meaning and significance of this statuette?
- What does it reveal about the people who lived in Northwest Central Asia in the Paleolithic Era?

Source: H. Moravske Museum, Brno, Czech Republic. © Werner Forman/Art Resource, NY.

Figure 1-2 The Steppe
This is a contemporary photograph of the Russian steppe in Siberia just north of Kazakhstan.
- What challenges would the Eurasian steppe present to people who chose to live there?
- What technology and kind of society would people need in order to live as sedentary farmers society on the Eurasian steppe?
- What technology and kind of society would people need in order to live as livestock herders on the steppe?

Source: Russia and Eastern Images.

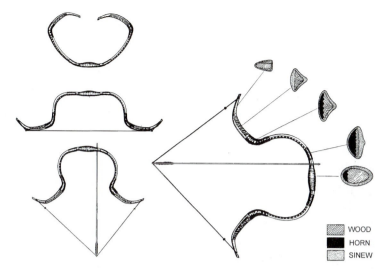

Figure 1-3 Bow Used by Steppe Nomads
    This is a drawing of the composite, compound bow used by steppe nomads. It is made by gluing together wood, horn, and sinew, and it provides for a long draw length with a relatively short bow. (The longer the draw length, the greater the power of the bow.)
    [*Scientific American*, vol 264, no. 6 (June 1991): 79.]
• Why did nomads need to invent a short bow?
• What does this reveal about the level of technology among the Scythians?
Source: Reprinted by permission of Hank Iken.

Figure 1-4 Scythian Shield Emblem.
    This is a gold figure of a stag that was used as an ornament on a shield. It was made by a Scythian artisan in the late seventh or early sixth century B.C.E.
• What does this reveal about the interests and lifestyle of the Scythians?
• What does it reveal about the level of their material culture and the nature of their society?
Source: The Bridgeman Art Library International Ltd.

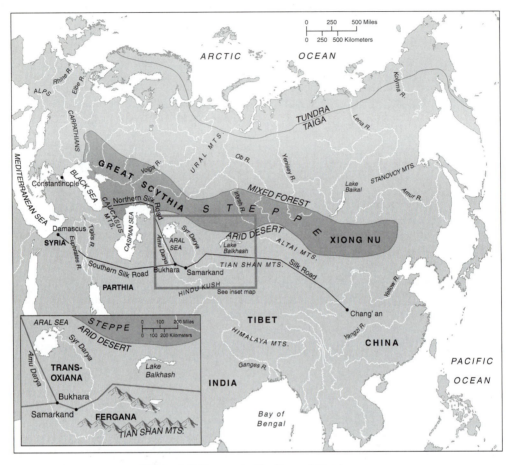

Figure 1-5 Europe in the Second Century B.C.E.

By the second century B.C.E., the Scythian Empire was in decline. The Outer Eurasian empires were at a peak of wealth and power, and for the first time the Silk Road extended all the way from China to the Mediterranean and Black Seas. However, nomad empires—the Scythians in the west and the Xiong Nu in the east still controlled the Eurasian steppe.

_____ FOR FURTHER READING _____

Barfield, Thomas J. *The Perilous Frontier: Nomadic Empires and China.* Cambridge, MA: Blackwell, 1989.

_____. *The Nomadic Alternative.* Upper Saddle River, NJ: Prentice Hall, 1993.

Chaliand, Gérard, *Nomadic Empires: From Mongolia to the Danube.* Trans. A. M. Berrett. New Brunswick, NJ: Transaction Publishers, 2004.

Christian, David. *A History of Russia, Central Asia and Mongolia. Volume 1: Inner Eurasia from Prehistory to the Mongol Empire.* Oxford: Blackwell, 1998.

Golden, Peter B. *An Introduction to the History of the Turkic Peoples.* Wiesbaden: Harrassowitz, 1992.

Khazanov, A. M. *Nomads and the Outside World.* Cambridge: Cambridge University Press, 1984.

Rice, Tamara Talbot. *The Scythians*, 3rd ed. New York: Thames and Hudson, 1961.

Sinor, Denis, Ed. *The Cambridge History of Early Inner Asia.* Cambridge: Cambridge University Press, 1990.

CHAPTER TWO

THE ORIGINS OF EAST SLAVIC CIVILIZATION, 500 TO 1000

Around 500 C.E., a people appeared in the western forests of Inner Eurasia who would turn the steppe tradition upside down. The Eastern Slavs entered the historical record first as tributaries of the Khazars, a pastoral empire of the steppe, and were soon afterward subordinated by the Vikings, river-traveling nomads from the north. By the beginning of the second millennium C.E., the Slavic agriculturalists began to assimilate their Viking rulers and to create the first self-sustaining, sedentary civilization of Inner Eurasia. The elites of this state (ultimately to be called "Russia") discovered the secret of governing a sedentary population: to fund their armies by taxation (and not periodic looting) and to secure the loyalty of their armies through ideology (and not charisma). The Russians, descendants of the Eastern Slavs, went on to build a larger Eurasian empire than any other conqueror except for Genghis Khan. If Russia could not match the Mongol Empire in extent, however, it far surpassed it in endurance. Russia is not only the northernmost civilization in world history, it is also, after more than one-thousand years, one of the longest-lived.

THE EURASIAN CONTEXT

China led Outer Eurasia in recovering from the invasions and imperial decay that had characterized the first half of the first millennium C.E. In 618, the Tang Dynasty was founded in cooperation with the same Turk tribes that had toppled the Han. Improved communications

Turn to page 39 for a map showing key geographic locations and features for this time period.

and expansion of irrigation fostered an economic revival that the Tang drew upon to fund its political expansion. Combining Chinese weapons (principally the crossbow) with Inner Eurasian cavalry skills, the Tang reestablished control over the Inner Eurasian borderlands all the way to the Fergana valley and reestablished trade with the West on the Silk Road. In the middle of the eighth century, the usual imperial overexpansion, court conspiracies, and provincial separatism set in; the Tang Dynasty ended in 907.

In 622, an Arab merchant, Muhammad, fled from Mecca to Medina, taking with him the followers of his new religion, Islam. He set in motion a series of events that led to the unification of the nomadic tribes of Arabia into a community and an army that, over the course of a century, built the largest empire in world history to that point. By 752, the Umayyad dynasty controlled the territory from the Indus River in the east through all of the Middle East (except for the Anatolian Peninsula), across North Africa, and up the Iberian Peninsula to the Pyrenees Mountains. In 752, the Umayyad Dynasty was overthrown everywhere but in the Iberian Peninsula and replaced by the Abbasid Dynasty. The Abbasids were a cosmopolitan ruling family who concentrated on promoting trade and prosperity instead of expanding their territory. They moved their capital from Damascus to the newly built Baghdad.

For the next five hundred years, the Abbasid empire was a center of world trade and a synthesizer of Eurasian knowledge. Abbasid merchants imported silk and porcelain from China; ivory, gems, and spices from India and Southeast Asia; gold and ivory from Africa; glass, linen, and pottery from Byzantium; horses and hides from the Steppe; and furs, wax, honey, and amber from the northern Eurasian forests. Arab and Persian artisans produced textiles, carpets, tiles, and paper. The Great Silk Road brought ideas as well as goods. From China came knowledge of astronomy and historical method, from India came mathematics, and from Greece came natural science, medicine, and philosophy. Muslim scholars made original contributions to all these fields, and they particularly excelled in algebra, chemistry, and medicine.

In 875, the Samanids, a Persian dynasty, asserted the independence of Transoxiana from the Abbasid empire. This did not affect trade patterns, however, since the Samanids made their capital in Bukhara, promoted industry and trade, and gave their protection to the middle section of the old Silk Road. The Samanid dynasty also fostered a Persian cultural renaissance.

After 500, the Roman Empire contracted dramatically. The western half of the empire, of which Rome was the capital, had been weakened by provincial separatism, economic decline, and invasions by Germanic and Central Asian armies. The last emperor in Rome was deposed in 476, and the provincial structure disintegrated, replaced by a number of pagan Germanic kingdoms. Then, from the middle of the seventh century to the middle of the eighth, as noted above, Arab armies took over Rome's southern Mediterranean territory from Syria to the border of Gaul.

The western (European) provinces of the old Roman Empire fared badly after Rome's collapse. The loss of Mediterranean trade routes to Muslim merchants continued the economic decline of the west, and Europe reverted to a subsistence economy. Cities disappeared as unemployed artisans sought refuge on the estates of rural magnates. Feudalism and manorialism solved the problems of survival and security for most of the population but at the cost of localism and poverty. Trade did not entirely disappear, and in the eighth century the increasing use of silver coins in Frisia signified the beginning of an economic revival. However, it was not for two hundred years that prosperity really returned to Europe.

The remaining Roman Empire included little more than the Balkan and Anatolian Peninsulas including the former eastern capital of the empire, Constantinople. This abridged empire was officially called the Eastern Roman Empire, but it is also referred to as the Byzantine

Empire, or Byzantium, after the name of the Greek city near which Constantinople had been built. Its agricultural productivity, high level of technology, and strategic location allowed the Eastern Roman Empire to continue as a major civilization for another millennium.

Constantinople was the largest, wealthiest, and culturally richest Eurasian city west of Baghdad. It was the western end of the Silk Road and the nexus of trade for the European and Mediterranean world. Emperors in Constantinople continued to think of themselves as *Roman* Emperors, and some of the greatest achievements of Roman Civilization, among them the codification of Roman law by the Emperor Justinian (527–65), took place there after the Empire in the west had fallen. Constantinople was also a Christian religious center.

The Emperor Justinian elaborated a theory of "symphony" between state and church, in which the secular government provided for the material needs of the population and the church provided for their spiritual needs. He created a church hierarchy that paralleled the imperial hierarchy at every level, except the very highest. He gave the bishops of five major cities (Constantinople, Rome, Antioch, Jerusalem, and Alexandria) the title "patriarch," and he apportioned the ecclesiastical administration of the provinces among them. There was no head of the church to parallel the position of emperor, since Justinian considered the Roman Emperor to be the head of both state and church.

The eastern patriarchs accepted this arrangement, but the bishops of Rome, who were beyond the control of the Eastern Roman Emperors, did not. They argued that the bishop of Rome, called the Pope, was the successor of St. Peter, who had been chosen by Jesus Christ to lead the Church. The considered that their office had supremacy over the whole Christian church in matters of both faith and government. An open break did not occur until after the turn of the millennium, but the trend toward an East-West division of the church had begun.

Across Inner Eurasia, no single nomadic empire arose to succeed the first Turk empire, whose decline had coincided with the rise of the Tang. In the East, between the seventh and ninth centuries, a second Turk empire and its successor Uighur Empire briefly ruled the steppe north of China. In the west, a Turk tribe known as the Khazars built a major and relatively long-lasting state.

Originating in the early seventh century in the territory between the Caspian and Black seas, the Khazars had, by the ninth century, mastered the western steppe from the Ural River to Danube and presented a serious challenge to the Abbasid and Byzantine Empires. Itil, the capital of the Khazar empire, was built where the Volga flows into the Caspian Sea on the intersection of two major trade routes—the northern branch of the Old Silk Road, and a route from Baghdad to Scandinavia via the Volga. Some Khazars settled down to farming, many continued to be pastoralists, and there was significant mining and smelting of iron in the southern Urals. However, the greatest source of wealth for the Khazar empire was trade, the taxation of trade, and the imposition of tribute on neighboring peoples.

The Bulgars, Turkic-speaking descendants of the Huns, were one of those subordinate peoples. Their principal city, Great Bulgar, was built where the Kama River flows into the Volga. Like Itil, Great Bulgar stood at the intersection of two trade routes—the Volga (mentioned above) and an east-west caravan route from the cities of Central Asia toward Europe. By the tenth century, the Bulgars economy was complex, including summer pastoralism, sedentary agriculture, and commerce. The most notable items of exchange were furs from the Finns and Lapps in north, silver coins from Central Asia and the Middle East, and hides, cattle, and agricultural goods produced by the Bulgars, themselves.

The northern end of the Volga trade route was dominated by Scandinavians who connected the reviving trade centers of northwestern Europe with the routes that intersected in Great Bulgar and Itil. Although a part of the European cultural zone and originally an agricultural people, the Scandinavians had begun to adopt the characteristics of nomadic adventurers. The invention of the long-boat (large, ocean-worthy vessels with a draft shallow enough to navigate rivers and which could be propelled by sails as well as oars) provided them mobility, and the quickening of inter-regional trade provided the incentive for clan leaders to organize young men into bands of treasure-seekers called Vikings. Vikings traded with the strong and plundered the weak.

In the late eighth century, trade had revived on the coast of the North Sea, and, before native princes were able to find ways to tax this wealth and translate it into military power, the Vikings looted it. Beginning with raids on the coasts of the British Isles, Vikings soon expanded their expeditions to the coasts of Portugal, Spain, and Italy. By the middle of the ninth century, Viking armies were even sailing up the Seine and demanding massive payments in silver from Paris.

In the East, the situation was somewhat different. There were no monasteries or cities with concentrations of portable wealth to plunder. Instead, riches were to be obtained by trade and by tribute in kind. As early as 750, a Scandinavian trading settlement, Staraia Ladoga, was built where the Volkhov River flows into Lake Ladoga. The Vikings obtained pelts of arctic fur-bearing animals from the local Baltic and Finnish tribes and became the principal suppliers of luxury furs to Europe. Hoards of Arabian silver dirhams in the north show that these Vikings had also discovered a market for fur on the Volga trade route. However, Great Bulgar, at the junction of the Volga and Kama Rivers, was too strong for the Vikings to conquer, and in their search for alternative routes south, they discovered the Dnieper River and the Slavs.

THE SLAVS

The Slavs speak an Indo-European language, they are culturally European, and they appear to have originated in the general territory between the Baltic Sea and the Danube River. Some East Slavic traditions hold that Slavs have lived in the Dnieper River valley from time immemorial, but so far there is no firm evidence to support this belief. The Slavs are not mentioned by name by Herodotus, but by the time of the Vikings and Khazars they were the predominant ethnic group west of the Volga and north of the steppe.

The Byzantine Empire felt threatened by the presence of a Slavic military organization on its Danube frontier around 500 C.E., and it is in Byzantine records that the Slavs first appear in written history. It is only from that point that we can detect the spread of Slavic culture eastward into the territory that is now Belarus, Ukraine, and Russia. There is evidence that some of this expansion was caused by population movement (not of entire communities escaping hard times but of groups of young families moving from overpopulated regions to lands of greater opportunity). However, the spread of Slavic culture was more rapid than can be explained by population growth alone. Part of the expansion must have resulted from the adoption of Slavic language and culture by the people who were already living there.

The Slavs, and the neighbors they settled among, were farmers. In the forests they practiced "slash and burn" agriculture. The first stage of this process involves killing trees by cutting a ring of bark from around the trunk and sowing grain in the now-unshaded soil around them. Some years later, after the initial fertility of the forest floor is used up, the trees are cut down and burned and the ashes are plowed into the soil. Once this restored fertility is used up, however, there is no other option than to move to another region of forest and begin the process again. In the wooded steppe, a two-field system was used. Farmland was used until it lost its productivity, then new fields were plowed and the old ones were left to lie fallow. Agriculture was not practiced on the steppe proper for two reasons: The turf was too thick to be cut by the Slavs' wooden plows (even the *sokha,* on which the wooden plow-share was covered with metal, did little more than scratch the surface of the soil), and the steppe was the realm of nomad pastoralists.

The Slavs lived primarily on grain. Black (rye) bread was their staple food. Rye is the only grain other than wheat than can be made into loaves, and rye is also the hardiest of the small grains. Wheat did poorly in the cold climate of the Inner Eurasian forest, and it was considered a luxury crop. The Slavs also ate oats, barley, and millet as porridge. Hemp and flax, which the Slavs grew for making cloth, also provided seeds for food and oil. The Slavs drank mead (honey wine) and kvass (a weak beer made from bread crusts or grain). They supplemented their cereal diet with meat from cattle and pigs, wild game (mostly deer, pheasants, and partridges) and fish.

Slavic society was patriarchal, conservative, and egalitarian. The Slavs believed that the world was perfect in its creation and that proper behavior was to adhere as closely as possible to the supposedly original forms and customs. Slavic chiefs, therefore, didn't have the power to innovate but were only authorized to put into effect what the tribal assembly agreed was required by tradition.

Ancient Neolithic animism lived on in Slavic religion. There were Slavic cults of stones, trees, and wells. Slavs believed that trees had spirits (every house was believed to have a *domovoi* or house-spirit, which came from one of the trees of which the house was made), and the birch was particularly sacred. *Rusalki* (the spirits of virgins who died violently and who lure men to their deaths in the forests and rivers) were probably also remnants of animism. Little is known of the traditional gods of the Slavs, but they don't seem to have had parallels with the sky gods of Greek and Norse mythology, since they appear to have lacked a father god or a god of war. The moon rather than the sun was their most venerated heavenly body.

Many scholars have emphasized the female elements of Slavic religion. They point out that "Venus statuettes" (stone figurines representing naked female figures with exaggerated breasts, stomachs, and buttocks) seem to have originated in the forests north of the Black Sea. They interpret these statuettes as fertility symbols associated with the worship of the Great Goddess, Mother Earth, and they believe that the Slavs acquired this gynocentric religion when they settled in the region. G. P. Fedotov asserts that "In Mother Earth, who remains the core of Russian religion, converge the most secret and deep religious feelings of the folk."[1]

This position has much to recommend it, but it must also be noted that the Slavic practice of ancestor worship (or worship of the clan) was male-centered, focusing on Rod, a male fertility deity who was worshiped in the form of a phallus. Moreover, the rights of women were not notably different from typical patriarchal societies. Marriage was universal, spouses were chosen by parents or elders, virginity was expected in brides, and, when multiple spouses existed, it was men and not women who were permitted them. Furthermore, the earliest known form of marriage among the Slavs was a ritualized form of bride abduction. Festivities were held in the late spring or early summer in honor of Lado, the Slavic god of marriage, during which men would carry away the women they had previously agreed to marry.

Slavic settlement patterns seem to have been based on tribal affiliation. The typical community was a cluster of villages only a few miles from one another containing several hundred inhabitants. The villages were made up of about a dozen houses each. The houses were small (probably holding no more than a single family) wooden structures dug halfway into the ground for warmth. In the eighth and ninth centuries such tribal clusters were typically located about twenty miles apart. The widespread diffusion of these small communities and the absence of great accumulated wealth suggests that the Slavic society was not particularly hierarchical or differentiated into specialized occupations.

Settled farmers though they were, the Slavs were aware of the advantages of trade. The appearance of silver coins dirhams and jewelry in Slavic towns of the ninth century suggests that they established some connection with the Volga—perhaps as guides for trading parties, perhaps as suppliers of agricultural goods, honey, wax, and squirrel pelts. In consequence, Slavic settlements at strategic locations on rivers acquired merchant and artisan suburbs and built protective stockades of earth and timber. By 900, several cities existed in the land of the Slavs, of which Kiev, on the Dnieper River, was the largest. Local chiefs appear to have had considerable power and were able to raise forces for defense against invaders, but there appears to have been no native drive to unify the Slavs into one state.

VIKINGS, SLAVS, AND THE ORIGIN OF "RUSSIA"

The traders and raiders who were based in the Viking community centered at Staraia Ladoga were known as the Rus by the Arabs and Rhos by the Greeks. *Rus* is a Finnish word that means "rowers" or "crew of oarsmen," however, and it does not necessarily refer to an ethnic group. The customs and language of the Rus (as the word is transliterated from Slavic) were Scandinavian (Swedes probably predominated), but from what we know of nomadic trading societies, we should expect that the Rus absorbed members of the peoples they came in contact with. They would have taken wives or concubines and accepted the services of ambitious young men from the peoples they traded among. Moreover, ethnicity is a learned and not a genetic characteristic. It is therefore most useful to think of the Vikings not as an ethnic group but as an occupational category—perhaps inspired and led by Scandinavians but behaving in ways typical of nomads who trade and raid.

In the course of their explorations southward, looking for routes to the wealth of Constantinople, Black Sea cities, and the Arab Middle East, the Rus discovered the Slavs. In the beginning, the Rus were a parasitic, tribute-gathering army of pirates who periodically appeared to demand submission and tribute of slaves, furs, wax, and honey. Slav communities submitted when they had to and rebelled when they could. However, the long-term development of Rus-Slav relations was of accommodation. The Rus tribute takers managed to moderate and regularize their exactions and to justify them by providing military protection. At the same time, a dual process of assimilation took place. Members of the Slavic elite began to enter the Rus ruling circles, while the Rus adopted the language and culture of the Slavs and intermarried with them. By 1000 C.E., the land of the Rus was well on its way to being a national state.

How this process occurred is reflected in the traditional, and legendary, *Primary Chronicle* or *Tale of Bygone Days,* compiled by Slavic Christian monks in the twelfth century. Though not to be taken at face value, it is a story with which all students of Russian history should be familiar. The *Chronicle* tells that in 862 the Slavic tribes were continually at war with one another. To end their fighting, they invited the "Varangian Rus" to rule over them and provide law and order. Three brothers, each with a *druzhina* (retinue) including Rurik, the eldest and the leader, settled in Novgorod. Rurik is the legendary progenitor to whom all Russian Grand princes and tsars, until 1598, traced their ancestry.

When Rurik died, he bequeathed his rule to a relative, Oleg, asking him to care for Rurik's young son Igor. In 882, Oleg led an army of Slavs and Rus down the Volkhov River to the Dnieper and took possession of the city of Kiev and imposed tribute on the local Slavic tribes. Oleg followed this success with an assault on Constantinople, and, though he failed to conquer the city, he won favorable trading terms and gifts. However, the Rus were neither allies of Constantinople nor the accepted rulers of the Slavs, and when Igor succeeded Oleg, he had again to lay siege to Constantinople to maintain trading rights and extort cash payments in exchange for peace. Igor also had to reconquer the Slavic tribes to maintain the payment of tribute. One tribe, the Derevlians, was strong enough to resist; they killed Igor and his druzhina when they came to collect their tribute in 945.

Olga, Igor's widow, ruled the Rus from 945 until 956, while their son, Sviatoslav, was young. Olga is famous in legend for her revenge on the Derevlians for the murder of Igor. Pretending three successive times to entertain the Derevlian prince's retinue, Olga used stratagems to bury the first delegation alive in a pit in her banquet hall, to burn the second delegation in a bathhouse, and to make the third delegation drunk with mead so they could be massacred. In fact, she appears to deserve credit for a new vision for the land ruled by the Rus. She attempted to reduce Rus-Slav conflict by reducing the amount of tribute levied on the Slavs and making its collection regular and predictable. Her relation with Constantinople was that of ally rather than an extortioner, and when she traveled there in 948 she was welcomed with the respect due to a head of state. Moreover, while in the Byzantine capital, Olga converted to Christianity.

Olga was unable to convert her son, Sviatoslav, to her new religion or her new vision of the Rus. Sviatoslav had no interest in becoming the ruler of a Christian people or a sedentary state in the orbit of Constantinople. Instead, he pursued imperial expansion. In the west, he mounted major campaigns against Constantinople and even moved his capital from Kiev to the southwest edge of the forest to be closer to the wealth of Byzantium. In the east, he seems to have aimed for direct contact with the trade caravans of Central Asia, since he attempted to conquer both the Volga Bulgars and the Khazars. The Bulgars were able to withstand him, but the Khazars were not, and Sviatoslav's victory over them in 965 marked the end of their power.

Sviatoslav also had to deal with a new society of nomadic pastoralists, the Pechenegs, who came out of the East to occupy the steppes north of the Black Sea. Although the later Christian compilers of the *Chronicles* portrayed the pagan nomads as fearful, godless enemies, in fact there was considerable cooperation between them and the Rus. Trade of agricultural goods for cattle was mutually beneficial, and the two peoples seemed to know one another well. Indeed, over the years, the Rus had come to resemble steppe nomads to a considerable degree. Originally the Vikings had been soldiers who, although they traveled in boats, fought on foot with swords and axes. However, after prolonged contact with the nomadic warriors of the steppe, the Rus learned to ride horses and use bows and arrows.

In the end, however, the Pechenegs were the death of Sviatoslav. In the spring of 972, on his way back from yet another successful expedition against Constantinople, while sailing up the Dnieper River, Sviatoslav was ambushed and killed by their chief. Surely few Slavs grieved to hear of their overlord's demise. Sviatoslav had not followed his mother's example and continued his forefathers' exploitative practices. He had sent his relatives with their druzhinas to occupy cities and gather tribute. Sviatoslav's oldest son, Iaropolk, ruled Kiev, and one of his younger sons, Vladimir, ruled Novgorod. This can hardly be called a government, since the only service they seem to have provided was to keep other tribute collectors away. Justice, the first sign of real government, was administered by the Slavs themselves according to their traditions.

For five years after Sviatoslav's death, his sons fought one another for the right to rule all the land of the Rus, and in 978 Vladimir emerged triumphant and established himself as Grand Prince of Kiev. Superficially, Vladimir appeared to carry on the same political and military traditions as his predecessors suppressing independent-minded Slavic cities, fighting the Pechenegs, and trading with Byzantium. At the same time, however, there is reason to think Vladimir was moving toward a new conception of the relation of the Grand Prince of Kiev to the population that paid him tribute.

From the beginning of his rule, Vladimir began to reverse the old traditions according to which Rus ruled Slavs. In 980 he had sent a band of Rus, who were demanding additional tribute from the local population, toward Greece with instructions not to come back. Vladimir seems to have wanted to show an emotional connection between himself and the Slavs, since he set up a temple with idols of Slavic deities. Moreover, Vladimir was also content to rule a nation of sedentary agriculturalists—predominantly Slavs but including some Lithuanian and Finnish tribes in the north—and not seek a larger empire. When he defeated the Bulgars, for example, he did not attempt to destroy them or incorporate them into the land he ruled. Instead, he signed a peace treaty that secured a friendly buffer to the East. Neither did Vladimir mount the predatory raids on Constantinople that had been characteristic of the past. Instead, Vladimir sought an alliance with Emperor Basil II and sent armies to help him suppress an internal revolt. Vladimir thus seems to have conceived of Kiev Rus as a state in a stable state-system, not as an expansive empire. Vladimir wanted to marry the Emperor's sister and was willing to accede to her father's condition that he first convert to Christianity.

Vladimir's reorientation from the steppe and toward Byzantine civilization has a number of possible explanations. One was economic. Trade with the East was dwindling, and the flow of silver dirhams had virtually ceased following Sviatoslav's defeat of the Khazars, the former trade link with Bukhara and Baghdad. Another likely reason was ethnic. If Vladimir was attempting to build ties with the Slavs, his orientation toward Constantinople makes perfect sense. Eastern Christianity could provide both a common religious bond and a common written language.

In the 860s, two Byzantine monks, Cyril and Methodius (after their deaths saints in the Eastern Orthodox Church), were invited by a Slavic prince north of the Danube to bring Christianity to his people. Cyril and Methodius created an alphabet (now known as Cyrillic), based on Greek letters, for the Slavic language, and they translated the Bible and the Eastern liturgy into the new written form. Christianity spread rapidly among the Western Slavs and was making progress in the East. Indeed, in the land ruled by the Rus, Olga, Vladimir's grandmother, had not been the only, or even the first, to convert. By the time of Vladimir's conversion in 988 Christian churches already existed.

This is not to suggest that Vladimir was responding to popular demand. Declaring Christianity to be the official religion of the Slavs, converting them by force, and publicly destroying their pagan idols (that he had so recently erected) did not make Vladimir popular. In Novgorod, for example, the people revolted against the imposition of the new religion. Moreover, the majority of the people remained pagan for several more centuries.

Nevertheless, from a long-term political viewpoint, the effort of conversion was worthwhile: Vladimir was importing more than a set of religious beliefs, he also was bringing literacy to the Rus. Because the Slavic language had not yet differentiated into regional forms, Old Church Slavonic, as the written language is now called, was understood throughout the Slavic world. Therefore, anyone who learned to read and write the language of sacred literature could also communicate with Slavs on other subjects. When Vladimir sent his sons, with their druzhinas, to rule the cities of Rus, they were accompanied by bishops, priests, and deacons who worked closely with them in political administration.

The Christian church also provided ideological support for the Grand Prince. The Chronicle said of Vladimir, "He is the new Constantine of mighty Rome, who baptized himself and his subjects; for the Prince of Rus imitated the acts of Constantine himself." Thus Vladimir recreated the role of Constantine as the earthly protector of the Church and the faithful. Moreover, by marrying the sister of the Emperor of the Eastern Roman Empire, he made it possible for his dynasty to claim imperial blood.

Vladimir represented his ties with Byzantium symbolically by issuing gold coins with his image on them, thus imitating the Byzantine coins that had replaced Arab dirhams as the currency of the Rus. He also began a program of church construction on the Byzantine model—most notably the Church of the Tithe in Kiev, built between 989 and 996. By the end of Vladimir's reign, Kiev was an impressive city with forty churches and eight marketplaces.

Christianity also helped fuse the Rus, Slav, Finn, and Lithuanian elements of the population into a single culture. Following conversion, an influx of Greek teachers brought with them Gospels, psalms, liturgy, sermons, and saints lives. The *Chronicle* reports that Vladimir took the children of the best families and sent them to be educated in "book-learning." The process of conversion occurred simultaneously with the assimilation of the Slavic and Rus ruling classes into one another, and from this point on, the *Chronicle* no longer distinguishes between the two. "Boiars," "druzhina," and "elders" are used interchangeably and refer to a mixed aristocracy with no reference to ethnicity. The land of the Rus came to mean the entire population of the territory ruled by the descendants of Rurik—the Rurikovichi (singular, Rurikovich).

A people is defined not only by what it believes and by who its friends are but also by its enemies. For enemies, Vladimir chose the Pechenegs. He built forts on his southern borders and pushed them from one to two day's travel from the borders of Rus. It is impossible to tell if the Pechenegs were any more aggressive, or if Vladimir used the "Pecheneg threat" as a means of mobilizing and uniting his population. We do know that the Church participated enthusiastically in this project, portraying the pagan Pechenegs as minions of the devil, and setting a precedent for the way future church writers viewed nomadic pastoralists.

CONCLUSION: VLADIMIR'S ACHIEVEMENTS

As Vladimir grew old, he must have felt a great sense of achievement. He had established himself as sole ruler of the land of the Rus. He was recognized as the legitimate ruler by the Emperor of Byzantium and had married into the imperial family. He more than held his own against the Bulgars and Pechenegs. He had imported a religion (and with it a written language and literature) that connected his people with Byzantine civilization. He had begun to overcome the Slav-Rus divide and to transform tribute-takers into the administrators of a state. An East Slavic state and nation had begun to emerge.

NOTES

1. George Fedotov, *The Russian Religious Mind: Kievan Christianity, The Tenth to the Thirteenth Centuries* (New York: Harper and Row, 1946), 12.

---------------------------------- **TEXT DOCUMENTS** ----------------------------------

Ibn Rustah on the Slavs

Ibn Rustah was an Arab travel writer who wrote about the Rus and Slavs at the beginning of the tenth century, C.E.

- What appears to be the connection between lifestyle and geography? Are the Slavs sedentary or nomadic?
- Ibn Rustah says the Slavs have no plowed fields, yet they harvest millet. How do you explain this?
- What does this reveal about gender?
- Comparing this with Herodotus's account of the Scythians, what cultural practice does Ibn Rustah not seem to understand?

A city by the name of Kiev is situated at the very border of the land of the Slavs. The route to their country goes through the steppes, through trackless lands, across streams and dense forests. The land of the Slavs is a level and wooded land; and they live in the forest. They have neither vineyards nor plowed fields.

They make objects like pitchers from wood and put them out to be bee hives in which they collect honey. . . . They herd swine as sheep are herded.

When one of them dies, they burn his corpse. Their women, when they are bereaved, cut themselves with a knife on their arms and faces. On the day following the cremation of the deceased, they set off for the place where this was carried out, they gather the ashes and put them in an urn, then they place it in a mound.

If the deceased had three wives and one of them asserts that she especially loved him, then she takes two posts to where his corpse is. They drive them solidly into the ground, then they place a third pole crosswise and tie a rope in the middle of the cross-piece. She stands on a bench and ties the end of the rope around her neck. When she has done this, the bench is taken from under her, and she stays hanging until she strangles and dies, and after her death they throw her in the fire [with the body of her dead husband] where she burns up.

They are all idolaters. They plant more millet than anything else. During harvesting they take millet seeds in a scoop, raise them to the sky, and say "Oh God! You who have provided us food in the past, now also provide for us in abundance."

They have various kinds of lutes, psalteries, and reed-pipes. Their pipes are two cubits long and their lutes are eight-stringed. They prepare an intoxicating drink out of honey. During the cremation of the deceased they give themselves up to noisy celebration, thereby expressing their joy at the mercy shown to [the deceased] by god. They have very few draft animals, and saddle-horses are owned only by the notable man. [King?]

Their weapons consist of javelins, shields, and spears; and they have no other weapons . . .

Source: Ibn Rustah, from *The Book of Precious Treasures*. P. I. Lebedev, *Khrestomatiia po istorii SSSR*, vol. 1, *s drevneishikh vremen do kontsa XVII veka* (Moscow: Gosudarstvennoe Uchebno-pedagogicheskoe Izdatel'stvo Ministerstva Prosveshcheniia RSFSR, 1951), 41–42.

The cold in their country is so strong that each of them digs for himself out of the ground a kind of cellar to which he attaches a pointed wooden roof like the roof of a Christian church and then put earth on the roof. They live with their families in these cellars and, having taken some firewood and stones, light a fire and heat the stones in the fire until they are red. When the rocks are as hot as possible, they pour water on them, which produces steam and warms the habitation so much that they must actually take off their clothes. They stay in this house until spring.

Ibn Rustah and Gardezi on the Rus (Vikings)

The first of the following passages also comes from Ibn Rustah who knew the Vikings as the "Rus." The translator uses the term "Russia" to refer to the central Viking base—probably the town of Staraia Ladoga. The second passage come from yet another Arab writer, Gardezi, who rewrote Ibn Rustah's account in the middle of the eleventh century, adding information from other sources.

- What do the Rus (Vikings) have in common with nomads of the steppes?
- What is their economic and political relationship with the Slavs?
- What evidence of ethnic mixing is there?

IBN RUSTAH

Russia is an island around which is a lake, and the island in which they dwell is a three day's journey through forests and swamps covered with trees and it is a damp morass such that when a man puts his foot on the ground it quakes owing to the moisture.

They have a king who is called Khaqan Rus, and they make raids against the Slavs, sailing in ships in order to go out to them, and they take them prisoner and carry them off to Khazaria and Bulgar and trade with them there.

They have no cultivated lands; they eat only what they carry off from the land of the Slavs.

When a child is born to any man among them, he takes a drawn sword to the new-born child and places it between his hands and says to him: "I shall bequeath to thee no wealth and thou wilt have naught except what thou dost gain for thyself by this sword of thine."

They have no landed property nor villages nor cultivated land; their only occupation is trading in sables and grey squirrel and other furs, and in these they trade and they take as the price gold and silver and secure it in their belts [or saddle-bags].

Source: C. A. Macartney, *The Magyars in the Ninth Century* (Cambridge: Cambridge University Press, 1930), 213, 214, 215. Reprinted with the permission of Cambridge University Press.

They are cleanly in regard to their clothing, and the men wear bracelets of gold; they are kind to their slaves and clothe them well for they engage in trade.

The Russians have many cities and they expend much money on themselves.

GARDEZI

The clothing of the people of Rus and the Slavs is of linen and their men have gold bracelets on their hands. In the island is great cities [sic], and within it is an abundance of Sulaymani swords. When they make war, they are all of one mind, and do not have disputes, especially when in sight of the enemy.

Their king seizes a tithe from the merchants. Constantly 100 or 200 of them come to the Slavs and by force seize from them maintenance while they are there. From the Slavs many men go and serve the Russians in order that through their service they may be safe.

When a great man is slain, they make a grave for him in the earth, wide and large, as spacious as a house, and they place with him all his body-clothes and a handful of rice and a jug of . . . [missing from original] and wine and food and money, and they place his wife, still alive, with him, and seal the top of his grave, so that his wife dies.

Yngvar's Saga

Yngvar's Saga was written in Iceland in the early thirteenth century and was based on an oral tradition regarding a Viking (here called Russian) leader Yngvar and his son Svein who traveled in what is now Russia. The stories contain many fabulous elements and separating truth from fiction is difficult. However, the following account is surely based on typical encounters between Vikings and the people in the lands they visited.

- What does this reveal of the Viking spirit and the experience of long-distance trade in the premodern world?
- How does this shed light on the relation of trading to raiding?

They had been sailing for some time when Svein noticed a creek cutting into the land, and told his men to steer towards it. Since many of them were youngsters, they were only too keen to obey, and as they approached land they could see . . . a good many farmsteads. Then

Source: Hermann Palsson and Paul Edwards, Trans. and Ed., *Vikings in Russia: Yngvar's Saga and Eymund's Saga* (Edinburgh: Edinburgh University Press, 1989), 60–61. Reprinted with permission of Edinburgh University Press.

they caught sight of eight men running at astonishing speed towards them. One of the natives had a feather in his hand, and first he pointed up the stem of the feather, then the blade, which seemed to be a token of peace, so Svein responded with a hand-sign of peace too. The natives gathered under the lee-side of a cliff, offering various kinds of merchandise. Svein told his men they could go ashore, and they traded with the natives though neither side could understand what the other was saying.

Next day, Svein's men went ashore yet again to trade with the natives and for a while they exchanged goods, until one of the Russians tried to break an agreement he had just made to buy some furs. When the heathen lost his temper and punched him on the nose so that the blood poured onto the ground, the Russian drew his sword and sliced the heathen in two. At that the heathen people ran off shouting and screaming but in no time they gathered in what seemed an invincible army. But Svein told his men to arm themselves for war and march against the heathen, and in the fierce battle that followed the heathen, having no protective armor, fell in huge numbers. When they saw that they had lost the battle, the heathen ran, and Svein and his men won a great deal of plunder left behind by the others, which they carried down to the ships.

The *Primary Chronicle* on Olga and Byzantium

The Primary Chronicle *or* Tale of Bygone Days *is the oldest of the East Slavic records of the history of Rus. It was compiled in the twelfth century, approximately three-hundred years after the events described here, and it cannot be considered completely reliable.*

- What seems likely to be the underlying truth, and what is likely to be just a good story?

Olga went to Greece, and arrived at Constantinople. The reigning Emperor was named Constantine, son of Leo. Olga came before him, and when he saw that she was very fair of countenance and wise as well, the Emperor wondered at her intellect. He conversed with her and remarked that she was worthy to reign with him in his city. When Olga heard his words, she replied that she was still a pagan, and that if he desired to baptize her, he should perform this function himself; otherwise, she was unwilling to accept baptism. The Emperor, with the assistance of the patriarch, accordingly baptized her.

Source: Samuel Cross and Olgerd Sherbowitz-Wetzor, *The Russian Primary Chronicle, Laurentian Text* (Cambridge, MA: The Mediaeval Academy of America, 1953), 82.

After her baptism, the Emperor summoned Olga and made known to her that he wished her to become his wife. But she replied, "How can you marry me, after yourself baptizing me and calling me your daughter? For among Christians that is unlawful, as you yourself must know." Then the Emperor said, "Olga, you have outwitted me." He gave her many gifts of gold, silver, silks, and various vases, and dismissed her, still calling her his daughter.

Accounts of Sviatoslav

Below are two accounts of Grand Prince Sviatoslav. The first comes from the Primary Chronicle. The second comes from a Byzantine writer.

- Compare Sviatoslav in both actions and appearance with his Rus ancestors. With the Scythians. How do you explain the similarities and differences?
- What is his relationship with Byzantium? With Kiev Rus?

From the *Primary Chronicle:* When Prince Sviatoslav had grown up and matured, he began to collect a numerous and valiant army. Stepping light as a leopard, he undertook many campaigns. Upon his expeditions he carried with him neither wagons nor kettles, and boiled no meat, but cut off small strips of horseflesh, game, or beef, and ate it after roasting it on the coals. Nor did he have a tent, but he spread out a horse-blanket under him, and set his saddle under his head . . .

Sviatoslav marched to the Danube to attack the Bulgarians. When they fought together, Sviatoslav overcame the Bulgarians, and captured eighty towns along the Danube. He took up his residence there, and ruled in Pereiaslavets, receiving tribute from the Greeks.

Sviatoslav advanced against the Greeks, who came out to meet the Rus. When the Rus perceived their approach, they were terrified at the multitude of the Greek soldiery, and Sviatoslav remarked, "Now we have no place whither we may flee. Whether we will or no, we must give battle. Let us not disgrace Rus, but rather sacrifice our lives, lest we be dishonored. For if we flee, we shall be disgraced. We must not take to flight, but we will resist boldly, and I will march before you. If my head falls, then look to yourselves." Then his warriors replied, "Wherever your head falls, there we too will lay down our own." So the Rus went into battle, and the carnage was great. Sviatoslav came out victor, but the Greeks fled. Then Sviatoslav advanced toward the capital fighting as he went, and destroying towns . . .

The Emperor accordingly requested Sviatoslav to approach no nearer, but to accept tribute instead. For Sviatoslav had indeed almost reached Constantinople. So the Greeks paid him tribute, and he took also the share of those Rus who had been slain, promising that their

Source: Cross, *The Russian Primary Chronicle,* 84–85, 88–89, 90. Lebedev, *Khrestomatiia po istorii SSSR,* vol. 1, 61.

families should receive it. He accepted many gifts besides, and returned to Pereiaslavets with great acclaim.

[He then set off up the Dnieper.]

When spring came in 972, Sviatoslav approached the cataracts, where Kurya, Prince of the Pechenegs, attacked him; and Sviatoslav was killed. The nomads took his head, and made a cup out of his skull, overlaying it with gold, and they drank from it.

[*From a Byzantine account:*]

Sviatoslav crossed the river in a sort of Scythian boat, and, sitting at an oar, rowed on an equal footing with the others. This is how he looked: he was of medium height not too tall, not too small, with thick eyebrows, blue eyes, a flat nose, a shaved beard, and a thick, long mustache hanging from his upper lip. His head was completely bald, except on one side there hung a lock of hair signifying the nobility of his birth. His neck was thick, his shoulders were broad, and his whole figure quite well-proportioned. He seemed gloomy and savage. In one of his ears there hung a golden ear-ring adorned with two pearls and a ruby set between them. His clothing was white, and not distinguishable from the others except in cleanliness . . .

Vladimir and the Conversion of Kiev Rus

Vladimir, Grand Prince of Kiev (978–1015) not only himself converted to Christianity, he also decreed that the entire territory he ruled should convert. The Chronicle's *explanation of Vladimir's decision appears here.*

- Which of the following seem convincing?
- Which seem to reflect the prejudices of the Christian chronicler?

Vladimir was visited by [the Volga] Bulgars of the Muslim faith who said, "Though you are a wise and prudent prince, you have no religion. Adopt our faith, and revere Muhammad." Vladimir inquired what was the nature of their religion. They replied that they believed in God, and that Muhammad instructed them to practice circumcision, to eat no port, to drink no wine, and after death, promised them complete fulfillment of their carnal desires. . . . They also spoke other false things which out of modesty may not be written down. Vladimir listened to them, for he was fond of women and indulgence, regarding which he heard with pleasure. But circumcision and abstinence from pork and wine were disagreeable to him. "Drinking," said he, "is the joy of the Rus. We cannot exist without that pleasure."

Then came the Germans, asserting that they were come as emissaries of the Pope. They added, "Thus says the Pope: 'Your country is like our country, but your faith is not as ours. For our faith is the light. We worship God, who has made heaven and earth, the stars, the

Source: Cross, *The Russian Primary Chronicle,* 96–97, 111.

moon, and every creature, while your gods are only wood."' Vladimir inquired what their teaching was. They replied, "Fasting according to one's strength. But whatever one eats or drinks is all to the glory of God, as our teacher Paul has said." Then Vladimir answered, "Depart hence; our fathers accepted so such principle."

The Jewish Khazars heard of these missions, and came themselves saying, "We have learned that Bulgars and Christians came hither to instruct you in their faiths. The Christians believe in him whom we crucified, but we believe in the one God of Abraham, Isaac, and Jacob." Then Vladimir inquired what their religion was. They replied that its tenets included circumcision, not eating pork or hare, and observing the Sabbath. the Prince then asked where their native land was, and they replied that it was in Jerusalem. When Vladimir inquire where that was, they made answer, "God was angry at our forefathers, and scattered us among the gentiles on account of our sins. Our land was then given to the Christians." The Prince then demanded, "How can you hope to teach others while you yourselves are cast out and scattered aborad by the hand of God? If God loved you and your faith, you would not be thus dispersed in foreign lands. Do you expect us to accept that fate also?"

[A delegate from Constantinople argues against the Bulgars, Germans, and Khazars, and tells Vladimir about Christianity. Vladimir does not choose Eastern Christianity until after he had sent envoys out to examine the ways the various religions were celebrated. The envoys reported:]

When we journeyed among the Bulgars, we beheld how they worship in their temple, called a mosque, while they stand ungirt. The Bulgar bows, sits down, looks hither and thither like one possessed, and there is no happiness among them, but instead only sorrow and a dreadful stench. Their religion is not good. Then we went among the Germans, as saw them performing many ceremonies in their temples; but we beheld no glory there. Then we went to Greece, and the Greeks led us to the edifices where they worship their god, and we knew not whether we were in heaven or on earth. For on earth there is no such splendor or such beauty, and we are at a loss how to describe it. We only know that God dwells there among men, and their service is fairer than the ceremonies of other nations. For we cannot forget that beauty."

Vladimir and Constantinople

During his reign, Vladimir did not attack Constantinople, but the Chronicle *does report that he forced the surrender of the Greek city of Chersonesus on the Crimean Peninsula. His goal was not to force better trade relations, but for quite another reason.*

- Compare Vladimir's relationship with Constantinople with Sviatoslav's.
- Can you speculate on the reason for and the significance of the change?

Vladimir and his retinue entered the city, and he sent messages to the Emperors Basil and Constantine, saying, "Behold, I have captured your glorious city [Chersonesus]. I have also heard that you have an unwedded sister. Unless you give her to me to wife, I shall deal with your own city [Constantinople] as I have with Chersonesus." When the Emperors heard this message they were troubled, and replied, "It is not meet for Christians to give in marriage to pagans. If you are baptized, you shall have her to wife, inherit the Kingdom of God, and be our companion in the faith. Unless you do so, however, we cannot give you our sister in marriage. When Vladimir learned their response, he directed the envoys of the Emperors to report to the latter that he was willing to submit to baptism . . .

Source: Cross, *The Russian Primary Chronicle,* 112.

VISUAL DOCUMENTS

Figure 2-1 Cathedral of St. Sophia, Istanbul

The Cathedral of St. Sophia in Constantinople (called Istanbul today) was completed in 537 C.E. As Constantinople's most magnificent architectural monument, it has been a must-see sight for any tourist (or foreign emissary) to visit that city ever since.

- What would you expect would be the impression of this building on a visitor to Constantinople who had come from a city in the forests of the Dnieper River valley?
- Judging from the *Chronicle's* account of the conversion of the Rus, do you think it likely that Vladimir's emissaries visited this cathedral?
- How convincing is the *Chronicle's* account?

Source: Hirmer Fotoarchiv.

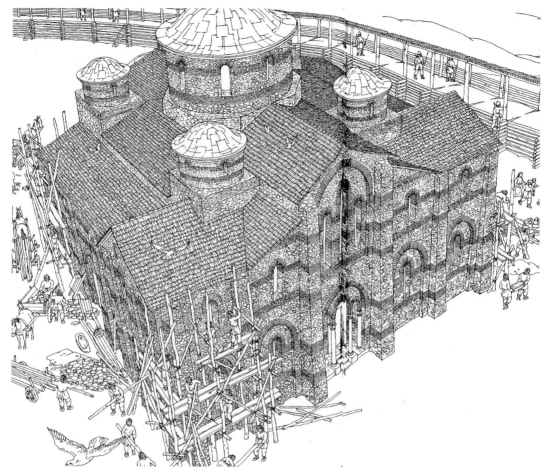

Figure 2-2 Church of the Tithe, Kiev

This is an artist's reconstruction of the Church of the Tithe, built by Vladimir in Kiev in 989 or soon after. It was incomparably bigger than any church previously built in the territory of Kiev Rus.

• What does the building of the Church signify for economy and society of Kiev Rus?
• What does it reveal about Vladimir's cultural orientation?

Source: Zdenek Vana, *Svet davnych Slovanu* (Prague: Artia, 1983).

Figure 2-3 Arab Dirham (815–816) of the Abbasid Period

Figure 2-4 Michael III. Byzantine Emperor (842–867)

In Michael's reign, the Varangians first appeared at the gates of Constantinople and Cyril and Methodius began their missionary work among the Eastern Slavs.

Figure 2-5 Kiev Rus Coin with the image of Vladimir (978–1015)

Coins can be much more than arbitrary tokens representing purchasing power. They can be valued in themselves, as precious metals (for making jewelry, for example), and they can serve a symbolic function.

- What are the similarities and differences among these coins?
- What do coins tell about trade routes and interactions among people?
- For what reasons might Vladimir have struck his own coins? Why were they similar to Byzantine and not Arab coins?

Source: Stanislav de Chaudoir, *Obozrenie Russkikh deneg i inostrannykh monet upotrebliavshikhsia v Rossii s drevnikh vremen* (St. Petersburg: Tipografiia Ekspeditsii Gosudarstvennykh bumag, 1835), Part 1, plate 1, drawing 6.

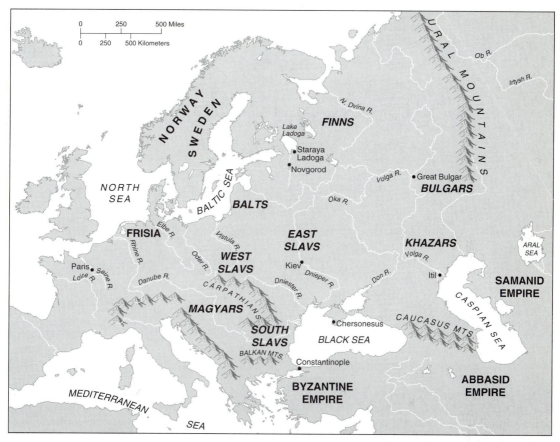

Figure 2-6 Western Inner Eurasia in the Ninth Century, C.E.

By the 800s,. when the Vikings began their eastern trading and raiding expeditions to the Byzantine, Abbasid, and Samanid Empires, Western Inner Eurasia was populated by the Slavs, Bulgars, and Khazars.

FOR FURTHER READING

(In addition to the book by Christian noted in Chapter One.)

Barford, P. M. *The Early Slavs: Culture and Society in Early Medieval Eastern Europe.* Ithaca, NY: Cornell University Press, 2001.

Cross, Samuel and Olgerd P. Sherbowitz-Wetzor. *The Russian Primary Chronicle, Laurentian Text.* Cambridge, MA: The Mediaeval Academy of America, 1953.

Franklin, Simon and Jonathan Shepard. *The Emergence of Rus, 750–1200.* London: Longman, 1996.

Levin, Eve. *Sex and Society in the World of the Orthodox Slavs, 900–1700.* Ithaca, NY: Cornell University Press, 1989.

Martin, Janet. *Medieval Russia, 980–1584.* Cambridge: Cambridge University Press, 1995.

Chapter Three

Kiev Rus, 1000–1240

During the reign of Vladimir (978–1015), a distinctive civilization began to appear among the Eastern Slavs. The state ceased to be an alien presence as its leaders adopted Slavic language and culture and provided security, law, and order to the population. The rather diverse population living in the territory governed by the emerging state of Kiev Rus acquired a homogenous and distinctive culture. The majority Slavs absorbed Scandinavian, Finn, Lithuanian, Khazar, Bulgar, and other communities. Christianity provided a literate high culture for urban elites, and Christian ceremonies began to replace pagan practices among the rural population. The creation of a Church organization (the Metropolitanate of Rus) to coincide with the boundaries of the state further reinforced the unity and homogeneity of Kiev Rus.

From the reign of Vladimir until the Mongol conquest (978–1240), Kiev Rus was tied to Europe economically, culturally, and dynastically. Novgorod was the easternmost outpost of the Hanseatic League, supplying Europe with furs and forest products, while Kiev maintained its connection with Constantinople, providing the Mediterranean world with slaves. Kiev Rus, like Western Europe, was a Christian society (though as time went on strains developed between the Western and Eastern churches). Vladimir's descendants married children of Polish, English, Swedish, Danish, and French monarchs, Byzantine and Holy Roman emperors, and Polovtsian khans. Indeed, Kiev Rus was the leading European country of its time. Kiev was larger and more magnificent than any other European city but Constantinople. The territory ruled by Vladimir's heirs was more urbanized, covered more territory, and had a larger population than any other country in Europe.

Turn to page 60 for a map showing key geographic locations and features for this time period.

THE EURASIAN CONTEXT

In the period 900 to 1250, eastern Outer Eurasia was fragmented, Central Asia and the Middle East experienced political instability and nomadic invasion, and a new civilization ("Western Civilization") arose in western Eurasia. The Eurasian economic boom continued, however, as goods and ideas flowed freely on the Great Silk Road.

After the fall of the Tang Dynasty in 907, China broke into three parts. The territory south of the Yangzi River valley was ruled by an ethnic Chinese dynasty, the Song. Northern China, divided in two, was ruled by steppe nomads: The northeast was ruled first by the Kitans then the Jurchens, while the northwest was ruled by the Tanguts. Nevertheless, the technological progress begun during the Tang continued. Chinese artisans discovered how to use gunpowder to fire projectiles, the compass was adapted to seafaring, and Song ships were the most technologically advanced in the world. The Chinese continued to produce the world's most prized silk, porcelain, iron, and steel.

In the Middle East, by 950, the Abbasid Empire existed in name only; Baghdad had lost the obedience of regional governors. Meanwhile, a Turkic chief named Seljuk had created a tribal confederation just south of the Syr Darya River. By the early eleventh century, his grandsons had conquered most of Central Asia and turned southward. In 1044, the Seljuk Turks conquered Iran, and in 1055, they were actually welcomed by the Caliph in Baghdad as a means of restoring the Abbasid Empire. The Seljuks not only restored the Empire by reuniting Iran with Mesopotamia, they also expanded it by defeating Byzantium in 1071 and seizing most of the Anatolian peninsula. This was followed by mass migration of Turks into Anatolia (which, thanks to them, would ultimately become known as "Turkey").

The Seljuk rulers created a state-supported system of public schools—the Madrassahs—that exerted considerable influence on western Eurasia. The immediate purpose of the schools was ideological—to promote Sunni and combat Shi'a doctrines—but they also advanced secular knowledge. Madrassahs systematically preserved and disseminated the Abbasid synthesis of Eurasian science, medicine, and technology not only throughout Southwest Asia, but, through Latin translations, to the Mediterranean world as well.

Seljuk rule lasted less than a hundred years. In the late eleventh century, dynastic rivalries appeared, and the Middle East was fragmented again. The last of the Middle Eastern empire-builders before the Mongol conquest was Saladin, a Kurdish general and governor of Egypt, who, by the time of his death in 1193, had consolidated under his rule all of the Middle East from Mesopotamia to Egypt. His dynasty, too, was brief; by the middle of the thirteenth century, Saladin's descendants lost their eastern lands to the Mongols and their western lands to the Egyptian Mamluks.

In the first quarter of the new millennium, Europe made a dramatic economic recovery. In the tenth century, Viking invasions abated, the climate improved, agriculture flourished, and the population grew. This made possible the revival of towns and trade. In the north the Germanic Hanseatic league exchanged wool textiles from the northwest for fish, furs, timber, and pitch from the northeast. In the south, Italian city-states connected Europe with Eurasia, exchanging salt, olive oil, wine, leather, and woolen cloth for Eastern luxury goods.

This economic upsurge made possible a dynamic new civilization at the center of which was the Christian Church. By 1000, Christian missionaries had converted all of the pagan nations that had replaced the western Roman Empire and the Church was the beneficiary of a popular piety which expressed itself in church construction and in support for monasteries and orders of friars. In high culture, the piety of the learned led to the development of Scholasticism, a systematic philosophy that attempted to express the Christian faith in Aristotelian terms. (The works of Aristotle, preserved by Arab scholars had been transmitted to

Christian Europe by way of Muslim Spain.) The Church also preserved and promoted the Roman idea of empire. The Pope, Bishop of Rome, stood at the head of an institutional structure that included all of western Europe, and he asserted his authority to lead the entire Christian community—including its secular rulers. Political power was personal and decentralized, and the monarchs of Europe were institutionally weak.

However, the idea of a national monarchy was developing (particularly in France and England) that contradicted the notion of a single Christian empire. European monarchs began to conceive of themselves as Roman emperors on a national (not imperial) scale. They claimed sovereign and indivisible governing and law-making authority within their territory—authority that was properly bequeathed to a single heir. Future conflict between the idea of empire and sovereign national state was inevitable.

Europe also became expansive and aggressive. After 1000, Christian armies began to push the Muslim Umayyad Dynasty from the Iberian peninsula. In 1095, Pope Urban II called for a Crusade, or "war for the cross," to do the same in the Holy Land. The coincidental collapse of the Seljuk dynasty meant that European armies faced little resistance, and they carved several Crusader states out of western Syria and Palestine. (These states lasted only as long as Muslim disunity did; Saladin drove the Europeans out.) The concept of Crusade was also applied to the pagan peoples in northern Europe. The King of Denmark and the Duke of Saxony sent armies to the Baltic to convert the Pagan Prus, Livs, Balts, and Finns to Christianity, and to rule them. This set the stage for conflict with the southeastern neighbors of these Baltic peoples—the Rus.

Meanwhile, the Byzantine Empire was besieged on all sides. In 1071, it suffered two major defeats; Seljuk armies seized most of the Anatolian peninsula, and Norman invaders conquered Sicily. Moreover, the Balkan provinces began to resist Byzantine rule, and by the middle of the thirteenth century, Greece, Serbia, and Bulgaria were independent. By 1240, the Byzantine Empire was limited to the northwest quarter of Anatolia and a small territory on the southern edge of the Balkan Peninsula.

In addition, the Byzantine belief that they were the successors of the Roman Empire was denied by the rising West. In 962, the German Otto the Great declared himself to be "Emperor of the Romans" (the title later known as "Holy Roman Emperor"). Simultaneously, the Pope, Bishop of Rome, pressed his claim to be the supreme ruler of the universal Christian Church. In the Great Schism of 1054, the Pope denounced the Eastern Church for violations of doctrine and excommunicated the Patriarch of Constantinople, who responded in kind. Then, to add injury to insult, when a Fourth Crusade was repelled by Muslim forces in the Holy Land in 1204, the Crusaders turned on Constantinople, which they conquered and sacked. They then installed a Roman Catholic regime, with a Patriarch appointed by the Pope, that ruled the city until 1261.

In the Caucasus in this period, the Kingdom of Georgia experienced its Golden Age. In the late ninth century, its Byzantine governor had declared Georgia's independence and declared himself its hereditary ruler. In subsequent centuries, his descendants united Georgia into one state. The height of Georgian power came in the reign of Queen Tamar (1184–1213) whose empire included most of the Caucasus region. The Golden Age came to an end when the Caucasus was overwhelmed by Mongol invaders in 1220.

The Pechenegs continued to control the steppe to the south of the Rus until the end of the eleventh century. In an attack on Constantinople in 1090, their army was destroyed, and their federation fell apart. Control of the steppe then passed to the Kipchaks, yet another association of Turkic tribes from northeast Eurasia. In the middle of the eleventh century, they had begun to cross the Don River, and after the Pechenegs were defeated by Byzantium, the Kipchaks assimilated the remnants of the Pecheneg federation. The Kipchaks did not attempt to conquer Byzantium or Kiev Rus or to create a sedentary empire. They lived off their herds, and carried on the typical nomadic "trade and raid" relationship with their neighbors.

POLITICS IN KIEV RUS

The rising prosperity of the Eastern Slavs, their conversion to Christianity, and Vladimir's work to turn a tribute-collecting system into a state all paralleled similar developments in the west. However, the structure of the state of Kiev Rus was strikingly different from the kind of national monarchy that was emerging in Western Europe. Vladimir did not declare himself to be the sovereign lord and source of law for all the Rus, he did not attempt to build a bureaucratic structure to implement his will, and he did not treat the land of the Rus as a single, indivisible realm to be inherited intact by his oldest son. Instead, Vladimir himself ruled the city of Kiev, and appointed his twelve sons to serve as princes of the dozen largest cities of the land. Furthermore, Vladimir did not attempt to create a unified national army under his command; instead, as the need arose, neighboring princes combined their military forces against the foreign threat. Thus Kiev Rus had the structural characteristics of a federation of city-states held together by family ties among the ruling princes. This ruling dynasty is known as the Rurikovichi, or descendants of Rurik.

The basic unit of government was the principality, which was composed of a major city and its surrounding towns and villages. In the beginning, these cities had served as winter residences and tribute collection depots, but as the Vikings assimilated into Slavic society and transformed themselves from plunderers into rulers, the cities became administrative centers. The prince, a Rurikovich, ruled the principality in cooperation with the residents of the city. Members of the city's wealthy elite were accepted into the prince's druzhina and so could influence policy. Additionally, each principal city had an assembly of all free males called a "veche." Little is known about the veche; it is mentioned in the *Chronicles* only during times of crisis when townspeople protested policies of or demanded action by the prince. On occasion, the veche even refused to accept the appointment of a particular prince. At no time did the people question the right of the Rurikovichi to rule, but they did occasionally restrict their prince's policy options.

A noteworthy feature of the Kiev Rus system was its lack of a codified method of passing political power from one generation to the next. Vladimir died without leaving written instructions regarding succession. It seems to have been understood, in accordance with the Rus principle of equal inheritance, that Vladimir's oldest son, Iaroslav, would move with his druzhina to Kiev to succeed his father as Grand Prince. His brothers would each move to the next most prestigious principality in order of seniority, and would wait their turn to inherit the right to be prince of Kiev when their older brothers died. When the last brother died, he would be succeeded by his most senior nephew, that is, the oldest surviving son of the oldest brother of the preceding generation.

However, the definition of "oldest son" was open to interpretation. Iaroslav was Vladimir's oldest natural son by his first wife. However, Vladimir later married a woman who had a son, Sviatopolk, by an earlier marriage who was older than Iaroslav. On the basis of his superior age, Sviatopolk challenged Iaroslav for the right to be Grand Prince of Kiev. Sviatopolk marched with his druzhina to Kiev, killed two of his younger brothers, Boris and Gleb, and declared himself Grand Prince. Iaroslav resisted what he considered a usurpation of power and waged war against Sviatopolk until 1019 when the latter died. Iaroslav then shared the leadership of Kiev Rus with his brother Mstislav. Iaroslav, Prince of Kiev, administered the territory to the east of the Dnieper while Mstislav, Prince of Chernigov, administered the western territories. After Mstislav died in 1036, Iaroslav was the undisputed senior member of the dynasty until his own death in 1054.

As his father, Vladimir, had done, Iaroslav sent his sons to rule the most important cities in the Kiev Rus state, no doubt expecting his eldest son to succeed him as Prince of Kiev and his younger sons to wait their turn in order of seniority. The seniority system, however, though perhaps reasonable in principle, was far from clear in practice. Iaroslav's oldest son, Iziaslav was challenged by a cousin who claimed seniority because his grandfather was an older brother of Iaroslav, who would have superceded him had he not died before Vladimir did. Once again, therefore, the descendants of Vladimir fought among themselves for the right to become Grand Prince.

As these examples show, this system produced a political history that is extraordinarily difficult to follow. The Rurikovichi had large families, a large and complex family tree grew, and the principles of seniority were open to interpretation, always self-interested. Nearly every succession was accompanied by an armed struggle, and, after the reign of Iaroslav the Wise (1019–1054), there was only one Grand Prince of Kiev, Vladimir Monomakh (1113–1125), who is credited with having ruled over a "united" Kiev Rus.

As a consequence, historians have tended to characterize Kiev Rus as chaotic, unruly, and always about to fall apart. Recent scholars, however, have discovered a fundamental coherence behind this apparent anarchy, so alien from the western nation-state tradition. Janet Martin has argued that succession struggles were not mere expressions of "might makes right."[1] Civil wars were not waged in violation of precedent, but to solve conflicting interpretations of how to apply precedent to a new (and ever more complicated) generation of princes. In addition, Simon Franklin and Jonathan Shepard suggest that the "civil wars" were comparatively nonviolent. The armed forces were quite small, often only a few hundred warriors on each side. The typical battle was either no battle at all—the weaker of the two sides backing down—or else a brief skirmish in which a few deaths decided the issue.[2]

The system makes sense if we think of sovereignty as being exercised not by an individual but by a family. Senior members of the clan might fight among themselves over the right to rule the cities of Rus, but no one disputed that the privilege was reserved without exception for direct descendants of Rurik (through Vladimir). The story of Kiev Rus is best understood, then, not as a series of individual rulers pursuing separate agendas but as a family that ruled collectively. A good example of this is the *Russkaia Pravda,* the first code of laws in Rus. It was attributed to Iaroslav, but it did not purport to be a statement of natural law issued in the name of a sovereign monarch. Instead it was a summary of past traditions issued on behalf of the ruling family. Later versions were referred to as "Iaroslav's Sons'" code.

The city of Kiev played a key symbolic role in this system. The capital city had mattered little to the empire-building Sviatoslav, but Vladimir chose it as a permanent capital for his state and church. Iaroslav the Wise not only continued his father's tradition, he elaborated on it. Iaroslav brought in Byzantine architects, builders, and artists, to construct and decorate four major churches, including St. Sophia, the biggest and most ornate church to be built in Rus for the next five-hundred years. Iaroslav also built new palaces and new city walls, and before he died, Kiev was by far the most magnificent of all Rus cities.

Iaroslav made Kiev a cultural and religious center as well. He introduced book culture into Kiev by bringing in translators from Byzantium to create a body of religious works in the common Slavonic language. He took an active role in Church affairs and appointed his own candidate, Ilarion, to be Metropolitan (one of only two Russians to serve in that office between 988 and 1240).

Thus Iaroslav used cultural symbolism rather than political institutions to hold the system together. The prestige of the office of Grand Prince was enhanced by the glory of his city. The junior Rurikovichi participated in the collective rule of Kiev Rus not because their obedience was compelled by the threat of force but because of their respect for Kiev and its prince. The grandeur of the city was expected to awe the Grand Prince's younger brothers and to incline them to support a system that would someday allow them to become the Grand Prince of Kiev.

RELIGION AND CULTURE

This system of collective rule was not the only factor keeping the principalities of Kiev Rus together. The unity of the state was also reinforced by the Christian Church, which supplied a centralized, hierarchical, and uniform structure, which was absent from the political realm. The Patriarch in Constantinople treated Kiev Rus as a province of the Empire. He appointed a Metropolitan of Rus with his capital in the city of Kiev. The metropolitan, in turn, appointed a bishop to each of the principalities. Within each principality (termed a diocese, another parallel with the Roman empire), the bishop was responsible supervising the priests and other church officials. Even though the Metropolitan was, in all but two cases, a Greek, the Church did not serve Byzantine political interests. In fact, the Church rarely intervened in politics and then only to prevent bloodshed.

Instead, the Church worked in full cooperation with the secular princes in administering their lands. Bishops had jurisdiction over violations of religions law, crimes committed by church people (monks, priests, etc.), and crimes against church property. This achieved two ends. It provided financial support for the Church by granting it the fees and fines. It also contributed to the development of a homogenous culture relating to family life (practices related to birth, marriage, and death), sexual behavior (outlawing, for example, polygamy, incest, and rape), and the daily, weekly, and seasonal rituals (prayer, mass, holidays, pilgrimages, and the celebration of Christmas and Easter).

Monasteries also served to integrate Rus culturally. They embodied Christian ascetic, pacifist, and humanitarian ideals not often found among princes or church hierarchy. The Monastery of the Caves in Kiev, for example, was created by the followers of certain holy hermits who lived in caves overlooking the Dnieper River. These followers received permission from Iaroslav's son to form a monastery. Feodosii, its second abbot, created a model that combined asceticism, discipline, and communal living with Christian social service. His monastery cared for prisoners, gave food and medical treatment to the poor and the physically disabled, and provided beds for travelers.

Another way in which monasteries promoted cultural unity was through their monopoly on book culture. It was in monasteries that books were translated, copied, and preserved. These works included not only religious works—liturgies, prayers, hymns, the Psalms, the Gospels, Saints' Lives, sermons, and antiheretical writings—but secular biographies and travel literature as well. Also in monasteries, monks complied chronicles, thus recording the history of the Rus. The major principalities each kept their own chronicle that recorded political events of local importance, but the authors consistently represented the Rus as a single people. This idea was also present in the writings of Ilarion, the first native Metropolitan of Rus. In his *Sermon on Law and Grace*, Ilarion implied that Rus was not a mere provincial extension of the Byzantine Church; it was its own country. He compared Vladimir with the Emperor Constantine as God's agent in converting his people, and he referred to the Rus as a "nation" given grace directly by God and not through the mediation of Constantinople.

A sense of identity can be sharpened by the creation of an "other"—an alien people that is both hostile and evil. Church writers found this "other" in the nomadic peoples of the steppe. They portrayed the Pechenegs and Kipchaks as wild, pagan, satanic enemies of civilization. They also blamed nomad victories over the Rus on a supposed "lack of unity" among the Rus princes. The reality of the matter was that although the Rus clashed occasionally with their steppe neighbors their relations were not exclusively hostile. There was significant exchange of goods and people across borders. Nomads enlisted in princely druzhinas; Slavs joined nomad tribes, Princely families from both sides intermarried, and Rus princes even used nomad allies in their civil wars.

It must be kept in mind that the cultural unity brought to Kiev Rus by the Christian Church applied at first only to the wealthy and powerful. Residents of the princely cities were the first to be converted. Each city had a bishop to educate and ordain priests and at least one cathedral with holy art (icons) to serve as a daily symbolic reminder of the Christian religion. The lower classes, particularly ordinary farmers, were the last segment of the population to be affected. Throughout the era of Kiev Rus, even after rural Slavs began to adopt Christian symbolism, such as making amber amulets in the shape of crosses or embroidering crosses into cloth, they still clung to their pagan traditions. They venerated household idols, they turned to sorcerers and witches for love potions, abortifacients, and cures for illness, and they held the old pagan fertility festivals featuring drinking, feasting, dancing, fighting, and sexual promiscuity.

ROLES AND STATUS OF WOMEN

The development of Christian civilization in Rus intensified patriarchal practices. As pagan, subsistence agriculturalists, young people had chosen their partners in spring marriage festivals. With the rise of a money economy, parents became more involved in the choice of spouses, and payment of a dowry from the bride's family to the groom's was introduced. The prospective bride's family would take her to the groom's house to meet his family, and, if an agreement was reached, the next day the bride's parents would return with the dowry payment. Christianity added a period of betrothal, a marriage contract, and a church ceremony performed by a priest.

Daughters in Kiev Rus did not have equal rights of inheritance with their brothers. When a father died his property was divided only among his sons, who were then responsible for taking care of their unmarried sisters (i.e., finding them husbands). Only if there were no sons could daughters inherit. In wealthy families, girls often received the same kind of education as sons, that is, grammar, mathematics, philosophy, astronomy, and foreign languages, especially Latin and Greek, but this did not confer any political rights. Mothers, sisters, and wives at times played important roles in political affairs, and in some cases wives even ruled in their husbands' absence, but no woman in Kiev Rus was officially recognized as a prince.

Christianity brought both benefits and limitations to the lives of women in Kiev Rus. On the positive side, it provided elite women opportunities for education and alternatives to the role of wife and mother. In 1089, the first convent, with a school for girls, was founded, and over the next two centuries monastic schools for girls became common. Nuns learned to read and write and copied books and compiled religious texts. Moreover, the Church tried to promote free choice in marriage by levying fines against any parents who forced a son or daughter to marry against their will.

On the other hand, the church also reinforced patriarchal practices. With the introduction of dowries, virginity acquired a monetary value. The Church sanctioned this by levying fines against women who had lost their virginity before marriage. Moreover, women could be divorced for sins that men were immune from: adultery, the attempted murder of a husband, and relations outside the home which "ruined her honor."

ECONOMIC TRENDS

Another force for unity was an interconnected urban economy, with Kiev at the center. Kiev received furs, wax, honey, amber, and slaves from the cities of the Rus and shipped back to them the luxury textiles, jewelry, glassware, wine, olive oil, spices, marble, glazed tile, and icons that it received from Constantinople. Moreover, as the Khazar Empire disintegrated, artisans from Itil moved to Kiev to ply their trades, and they were joined by Byzantine craftspeople who came to avoid the middleman and to produce directly for the Kievan market. These foreigners shared their skills with local artisans, and over the course of the eleventh century, Kiev became a center for the native production of pottery, leather goods, glassware, and gold and silver jewelry. The stonecutters, brick-makers, and masons who were brought to Kiev to build churches began a native construction industry.

Other cities thrived as well. Novgorod had its own economic base—obtaining furs, walrus ivory, and amber from the north by trading locally produced goods. It also continued to serve as a commercial link between northern Europe and the Volga trade route to the Muslim East. Novgorod supplied Kiev and the other cities of Rus with woolen cloth, salt, pottery, weapons, alcoholic beverages, and silver from Europe, and the usual luxury textiles from the East. Other principalities experienced economic booms as their princes instituted building projects and fostered trade. Towns multiplied. Kiev Rus had 89 towns in the eleventh century, 223 in the twelfth, and as many as 300 by the early thirteenth century.

The growth of towns could not have occurred, however, without a simultaneous expansion of agriculture. This, in turn, implied territorial expansion. Agricultural techniques changed little between 1000 and 1240, so increased production of food was made possible only by the tilling of new fields. Slash and burn agriculture was still practiced, the sokha was the most commonly used implement for tilling the soil, sickles were used to harvest grain, and scythes were used for cutting hay. Rye remained the principal crop, although millet, buckwheat, oats, barley, and wheat were also planted. Other foods included peas, lentils, and flax and hemp seeds. The agricultural population continued to keep beehives for their honey and wax, and to raise cattle, pigs, sheep, goats, and poultry. Like their ancestors, they hunted and fished, and they gathered wild berries, fruit, nuts, and mushrooms. Beginning in the twelfth century, East Slavic farmers planted apple orchards with stock which originated in Central Asia.

Though production methods did not change, patterns of landholding did. The first was the rise of the territorial commune or *mir*. Population movement and intermarriage broke down the clan or family-based farm community and produced villages of unrelated households. Each family owned its own house, livestock, and tools, and worked as an economic unit. The family owned the land they cultivated and could bequeath it to its children. All villagers had equal rights to use the commune's pastures for grazing cattle and forests for wood gathering, hunting and fishing. The mir was used as a local unit of taxation, administration, and law enforcement. Members shared the obligation to pay taxes. They followed traditional practices for dealing with violations of social norms among themselves, but when outsiders were involved, the commune was bound to follow the law of the state. If an outsider suffered a loss, or was injured or killed on communal lands, it was the responsibility of the entire community to make restitution.

The second major change was the movement of the wealthy elite and the Church into landholding and agricultural production. As the Rurikovichi transformed themselves from tribute-gatherers to administrators, their incomes shrank. To make up for the loss of plunder, they took possession of land (either by appropriating unused wilderness or by seizing a settled mir) and organized the production of goods for the market. These agricultural estates were managed by hired stewards and worked by indentured servants, slaves, or farmers who had lost their freedom when their land was confiscated. Princes' lands produced the same kinds of crops and cattle as free mirs, except they bred more horses. Over time, as princes made gifts of land to churches, monasteries, and their druzhinas, land ownership became a major source of income for all social elites. However, throughout this period, most of the land was still in the hands of the independent, self-governing mir.

SOCIAL STRUCTURE

Economic growth and diversification generally gives rise to social differentiation, and Kiev Rus was no exception to this rule. At the top of the social scale were the princes, the descendants of Rurik. They had a monopoly on the right to administer the cities of Kiev Rus and to lead its armies. Vladimir's sons and grandsons all seem to have had an equal right (based on seniority) to inherit the position of Prince of Kiev, but in later generations the family began to resemble a stratified class. Some branches entirely lost the right to become Prince and could hope to rise no further than prince of a lesser city. The youngest sons of youngest sons were often unable to administer any city at all and could only serve other princes.

The consolidation of Rus and Slavic elites that had begun in Vladimir's time continued, and by the end of the twelfth century the term *boiar* referred to a single, homogenous, Christian, Slavic-speaking, wealthy, landed elite. The Prince's druzhina, which awarded high status to its most prominent members, played the central role in this process by admitting servitors from all ethnic groups or social levels. Over the course of the eleventh century, grants of land replaced direct payments and boiar status became synonymous with estate ownership. These estates were considered payment for past services, not a contract for future service (as in feudal Europe), and were owned outright. The beneficiary of the land was free to enter the service of another prince.

Social structure became stratified in towns as well. The wealthiest merchants, while not sharing the aristocratic privileges of the boiars, nevertheless dominated city affairs. There was the usual hierarchy of wealth: merchants, skilled artisans, free unskilled laborers, and two kinds of unfree labor—temporarily unfree and permanent slaves. One form of unfree labor was contractual; in exchange for a payment of money, a worker would agree to work for a set period of time. Until the time limit expired, the worker was obligated to serve his or her master without further pay. Another form was servitude as interest on a loan. The borrower would become an indentured servant, required to work for the grantor of the loan until the principal was repaid. Indentured servants hardly ever regained their freedom, since they were rarely able to find the money to pay back the loan. However, they were distinguished from slaves in two ways: they could not be killed or mistreated, and their indentured status could not be inherited by their children.

Slaves, on the other hand, had no legal protection from murder or physical punishment, they had no right to own property, and their children became the property of their masters. The chief source of slaves was prisoners of war. All soldiers and inhabitants of captured cities were considered to be the possessions of the victors, and those who could not be ransomed were sold. Slaves were a major export to Constantinople. Sometimes Rus armies marched against the Kipchaks on purely slave-raiding missions (and vice versa). Another source of slaves came from the punishment of bankrupt merchants. Finally, slavery could be accepted voluntarily by selling oneself, by marrying a female slave, or by becoming a steward on a prince's estate. The Church did not try to eliminate slavery, but encouraged masters to treat slaves humanely and to grant them freedom in their wills.

The structure of the Church paralleled the secular social hierarchy. The leaders of the Church—bishops and abbots of major monasteries—came largely from the princely and boiar classes. They were required to be celibate. Parish priests, known as the "white clergy," were permitted to marry, and, since they were in a position to teach their sons church doctrine and practice, the priesthood tended to become a closed caste. The white clergy could not rise in the church hierarchy, and they remained in the same social class as their parishioners. Monks, the "black clergy," could not marry, and this qualified them for higher positions in the church hierarchy. Thus, the church provided for some social mobility; sons and daughters of commoners could enter monasteries and have the opportunity to rise to leadership positions. The Church was also the home of the *izgoi*, people who lost their class status. These included illiterate sons of priests, freed slaves, bankrupt merchants, and orphaned princes—all people who were unable to support themselves. They were accepted into monasteries where they were given jobs appropriate to their former social status.

The Rus law code had more to do with raising money in the form of court fees and fines than it had to do with providing justice. In cities and among upper social levels, injuries were remedied primarily through retaliation; the *Russkaia Pravda* provided cash payments only if the victim's family could not exact revenge. For the most part, the *Russkaia Pravda* served the economic interests of the princes by levying cash fines against those who damaged their property. All those who worked on the estates of princes were slaves, and so had economic value, and the murder of such a person was treated as a crime against property. The murder of a steward or master of the stable carried a fine of eighty grivnas, the murder of a page or cook forty, the murder of a village manager, tutor, or nurse twelve. The murder of an ordinary laborer carried a fine of only five grivnas, the same as the murder of a free person.

LATER POLITICAL DEVELOPMENTS

Despite the forces for unity discussed in this chapter, by the early thirteenth century, three regions seemed to be developing in distinctive directions. In the Southwest, Galicia was notable for the power of its boiars, who, on a number of occasions, forced their prince to leave. For a short period in the early thirteenth century, the boiars allowed a Hungarian prince to rule for a time. Volynia, Galicia's neighbor to the north, was ruled by a line of princes who worked to unite the two principalities under their authority. In 1240, when the Mongols invaded, a Rurikovich named Daniil not only ruled both Volynia and Galicia, he had become Grand Prince of Kiev, as well.

In the principality of Novgorod, the commercial capital of the north, merchants became the dominant political force. The merchant elite quickly learned how to use the veche to limit the power of the prince. First, it reserved the right to reject a prince it did not want. Then, by the late eleventh century, the veche was able to elect a *posadnik* (governor), who handled the day-to-day administration of the city, a *tysatskii* (military commander), who headed the citizens' militia and who evolved into the spokesperson for the common people, and a panel of judges for administering commercial law. Finally, in 1156, the veche asserted the right to elect its own prince, provided that he was a Rurikovich, and its own bishop, provided that the Metropolitan would agree to consecrate him. Having no hereditary princely line with an incentive to create principalities for younger sons to rule, the city of Novgorod itself annexed northern lands and became the largest principality in Rus.

In Vladimir's day, none of the towns in the Northeast—on the headwaters of the Volga—had been significant enough to be made a princely seat. As the agricultural population of Rus grew, however, this sparsely settled region offered an opportunity for expansion. Vladimir Monomakh had realized the potential wealth of the region and began to develop it, and his descendants formed it into a principality called Vladimir-Suzdal, after its two major cities. Its princes derived their wealth not only from the colonization of land, but by taking control of the Volga trade route. They prevented Novgorod and Bulgar merchants from passing through, and instead required them to trade their goods in the Vladimir-Suzdal markets where they could be taxed by the prince.

Even more significantly, Vladimir-Suzdal princes did not try to become Grand Prince of Kiev; instead they tried to make the title of Grand Prince of Vladimir the superior of the two. Andrei Bogoliubskii (d. 1175) built a magnificent Cathedral of the Dormition of the Virgin in Vladimir and asked Constantinople to send Vladimir-Suzdal its own Metropolitan. (The Patriarch refused.) In 1169, Andrei seized Kiev while participating in a civil war on behalf of a brother, but instead of ruling the city, he sacked it and carried off icons and religious artifacts to decorate churches in his own principality. He and his descendants dropped out of the struggles to be Grand Prince of Kiev, and they turned their attention to the east, where they expanded at the expense of the Volga Bulgars and the Mordvins.

Whether these separatist trends could have been overcome by energetic action by the Grand Prince of Kiev and the Metropolitan of Rus is an unanswerable question. Mongol armies began to invade the lands of the Rus in 1237, and in 1240 Kiev was looted and burned. The Northeast was absorbed into the Mongol Empire, and over the next two centuries Kiev Rus fragmented along the fault lines just described.

NOTES

1. Janet Martin, *Medieval Russia, 980–1584* (Cambridge: Cambridge University Press, 1995), 27–35.
2. Simon Franklin and Jonathan Shepard, *The Emergence of Rus, 750–1200* (London: Longman, 1996), 195.

--- **TEXT DOCUMENTS** ---

The Mother of God's Travels in Hell

This apocryphal story circulated widely in the early Christian church. This version was written in Kiev Rus in the twelfth century.

- What religious functions does this writing fulfil?
- What does it reveal about East Slavic spirituality? construction of gender?

The Mother of God wanted to witness how souls were tortured, and she asked the Archangel Michael [to show her]. . . .

Hell was opened. And she saw. . . . very many men and women who were weeping. And she asked the archangel: "Who are these people?" And the archangel answered: "These are ones who did not believe in the Father, the Son, and the Holy Ghost, but forgot God. . . . They called the sun and the moon, beasts and reptiles, earth and water gods . . . And they made gods out of Troian, Khors, Veles, and Perun, and they worshiped evil demons. . . ."

The cherubim and seraphim and four hundred angels took the Mother of God. . . . to where there was a river of fire. A great number of men and women who stood in this fiery river, some to their waists, some to their shoulders, some to their necks, and some over their heads. And seething this the holy Mother of God cried out and asked, "Who are those that stand in the fire to their waists?" And the archangel replied: "They are those that have been cursed by their fathers and mothers. . . ." And the Mother of God asked who were the ones who stood in the fire to their shoulders, and the archangel replied: "They are those who have cursed at their own godparents and have committed fornication. . . . "And the Mother of God then asked: "Who are those who are over their heads in the river of flame?" The archangel replied: "They are those, Lady, who have sworn falsely while holding the cross. . . ."

And there was a great cloud of fire, and in it were beds of burning fire and on them lay many men and women. . . . And the archangel said, "Lady, those are the ones who during the holy weeks did not get up for the midnight service, but lazily lay in bed as if they were dead."

And the Holy Mother of God saw a tree of iron with branches of iron on which there were iron barbs instead of fruit. On these barbs a great many men and women were hung by their tongues. . . . And the archangel said: "These people are slanderers and gossipers who separate brother from brother and husbands from their wives.". . .

And the most Holy One saw women hanging by their fingernails, and fire came from their mouths, and burned them all over. . . . And the archangel said: "They are priests wives who did not respect priesthood, and married again after their husbands died. . . ."

Source: N. K. Gudzii, Ed., *Khrestomatiia po drevnei Russkoi literature XI–XVII vekov*, Moscow: Gosudarstvennoi Uchebno-pedagogicheskoe izdatel'stvo RSFSR, 1955, 92–98. Excerpted and translated by the author.

And she saw other women lying in fire and various serpents were eating them, and Michael answered: "These are nuns from monasteries who sold their bodies for fornication. . . ."

. . . In the middle of a river of flames were a great multitude of sinners. . . . And the Archangel said: "These are whores and adulterers, thieves, eavesdroppers, matchmakers and slanderers, drunkards, unmerciful princes, bishops, and patriarchs, and tsars who did not obey God's will, money-grubbers who charged interest, and lawbreakers.". . .

[Upon showing the Mother of God another burning river, the Archangel Michael said:] "This is a river of pitch, and its waves are on fire, and the Jews are tormented here because they tormented our Lord, Jesus Christ, the Son of God, and the heathens [are tormented] who were baptized in the name of the Father, the Son, and the Holy Ghost but who continued to believe in demons and rejected God and baptism, and [those are also tormented here] who fornicated with their godmothers or mothers or daughters, and those who killed people with poison or who killed people with weapons or who suffocated their children. . . ."

. . . And [the cherubim and seraphim] carried the Blessed One to the heavenly height, and put her by the throne of the invisible Father. She raised her hands to her Blessed son and said: "Have mercy, O Lord, upon the sinners, for I have seen them, and I could not bear it; let me suffer with the Christians." And a voice came to her saying: "How can I have mercy? I see nails in my Son's hands." And she said, "Lord, I do not pray for the unbelieving Jews, but for the Christians I pray for your mercy." . . .

[Then the Mother of God called to all the angels, and Moses, and the prophets, and Paul, and John and the archangel Michael. And they all begged the Lord to have mercy.]

The Lord, seeing the prayers of the saints, became merciful for the sake of his only begotten son and said: "Come down, my beloved Son, and listen to the prayers of the saints and show your face to the sinners."

And the Lord came down from the invisible throne, and those who were in the utter darkness heard of this and cried out with one voice: "Have mercy upon us, Son of God; have mercy upon us, Tsar of all the ages." And the Lord said: "Listen everyone! I made paradise and I created man in my own image and made him lord of paradise, and gave him eternal life, but they disobeyed and earned death; but because I did not want to see the work of my hands suffer from the devil so I came to earth and became incarnate through the Virgin and was raised from the cross to free people from slavery and original sin. . . . But you did not care to repent for your sins. You became Christians in word only and you did not keep my commandments. For this you are placed in eternal fire, and I should not have mercy on you! But today, through the mercy of my Father who sent me to you, and for the prayers of my Mother who has wept much for you, and through the archangel Michael, and through the multitude of my martyrs who have labored greatly for you, I give to you tormented ones day and night, from Good Thursday to Holy Pentecost, for respite and for praising the Father, and the Son, and the Holy Ghost," And they all answered: "Glory to thy mercy!"

Glory to the Father, and to the Son, and to the Holy Ghost, now and for eternity. Amen.

The Church Statute of Kiev Rus

When Vladimir converted to Christianity and established Church institutions in Kiev, he gave the Church a series of rights and privileges which were extended by Iaroslav. These excerpts are from Iaroslav's Church Statute.

- What do these laws reveal about class structure, gender relations, and the economic system?
- About the relation between church and state?
- About Rus concepts of justice and law?

1. Whoever shall carry away and then violate a maiden, if she is a daughter of an [influential] *boiar*, shall pay her five *grivnas* of gold for her indignity, and the bishop shall receive five *grivnas* of gold; if she is a daughter of a less [influential] *boiar* [she shall receive for her indignity] only one *grivna* of gold and the bishop [shall receive] one *grivna* of gold; and if she is a daughter [only] of a distinguished person she shall receive for her indignity five *grivnas* of silver and the bishop shall receive five *grivnas* of silver. The kidnappers shall [in addition] pay one *grivna* of silver to the bishop. The prince shall administer justice [in these matters in accordance with ancient customs and traditions].

3. If, without any valid reason, a distinguished *boiar* puts his wife away, she shall receive three gold *grivnas* for her indignity and the bishop shall receive three gold *grivnas*; for the same action [the wife of] a distinguished citizen shall receive three *rubles* and the bishop shall receive three *rubles*; for the same action [the wife] of a commoner shall receive fifteen *grivnas* and the bishop shall receive fifteen *grivnas*. The prince shall administer justice . . .

4. If a daughter who has her father and mother [still living] should give birth to an illegitimate child, she should be reprimanded [by the bishop] and then placed in the bishop's court. The family may then ransom her out.

5. If someone should entice a maiden to his dwelling and then force her to have sexual intercourse with others, the bishop shall receive three *grivnas* [for this crime] and the maiden [shall receive three *grivnas*] for her dishonor. All the participants who dishonored her shall be fined one *ruble*. The prince shall administer justice. . . .

6. If a husband should force his wife into prostitution, this is a religious crime. The prince [however] shall administer justice. . . .

7. Should a husband marry another woman without divorcing his wife, the bishop shall have the jurisdiction in this matter. The new wife shall be placed in the bishop's court and the husband shall be made to live with his [first] wife.

8. Should a wife become very ill, or become blind, or be afflicted with a prolonged illness, [her husband] shall not be allowed to divorce her; the same rule shall apply to the husband [in case of his illness].

9. If the godfather should have sexual intercourse with the mother [of his godchild], the bishop shall receive one *grivna* of gold and at his discretion he shall also impose [an appropriate] penance.

Source: "Yaroslav's Church Statute" in Basil Dmytryshyn, *Medieval Russia: A Source Book, 850–1700* (Gulf Breeze, FL: Academic International Press, 1999), 41–45. Copyright Academic International Press, Gulf Breeze, FL. Used by permission.

11. The bishop shall receive 100 *grivnas* as the fine from whomever shall have sexual intercourse with his sister. The bishop shall also impose [an appropriate] penance. The punishment for this crime shall be administered in accordance with [the existing] laws.

12. The bishop shall receive eighty *grivnas* from whomever marries a close blood relative. The bishop shall separate them and impose [an appropriate] penance.

14. If a husband and wife decide to separate voluntarily, the bishop shall receive twelve *grivnas*. If they were not married legally [in the Church] the bishop shall receive only six *grivnas*.

15. The bishop shall receive 100 *grivnas* from whomever shall have sexual intercourse with a nun.

16. The bishop shall receive twelve *grivnas* from whomever shall commit sodomy. He shall also impose [an appropriate] penance.

17. If a father-in-law should have sexual intercourse with his daughter-in-law, the bishop shall receive 100 *grivnas;* in accordance with the [existing] law he shall also impose [an appropriate] penance.

18. If a brother-in-law should have sexual intercourse with his sister-in-law the bishop shall receive thirty *grivnas*.

22. If a maiden does not want to marry and her father and mother force her into it, and if she then does some harm to herself, her father and mother are guilty and must pay the bishop a fine; the same applies to the young lad [she was forced to marry].

35. Local officials of the prince shall have no jurisdiction over crimes committed by a bishop's servants, the church people, and those living within monasteries. Crimes committed by these people shall be under the exclusive jurisdiction of the bishop's officials as is also their property.

Kiev Rus Relations with the Kipchaks

The Kipchaks were a Turkic people who occupied the steppes to the south of Kiev Rus from the eleventh century until the Mongol conquest. These selections come from the Primary Chronicle. *(Dates are given in the Jewish calendar, used by the Eastern Slavs until 1700, with the Gregorian calendar year in parentheses.)*

- How does the author of the *Chronicle* portray the Kipchaks? Why do you think this is the case?
- If one pays attention to the behavior of the actors, instead of the value judgments of the chronicler, what appear to be the real relations between the Rus and the Kipchaks?

[The following passage comes from introductory material regarding nomads.] Just so, even in our own day, the Kipchaks maintain the customs of their ancestors in the shedding of blood and in glorifying themselves for such deeds, as well as in eating every dead or

Source: Cross, *The Russian Primary Chronicle,* 58, 143, 146, 165, 179–180, 200, 201.

unclean thing, even hamsters and marmots. They marry their mothers-in-law and their sisters-in-law, and observe other usages of their ancestors. But in all countries we Christians who believe in the Holy Trinity, in one baptism, and in one faith, have but one law, as many of us have been baptized into Christ Lord and have put on Christ.

6569 (1061) The Kipchaks invaded Rus to make war for the first time. On February 2, Vsevolod went forth against them. When they met in battle, the Kipchaks defeated Vsevolod, but after the combat they retired. This was the first evil done by these pagan and godless foes. Their prince was Iskal.

6576 (1068) A multitude of those nomads known as the Kipchaks attacked the land of the Rus, and Iziaslav, Sviatoslav and Vsevolod went forth against them as far as the Alta. They joined battle in the dead of night, but since God had let loose the pagans upon us because of our transgressions, the Russian princes fled and the Kipchaks were victorious.

God in his wrath causes foreigners to attack a nation, and then, when its inhabitants are thus crushed by the invaders, they remember God. Intestine strife is incited by the craft of the devil. For God wishes men not evil but good; while the devil takes his delight in cruel murder and bloodshed, and therefore incites quarrels, envy, domestic strife, and slander. When any nation has sinned, God punishes them by death of famine or barbarian incursion, by drought or a plague of caterpillars or by other chastisements, until we repent of our sins and live according to God's commandment.

6586 (1078) While Sviatopolk, the son of Iziaslav, was ruling at Novgorod in his stead, and while Iaropolk was reigning in Vyzhgorod and Vladimir at Smolensk, Oleg and Boris led the pagans to attack Rus, and fell upon Vsevolod with their Kipchak reinforcements.

6600 (1094) Sviatopolk made peace with the Kipchaks, and took to wife the daughter of their prince Tugorkan. In this same year, Oleg arrived from Tmutorakan before Chernigov with a force of Kipchaks. Vladimir fortified himself in the city. Oleg then approached and burned the environs, including the monasteries. Vladimir made peace with Oleg, and departed from Chernigov to occupy his father's throne in Pereyaslavl, while Oleg took possession of the city that had been his own father's. The Kipchaks committed many depredations in the vicinity of Chernigov, and Oleg made no attempt to restrain them for the reason that he himself had inspired their raids. This was, in fact, the third time that he had led a force of pagans to attack Rus. May God forgive his sin, for many Christians were destroyed, while others were taken captive and scattered throughout the lands.

6609 (1103). God inspired a noble project in the hearts of the Russian princes Sviatopolk and Vladimir. . . . They then sent to Oleg and David and invited them to make a life-or-death stand against the Kipchaks.

The princes of Rus and all the soldiery offered their prayers to God and made their vows to God and to the Blessed Virgin; some promised presents of food, others alms to the poor, and others supplied for the monasteries. After they had prayed thus, the Kipchaks advanced. . . . The Russian princes likewise sent forward their advance party. They thus surprised the vanguard of Altunopa, upon whom they fell, slaying him and his followers. Not one of them escaped, for the Rus slew them all. The nomad troops came on like the trees of the forest, and their mass was impenetrable. The Rus straightway advanced to meet them. Now God on high inspired an awful fear in the Kipchaks, so that terror and trembling beset them at the sight of the Russian forces, and they wavered. Even their steeds possessed no more swiftness of foot. But our soldiery, both foot and horse, advanced joyously to the combat.

Upon beholding the effort of the Rus against them, the Kipchaks fled before the Russian troops without even waiting to meet them, and our men gave chase and cut them down. On April 4, God thus performed a great salvation and bestowed upon us a mighty victory over our foes.

Everyday Life in Novgorod

Each important city kept its own Chronicle. *This is a selection from the* Chronicle of Novgorod.

- What can you infer about life in Novgorod–its difficulties, political concerns, and religious attitudes and practices.
- Which features and characteristics were probably general in the cities of Kiev Rus, and which are probably specific to a merchant town like Novgorod?

6631 (1123) Vladimir the Great, Son of Vsevolod, died in Kiev; and they put his son, Mstislav, on the throne of his father. The same year there was a great storm with thunder and hail; it rent houses and it rent tiles off shrines; it drowned droves of cattle in the Volkhov [River], and others they hardly saved alive. The same year they painted [frescoes in] the Anton chapel in the monastery.

The same year the people of Novgorod put Vsevolod on the throne.

6634 (1126) Vsevolod went to Kiev to his father and he came back to the throne in Novgorod on February 28. The same year they gave the office of Posadnik to Miroslav Giuriatinich.

6635 (1127) Vsevolod founded the stone church of St. Ioan in Novgorod, in the name of his son, in Petriata's Court. The same year a blizzard fell thick over land and water and houses during two nights and four days. The same year the water was high in the Volkhov and snow lay until [May 1]. And in the autumn the frost killed all the grain and the winter crop; and there was famine throughout the winter; an osminka of rye cost half a grivna.

6636 (1128) Kiuriak, Hegumen of St. Georgi, died. The same year Ioan, son of Vsevolod, grandson of Mstislav, died on April 16. The same year David Dmitrovich was made Posadnik in Novgorod. This year it was cruel; one osminka of rye cost a grivna; the people ate lime tree leaves, birch bark, pounded wood pulp mixed with husks and straw; some ate buttercups, moss, horse flesh; and thus many dropping down from hunger, their corpses were in the streets, in the market place and on the roads, and everywhere. They hired hirelings to carry the dead out of the town; the servants could not go out; woe and misery on all! Fathers and mothers would put their children into boats in gift [as slaves] to [foreign] merchants, or else put them to death; and others dispersed over foreign lands. Thus did our country perish on account of our sins. This year, the water was high in the Volkhov, and carried away many houses; . . .

6637 (1129) Daniel came from Kiev to be Posadnik of Novgorod.

6638 (1130) Vsevolod with the men of Novgorod went against the Chud people in the winter during the Feast; them he slaughtered, their dwellings he burned, and their wives and children he brought home [as slaves]. The same year he went to Kiev to his father. The same year they finished the Church of St. John. This year coming from beyond sea from the Goths, seven boats sank; they themselves all sank and their goods; but some escaped, though naked, and came from [Denmark] in health. . . . And they let Petrila be Posadnik over Novgorod.

Source: Robert Michell and Nevill Forbes, *The Chronicle of Novgorod, 1016–1471* (London: The Royal Historical Society, 1914), 10–14. (c) Royal Historical Society, reprinted by permission.

6642 (1134) The people of Novgorod began to talk of a war with Suzhdal, and they killed one of their own men and threw him from the bridge on Pentecost Saturday. The same year the business side caught fire, from the Carpenters' brook to the end of Kholm, as it had caught fire before; and ten honorable churches were destroyed by fire on August 4. The same year Vsevolod marched with the men of Novgorod, wishing to place his brother in Suzhdal, and at the Dubna they turned back. . . .

6644 (1136) . . . The men of Novgorod summoned the men of Pskov and of Ladoga and took counsel how to expel their Prince Vsevolod, and they confined him in the court of the Bishop, together with wife and children and mother-in-law, on May 28, and the guards with arms guarded him day and night, thirty men daily; and he sat two months and they let him out of the town on July 15, and they received his son, Vladimir. And they made these his faults: 1. He had no care for the serfs; 2. Why didst thou wish to take thy seat in Pereyaslavl? 3. Thou didst ride away from the troop in front of all. . . .

6696 (1188) The same year the whole town of people gathered together, and decided to appoint as Bishop for themselves, Arkadi, a man chosen of God; and the whole people went and took him out of the monastery of the Holy Mother of God, both prince Mstislav Giurgevich, and the whole choir of St. Sophia, and all the town priests, and the Hegumen and the monks, and they led him in, having entrusted him with the bishopric in the Court of St. Sophia, till the Metropolitan should come to Russia, and then you shall go to be appointed. The same year the oversea merchants put up the Church of the Holy Friday on the market place.

VISUAL DOCUMENTS

Figure 3-1 Cathedral of St. Sophia, Kiev

The Cathedral of St. Sophia was built on the order of Iaroslav the Wise in 1037.

- What does this reveal about Kiev's economic condition and cultural orientation?
- Iaroslav said that he built this church to commemorate his victory over the Pechenegs and to glorify Christianity. What other reasons might he have had for building it?

Source. Photo by Bernard Cox/John Bethell PhotoLibrary, St. Albans.

Figure 3-2 The Mother of God of Vladimir

This is the most revered of all Russian icons. It was painted in Constantinople and brought to Kiev in 1131. In 1155, Prince Andrei Bogoliubskii obtained the icon and took it to the city of Vladimir. In 1395, the icon was taken to Moscow.

- What does it reveal about early Rus civilization?
- In Western Europe, Jesus' Mother is most frequently referred to as "the Virgin Mary" or "the Holy Virgin." Among the Rus and their successors, she is typically referred to as "the Mother of God" (*bogoroditsa*). What significance might this have for gender issues in East Slavic culture?

Source: Tretiakov Gallery, Moscow.

Source: Tretiakov Gallery, Moscow.

Figure 3-3 The Vernicle or "Holy Face"

This icon dates from the twelfth century. It is a representation of Jesus as God.

- What attributes of God do you think the painter wanted to convey?

Figure 3-4 St. Nicholas

St. Nicholas, a legendary bishop of the fourth-century Christian church, was famous for miracles he performed to help the poor and the unfortunate, and he became the patron saint of many cities and many kinds of people, including sailors, travelers, merchants, working people, unmarried girls, and children. St. Nicholas became the patron saint of Russia.

This icon was painted in the late twelfth or early thirteenth century.

- What does the veneration of St. Nicholas reveal about Rus culture, society, and religiosity?

Source: Tretiakov Gallery, Moscow.

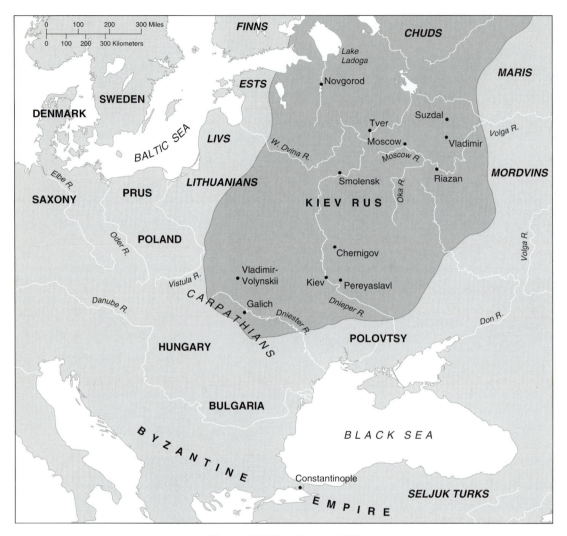

Figure 3-5 Kiev Rus in 1200

In 1200, Kiev Rus had lost control over the northern Black Sea steppe to the nomadic Polovtsy, but it remained the largest state in Europe and Kiev was second to Constantinople in size and magnificence..

_____ FOR FURTHER READING _____

(In addition to the books by Christian, Cross, Franklin and Shepard, Levin, and Martin from the previous chapter.)

Blum, Jerome. *Lord and Peasant in Russia.* Princeton, NJ: Princeton University Press, 1961.
Fedotov, George P. *The Russian Religious Mind,* 2 vols. Belmont, MA: Norland, 1975.
Fennell, John. *The Crisis of Medieval Russia, 1200–1304.* New York: Longman, 1983.
_____. *A History of the Russian Church to 1448.* New York: Longman, 1995.
Obolensky, Dimitri. *Byzantium and the Slavs.* Crestwood, NY: St. Vladimir's Seminary Press, 1994.

CHAPTER FOUR

THE EASTERN SLAVS AND THE MONGOL EMPIRE, 1240–1360

In the thirteenth century, the Mongols conquered most of the Eurasian continent, including the Eastern Slavs, and after the Mongol invasion and conquest, the divisive tendencies of the twelfth century became irreversible. The southeast principalities of Kiev Rus were absorbed by Poland and Lithuania. Novgorod grew in wealth and independence and began to take on the characteristics of a merchant empire. The northeast was incorporated into the Mongol empire, and Vladimir replaced Kiev as the residence of the senior member of the Rurikovich dynasty. In addition, a junior line of Rurikovichi in the previously insignificant city of Moscow initiated policies that violated the old Kiev Rus tradition of collective rule and set the foundation for the rise of a unitary, centralized state. By the end of the 1350s, as the Mongol Empire began to disintegrate, Moscow was on the verge of dramatic expansion and transformation.

THE EURASIAN CONTEXT

The greatest of all the empires built by steppe nomads was the work of the Mongol leader, Temujin (1162–1227), a military and political genius who was driven by a vision of universal empire. Temujin acquired a loyal and disciplined army as he brought order to feuding

---

Turn to page 80 for a map showing key geographic locations and features for this time period.

Mongol clans, and he was proclaimed Genghis ("universal") Khan by his generals in 1206. In the next year, he began to lead his armies against the sedentary civilizations of Outer Eurasia, and, before his death, Genghis Khan had conquered China as far south as the Yangzi River and Central Asia as far west the Amu Darya.

His sons inherited this empire, but it was his grandsons who expanded it to its furthest extent. Batu inherited the right to rule the western half of Inner Eurasia, and, after conquering the steppes beyond the Aral Sea, he moved north, capturing Great Bulgar in 1236, Riazan in 1237, Vladimir and Suzdal in 1238, and Kiev in 1240. In 1241 Batu defeated Hungarian, Polish, and German armies west of the Carpathians, but he chose not to advance further into Europe. His realm became known as the Kipchak Khanate (after the nomads who had ruled the steppe). Güyük inherited the Chagatai Khanate, which covered all of Central Asia from the Amu Darya in the Southwest to the Altai Mountains in the Northeast. Hulegu was bequeathed the right to the Middle East south of the Syr Darya, which became known as the Il-Khan Empire. He conquered Persia (including present-day Afghanistan and Pakistan) in 1258, captured Baghdad in the same year, and reached the border of Syria in 1260. Hulegu also conquered Armenia, and most of the Caucasus (only the western side of Georgia remained independent). A fourth grandson, Kubilai, was made ruler of the Empire of the Great Khan, which included the Mongolian heartland and all eastern Eurasia. He completed the conquest of China in 1279 when he defeated the last Song forces. Together these four Khanates made up an empire that included the entire Inner Eurasian steppe and most of Outer Eurasia.

The Mongol empire brought to a climax the economic development and cultural interchange that had begun when the Silk Road had first connected Han China with Rome in the second century B.C.E. Now the Silk Road was under the control of a single political entity that provided safe and reasonably fast transportation from one end to the other. (It took a little less than a year to travel from the Black Sea to Beijing.) This central trading link quickened economic life throughout the continent. The major maritime trading systems on the perimeter of Eurasia benefitted as well from the Mongols' fostering of world trade.

There was an invigorating flow of ideas and culture from one end of Eurasia to the other. China experienced a golden age of literature and art. Persian astronomers studied Chinese observations of planetary motion and developed the model that would later inspire Copernicus. Persian mathematicians learned the use of fractions from Chinese astronomers and discovered how to express them as decimals. It was at this time that Europeans borrowed "Arabic" numerals from Persia, just as the Persians had borrowed them from India much earlier. Chinese painting techniques also influenced Persian artists. It was because of the Silk Road that Europeans like Marco Polo were able to make direct contact with China for the first time.

Nevertheless, this Eurasian cultural and economic golden age came at an incalculable human cost. For most people in the lands of the Mongol Empire, according to David Morgan, "the Mongol conquests were a disaster on a grand and unparalleled scale."[1] First, the Mongols used systematic terror as a military tactic. Cities that surrendered immediately were subject only to payment of tribute, those which resisted were looted and burned and their residents killed or enslaved. Central Asia and Eastern Persia resisted and experienced near genocide as a result.[2] Second, the purpose of Mongol conquest seems not to have been to provide peace and justice (as Genghis, himself, claimed), but to provide a livelihood for the army, who were paid in booty and tribute. Once the empire had expanded as far as possible, it existed only as an army of occupation extracting the maximum possible wealth from the population. The effects on the local population were devastating. In China, farmers were starved by overtaxation, and, because the Mongol rulers failed to maintain public works, the

Yellow River flooded causing famine and population displacement. Between 1200 and 1290, China lost 30 percent of its population. A similar fate befell Central Asia and Persia where the Mongols allowed the irrigation networks to deteriorate, and where tribute was gathered from the population twenty or thirty times a year. As much as 90 percent of the agricultural population in Persia died or fled.

Luckily for Europe, however, Batu Khan decided not to conquer the extreme western end of Eurasia, and Europe prospered throughout the thirteenth century. The population grew, tilled acreage expanded, and international trade increased. The thirteenth century was the age of Thomas Aquinas (whose *Summa Theologiae,* a systematic exposition of Christian doctrine, was the highest achievement of Scholasticism) and the blossoming of what Europeans later called the "High Middle Ages." In political life, the principle of regional, territorial sovereignty waxed while the idea of a single Christian empire waned. The pope was unable to assert political authority equal to his religious authority. The Holy Roman Empire also lost power; by the early fourteenth century, Italian city-states were independent and German princes had become autonomous. Monarchs in western Europe further consolidated their claims to be the sovereign lords of their lands, and they integrated the wealthy and powerful social elites into their governments by creating representative institutions, such as the English Parliament or French Estates-General.

The Mongol conquest of the Middle East briefly aided the Byzantine Empire by weakening and distracting the Seljuk Turks who occupied the Anatolian Peninsula. This allowed Byzantine armies to focus their attention on Constantinople (occupied by western European forces since the Fourth Crusade), and in 1261, they finally drove out the Emperor and Patriarch, which had been installed by Rome. The Byzantine Patriarch was highly regarded and Byzantine monasteries were influential throughout the Eastern Christian Church, but Byzantine military power was weak. Its temporary success was caused by its enemies' weakness rather than its own strength. By the middle of the fourteenth century, Byzantium was again on the defensive against Western Europe, Serbia, and the Turks.

In Northeast Europe, three expansive neighbors—the Teutonic Knights, Poland, and Lithuania—pressed on the western borders of the Eastern Slavs. The Order of Teutonic Knights had originated as a medical service sent to the Holy Land during the Crusades but which transformed itself into a military body and created branches in eastern Europe to participate in the "Northern Crusades" against the pagan Prus and Baltic peoples. Between 1233 and 1283, the Teutonic Knights gained control over Prussia, and by 1346 they had incorporated the eastern Baltic (Courland, Livonia, and Estonia) into their feudal state. They were stopped from further expansion eastward by the principality of Novgorod and southward by Poland and Lithuania.

Poland had begun to emerge as a distinctive nation of Western Slavs at the same time as Kiev Rus was forming in the east. Poland's first known king, Mieszko I (d. 992), converted to Christianity in 966 and accepted a crown from the Pope. The Western Slavs became distinguished from Eastern Slavs by their religious allegiance to Rome and by their use of the Latin alphabet to write their language. Under Mieszko I, Poland extended from the Baltic Sea to the Carpathian mountains and from Bohemia to Kiev Rus. In 1241, Poland was defeated by the Mongols, but it was neither occupied nor incorporated into their empire. In the middle of the thirteenth century, Poland lost its northern territories to the Teutonic Knights, and for the remainder of the century it attempted to expand eastwards at the expense of the Rus.

The Lithuanians are an ancient Baltic people who first appear in European political history in 1251 when their ruler was baptized a Roman Catholic and recognized by the Pope as a king. The royal family subsequently reverted to paganism, however, and, they were therefore targeted by the crusading Teutonic Knights. Lithuania successfully defended its independence—the only Baltic people who were able to do so. In the fourteenth century,

Lithuanian kings began to compete with Poland for control of the western territories of the former Kiev Rus. They again converted to Roman Christianity in 1387.

POLITICAL DEVELOPMENTS

Batu's empire—the western half of Inner Eurasia, from the Aral Sea to the Carpathian Mountains—was called the Kipchak Khanate by the Mongols. The Rus, however, for reasons that are now unclear, knew the Mongol state as the Golden Horde, and that is the term that will be used in this book. The Golden Horde was a major Eurasian state, one of the four subdivisions of the Mongol Empire and an economic and political power in its own right. Batu built his capital city, Sarai, where the northern branch of the Silk Road crossed the Volga River, and it quickly became a cosmopolitan metropolis. Merchants from Byzantium, Southwest Asia, Central Asia, and Italy resided there. Sarai was also a manufacturing center since Batu brought in artisans and slaves conscripted from the conquered cities of Rus and Central Asia. Finally, as the residence of the Khan and his central bureaucracy, Sarai attracted ambassadors from all of western Eurasia.

Batu's was the most traditional pastoral empire of all the four Khanates in the empire. His Mongol soldiers, with the Turks, Kipchaks, Mordvins, and others who joined them, continued their nomadic way of life, and regiments were assigned pastureland on the steppe. Therefore Batu had no interest in occupying and directly ruling the sedentary and agricultural Slavs in the way that the Yuan dynasty ruled China or the Il Khans ruled Persia and Mesopotamia. Instead, he was willing to recognize the authority of the Rurikovichi to govern, providing they served his interests. Rus princes were expected to provide armies to fight on behalf of the Mongols and to regularly deliver tribute to Sarai. The prince of each principality of Rus was required to travel to Sarai to swear loyalty to the Kipchak Horde when he first became prince and later if a new Khan succeeded to the throne. In recognition of the oath of loyalty, the prince was given a iarlyk—an official document confirming that the Khan recognized him as a legitimate prince.

The principalities of Galicia and Volynia, on the periphery of the Golden Horde, were allowed considerable autonomy. Their princes had to acknowledge their subordinate status and provide armies to aid the Khan, but they were not forced to accept census takers, tribute gatherers, or an army of occupation. As a result, they lost their ties with other Rus princes and became involved with their Hungarian, Polish, and Lithuanian neighbors. Prince Daniil of Volynia had been Grand Prince of Kiev before the Mongol invasion. However, when he went to Sarai to receive a iarlyk, the Khan confirmed him only as prince of Volynia and Galicia, and he had to abandon Kiev. For the next century, Galicia and Volynia were ruled by his descendants—sometimes separately, sometimes united under the rule of one prince.

In 1323, however, the last Daniilovich died, and the region was plunged into turmoil. Boiars from both principalities elected a Polish cousin of Daniil's line, but they soon had him killed for being too pro-Catholic and pro-Polish. Then Poland and Lithuania fought over the region until a settlement was reached in 1366: Poland gained Galicia and western Volynia, while the remainder of Volynia went to Lithuania. Overall, however, it was Lithuania who took the greatest advantage of the power vacuum in the territory of Kiev Rus after the Mongol conquest. By 1342, Lithuania had absorbed the former principalities of Polotsk, Grodno, and Turov, and in 1362, it seized the principality of Kiev.

The experience of Polish- and Lithuanian-occupied areas of former Rus were very different. As Roman Catholics, the Poles considered themselves to be crusaders defending the Latin church against pagan Lithuania and Orthodox Rus. They remained alien from the population. Land populated by Orthodox, Eastern Slavic farmers was given to Polish, German, Czech, and Hungarian nobles. German merchants were invited in to develop the cities. Latin was the official language, and in 1375 a Catholic archdiocese was formed in Lvov.

The Lithuanians, by contrast, made their territorial gains not by fighting the native princes but by defeating the Mongol occupiers. They were, therefore, welcomed by the population as liberators. In stark contrast with the Polish occupation of Galicia, Lithuanian nobles who were given land in the former Kiev Rus assimilated themselves into Rus culture. They accepted the Rus boiars into their ruling class, they converted to Eastern Orthodoxy, and they used Slavic as their official state language. They even talked of "gathering the lands of Rus" and reuniting all of old Kiev Rus under their leadership. There was a tension, however, between Lithuanians in Eastern Slavic lands, who converted to Orthodoxy, and the Lithuanians in their original Baltic homeland who converted to Roman Catholicism in order to form closer ties with Poland.

Novgorod was spared pillage by the Mongols. At the time of the Mongol invasions, the prince of Novgorod, Aleksandr, prevented the sack of his city by accepting Batu as his overlord and by personally guaranteeing the delivery of tribute from Novgorod to the Khan. Aleksandr's critics blame him for not resisting and for using Mongol armies to collect tribute from the unwilling citizens of Novgorod. His supporters point out that resistance was useless, and that subordination to the Mongols both preserved Novgorod from destruction and permitted the prince to defend his people from Western invaders. Aleksandr defeated the Swedes on the Neva River in 1240, after which he was known as Aleksandr Nevskii. In 1242, he decisively defeated the Teutonic Knights in a battle on the ice of Lake Chud and put a permanent end to their eastern expansion.

As a loyal subordinate of the Golden Horde, Novgorod benefitted from the Eurasian economic boom of the Mongol Era. Novgorod continued to serve as connecting point between the Baltic and Volga trade routes. Woolen cloth, beer, wine, salt, metal tools, and silver came from northern Europe, luxury textiles and manufactured goods came from Central Asia, and for them Novgorod traded the fur, wax, and walrus tusks that it obtained from its northern empire. Novgorod led all of Rus in recovering economically from the effects of the Mongol invasions, and it was the largest and wealthiest East Slavic city of this period.

Over the course of the thirteenth century, Novgorod's boiar commercial elite grew even more powerful and their influence over city government increased at the expense of the veche and ordinary citizens. They created a city council, composed of former posadniks, that represented each of the five sections of the city and all of the boiar families. The posadnik was elected yearly, and hence was more closely controlled by the city council.

Vladimir-Suzdal was more closely controlled by the Khans of the Golden Horde than either Galicia-Volynia or Kiev, no doubt because it was located on the Volga trade route and was the key to accessing the wealth of Novgorod and the north. At first the Mongols used their own officials to take the census and collect tribute, and they sent their own military forces to protect the officials and keep roads safe for tribute gathering and trade. By the early fourteenth century, however, princes in the Northeast had proven their reliability and were allowed to take over tribute collection and delivery. Mongol tax officials began to reside in Sarai, and they supervised the princes from a distance.

The Rurikovich family continued to grow and to establish new principalities. Its members also continued to observe the political traditions of Kiev Rus, except that Vladimir now replaced Kiev as the most prestigious principality in Rus, and the position of Grand Prince of Vladimir became the rightful office of the most senior member of the dynasty. Determining who, exactly, was the senior member of the dynasty was no easier than it had been in the past, and struggles among cousins for the right to the title of Grand Prince of Vladimir continued, but Mongol rule changed the means by which these struggles were decided. For the first time, the Rurikovichi had a superior power, the Khan of the Golden Horde, to adjudicate their disputes, and it was he who confirmed the Grand Prince of Vladimir in his office.

It was during the period of Mongol domination that the princes of the Moscow began a process by which their descendants would themselves become Eurasian empire-builders. Through a series of unplanned and fortuitous events, Moscow broke out of the Kiev Rus political arrangement of collective rule and lateral succession. The territory of the principality became indivisible, the right to rule began to pass from father to oldest son, its princes acquired a preponderant military force and were able to subordinate their fellow princes and annex their principalities. However, in the thirteenth and fourteenth centuries, there was little to distinguish Moscow from any other of the cities of the northeast, and the rise of Moscow was gradual and far from inevitable. It is only in retrospect that the direction of Moscow's development seems clear and purposive.

Moscow was first mentioned in the chronicles under the year 1147, but it did not become a principality until the mid-1280s when Aleksandr Nevskii (formerly Prince of Novgorod but by that time Grand Prince of Vladimir) made his son, Daniil, its prince. Daniil annexed cities and territories, and by his death, Moscow was a self-sufficient economic unit that controlled the main waterway between Suzdal and Novgorod. Daniil was succeeded as prince of Moscow by his oldest son, Iurii (1303–1325), who continued his father's policies of annexation and is known to posterity as Iurii Dolgorukii ("of the long arms").

In 1304, Mikhail of Tver, the senior member of the Rurikovich clan, became Grand Prince of Vladimir. He was accepted by his fellow princes and was duly awarded the iarlyk by the Khan of the Golden Horde. In 1318, when Mikhail died, however, Iurii Dolgorukii challenged the Rurikovich system by claiming the right to succeed him as Grand Prince of Vladimir. Iurii was, in fact, the senior member of the dynasty, but his father, Daniil, had never served as Grand Prince of Vladimir, and, according to long-standing tradition, this meant that Daniil's descendants had lost forever the right to become Grand Prince.

Iurii was opposed by his cousins, and, he would probably have lost a civil war over the issue, since he would have had to face the combined forces of all princes who upheld the old system of succession. However, there was now a sovereign overlord of Rus, the Khan of the Golden Horde, and Iurii took advantage of this fact. He went to Sarai bearing gifts and Novgorod's tribute payment, and while there he married the Khan's sister. When Iurii returned to the Northeast, he brought with him not only the iarlyk for Grand Prince of Vladimir but a Mongol army as well.

For more than a decade the sons of Mikhail of Tver resisted, and in the end they managed to recover the Grand Princeship of Vladimir. Luckily for Moscow, however, the people of Tver revolted against Mongol tax collectors. Ivan I (1325–1341), also known as Ivan Kalita ("moneybags"), Iurii's youngest brother and successor as Prince of Moscow, took advantage of Tver's disloyalty to obtain both the iarlyk and Mongol troops. In 1327, Ivan defeated and sacked Tver. From this point on, the title of Grand Prince of Vladimir was kept in the family of the Daniilovichi of Moscow. Ivan Kalita was succeeded by his two sons, Semen (1341–1353) and Ivan II (1353–1359). These princes continued to augment their principality by purchase, by annexation, by contracting marriages with other princely families, and by gaining the allegiance of large landholders who wanted to tie their fortunes to a rising political power.

Religion and Culture

The Mongols were tolerant, even supportive, of all the religions in their Eurasian empire. The Khan of the Mongol Horde, in accordance with this policy, confirmed the authority of the Metropolitanate of Rus and exempted it from all taxes, tribute, and conscription. As a result, the Church grew enormously wealthy. Princes gave lands to churches and monasteries both to support the church and to avoid paying tribute. Church lands, populated by peasants, contributed to the wealth of the principality but were not taxed by the Mongols. The wealthy elite gave land to churches and monasteries out of piety and so that prayers would be said for their souls.

The Church became the most important force for preserving the unity of the Eastern Slavs. Even though the state of Kiev Rus had been fragmented, the Metropolitanate of Rus remained. For sixty years after the conquest, the Metropolitan in Kiev continued to appoint bishops to each of the former principalities of Kiev Rus—including those under Polish and Lithuanian control. In 1299, Metropolitan Maxim moved the capital of the Metropolitanate of Rus from Kiev to Vladimir. Because of the pressure from Catholic influences in the southwest, it was natural for him to look for support to the Orthodox princes of the Northeast. Vladimir was also a more convenient location for dealing with the Mongols.

The Metropolitan soon threw his support behind the rising principality of Moscow, and it was with enthusiastic Church encouragement that Moscow annexed the principalities of the Northeast and began to compete with Lithuania to "gather the lands of Rus." For example, in their conflict with the princes of Tver, the princes of Moscow were aided by Metropolitans Peter (1305–1326) and Feognost (1328–1353) who used excommunication, withholding of blessings, removal of bishops, and closing of churches to advance the cause of Moscow.

Peter also helped to make Moscow a religious center by co-sponsoring the building of the Church of the Dormition in 1327. While the church was under construction, Peter died, and he was entombed in one wall of the church. Peter was sainted in 1329, and the church became a shrine. Ivan Kalita built four more churches inside the Kremlin. Thus, in the tradition of Iaroslav the Wise, the princes of Moscow used church architecture to raise their city to preeminence among the principalities of the Rurikovichi.

The fourteenth century was also a great age of monastery construction. The most famous was the Trinity Monastery built in Radonezh, near Moscow, in 1337 by an impoverished boiar who took the name Sergei when he became a monk. Under his leadership, the Trinity Monastery paralleled Kiev's monastery of the Caves in several important ways. It adopted the cenobitic model of discipline, poverty, and communal living; it spawned a host of imitators as monks left it to form monasteries in more remote locations; and its association with Moscow contributed religious legitimacy to Moscow's claim to succeed Kiev as the capital city of the Rus.

As the centuries passed since the official conversion of the Rus to Christianity, pagan practices were abandoned or transformed into incidental rituals, while the major life experiences and the changes of the seasons were observed in Christian forms. During the period of Mongol rule, it seems to have become generally accepted that only priests could perform weddings, and that the Christian rites of mass, baptism, marriage, and burial were essential for salvation. Church attendance to celebrate Christmas and Easter was nearly universal.

The church also imparted its sexual mores to the population. It set penalties for infanticide, abortion, and birth control. The Church taught that celibacy was the ideal life and that sex was basically sinful, although acceptable as long as it was intended to produce children. Conjugal sex was considered an unclean act, and sexual relations were forbidden on holy days or fast days. In addition, after giving birth a woman was considered unclean for forty days, during which time she was forbidden to prepare meals, attend church, or go out in public.

It seems appropriate that it was in the Mongol era that the term *krestian* ("Christian") came into use as the word for "peasant." As the wealthy elite (and the church) came to depend more and more directly on the labor of peasants for their income, they probably began to recognize them as important members of the Christian Rus community rather than as alien pagans. With the spread of churches and monasteries—the visible signs of Christianity—the peasants, too, probably began to feel a greater sense of membership in this community. Ordinary farmers bore the brunt of Mongol devastation and tribute-gathering, and it was only natural for them to look for protection from the Church. A rise in religiosity is always associated with times of economic disruption and political upheaval, and participation in church ceremonies and festivals must have offered solace to the peasantry.

ROLES AND STATUS OF WOMEN

Relations between men and women changed little during this period. Politics of church and state were male prerogatives, and women of the nonproductive classes devoted themselves to the family, managing the household and raising children. Farm women cared for home and children and also worked the land and raised livestock. From the thirteenth century, the marriage contract was signed by bride and groom as well as by their parents, but it was normal for parents to choose spouses for their children. The Russian word for bride, *nevesta*, means "unknown woman," and this suggests that at one time it was common for the husband and wife to meet for the first time at the wedding ceremony.

Patriarchal practices continued. The Church taught that the ideal wife should be humble, silent, and submissive. It became a practice for the groom to send his fiancé a chest with needles and pins, signifying that making cloth and sewing clothing was her duty, and a small whip, symbolizing her subordination to him. In the fourteenth century, a new marriage ritual arose that celebrated (female) pre-marital chastity. Retiring to a bedroom, while the guests continued to feast, the couple would consummate their marriage. Afterwards, when they reappeared, the groom would signify to the guests whether or not his wife had been a virgin.

On the other hand, in the thirteenth century women gained new rights to divorce. If a husband sold himself into slavery, if he slandered her character, if he physically abused her, or if he went off to war for more than three years, his wife was permitted to divorce him and remarry. Moreover, women's property rights increased. Starting in the thirteenth century, daughters received an equal share of property with brothers. Women could engage in commerce and could buy and sell property. Some lands could be inherited only through the female line, and a widower had no rights to his dead wife's property, which passed to her children. Women had the right to make their own wills and to appear in court. Prince's wives could serve as judges. Finally, women were venerated as mothers, and mothers could exert a powerful influence on their grown children by bestowing or denying their blessing.

ECONOMIC AND SOCIAL TRENDS

For all the damage done to the Eastern Slavs by Mongol armies, they still did not suffer as much as other regions of Eurasia such as China and Persia. More cities were undamaged (including Novgorod, Rostov, Yaroslavl, and Tver) than were destroyed. In the principality of Vladimir, for example, it has been estimated that only fourteen out of three hundred towns were looted and burned. Additionally, the economy of the Northeast, and especially Novgorod, benefitted from Mongol encouragement of trade.

Nevertheless, aggregate social and economic statistics do not alter the fact that the Mongol invasions were an unimaginable human catastrophe for the generation who experienced them. Tens and maybe hundreds of thousands of people were killed. Even more people were captured and sold into slavery. (The slave trade was a significant component of Mongol trade with the Southwest Asia and Europe.) Rus cities were depopulated of artisans, as the

Mongols conscripted skilled workers, particularly those who made weapons, and deported them to Sarai and other cities of the Golden Horde. Livestock was slaughtered and crops destroyed; the countryside was devastated. Church construction, an indicator of economic prosperity, came to an end. It was fifty years before building projects were begun again, and a century before the rate of church-building reached pre-Mongol levels.

Economic recovery was begun by the hardy and resilient Slav agriculturalists who gradually recovered war-ravaged land, cleared new fields, and started new families. These farmers produced the wealth that made it possible for princes to pay tribute and for the general economy to recover. The village community of the pre-Mongol era disappeared and was replaced by single-family farms or small hamlets of two or three families. These families were associated in autonomous, self-governing communes which administered the use of forests, commons, and streams and which coordinated the collection and payment of tax obligations.

Free peasant farmers (known as "black people" because land not owned by aristocratic landlords was called "black land") treated the land they tilled as their private property. They bought and sold it and bequeathed it to their children. They were free to grow whatever crops they wanted, and they were free to move to farm new land. Their only obligation was to pay taxes to the prince. Most of the taxes were in kind—grain (rye, oats, barley, wheat), flax, butter, and slaughtered livestock. Taxes were allocated among the families based on their ability to pay (determined by family size, livestock, and tools). The peasants also provided labor for public works—roads, fortifications, transportation, and delivery of mail.

Ever more land passed into the hands of the wealthy elite, although in this period black land probably still predominated. In the new economic circumstances, however, the landed elite no longer organized production for the market on its estates as it had done previously. To begin with, in the aftermath of the Mongol invasion, there was no market to produce for. Moreover, because property was equally divided among children, parcels of land became too small to organize for large-scale estate production. As a result, landowners acquired wealth from their land by allowing peasant communities to farm it and by charging them rents, fees, and service payments.

Thus, the ownership of land populated with agricultural workers became the principal source of wealth for the Rus elite. The princes owned huge amounts of land in their own names—independently of their princely office—and they continually sought to acquire more. Furthermore, each prince considered that all the land in his principality was his to dispose of, and he felt free to give it to private individuals, the church, or monasteries. Any agriculturalists who tilled that land then came under the jurisdiction of the new owner who would then demand rent. These landlords also acquired the power to govern the agriculturalists living on their land. They collected taxes on behalf of the government, they supervised the commune administrators, and they acted as judges administering law and order.

Since estate owners did not organize production themselves, agricultural labor was highly valued, and landowners competed with one another to attract farmers. They did so by offering free land, loans of money to buy animals and tools, and promises of future aid in case of emergency. Princes were so anxious to attract people to their vacant land that they often granted charters of immunity from tax or tribute obligations to landlords. The landlords, in turn, were able to attract farmers by offering them immunities from various tax, tribute, or service obligations for a set number of years (usually two or three).

Land could be bought by anyone with the money to purchase it, but it could not always be freely sold. Land was considered a possession of the extended family and could not be sold without its permission. A relative who was not informed of a sale of land had the right to buy it back from the purchaser at the sale price. The only exception to this rule was if the land was lost through bankruptcy.

The social structure of the laboring population changed little. Indentured servitude continued, but now these bondspeople had the right to appeal to courts for legal protection. Slavery continued, but slaves could no longer be killed by their owners without impunity. There was also a tendency for landowners who did not manage their own estates to turn their slaves into independent (rent-paying) peasants. The black peasants had the same legal status as all other free people and could move to new land.

Elite social structure changed considerably. Rurikovich princes continued to multiply. Since princes divided land equally among their sons, many princes were no wealthier than boiars, and some owned no land at all. Those who could not support themselves on their rents entered the service of the major princes and became known as "serving princes." This category also included foreign princes, Mongol and Lithuanian for the most part, who decided to tie their fortunes to the rising principality of Moscow.

The druzhina disappeared. People in the direct service of princes were now called the *dvor* ("courtyard"). Some were free servitors, others either contracted for a set period of service or were slaves. Servitors could be paid for their service by grants of land, or by a new system of support called *kormlenie* (literally "feeding"), in which the servitor would be given the right to collect fees from a town or region for set number of years.

The term boiar had been used in Kiev Rus to refer to the wealthiest elite, and this usage continued in the Northeast. In the principality of Moscow, however, boiar began to have a unique significance. A small group (in the beginning no more than half a dozen) of Moscow boiars coalesced at the court creating a more or less formal institution that provided advice and aid to the Grand Prince. They were principally military servitors, and they commanded retinues made up of servitors of their own, which they put at the disposal of the Grand Prince. They also served as advisers and administrators. They were rewarded with grants of land, booty won in war, and other gifts. They were landowners in their own right and lived on their own estates.

Conclusion

In retrospect, the most momentous development in the northeast in this time period was the expansion of Moscow and the rising prestige of its princes. However, when Ivan II, Prince of Moscow and Grand Prince of Vladimir, died in 1359, the future of the lands between the Baltic and Black Seas was far from predictable. The Golden Horde was beginning to show signs of decline, but it continued to dominate western Inner Eurasia. Lithuania continued to annex territory from the former Kiev Rus. Novgorod was a major commercial empire that asserted its autonomy. Each time a Muscovite prince died, the passage of the office of Grand Prince to his heirs was challenged by other Rurikovichi. There was internal conflict among Moscow's boiars. There would have been no reason, at the time, to have predicted a great future for the Principality of Moscow.

Notes

1. David Morgan, *The Mongols* (Oxford: Blackwell, 1986), 74.
2. Ibid.

_____ **TEXT DOCUMENTS** _____

Mongol Warfare

In 1245 Pope Innocent IV sent an ambassadorial mission to the Mongols. The monk John of Plano Carpini, who led the mission, visited the camp of Batu as well as the capital of the Great Khan at Karakorum. After his return, Carpini wrote "A History of the Mongols" from which this passage is taken.

- Are Carpini's descriptions of the Mongol army convincing? (Compare with other text documents in this chapter.)
- What does the Mongol army have in common with earlier nomad armies? How is it different?

Genghis Khan ordained that the army should be organized in such a way that over ten men should be set one man and he is what we call a captain of ten; over ten of these should be placed one, named a captain of a hundred; at the head of ten captains of a hundred is placed a soldier known as a captain of a thousand, and over ten captains of a thousand is one man. . . . Two of three chiefs are in command of the whole army, yet in such a way that one holds the supreme command.

When they are in battle, if one or two or three or even more out of a group of ten run away, all are put to death; and if a whole group of ten flees, the rest of the group of a hundred are all put to death, if they do not flee too. In a word, unless they retreat in a body, all who take flight are put to death. Likewise if one or two or more go forward boldly to the fight, then the rest of the ten are put to death if they do not follow and, if one or more of the ten are captured, their companions are put to death if they do not rescue them.

They all have to possess the following arms at least: two or three bows, or at least one good one, three large quivers full of arrows, an axe and ropes for hauling engines of war. As for the wealthy, they have swords pointed at the end but sharp only on one side and somewhat curved, and they have a horse with armor; their legs also are covered and they have helmets and cuirasses. . . .

When they are going to make war, they send ahead an advance guard and these carry nothing with them but their tents, horses, and arms. They seize no plunder, burn no houses, and slaughter no animals; they only wound and kill men or, if they can do nothing else, put them to flight. They much prefer, however, to kill than to put to flight. The army follows after them, taking everything they come across, and they take prisoner or kill any inhabitants who are to be found. Not content with this, the chiefs of the army next send plunderers in all directions to find men and animals, and they are most ingenious at searching them out. . . .

It should be known that when they come in sight of the enemy they attack at once, each one shooting three or four arrows at their adversaries; if they see that they are not going to be able to defeat them, they retire, going back to their own line. They do this as a blind to

Source: "The Travels of John of Plano Carpini," in Christopher Dawson, Ed., *The Mongol Mission. Narratives and Letters of the Franciscan Missionaries in Mongolia and China in the Thirteenth and Fourteenth Centuries* (London and New York: Sheed and Ward, 1955), 32–3, 35, 36–38.

make the enemy follow them as far as the places where they have prepared ambushes. If the enemy pursues them to these ambushes, they surround and wound and kill them. Similarly if they see that they are opposed by a large army, they sometimes turn aside and, putting a day's or two days' journey between them, they attack and pillage another part of the country and they kill men and destroy and lay waste the land. If they perceive that they cannot even do this, then they retreat for some ten or twelve days and stay in a safe place until the army of the enemy has disbanded, whereupon they come secretly and ravage the whole land. . . .

They reduce fortresses in the following manner. If the position of the fortress allows it, they surround it, sometimes even fencing it round so that no one can enter or leave. They make a strong attack with engines and arrows and they do not leave off fighting by day or night, so that those inside the fortress get no sleep; the Mongols however have some rest, for they divide up their forces and they take it in turns to fight so that they do not get too tired. If they cannot capture it in this way they throw Greek fire; sometimes they even take the fat of the people they kill and, melting it, throw it on to the houses, and wherever the fire falls on this fat it is almost inextinguishable. . . .

If they are still unsuccessful and the city or fort has a river, they dam it or alter its course and submerge the fortress if possible. Should they not be able to do this, then undermine the city and armed men enter it from underground; once inside, some of them start fires to burn the fortress while the rest fight the inhabitants. If however they are not able to conquer it even in this way, they establish a fort or fortification of their own facing the city, so as not to suffer any injury from the missiles of the enemy; and they stay for a long time over against the city, unless by chance it has outside help from an army which fights against the Mongols and removes them by force. While they are pitched before the fortification they speak enticing words to the inhabitants making them many promises to induce them to surrender into their hands. If they do surrender to them, they say, "come out, so that we may count you according to our custom," and when they come out to them they seek out the artisans among them and keep these, but the others, with the exception of those they wish to have as slaves, they kill with the axe. If they do spare any others they never spare the noble and illustrious men, so we are told. . . .

All those they take prisoner in battle they put to death unless they happen to want to keep some as slaves. They divide those who are to be killed among the captains of a hundred to be executed by them with a battle-axe; they in their turn divide them among the captives, giving each slave to kill ten or more or less as the officers think fit.

Gender Roles and Relations Among the Mongols

In 1253, Louis IX of France sent the Franciscan friar, William of Rubruck, to Karakorum to suggest an alliance between Europe and the Mongols against the Muslim world. The mission failed, but the ambassador published an account of his journey after he returned.

- How do Mongol gender practices compare with those of the Scythians? With the Rus?

It is the duty of the women to drive the carts, to load the houses on to them and to unload them, to milk the cows, to make the butter and curd, to dress the skins and to sew them, which they do with thread made out of tendons. They split the tendons into very thin threads and then twist these into one long thread. They also sew shoes and socks and other garments. . . . The women also make the felt and cover the houses.

The men make bows and arrows, manufacture stirrups and bits and make saddles; they build the houses and carts, they look after the horses and milk the mares, churn the koumis, that is the mares' milk, and make the skins in which it is kept, and they also look after the camels and load them. Both sexes look after the sheep and goats, and sometimes the men, sometimes the women, milk them. They dress skins with the sour milk of ewes, thickened and salted.

. . . As for their marriages, you must know that no one there has a wife unless he buys her, which means that sometimes girls are quite grown up before they marry, for their parents always keep them until they sell them. . . . No widow among them marries, the reason being that they believe that those who serve them in this life will serve them in the next, and so of a widow they believe that she will always return after death to her first husband. This gives rise to a shameful custom among them whereby a son sometimes takes to wife all his father's wives, except his own mother; for the household of a father and mother always falls to the youngest son and so he himself has to provide for all his father's wives who come to him with his father's effects; and then, if he so wishes, he uses them as wives, for he does not consider an injury has been done to him if they return to his father after death.

And so when anyone has made an agreement with another to take his daughter, the father of the girl arranges a feast and she takes flight to relations where she lies hid. Then the father declares: "Now my daughter is yours; take her wherever you find her." Then he searches for her with his friends until he finds her; then he has to take her by force and bring her, as though by violence, to his house.

Source: "The Journey of William of Rubruck," in Dawson, *The Mongol Mission,* 103–104.

The Mongol Invasion of Rus

The following passage comes from the Chronicle of Novgorod. (Note: "Tatar" is the name of an Inner Eurasia nomadic people whom Genghis Khan defeated and incorporated into his empire. The Russians used the name "Tatar" to mean "Mongol.")

- How accurate do you think this account is in its factual description (consider it in light of Carpini's account of the Mongol army)?
- How does this compare with how the *Primary Chronicle* described their nomad neighbors?
- How does the chronicler explain the Mongol victory? What are the implications of this explanation?

1238 . . . Foreigners called Tatars came in countless numbers, like locusts, into the land of Riazan. . . . And the princes of Riazan sent to Iurii of Vladimir asking for help, or himself to come. But Iurii neither went himself nor listened to the request of the Princes of Riazan, but he himself wished to make war separately. But it was too late to oppose the wrath of God . . . Thus also did God before these men take from us our strength and put into us perplexity and thunder and dread and trembling for our sins. And then the pagan foreigners surrounded Riazan and fenced it in with a stockade. . . . And the Tatars took the town on December 21, and they had advanced against it on the 16th of the same month. They likewise killed the Prince and the Princess, and men, women, and children, monks, nuns and priests, some by fire, some by the sword, and violated nuns, priests' wives, good women and girls in the presence of their mothers and sisters. . . .

    The pagan and godless Tartars, then, having taken Ryazan, went to Vladimir, a host of shedders of Christian blood. And Prince Yuri went out from Vladimir and fled to Yaroslavl, while his son Vsevolod with his mother and the bishop, and the whole of the province shut themselves in Vladimir. And the lawless Ishmaelites approached the town and surrounded the town in force, and fenced it all round with a fence. . . . And when the lawless ones had already come near and set up battering rams, and took the town and set it on fire on Friday before Sexagesima Sunday, the Prince and Princess and Bishop, seeing that the town was on fire and that the people were already perishing, some by fire and others by the sword, took refuge in the Church of the Holy Mother of God and shut themselves in the Sacristy. The pagans breaking down the doors, piled up wood and set fire to the sacred church, and slew all, thus they perished, giving up their souls to God. Others went in pursuit of Prince Iurii to Yaroslavl. . . . And it happened when he reached the river Sit they overtook him and there he ended his life. And God knows how he died; for some say much about him. And Rostov and Suzhdal went each its own way. And the accursed ones having come thence took Moscow, Pereyaslavl, Yurev, Dmitrov, Volokolamsk, and Tver; there also they killed the son of Yaroslav, And thence the lawless ones came and invested Torzhok on the festival of the first Sunday in Lent. They fenced it all round with a fence, as they had taken other towns, and here the accursed ones fought with battering rams for two weeks. And the people in the town were exhausted and from Novgorod there was no help for them; but already every

---

Source. Michell, *The Chronicle of Novgorod*, 82–85. (c) The Royal Historical Society. Reprinted by permission.

man began to be in perplexity and terror. And so the pagans took the town, and slew all from the male sex even to the female, all the priests and the monks, and all stripped and reviled gave up their souls to the Lord in a bitter and a wretched death . . . And the accursed godless ones then pushed on from Torzhok by the road of Sergei right up to Ignati's cross, cutting down everybody like grass, to within 100 versts of Novgorod. God, however, and the great and sacred apostolic cathedral Church of St. Sophia, and St. Kiril, and the prayers of the holy and orthodox Bishop, of the faithful Princes, and of the very reverend monks of the hierarchical Veche, protected Novgorod. And who, brothers, fathers, and children, seeing this, God's infliction on the whole Russian Land, does not lament? God let the pagans on us for our sins. God brings foreigners on to the land in his wrath, and thus crushed by them they will be reminded of God. And internecine war comes from the prompting of the devil: for God does not wish evil amongst men, but good; but the devil rejoices at wicked murder and bloodshed. And any land which has sinned God punishes with death or famine, or with infliction of pagans, or with drought, or with heavy rain, or with other punishment, to see whether we will repent and live as God bids; for He tells us by the prophet: "Turn to me with your whole heart, with fasting and weeping." And if we do so we shall be forgiven of all our sins. But we always turn to evil, like swine ever wallowing in the filth of sin, and thus we remain; and for this we receive every kind of punishment from God; and the invasion of armed men, too, we accept at God's command; as punishment for our sins.

Mongol Charter of Immunity Granted to the Church

The Mongols were tolerant and respectful of the religions of all the peoples they conquered.

The following is a charter (iarlyk) granted to the Metropolitan of Rus in 1267.

- What does this iarlyk grant? What does it require?
- What effect would this have had on the Church?
- What does this reveal about the nature of Mongol treatment of the non-Church population?

By the power of Eternal Heaven and by the Will of Eternal Heaven! [Khan] Temir hereby issues the following instruction to all of his people, officials, princes and high-ranking military commanders as well as to all tax collectors, office secretaries, circuit envoys, falconers, and officials in charge of hunting.

Source: "Yaroslav's Church Statute" in Dmytryshyn, *Medieval Russia: A Source Book, 850–1700* (Gulf Breeze, FL: Academic International Press, 1999), 175–176. Copyright Academic International Press, Gulf Breeze, FL. Reprinted by permission.

Emperor Genghis Khan had once decreed that there be no collection of tribute or of food provisions from those [subjects of the Mongol rule] who genuinely prayed to God for us and for our nation and who gave us their genuine blessings. Subsequent [Mongol] emperors have respected this injunction and have bestowed favors on priests and monks [of all other faiths]. [This injunction applies to the collection of] tribute as well as anything else, including a tax on trade goods, a tax on ploughshares, postal fees, recruit levies, and whatever may be requested. We have agreed to reconfirm these original benefits [to the Orthodox Church] and hereby are making them known to everyone. And, invoking God's name, we are not amending any former existing charters.

Consequently, regardless of his position or status [no Mongol official] may request or collect from them [that is, officials of the Orthodox Church], any tribute, or ploughshare tax, or transport obligation, or food provisions. The same rule applies to the collection of postal fees, recruit levies, and a tax on trade goods. Likewise, no one should appropriate anything that belongs to the Orthodox Church, such as their buildings, land holdings, water resources, orchards, flour mills, winter homes (and forests), and summer lodges (and pastures). And those who may do so are hereby required to return it back [to the church]. Also no church craftsman, or a falconer, or any other church employee may be either taken away [by local Mongol official] or be subjected to a close supervision. Moreover, whatever legally belongs to the Orthodox Church and is duly registered in their records, should be neither occupied, expropriated, alienated, or destroyed. And anyone who would dare to blaspheme their [Orthodox] faith will be guilty of committing a crime and will be executed.

Priests [of the Orthodox faith] who may live in the same home or whose brothers or sons have committed themselves to priesthood are entitled to the same [existing] benefits and protection as long as they are actively involved in it. However, once they leave the profession, they must pay the required tribute and do whatever is requested from them. Priests, who have received benefits from our earlier [charter], and who pray for us and bless us are to continue to enjoy their rights. Those, however, who fail to say prayers or who do not express their genuine feelings are hereby considered sinners and they will be punished accordingly. Finally, those individuals who are not priests, but who pray to God in our behalf, will also enjoy these benefits.

We have granted this charter to Metropolitan [Feognost]. Those who may see or hear the content of this charter are hereby prohibited from collecting any tribute or anything else from priests or monks [of the Orthodox Church]. Consequently, any Mongol official, or a secretary of the prince, or a tribute collector, or a collector of trade dues, or any one who may try to correct or requisition anything that is contrary to the intent or the letter of this imperial [charter], which is based on Genghis Khan's original injunction, will be guilty of a very serious crime and will be executed.

This [charter] was issued in the steppe on the first day of the hunting season [August 1, 1267].

An Uprising Against Mongol Rule

This account of Rus resistance to Mongol oppression comes from the Tver Chronicle for the year 1237.

- What does this reveal about relations between the Rus and the Mongols? Between the townspeople and the prince and the role of the veche?
- What does this reveal about the attitude of the Church toward the Mongols in 1534? Might the Church have had a different attitude in 1326?

God permitted the Devil to instill evil in the hearts of the godless Tatars, to say to the lawless tsar [i.e. the Khan of the Golden Horde]: "Unless you destroy Prince Aleksandr [Mikhailovich] and all the Russian princes, you will not have power over them." And Shevkal, the lawless and accursed instigator of all evil, the scourge of Christians, opened his foul mouth and began to say as the Devil had taught him: "Lord Tsar, if you command, I will go to Rus, and destroy Christianity, and kill their princes, and bring their princesses and children to you." And the tsar commanded him to do thus. The lawless Shevkal, scourge of Christians, went to Rus with many Tatars, came to Tver, and drove the grand prince from his palace, and himself, in his great insolence, stayed in the palace of the grand prince; and he stirred up a great persecution of Christians, with violence, and plunder, and killing, and desecration. The people, constantly hurt in their pride by the pagans, complained many times to the grand prince that he should defend them; but he, although he saw the injuries done to his people, could not defend them and ordered them to be patient; but the people of Tver could not endure this and waited for a suitable moment. And it happened that on the fifteenth day of August, in mid-morning, during the market hours, a certain deacon, Tveritin, surnamed Diudko, was leading a small and very fat mare to drink the water of the Volga; the Tatars saw her and carried her away. The deacon was grieved and began to cry out loudly, saying: "Oh men of Tver; do not let me down!" And a fight took place between them; the Tatars, relying on their unlimited authority, began to use weapons, and straightway men gathered, and the people rose in tumult, and sounded the bells, and assembled in a veche; and the entire city turned [against the Tatars], and the people all gathered right away, and there was agitation among them, and the men of Tver gave a shout and began to kill the Tatars, wherever they found them, until they had killed Shevkal himself and all of them in turn. . . .

And after he had heard this, the lawless tsar [khan] sent an army in winter into the Russian land, with the voevoda Fedorchiuk, and five temniki [commanders of units of 10,000 soldiers each]; and they killed many people, and took others captive, and put Tver and all the towns to flame.

Source: "The uprising in Tver in 1327," in George Vernadsky, Ed., *A Source Book for Russian History from Early Times to 1917*, Vol. 1 (New Haven, CT: Yale University Press, 1972), 52-3. (c) Yale University Press. Reprinted by permission.

Figure 4-1 The Dormition of the Mother of God

This icon depicts the dormition, or death, of the Virgin Mary. It is also called "the assumption" since the Orthodox Church teaches that Mary was bodily assumed into heaven at her death. It was painted in the style of the Novgorod school in the second half of the fourteenth century.

- Comparing this with previous icons, can you speculate on trends in icon painting?
- What is the significance of the subject of this icon for Russian culture?

Source: Tretiakov Gallery, Moscow.

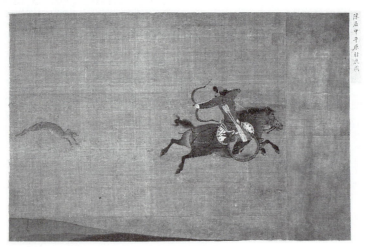

Figure 4-2 A Mongol Warrior

This is a contemporary Chinese drawing of a Mongol warrior.

- What typical features of steppe warriors does this figure exemplify?
- How did the Mongol conquest of Russia recapitulate earlier patterns of nomadic-sedentary interactions?

Source: Collection of the National Palace Museum. Taiwan, Republic of China.

Figure 4-3 Birchbark Document

Archeologists have found hundreds of documents written on birchbark in the cities of Kiev Rus, and especially in Novgorod, some dating from the eleventh century. They include contracts, business letters, love letters, and prayers. This is a page from a booklet of evening prayers that was probably written in the thirteenth or fourteenth century.

- What does this suggest about literacy in Novgorod and Rus?
- About Rus society in this era?

Source: Drawn by the author from a photograph in Kolchin, Yamshchikov, and Yanin, *Drevnii Novgorod: prikladnoe iskusstvo i arkheologiiia* (Moscow: "Iskusstvo," 1985), 21, plates 8 a, b, v, g, with reference to the copy of Document 419 in A. V. Artsikhovskii and V. L. Ianin, *Novgorodskie gramoty na bereste, Vypusk 7* (Moscow: "Nauka," 1978).

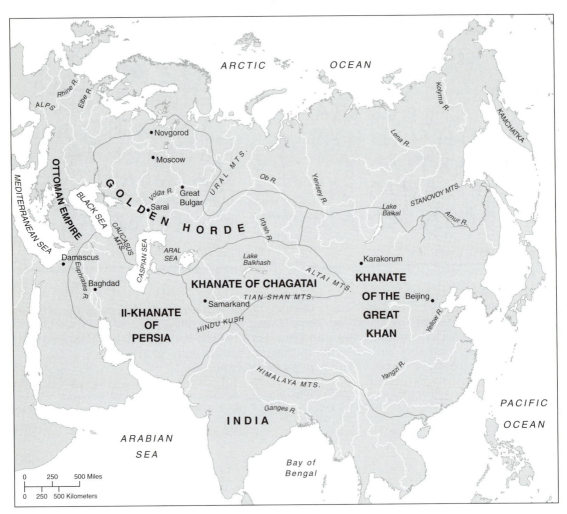

Figure 4-5 The Mongol Empire approximately 1300

Genghis Khan's heirs created the greatest of the nomadic empires of the steppes; in fact, the largest contiguous empire the world has ever seen. This map shows the Mongol Empire at its height, shortly before it was struck by the Black Death, and its decline began.

Credit: Author.

_____ FOR FURTHER READING _____

(In addition to the books by Blum, Christian, Fennell, Levin, and Martin from the previous chapter.)

Abu-Lughod, Janet L. *Before European Hegemony: The World System A.D. 1250–1350.* New York: Oxford University Press, 1989.

Crummey, Robert O. *The Formation of Muscovy, 1304–1613.* New York: Longman, 1987.

Fennell, John. *The Emergence of Moscow, 1304–1359.* Berkeley: University of California Press, 1968.

Halperin, Charles J. *Russia and the Golden Horde: The Mongol Impact on Medieval Russian History.* Bloomington, IN: Indiana University Press, 1985.

de Hartog, Leo. *Russia and the Mongol Yoke: The History of the Russian Principalities and the Golden Horde, 1221–1502.* London: British Academic Press, 1996.

Morgan, David. *The Mongols.* Oxford: Blackwell, 1986.

Ostrowski, Donald. *Muscovy and the Mongols: Cross-cultural Influences on the Steppe Frontier, 1304–1589.* Cambridge: Cambridge University Press, 1998.

Ringrose, David R. *Expansion and Global Interaction, 1200–1700.* New York: Longman, 2001.

CHAPTER FIVE

THE RISE OF MOSCOW, 1360–1460

The trends that had been only tentatively underway in the principality of Moscow in 1360 had become irreversible a century later. By the late fifteenth century, the Kiev Rus pattern of collective rule by a family of princes was gone, and Moscow had become a unitary state with one sovereign prince. The Grand Prince of Moscow had subordinated his cousins and had annexed most of their former territories. Moscow was also the capital of a newly independent branch of the Christian Church, and it was putting itself forward as the legitimate "gatherer of the lands of the Rus." Moreover, by 1460 Moscow was independent of the Mongol Khan in fact if not in law. Over the course of the century, from the middle of the fourteenth to the middle of the fifteenth centuries, Mongol power disintegrated, and Moscow was preparing to step forward as one of the heirs of their Eurasian empire.

THE EURASIAN CONTEXT

In the middle of the fourteenth century, after a century of unprecedented prosperity, the world economy collapsed. Intercontinental trade came to a virtual standstill, and most of Eurasia descended into a deep economic depression that lasted for nearly 150 years. Just as the Mongol conquests had stimulated the economic boom of the thirteenth century, so also were they responsible for the depression of the fourteenth century.

The most direct cause of the economic decline was the devastation of the agricultural population in China and the Middle East described in the previous chapter. In the short run,

Turn to page 103 for a map showing key geographic locations and features for this time period.

the looting of Eurasian cities and agricultural communities had stimulated international trade. It had transferred huge amounts of wealth from populations that consumed locally produced goods to a ruling elite that consumed luxury goods from distant lands. This produced an immediate economic bonanza for intercontinental traders, but in the long run, the oppression of agricultural populations caused farmers to flee (or die), and the agricultural surplus upon which civilization is based declined precipitously. The Mongols had killed the goose that laid the golden egg.

The Mongol Empire also facilitated another major cause of economic downturn—the spread of plague. William H. McNeill has shown that the Black Death first broke out in a Mongol-controlled area of the Himalayas, and that it was carried by Mongol soldiers or couriers to China in the 1330s. From China, the disease moved north to the steppe where it spread among the general Mongol population. Next it followed the Old Silk Road and appeared in Caffa on the Black Sea Coast in 1346, in Italy in 1347, and in Moscow in 1351.[1] The Black Death was a calamity even more disastrous than the Mongol invasions of the previous century. In China, in Mongolia, and in Europe between one-third and one-half of the population died during the first plague epidemic.

The end of Mongol rule followed. As we have seen, steppe empires are typically short-lived, for reasons of overextension, clan rivalries, and recovery by conquered peoples. All four divisions of the Mongol Empire were exhibiting these characteristics shortly before the Black Death struck, but the catastrophic depletion of Mongol armies by the disease hastened the process. As the Mongol empire disintegrated, it could no longer protect and promote what little international trade remained, and so the downward economic spiral continued.

In 1368 a rebellion by native Chinese overthrew the Mongol Yuan Dynasty and replaced it with a new dynasty, the Ming. The Chinese economy quickly recovered under the Ming, but they refused to trade with the Mongols. Thus the Silk Road lost contact with the wealthiest economy in Eurasia. In Persia, local elites rebelled against the Il-Khan regime, and after 1349 when the last Il-Khan ruler died, the empire dissolved.

In Central Asia, by contrast, the Chagatai Empire was brought down not by native resistance to Mongol rule, but by the rise of yet another charismatic, nomadic empire-builder—a Turk named Timur (known in Europe as Tamerlane). By 1370, Timur had completed the conquest of Central Asia, making Samarkand his capital, and he then sought to fill the power vacuum in Southwest Asia created by the collapse of the Il-Khan empire. Timur conquered the Caucasus Mountains and all of Southwest Asia from the Indus River to the Euphrates.

Timur's conquest of the Caucasus was even more devastating than the Mongol had been. The western part of the Kingdom of Georgia had managed to remain free of Mongol rule and Georgia's Golden Age had continued through the fourteenth century, but it did not long survive Timur's invasion. Timur then attacked the Golden Horde, the only remaining Mongol state. Although he defeated Mongol armies and sacked Sarai and other key cities, Timur was unable to consolidate his rule over the north. He retreated, and then he invaded India, where he died in 1405.

Meanwhile, in the Anatolian Peninsula, a new military power had arisen. In 1299, a Turkish clan leader by the name of Osman had declared his independence of the Seljuk Sultan, and had begun to encroach on the territory of the Byzantine Empire. By the 1380s, his descendants (known as Ottoman Turks) had crossed the straits and conquered parts of Serbia and Bulgaria. In 1402 Timur defeated and subordinated the Ottomans, but after his death they regained their independence and resumed their expansion northwards.

Byzantium never fully recovered from the Fourth Crusade (1204) and Roman rule over Constantinople. Even after regaining Constantinople in 1261, the Byzantine Empire remained only a shadow of its former self. The Black Death struck in 1346, and enemies pressed on its western and eastern borders. Throughout the fourteenth century, Byzantine rulers appeased the Ottomans by allowing the empire to become essentially a vassal state. After the Ottomans were defeated by Timur in 1402, however, Constantinople switched tactics and began to resist them. To enlist the support of the Pope and of western Europe, leaders of the Orthodox church met with representatives of Rome at the Council of Florence in 1439 and agreed to the Pope's terms for the reunion of the churches. They added the phrase "philioque" to the Nicene Creed, and they accepted the Pope as the head of the Christian church. Capitulation to the Papacy did not work, however; Western Europe did not provide military aid. In 1453, Ottoman armies overran Constantinople, and the Eastern Roman Empire came to an end. (Soon thereafter the Patriarch renounced the concessions he had made at the Council of Florence.)

Europe was experiencing crop failures and political turmoil even before the Black Death hit in 1347–1350, but the plague made Europe's troubles even worse. The demographic disaster was accompanied by a crisis in medieval society. The wealth and worldliness of the Papacy were criticized by clerical reformers within the Church and by dissenters and heretics outside it. The prestige of the Pope was damaged by the ironically named "Babylonian Captivity"; for most of the fourteenth century, popes lived in France and were considered to be puppets of the French king. The medieval national monarchy disintegrated because of contradictions between centralizing monarchies and feudal aristocracies and between feudal values and the rising commercial middle-class. The Hundred Years' War between France and England (1337–1453) was accompanied by aristocratic civil wars in which armies dissolved into gangs of mercenaries and thieves. The resulting devastation gave rise to peasant rebellions and urban insurrections.

Over the course of the century between 1360 and 1460, the Golden Horde also disintegrated. It was weakened by the Black Death and by the decline in trade along the Silk Road, and it was shaken by palace coups and regional separatism. One such power struggle made it possible for the Grand Prince of Moscow to defeat—temporarily—the forces of the Golden Horde. A far more serious blow to the Horde, however, was its defeat at the hands of Timur, mentioned above, in the 1390s. Timur looted Sarai and the major centers of production and commerce and this further contributed to the Mongol decline. In the 1420s, a junior branch of the ruling family separated the Crimean Peninsula and lower Dnieper River from the Golden Horde, and called itself the Khanate of Crimea. By 1445 the Khanate of Kazan, centered on Kazan in the middle Volga and including Bulgar, also broke free. In the end, all that was left of the territory of the Golden Horde, now known as the Great Horde, was the lower Volga and the steppe to the east of it. The successor states to the Golden Horde were all major regional powers, but the era of Mongol invincibility was over.

Lithuania benefitted greatly from the disintegration of Mongol power. By 1360, Lithuania had annexed Chernigov, Pereyaslavl, and Kiev, and by 1430, Lithuania extended from the Baltic Sea to the Black Sea and from the border with Poland in the west to within one hundred miles of Moscow in the east. The Lithuanian landed nobility continued to draw closer to Poland, attracted by the power enjoyed by the Polish *szlachta* (nobility), which had acquired legal protection against arbitrary arrest or confiscation of property and had forced a separation of powers between the executive and judiciary. This model of limited kingship was more attractive to the Lithuanian nobility than the strong monarchy developing in Moscow, and they encouraged their grand duke to create closer ties with Poland.

The first step was taken in 1385 when Jagiello, Grand Duke of Lithuania, married Jadwiga, Queen of Poland. The two countries were not united institutionally, but Jagiello and his descendants ruled both kingdoms. Jagiello introduced Western feudal institutions in Lithuanian territory, and in 1387, he made Roman Catholicism the official state religion. Jagiello encouraged the aristocracy in the territories of the former Kiev Rus to convert, but he allowed the East Slavic agricultural population to continue to practice Eastern Orthodoxy. He did not want the Orthodox church in his land to be governed by the Metropolitan in Moscow, and he therefore asked the Patriarch in Constantinople to create a separate metropolitanate for Lithuania. There was precedent for this, since in 1371 the Patriarch had appointed a metropolitan for Galicia, because Poland had threatened to convert by force the population to Catholicism if he did not. This time, however, the Patriarch balked; Moscow was vehemently opposed to any division of the Metropolitanate of Rus, and the Patriarch preferred to cultivate good relations with Moscow.

THE RISE OF MOSCOW

By the death of Ivan II in 1359, the Daniilovichi had established themselves as the dominant principality in the Northeast, and they had successfully asserted their right to inherit the title of Grand Prince of Vladimir in their line. In most respects, however, they shared the same political culture as their Kiev Rus ancestors. They inherited the position of prince laterally. (Iurii Dolgorukii had been succeeded by his brother Ivan Kalita, and Semen had been succeeded by his brother Ivan II.) Moreover, each of the other principalities of the Northeast—Tver, Riazan, Suzdal, etc.—were ruled by their own line of Rurikovichi. As before, the forces of unity were cultural: The princes saw themselves as a single family, and the Church thought of the population as a single nation.

During the reigns of Dmitrii Donskoi (1359–1389), Vasilii I (1389–1425), and Vasilii II (1425–1462), however, a new political system emerged. The title of Grand Prince began to be passed from father to son, and the equal division of property among sons ended. As their territory (and hence their army) increased in size, the power of the Grand Prince to compel obedience was enhanced. Grand Princes of Moscow began to curtail the ability of servitors to transfer their allegiance to a new lord, and they punished disloyalty with death and confiscation of property. In short, the Grand Prince of Moscow began to look more like a national monarch on the European pattern and less like the senior member of a family of princes that ruled collectively.

Ivan II died in 1359, and his son, Dmitrii, initiated of a number of significant political developments. First, and quite by chance, a tradition of linear succession from father to son began. Dmitrii inherited the title of Grand Prince and the undivided Principality of Moscow from his father, and he passed it on in the same way to his oldest son. In both cases, however, there were no surviving uncles to claim the right of succession, so tradition was not willfully violated.

Second, Dmitrii, through annexation and purchase, doubled the area ruled by Moscow. No single prince of Rus had ever commanded such a preponderant economic and military power over his cousins. With this power, he could enforce the obedience of a number of other northeast princes, so that he was able to put together something very close to a united army of the northeast.

Third, Dmitrii was able to defy the will of the Khan, to assert his right to be Grand Prince of Moscow, and to defeat a Mongol army for the first time. In 1375 the Mongol general, Mamai, taking advantage of the turmoil that followed the palace coup in Sarai several years earlier, assumed the power of the Khan and confirmed Mikhail of Tver as Grand Prince of Vladimir. Dmitrii, who claimed the title himself, ignored Mamai, led an army to Tver, defeated Mikhail, and forced him to sign a treaty recognizing Dmitrii as his "older brother" and the rightful Grand Prince of Vladimir. Mamai, incensed at this disrespect and at Dmitrii's failure to deliver tribute payments to him, made an alliance with the Grand Duke Olgerd of Lithuania (who was the brother-in-law of Mikhail of Tver and therefore an opponent of Moscow), and marched toward Moscow to punish Dmitrii. The two armies met at Kulikova Field on the upper Don River. Before the Lithuanian army arrived, Dmitrii attacked and defeated the Mongol army. (It was for this victory that Dmitrii was given the appellation "Donskoi.")

This event did not signify the liberation of the Northeast from Mongol overlordship. In 1381, Tokhtamysh, the rightful Khan (by descent), defeated Mamai and restored the unity of the Golden Horde, and in 1382 he defeated and sacked Moscow. However, Dmitrii Donskoi's victory did mark a significant turning point in Moscow's relationship with the Mongols. Tokhtamysh did not attempt to punish Dmitrii for his disobedience. Probably realizing that only the Grand Prince of Moscow had the power to collect and deliver tribute, Tokhtamysh accepted Dmitrii's right to the title of Grand Prince of Vladimir. Before he died, Dmitrii wrote a will that passed to his son, Vasilii I, the combined title of Grand Prince of Vladimir and Prince of Moscow. Tokhtamysh officially confirmed it, and henceforth the office Grand Prince of Vladimir was permanently attached to the Prince of Moscow.

When Dmitrii died, the office of Grand Prince once again passed from father to son. Dmitrii had outlived all his brothers, and Vasilii thus had no uncles to challenge his right of succession. Vasilii continued to pay tribute to Tokhtamysh, and led an army to help defend the Golden Horde from Timur. Timur's victory, however, benefitted Moscow. Tokhtamysh was forced to flee and Sarai was pillaged, and Vasilii stopped making tribute payments. Independence was only temporary, however; in 1408, a new Khan, Edigei, reorganized the Golden Horde, sent an army to Moscow, and forced Vasilii to resume the payment of tribute.

Vasilii expanded his territory eastward, annexing the principalities of Nizhnii Novgorod and Murom, thereby increasing Moscow's control over the central Volga region. He was unable to expand to the west or north because Lithuania and Novgorod were too powerful. Vasilii managed the expansive Lithuania through dynastic politics rather than war. He married a daughter of Vytautas ("Vitovt" in Russian), Grand Duke of Lithuania. Vytautas cut his ties with Moscow's rival, Tver, and agreed not to annex Pskov or Novgorod.

In 1425 when Vasilii died, his will provided that his son, Vasilii II, should succeed him as prince of Moscow and Grand Prince of Vladimir. In light of recent tradition, this might not seem an unusual thing. After all, the rule of Moscow had passed from father to eldest son for three preceding generations and over a span of seventy-five years. However, Vasilii I, unlike his recent ancestors, left several surviving brothers, and the eldest, Iurii, demanded the traditional right of lateral succession. Vasilii II, supported by Grand Duke Vytautas and Metropolitan Fotii, insisted on his right to succeed his father, and Yuri agreed not to press his case. As soon as Vasilii's protectors died (Vytautas in 1430, Fotii in 1431), however, Iuri gathered an army, marched on Moscow, defeated Vasilii II, sent him into exile, and declared himself Grand Prince.

Iurii lived only three more years, and when he died in 1434 Vasilii resumed his reign as Grand Prince. This time Vasilii's action was in full accord with Rurikovich tradition, since he had no more living uncles and was now senior member of the dynasty. Now, however, it was the turn of Iurii's sons to violate tradition and to attempt to secure the grand princeship for their oldest brother. Vasilii II resisted, defeated his oldest cousin in 1436 and had him blinded. In 1444, the civil war resumed, and in 1446, Vasilii was himself defeated, captured, blinded, and exiled by Iurii's second oldest son. Finally, in 1447, aided by his boiars, Vasilii gathered an army, defeated his cousin, resumed his reign, and ruled without further challenge until his death in 1462.

Vasilii added little new territory to his realm, but he added substantially to Moscow's power and prestige. He initiated a fundamental change in the relationship between the Grand Prince and elite landowners. In Kiev Rus, land was held outright and carried no political obligations. Landowners could transfer their allegiance to any prince they chose. However, as the power of the Grand Prince of Moscow grew, and as Lithuania moved toward the Polish model of aristocratic rights, some princes and other landowners began to switch allegiance from the Grand Prince of Moscow to the Grand Prince of Lithuania. Vasilii II considered this to be treason, and brought the practice to an end. He forbade Rurikovich princes and boiars alike to transfer their allegiance to another prince on pain of death and forfeiture of land. Vasilii also began to make a new kind of land grant, called a *pomestie* that was held by the grantee only while in active service of the Grand Prince.

Vasilii II also subordinated (but did not annex) Tver, Suzdal, and Riazan to his authority, and he began the process of subordinating Novgorod. Novgorod's leaders had been increasingly jealous of their autonomy, and they, like some princes, had looked to Lithuania as a less onerous overlord than Moscow. On occasion, Novgorod had invited Lithuanian princes to serve as its prince (instead of a Rurikovich–as tradition required). Vasilii II sent armies Novgorod in 1441 and 1456, and Novgorod agreed to pay higher taxes and a greater share of Mongol tribute and to transfer some of its northern territories to Moscow. It also promised not to deal with foreign powers without Moscow's consent.

By the reign of Vasilii II, Moscow was subordinate to the Mongols in name only. It was convenient for Moscow to recognize the Mongol Khan as overlord, both because the Khan recognized the Grand Prince of Moscow as the ruler of the Northeast and because it gave Moscow the excuse for continuing to collect tribute on the Khan's behalf (little of which was actually sent to Sarai). Moscow had been inferior in power to the combined Golden Horde, but after the Golden Horde fragmented, it was at least the equal of any one of the successor states. It was only a matter of time before Moscow formally declared its independence.

THE NEW POLITICAL ARRANGEMENT

Vasilii II must not have felt entirely confident that his Rurikovich relatives had accepted the principle of lineal succession from father to son over the old system of lateral succession from elder to younger brother. He therefore took great care to reinforce the claims of his eldest son, the future Ivan III, to succeed him. In 1447, Vasilii formally declared Ivan co-ruler, and he confirmed the passage of the title of Grand Prince to Ivan in his will. Luck, once again, was on the side of linear succession, since, when Vasilii died in 1462, none of his brothers were still alive to challenge Ivan's right of inheritance.

The political system that Ivan III (1462–1505) inherited was qualitatively different from that in which Daniil, the first Prince of Moscow, had operated. Collective rule by a family of princes had disappeared, replaced by a single prince and his aristocratic retainers. The Grand Prince of Moscow began to exhibit the characteristics of a sovereign ruler—enforcing personal decisions without reference to tradition or consensus among his fellow princes of the Rurikovich clan. In addition, the practice of equal division of a father's property among his surviving sons had ended. Younger brothers were each given a principality to administer, but it was too small to detract from (or challenge) the power of the Grand Prince of Moscow. Moreover, a younger brother was not allowed to bequeath the right to rule that principality to his sons; instead it reverted to Moscow. The sons of these princes had to make their own way in the world by acquiring property through purchase or by serving the Grand Prince.

Since, the cities and regions that would formerly have been governed by a junior prince were now retained by the Grand Prince of Moscow, the prince appointed regional governors and district administrators. The district administrators traveled on regular circuits through their districts, collecting taxes and administering justice to black peasants. This rudimentary administrative system came at no expense to the Grand Prince; his officials were supported by *kormlenie,* fees and payments given them by the local population.

The diminished power of the junior Rurikovich princes deprived the Grand Prince of a group of leaders endowed by social prestige with the authority to lead armies, represent the prince as ambassadors, and serve as governors. These political functions were taken over by a new ruling elite—the Moscow boiars. The previous chapter noted that a group of boiars coalesced around the princes of Moscow and played a critical role in the rise of the Dani-ilovichi. The importance of these boiars was particularly evident in the reign of Vasilii II who consistently received their support in his struggles with his uncle and nephews.

Indeed, it is reasonable to suppose that the expansion of Moscow and the initiation of lin-eal succession was at least as much in the interests of the boiars as it was of the prince. In the system of lateral succession of Kiev Rus, when a Rurikovich inherited the right to rule a principality, he brought his own elite servitors with him, and the servitors of the former prince would have to find other princes to serve (or perhaps be allowed to serve the new prince in a junior capacity). By supporting lineal succession from father to son, the Moscow boiars therefore perpetuated their own power. On the death of the Grand Prince, they would continue on as servitors of his son and heir.

Thus, the Moscow boiars must be thought of not as mere servants of the Grand Prince but as a key part of the new kind of centralized government that was evolving in the Northeast. The Grand Prince consulted with his boiars before starting wars, beginning major construc-tion projects, and choosing a wife. They are often referred to as the "Boiar Duma," which evokes the notion of a formal institution like a parliament. This is not the case, however. Boiars met as a group when summoned by the Tsar, but they never developed an indepen-dent structure or formal operating procedures. They were present at the Grand Prince's court when embassies were received and treaties were signed. They also participated in the major religious observances of which the grand prince was a part. The Moscow boiars were a close-knit elite, who tended to maintain their cohesiveness through intermarriage, but they also competed among themselves for prestige and power. The Grand Prince was necessary to them as both the source of prestigious appointments and as an arbiter of disputes to in-sure that competition did not become violent. The relationship thus benefitted both parties.

In yet another innovation, the new Moscow political system gave important political and religious roles to the women of the grand prince's family. Isolde Thyret has pointed out that Church leaders included the princes' wives in the ideology of Christian rule that was elabo-rated in this period. "These hierarchs even went so far as to support the creation of a power-ful myth that presented the wives of the Muscovite rulers as vessels of divine grace."[2] On a more mundane level, mothers were expected to advise their sons in affairs of state. When Dmitrii Donskoi willed the grand princeship to his oldest son, he made his wife, Evdokiia, the guardian of his children. Vasilii I told his son to obey his mother, Sofia Vitovtovna, in place of himself, and Vasilii II said the same to Ivan III. Vasilii also named his widow to be the guardian of his younger children. Wives were frequently consulted by Grand Princes, and when daughters were married to the rulers of other states, they were expected to use their influence on behalf of Moscow. Muscovite princes' wives also had the authority to grant fiscal and judicial immunities.

RELIGION AND CULTURE

A key factor in the rise of Moscow was the support provided by the Orthodox Church and its Metropolitan. From the first conversion of the Rus, the Eastern Church had conceived of all East Slavic Orthodox believers as a single community—the Metropolitanate of Rus—and even after Kiev Rus disintegrated after the Mongol conquest it kept alive the idea of a united Rus. Church leaders allied themselves with the Grand Prince of Moscow and encouraged him to "gather the lands of the Rus." The Muscovite grand princes welcomed the Church's support, especially because, having violated the traditional principles of collective rule, they had particular need of alternate sources of legitimacy. A religious mission to unite the Eastern Slavs not only provided legitimacy, it also justified continued territorial expansion.

When Dmitrii Donskoi became Prince of Moscow in 1359, he was only nine years old, and Metropolitan Aleksei, a man from a powerful boiar family, served as regent. Not only was Aleksei an effective mediator and political adviser, he also used his religious authority on Dmitrii's behalf. He blessed Moscow's armies, he prevailed upon the Patriarch to call on all Rurikovichi to obey the Prince of Moscow, and at one point he even excommunicated Mikhail of Tver for challenging Dmitrii's right to be Grand Prince.

Aleksei was so partisan in his support of Moscow that Olgerd of Lithuania (who was an ally of Tver), complained to the Patriarch, and in 1375 the Patriarch appointed a Greek, Kiprian, to be "Metropolitan of Kiev, Rhosia, and Lithuania" with his seat in Kiev. This did not, however, create the separate metropolitanate that Lithuania desired. First, it was only to last for Aleksei's lifetime, and, when Aleksei died, his duties were to be taken over by Kiprian, restoring the unity of the Metropolitanate of Rus. This might have been acceptable to Olgerd if Kiprian had kept his capital in Kiev, but, instead, Kiprian moved to Moscow and became an enthusiastic supporter of Moscow's cause.

Church writers became propagandists for Moscow. The *Primary Chronicle* had ended with the Mongol invasion, and when *Laurentian Chronicle* brought the historical record up-to-date, it included materials from all the Rurikovich principalities in order to create the idea of a single Christian community. The *Trinity Chronicle* placed Moscow at the center of political development, portraying it as the legitimate successor of Kiev linked through the office of the Metropolitan who moved from Kiev to Vladimir to Moscow. Kiprian himself contributed to this with his rewriting of the vita of the Metropolitan Peter, in which he said that Peter had chosen Moscow for the capital of the Church and that he had worked closely with Ivan Kalita. The Church also produced a vita of Dmitrii Donskoi which traced his ancestry back to St. Vladimir and referred to him as "tsar," the Slavonic word for "caesar" that was applied both to the Byzantine Emperor and the Mongol Khans. When Kiprian's own life was written, he was given credit for saving Northeast Rus from Timur by bringing the miracle-working icon *Our Lady of Vladimir* to Moscow and invoked Her protection. A chronicle subsequently reported that a vision of the Mother of God with an army of angels defending Moscow appeared to Timur and caused him to withdraw.

It is worth noting that the attitude of the Church toward the Mongols became more negative as the power of the Moscow Grand Princes increased. During the first century of Mongol rule, the Church, in exchange for the immunities and protection it received, dutifully said prayers for the Khan's soul and referred respectfully to the Khan and the Golden Horde. By the middle of the fifteenth century, however, when Church writers recopied old manuscripts, they inserted adjectives such as "accursed," "lawless," "foul," "evil," and "godless" to refer to the Mongols.

After Kiprian turned out to be a partisan of Moscow, Lithuania continued to press the Patriarch for its own Metropolitan, and the Patriarch from time to time allowed two Metropolitans, one in Moscow and one in Kiev, without formally resolving the question. The conflict was resolved in a most unexpected way in fifteenth century. In 1435, the Patriarch chose a Greek by the name of Isidore to serve in Moscow and once again unify the Metropolitanate of Rus. Then, in 1439, Isidore was asked by the Patriarch to participate in the Council of Florence (at which representatives of the Byzantine Church reversed the Eastern position on the issues that had originally caused the schism of 1054, including accepting the Pope as the head of the Christian Church). Isidore was then expected to return to Moscow and defend the decisions of the Council of Florence. Immediately after Isidore declared the supremacy of the Roman Pope, however, Grand Prince Vasilii II had him arrested. (Isidore was later allowed to escape from prison so he would not have to be burned as a heretic.)

It was now out of the question to ask the Patriarch to make another appointment, so Vasilii asked the bishops of the Moscow church to elect a Metropolitan from among themselves. They elected Iona (1448–1461) and thereby declared the *de facto* independence of the Rus Church from the authority of Constantinople. This, in turn, led to the formal division of the Metropolitanate of Rus. The Patriarch in Constantinople did not recognize the new Metropolitan in Moscow, so he appointed one himself. His appointee, obviously could not serve in Moscow and therefore took up residence in Kiev. Finally, therefore, the Grand Prince of Lithuania got what he wanted: a separate Metropolitanate for the Eastern Orthodox population living under his rule.

This development, combined with the conquest of Constantinople by the Ottoman Turks in 1453, had far-reaching consequences for Moscow. Since the time of Justinian, the Eastern Church had believed in the "symphony" between church and state. The Patriarch of Kiprian's day expressed this sentiment thus: ". . . for Christians, it is not possible to have a church, and not to have an emperor, for the empire and the church have a great unity and a commonality, and it is impossible to separate them."[3] The collapse of the Eastern Roman Empire thus suggested the need for a new empire. It was far from coincidental, then, that Church leaders regularly referred to Vasilii II as "tsar" and "autocrat," and chronicles and church writings praised him as the "defender of the faith" and "protector of orthodoxy." The idea would soon bear fruit.

Not all church people were comfortable with the rise in the wealth and the secular influence of the church. In Novgorod during the 1370s to 1380s a heretical sect, the Strigolniki (the term can be translated as "shearers" but its significance is unknown) accused the clergy of greed, objected to the practice of offering prayers in exchange for money, and protested against the practice of bishops charging a fee to ordain priests. The latter practice they called simony, and because of it they denied the validity of the entire Church hierarchy. The Strigolniki ultimately rejected all the sacraments except baptism, and an extreme faction of the movement even ceased believing in the New Testament and the essential tenets of Christianity. They were suppressed by the Church and had disappeared by the middle of the fifteenth century.

ROLES AND STATUS OF WOMEN

One school of historians has attributed a deterioration of the status of women to the influence of the Mongols, but it seems that this is one offense that cannot be laid at their door. In this period there was no essential change in gender roles or status, or diminution of the rights and privileges of women. Women could still buy and sell landed property, inherit estates, sue in courts and appear as witnesses, and administer justice in their own territories. Princes' wives and mothers continued to play important political roles. The deterioration of women's rights was yet to come, and occurred only after the "Mongol yoke" was lifted.

ECONOMIC AND SOCIAL TRENDS

Over the course of the fifteenth century, the economy of the Northwest gradually recovered from the catastrophes—pillage, tribute, and plague—brought by the Mongols. The recovery began with agriculture. The population grew and brought more land under cultivation.

Farmers began employing crop rotation (the three-field system) to rejuvenate the soil, and in some regions iron plows were introduced. The principal food crops were rye, barley, buckwheat, millet, wheat, oats, and peas. Farmers grew flax for cloth, hemp for sacking and cordage, and hops to flavor beer. (The increase in cultivated land meant fewer wild bees. Mead became a rich person's drink and peasants began to drink beer instead.) Typical livestock included cattle, sheep, pigs, and horses. East Slavic agriculturalists also engaged in industry: They produced salt from brine ponds; pitch, tar, and turpentine from coniferous trees; and they smelted iron. They also built water- and wind-powered mills to grind grain into flour.

Grain became the most important factor in internal trade. Novgorod had never been self-sufficient in grain, and by the fifteenth century Moscow had grown too large to feed itself. Moscow benefitted, in this respect as in many others, from its position on the headwaters of the Volga and near those of the Dnieper. (Roads were poorly developed and transportation continued to be mostly by river.) This increase in trade led to a general revival of cities across the region. Weekly markets and annual fairs appeared. Artisans reappeared in cities, and skills that had been lost in the first century of Mongol conquest were reacquired. Government purchasing also stimulated the economy; the casting of cannons and church bells became a major industry, and more stone masons were employed as a result of church construction. Another sign of the increase in internal trade was the minting of coins. No coins had been minted in Kiev Rus since the time of Vladimir Monomakh (1113–1125). Squirrel skins had been used for ordinary purchases (or more accurately, goods were traded on the basis of their value in squirrel skins; the skins, themselves, were rarely used), and small silver bars were used by the wealthy for large transactions. Beginning in the reign of Dmitrii Donskoi coins began to be minted again, and almost immediately grand princes learned they could increase their purchasing power by debasing them (by decreasing their silver content).

Trends in land ownership that had begun in the first century of Mongol rule continued. Farmers were the major source of income for the elite; they paid taxes to the prince and rent to landlords. Because of the increasing demand of the elite for income, the black land was increasingly given away by princes to their servitors and dependants, and the proportion of black land in the central region continued to fall. Princes gave away parcels of land without regard to mir boundaries so that agricultural communities were fragmented. Landowners then began to appoint their own agents to take over the mir functions of administering local justice and apportioning obligations. Additionally, peasants on nobles' estates fell under the judicial authority of the owner. They could not take legal complaints to the representatives of the Grand Prince, but were judged by their landlord.

At the same time, the ability of peasants to move was being restricted. Traditionally, agriculturalists had absolute freedom of movement, but a category of bound farmers, *starozhiltsy* (long-time residents), began to appear. Charters granted by princes to various cities and monasteries permitted them to prevent the starozhiltsy from moving to different land and to bring back those families who had already moved away.

Additionally, some landlords were given the power to limit the movement of all peasants, whether long-time residents or not, to a two week period in the autumn–typically the weeks before and after St. George's Day (November 26) or St. Philip's Fast (November 12). Before the family could leave, it had to pay all debts plus an exit fee based on how long it had lived there. In practice, this was not too onerous a restriction. Most peasants would not want to move until after the fall harvest anyway, and there were always landowners wanting more agricultural workers on their land who would pay the debts and exit fees. Nevertheless, the precedent of legal limitations on peasant movement was established.

CONCLUSION

When Vasilii II died in 1462, the Principality of Moscow had become a large, powerful, and, in reality if not law, sovereign state. The territory he ruled, however, was a disorganized jumble of annexed principalities and districts, his title of Grand Prince was an anachronism and did not convey his real power or status, and technically, Moscow was subordinate to the Mongol Khan. It remained for Vasilii's descendants officially to declare their sovereignty, to define and justify their position as rulers, and to organize, centralize, and standardize the administration of their state.

NOTES

1. William H. McNeill, *Plagues and Peoples* (New York: Doubleday, 1977).
2. Isolde Thyrêt, *Between God and Tsar: Religious Symbolism and the Royal Women of Muscovite Russia* (DeKalb: Northern Illinois University Press, 2001), 45.
3. Robert O. Crummey, *The Formation of Muscovy, 1304–1613* (London and New York: Longman, 1987), 61.

_____ **TEXT DOCUMENTS** _____

Afterword to "Zadonshchina"

"Zadonshchina" was a poem written to commemorate Dmitrii Donskoi's victory over the Mongols in the Battle of Kulikova Field in 1380. This is the final section of the poem.

- How does the poet characterize Dmitrii Donskoi's army? Who served in it, and what is the point of telling where they all came from? What was its goal?
- How might this poem serve the interests of the Grand Prince of Moscow?
- How might it serve the interests of the Orthodox Church?

We love the Russian land as a mother loves her dear children,
The mother caresses her child and praises it for good deeds,
but she also punishes it for bad deeds.
In the same way, our Lord God
was merciful unto the Russian princes
who fought between the Don and the Dnieper,
unto the Great Prince Dmitrii Ivanovich,
unto his brother, Vladimir Andreevich.

And so Princes Dmitrii Ivanovich and Vladimir Andreevich
remained victorious on the bone-strewn prairie of Kulikovo,
on the river Nepriadva.

And Prince Dmitrii Ivanovich said:
"It is horrible, brethren, to see the earth
covered with the corpses of Christians,
even as the field is covered with haystacks.
And it is horrible to see that the river Don
has flowed blood red for three days."

And then Prince Dmitrii Ivanovich commanded:
"Count how many *voevodas* perished,
count how many young men were killed."
And Mikhail, a boiar of Moscow replied:
"Our lord, Great Prince Dmitrii Ivanovich,
we are missing forty boiars from Moscow,
twelve princes from Belozersk,
thirty *posadniks* from Novgorod,
twenty boiars from Kolomna,
forty boiars from Serpukhov,

_____

Source: "Zadonshchina" by Sofony of Riazan, from *Medieval Russia's Epics, Chronicles, and Tales,* edited by Serge A. Zenkovsky, translated by Serge A. Zenkovsky, copyright (c) 1963, 1974 by Serge A. Zenkovsky; renewed (c) 1991 by Betty Jean Zenkovsky. Used by permission of Dutton, a division of Penquin Group (USA) Inc.

thirty magnates from Lithuania,
twenty boiars from Pereslavl,
twenty-five boiars from Kostroma,
thirty-five boiars from Vladimir,
eight boiars from Suzdal,
forty boiars from Murom,
seventy boiars from Riazan,
thirty-four boiars from Rostov,
twenty-three boiars from Dmitrov,
sixty boiars from Mozhaisk,
thirty boiars from Zvenigorod,
and fifteen boiars from Uglich.
And altogether 253,000 Russian men were
cut down by the infidel Emperor Mamai.
But God was merciful to the Russian land,
and still more Tatars fell on the battlefield."
And then Prince Dmitrii Ivanovich addressed the dead.
"Fellow princes, boiars, and sons of boiars,
you have found peace everlasting here, between
the Don and the Dnieper, on the prairie of Kulikovo.
Here you gave your lives for the holy Church,
for the Russian land and for the Christian faith.
Forgive me, brethren, and give me your blessing,
for this life and for the life everlasting."

And then Prince Dmitrii Ivanovich addressed his brother:
"Let us go, my brother, Vladimir Andreevich,
back to the Russian land,
back to the glorious city of Moscow.
And let us rule there on our throne,
for we have won glory and veneration.
Glory be to God!"

The Life of St. Sergei

St. Sergei Radonezhskii (1314–1392), the son of an impoverished boiar, began his religious career as a hermit in the wilderness north of Moscow near the town of Radonezh. Sergei built his own shelter, cleared land, and grew his own food. His example of asceticism and manual labor attracted other hermits, and, in 1354, they established the Holy Trinity Monastery. Sergei became Russia's most revered saint.

Sergei's hagiography (the biography or "Saint's Life" that was an essential element in the process of canonization in Russia) was written in the first half of the fifteenth century by Epifanii the Wise.

- What marked Sergei as a saint?
- What does this reveal about Russian spirituality?
- How would this contribute to the development of Russian national identity?

There spread a rumor that, as God's punishment for our sins, Khan Mamai, had gathered a great force—the whole godless Tatar horde—and was heading for the Russian land. All the people were in despair. The Grand Prince in Moscow, then holding the scepter of all the Russian lands, was the renowned and mighty Dmitrii. Having great faith in the Venerable Sergei, and knowing him as a man with the gift of foresight, went to the holy Elder and asked him: would he advise him to go out against the godless Tatars? Having heard the Grand Prince, the Saint blessed him and strengthened him with prayer, saying: "It is your duty, Lord, to care for the flock that God has entrusted to you and to go out against the godless ones. God will help you. You will be victorious and will return to your land uninjured and with great glory." The Saint also sent two monks with the Grand Prince to aid him . . .

Having received the blessing, Dmitrii immediately went to Moscow, gathered all his troops, and soon appeared before the godless Tatars. But, discovering the great multitude of their forces, he halted in doubt, and all his troops were overcome with great fear. But at that very instant, a messenger arrived with a message from the Saint, which reassured and commanded them "to go bravely forward without doubts to attack the savages and to fear nothing; God will help you in all possible ways." The Grand Prince Dmitrii and all his troops were immediately inspired with great bravery and went against their enemies. . . . God helped the great and invincible prince Dmitrii: the Tatars were defeated and thoroughly destroyed. . . .

All this time, Saint Sergei was engaged in prayer with his brother monks, praying for victory over the enemy and, having the gift of foresight, knew all that was happening there. . . . Within a very short time after the enemy was conclusively defeated, the Saint related to the monks everything that had happened there—the victory and the great courage of the Grand Prince Dmitrii Ivanovich . . . He named all the Orthodox warriors killed by the Tatars and asked for God's blessing on them.

Source: *Zhitie prepodobnago i bogonosnago otsa nashego Sergiia, igumena Radonezhskago chudotvortsa i pokhval'noe emu slovo, napisannyia uchenikov" ego Epifaniem" premudrym,"* 2nd ed. (Sviato-troiktskaia Sergeieva Lavra: Sobstvennaia tipografiia, 1908), 97–99, 103–105, 107–108, 109–111. Translated by the author.

. . . Once the blessed father Sergei was praying according to his usual practice in front of the image of the Most-pure Mother of our Lord Jesus Christ, and often gazing in the icon, he said: "Most-pure Mother of Christ, intercessor and defender and strong helper of the human race! Please intercede for us unworthy ones" . . . After finishing his prayers, he sat a moment to rest, and suddenly he said to his pupil. . . . "Be alert, child, and be vigilant, we are about to receive a miraculous and awesome visitation." Even as he said this a voice was heard saying "The Most-pure One comes." The saint hurried out of the cell into the hall and suddenly an unusual light flooded over him, which shone brighter than the sun. He saw the Most-pure One with two Apostles, Peter and John, radiant in ineffable light. Having seen this miraculous vision, the Saint fell to the floor, unable to endure the unbearable brightness. The Most-pure One, with her own hands, touched the Saint, saying "Do not be afraid, My favored one! I have come to visit you. Your prayer for your disciples has been heard, concern yourself about monastery no longer. From now on it will prosper in every way, and not only while you walk this earth. After you depart to God, I will always be with your monastery, abundantly providing everything it needs. . . ." Having said this, She became invisible. The Saint, in rapture, was seized with great awe and wonder.

. . . Time passed, and there came from Constantinople to Moscow a certain bishop who had heard much about the Saint, since word of him had spread everywhere and had even reached as far as Constantinople. But this bishop was possessed with doubt regarding the Saint and said "How is it possible that in this land there appeared such a luminary and especially in these latter days?" He decided to go to the monastery in order to see the blessed one himself. On the road, when he was already coming near, he was overcome with fear, and when he arrived at the monastery just as he saw the Saint, blindness fell upon him. The venerable one took him by the hand and led him into his cell. The bishop then involuntarily confessed his disbelief to the saint, and prayed for the recovery of his sight, calling himself sinful and errant from the true path. The forgiving and humble Sergei touched his blinded eyes, and it was as if scales fell from them and he could suddenly see. . . . After this the bishop, who before had not believed, now fully believed and loudly proclaimed to everyone that indeed Sergei was a man of God. He said it was a blessing from God that he had been allowed to behold this heavenly man and earthly angel.

. . . There was a man who lived not far from the Saint's hermitage, who often oppressed others, as the powerful usually oppress the poor. This person caused the following injury to one orphan who lived near to the Saint: he took his hog, that he was fattening up to eat, without paying for it, and ordered for it to be butchered. The mistreated orphan, greatly upset and weeping, came and prostrated himself before the Saint, begging him to intercede for him. That gracious soul, that comforter of the humiliated, defender of the downtrodden, and helper of the poor summoned the aforesaid offender, and rebuked him, saying "Do you believe, child, that God is a judge of the righteous and of sinners, a father to orphans and widows, that he takes vengeance on offenders, and do you not know that *It is a fearful thing to fall into the hands of the living God?* (Heb. 10:31) If this is so, how do we not tremble when we, stealing, take by force and do a thousand evils? We do not deserve the blessings that God gives us; we constantly want what belongs to others and scorn His patience. . . . Many of the powerful forget this here, but in the other world eternal torment awaits them." The Saint instructed him for a long time and finally ordered him to pay the orphan for the hog, saying: "And henceforth do not oppress the poor." The man, in fear, promised to correct his ways and live better and promised to pay the injured one. But soon after his intention . . . weakened, and it came into his mind not to pay the orphan anything. Occupied with this idea, he went as usual into his storeroom and saw that the carcass of the butchered hog was swarming with maggots, even though it was winter. He was smitten with horror. . . . He immediately paid the orphan and ordered the carcass of the hog to be thrown for the dogs and birds to eat. But they would not go near it—in order to unmask the usurer, to teach him not to oppress anyone.

. . . Having lived many years in praiseworthy labors and in abstinence and having performed innumerable and ineffable miracles, the Saint attained a very old age. . . . He gave up his pure and holy soul with a prayer to God in the year 6900 (1393) on the twenty-fifth day of September, having lived 78 years in all.

After the Saint's death there diffused from his body an abundant and ineffable fragrance. . . . The saint's face glowed with a whiteness like snow, not like death but like the living or like angels, revealing the purity of his soul and testifying to the reward he received from God for all his labors. His body was interred in the hermitage that he had created. And there were many miraculous cures at the passing away and after the death of the Saint! From only once touching his grave, weak limbs were strengthened, people were freed from the possession of unclean spirits, the blind were given sight, and hunchbacks were straightened. Although the Saint did not wish for glory, neither during his life or after death, nevertheless the almighty power of God glorified him. His passing was attended by angels who accompanied him to heaven, opening for him the gates of paradise and leading him to the hoped-for blessedness, the righteous peace, the angelic brightness, and—what he had always wished for—the brilliance of the Blessed Trinity. . . .

Peasant Obligations

The following charter was given by the Metropolitan Kiprian to the Emperor Constantine Monastery in Vladimir on October 21, 1391. (Note: The term "orphan" does not literally mean orphan, but was used to refer to all peasants who worked on monastery or church lands.)

- What does this document reveal about the peasants' ideas of justice?
- What kinds of obligations did peasants owe to landlords?
- What can you tell about the monastery's farming operation?
- What evidence is there of stratification in the peasant community? How does this affect obligations?

Now I, Kiprian, Metropolitan of All Rus, have given this deed to the Saint Constantine Monastery and to the abbot. The monastery orphans complained to me against Efrem the abbot, saying; he imposes . . . things not as of old, such as used not to be under the first

Source: R. E. F. Smith. *The Enserfment of the Russian Peasantry.* Cambridge: Cambridge University Press, 1968: 40–41. Reprinted with the permission of Cambridge University Press.

abbots; he takes from us, lord, customary dues which other abbots did not have. And the abbot said . . . I, lord, am going according to the old custom as it was under the first abbots . . . [I]n Moscow is Abbot Tsarko who was abbot at Saint Constantine before me, ask him, lord. . . . And Abbot Tsarko answered . . . thus it was in my abbacy in Saint Constantine: the big people from the villages of the monastery had to put the church in order, to fence in the monastery and its courtyard, to put up buildings, compulsorily to till the whole portion of the abbot's demesne arable; to sow, to reap, and to carry; to mow hay by desiatinas and bring it into the yard; to make weirs in both spring and winter; to fence the orchards with wattle; to man the seine nets, to make ponds, to hunt beaver in autumn, to block up the springs; and at Easter and St Peter's they each come to the abbot with something in their hands; and the horseless peasants from the villages thresh rye for the feast day and bake bread, grind malt, brew beer, thresh rye for seed; and the abbot gives flax to the villages and they weave nets and arrange the parts of the seines; and all the people from the villages on the feast day give a heifer, but once they besought me, lord, but not according to custom, with three sheep, and I excused them the heifer as I had no need of the heifer, but according to the old custom there is always a heifer on the feastday; and if the abbot rides into any village for a celebration feast, the hopper men give each a basket of oats to the abbot's horses.

. . . .And afterwards I, Kiprian, Metropolitan of All Rus, questioned in Vladimir my boiars Mikhail Bireev, Yuri Protopopin and Ivan my cook, of the custom of that monastery and of the festival heifer [payment] and they told me the same things, both of the lakes and the springs and the beaver hunt. And Kiprian, Metropolitan of All Russia, said thus to the abbot and the monastery peasants: all of you follow my charter, the abbot is to maintain the orphans, and the orphans are to obey the abbot and to do the monastery work. And if there shall be any other abbot after this abbot, he too shall follow this my charter. And I have ordered this charter to be placed in the church for the abbot and the people, and no abbot shall carry this charter from the monastery; if he does, he shall have neither God's mercy, nor my blessing.

Grant of Immunity

In Muscovite Russia, the main source of wealth for the landed elite was income from the farmers who lived on it, therefore wealth depended not on how much land one owned, but on how many farm families one had as tenants. One way the Grand Prince could reward a servitor was to allow him immunity from tax payments and obligations, so he could attract peasant families to his land by offering them lower taxes than they would otherwise pay.

In this document, dated April 1435, Grand Prince Vasilii II confirms the grant of certain immunities to Mikhail Iakovlevich for estates he owns.

(Note: "Stan people" are under jurisdiction of the prince's officials, not under that of a private landowner.)

- What exactly were the "immunities" that were granted?
- How did the landlord benefit from this? What is the significance of the landowner being allowed to judge his peasants?
- How did the peasants benefit from this?

Now I, the Grand Prince Vasilii Vasilevich . . . have made a grant to Mikhail Iakovlich and his children. As to their villages in Kinela and in the town . . . my . . . royal representatives and the Kinela volost heads . . . are not to send in to them their court investigators for any reason . . . and are not to judge them apart from murder and theft . . . but they [i.e. Mikhail Iakovlevich and his children] . . . are to judge their people themselves. If there is a joint court with the townspeople or the volost people, both the royal representatives and the volost heads and their servants are to judge and Mikhail and his children . . . judge with them; and the court tax is to be divided. And the royal court officials and the stan officials are not to send into those villages to their people for any reason, either for any service of mine, or for communal obligations, or for hay tax. And when my tribute comes [to be collected], those orphans, too, pay my tribute according to their ability, apart from the stan people, nor have they any need to pay the goods tax, nor the eighth tax, nor the customs due, nor the tax *[kostki]*; [they need pay] no customary dues; and when the post-horse due comes [to be collected], then they are to give that post-horse due to the town, apart from the stan officials. And whatever people they summon into those villages from other principalities, and not from my [i.e. the Grand Prince's] estate, those people who are [new] arrivals have no need to pay any of my tribute, the post-horse due, or the census tax, or provision of horses, no customary dues for ten years and they are to be judged by the same Mikhail and his children . . . And when their term is up, those people are liable to pay my tribute according to their ability with their people, apart from the stan officials.

Source: Smith, *The Enserfment of the Russian Peasantry,* 56–57. Reprinted with the permission of Cambridge: Cambridge University Press.

Restrictions on Peasant Movement

The preceding document showed how the Grand Prince could reward a servitor by helping him to attract new tenants. However, when one landlord gained a tenant, another landlord lost one. Consequently, another way the Grand Prince could show favor to a landowner was to allow him (or sometimes her) to limit the ability of their farmers to leave. This grant of the power to restrict peasant movements is dated 1448.

(Note: A "silver-man" is a peasant who owes either rent or a loan repayment to the landlord. A "St. George's Day person" is someone who has contracted not to move away until St. George's Day—November 26.)

- How serious a limitation on peasant movement does this represent?

From Prince Mikhail Andreevich to Beloozero, to my representative and to all the boiars and junior boiars and chamberlains and my village overseers, to all without exception. My father [confessor] the Abbot Kasyan of St. Kiril monastery petitioned me and says that you are withdrawing from him the monastery's silver-men and share-croppers and St. George's [day] people on contract. And you withdraw them other than at St. George's day [November 26], some at Christmas and others at St. Peter's day [29 June]. And you should not withdraw silver-men and share-croppers and free settlement people. But the silver-men and the share-cropper is to be withdrawn at St. George's day and is to pay the silver. But after St. George's day there is no withdrawal for the silver-man. But if he pays the silver, then he may be withdrawn. And I have ordered the abbot not to let the silver-men go after St. George's day. And whoever disobeys this my deed shall be punished by me.

Source: Smith, *The Enserfment of the Russian Peasantry*, 68–69. Reprinted with the permission of Cambridge University Press.

VISUAL DOCUMENTS

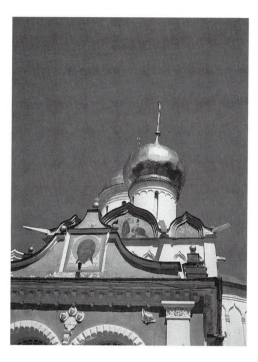

Figure 5-1 Trinity Cathedral in Monastery of the Holy Trinity and St. Sergei
This cathedral was built in 1422 to 1423, thirty years after the saint died.
• What does this reveal about the success of the Holy Trinity Monastery.
• What does it suggest about the principality of Moscow?
Source: Getty Images, Inc.—Photodisc

Figure 5-2 The Redeemer
Many art critics think that Andrei Rublev (c. 1360–1430) was the greatest of all Russian icon painters. Rublev, probably a monk at the Savior Andronikov monastery in Moscow, painted this icon around 1409.
• Compare this with earlier icons. Do you see any developments?
• What ideas about Jesus do you think Rublev was trying to convey? Does this suggest anything about Russian spirituality?
Source: Tretiakov Gallery, Moscow.

Figure 5-3 The Crucifixion
This icon was painted in 1500 by Dionisii, one of Rublev's students.
• What message does this add to that of the previous image?
Source: Tretiakov Gallery, Moscow.

Figure 5-4 St. Sergei Plowing
This is a miniature taken from the Life of St. Sergei written (and illustrated) in the early fifteenth century.
• St. Sergei is using a sokha. What are the characteristics of the sokha and in what kind of soil is it used?
• What is the significance of Sergei's working the land himself?
Source: A. V. Artsikhovskii, *Drevnerusskie miniatiury kak istoricheskii istochnik* (Moscow: MGU, 1944, Figure 50.

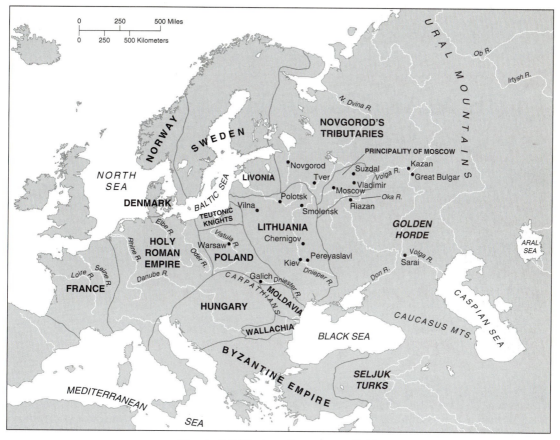

Figure 5-5 Western Eurasia, ca.1360

In 1360, Moscow had grown from a single city to a significant principality in the northeast. The Moscow princes termed themselves "princes of all Russia," but they remained subject to the Golden Horde, and appeared as if it was the rulers of Lithuania who had the greatest right to that title. Nevertheless, Moscow's rise continued.

FOR FURTHER READING

(In addition to the books by Blum, Crummy, de Hartog, Fennell, Levin, Martin and Ostrowski from the previous chapter.)

Nancy Shields Kollmann, *Kinship and Politics: The Making of the Muscovite Political System, 1345–1547*. Stanford, CA: Stanford University Press, 1987.

Isolde Thyrêt, *Between God and Tsar: Religious Symbolism and the Royal Women of Muscovite Russia*. DeKalb, IL: Northern Illinois University Press, 2001.

Chapter Six

The Making of the Muscovite State, 1460–1560

Between 1240 and 1460, as Moscow, Poland, and Lithuania expanded, dividing the territory of old Kiev Rus among them, there was a corresponding division of the Eastern Slavs into distinctive ethnicities. It was not that the rulers intended to create new peoples but that, by drawing and enforcing boundaries around their territories, they isolated the populations from one another. Church organization reinforced these divisions. In 1448, the eastern Rus church became independent from Constantinople. The Patriarch then began to appoint a Metropolitan for Kiev, and so the church was split into eastern and western halves. Over the centuries, isolated from one another by political and religious divisions, three distinctive variants of East Slavic culture and language evolved. These would ultimately become known as Ukrainian in the south and west, centered on Kiev, Belarusian in the northwest, centered on Polotsk, and Russian in the northeast, centered on Moscow.

The future nations of Ukraine and Belarus were slow to emerge, since they were ruled by alien governments; their elites developed national consciousness only in the nineteenth century. The territory ruled by Moscow, however, quickly assumed many of the characteristics of what would be called in Western Europe a "national monarchy." It was a territorial state containing a distinctive people who shared the same religious faith, and it was administered by a land-owning elite serving a hereditary ruler who claimed that sovereign power had been invested in him by God. The process of transformation that had begun with Iurii Dolgorukii was completed by Ivan III (1462–1505), his son Vasilii III (1505–1533), and his grandson Ivan IV (1533–1584). The country they ruled was variously known in western Europe as

Turn to page 126 for a map showing key geographic locations and features for this time period.

Muscovite Russia, the Tsardom of Muscovy, or simply Muscovy. The people became known as "Russians" and the church as the "Russian Orthodox Church."

THE EURASIAN CONTEXT

In China, the Ming Dynasty (1368–1644) was at its height in this period. Ming rulers extended their rule from Mongolia and Korea in the north to Vietnam and Myanmar in the south. The Ming was an age of great achievement in literature, painting, and the decorative arts. Despite this, the Ming has a reputation for cultural conservatism and self-absorption. After 1460, Ming emperors lost interest in establishing contact with the outside world; symbolic of their isolationism is the 1550-mile-long Great Wall they built to keep out the northern nomads.

In Central and Southwest Asia, the sixteenth century was a time of regional empire-building. Central Asia was invaded by a wave of Mongol-Turkic tribes, the Uzbeks, and by 1500 they had conquered all the land between the Amu Darya and Syr Darya Rivers, known as Uzbekistan today. The Shaybanid Dynasty, which ruled the region from 1500 to 1598, sponsored Sunni Islam and patronized arts, architecture, and literature. They fostered limited trade with the Ottoman Empire by way of Astrakhan and the Black Sea. However, English merchants who hoped to use the Volga River as a "Northeast Passage" to the riches of the East were disappointed at the poverty of Central Asian Markets. At the same time, several Uzbek tribes, preferring to maintain their pastoral way of life, fled north of the Aral Sea and became known as Kazakhs, a Turkic word for "adventurer" or "free man."

At the same time an Iranian dynasty, the Safavids, formed in Iran. In 1502, Isma'il I, the founder of the dynasty, allied with Turkmen tribes to rule Azerbaijan, and the next year he established himself as Shah of Iran. The Safavid dynasty established Shiite Islam as the state religion, and on this foundation it fostered the development of a unified Iranian national identity. However, the peak of its power and prosperity was yet to come. For most of the sixteenth century, the Safavids were on the defensive against the Uzbeks to the north and the Ottomans to the west.

In the sixteenth century, the Ottoman Empire, under the leadership of Süleyman I (known in the West as "the Magnificent," (1520–1566), achieved its height of wealth and power. At its peak, the empire included Turkey, North Africa, Southwest Asia west of the Tigris River, Greece, the Balkan Peninsula, and Hungary. Critical to Ottoman success were the Janissaries, elite military regiments whose soldiers were bought as young boys in Christian slave markets in the Balkan peninsula. The boys were converted, trained, and appointed on the basis of merit, the brightest serving as officers and government officials. They had the advantage, from the point of view of the government, of having no aristocratic family interests to promote that might conflict with state interests. The Janissaries were intensely loyal, had high morale, and were a highly effective fighting force. For the next century, Europe lived in fear of Ottoman expansionism; several times Ottoman armies advanced as far as the gates of Vienna. The Ottoman Empire controlled trade in the Black Sea, the Eastern Mediterranean, the Red Sea, and the Persian Gulf and enjoyed a period of prosperity unmatched in Eurasia. Nevertheless, its hostility toward Safavid Iran, and its aggressive expansion in Europe was not conducive to economic cooperation. Its neighbors sought to bypass, rather than share, Ottoman trade routes.

In the Caucasus, the Kingdom of Georgia had lost its best ally when the Byzantine Empire fell to the Ottoman Turks in 1453. For the next century, the Ottoman and Savafid Empires fought over the region and whittled away at Georgian territory. Finally, in 1578 the Turks overran the entire Caucasus and occupied Tbilisi.

From the middle of the fifteenth to the middle of the sixteenth century, Western Europe experienced religious, political, and economic revolutions that began a new era in its history. In the fifteenth century the Renaissance, beginning in Italy and spreading northward, secularized European civilization by reviving the humanism, individualism, and rationalism of the classical world, and by asserting the autonomy of science. The Protestant Reformation, begun by Martin Luther in 1517, ultimately rejuvenated Christianity in Europe, in both its Catholic and Protestant forms, but it ended forever the Pope's claim to the leadership of all Europe. Simultaneously, the "new monarchs" in Western Europe, the Tudors in England, the Habsburgs in Spain, and the Valois in France, contributed to the further development of the national state. They destroyed the power of the feudal nobility, built centralized administrative structures, and used representative institutions to project their authority. Finally, it was in this period that European navies from the Iberian Peninsula established direct contact with Africa, southern Eurasia, and the Americas. In 1488, Portuguese sailors discovered the Cape of Good Hope and the Indian Ocean, and by 1550, the Portuguese had used their superior firepower to monopolize trade in the Indian Ocean and, bypassing the Ottoman Empire, to trade directly with China and the East Indies.

In Sweden, Gustaf I Vasa (1523–1560), elected king in 1523, followed policies parallel with the "new monarchs" of Western Europe. In 1527, he confiscated the properties of the Roman Catholic Church, and established Lutheranism as the state church. In 1544, he declared the monarchy to be hereditary in his line and asserted his absolute power to govern. He established a centralized and obedient administrative system, subordinated the nobility, convened the Diet only for propaganda purposes, and built a powerful army and navy. When Gustaf died in 1560, Sweden was the dominant power in the Baltic region, on the verge of conflict with Russia.

At the same time, attempts to build a "new monarchy" were also under way in Poland. Poland's kings asserted their authority as the state's highest judge, its source of law, chief executive, and commander of the army. Theoretically kings were elected by the *szlachta* (nobility), but because of the marriage of Grand Duke Jagiello and Queen Jadwiga in 1385, the kingship of Poland was hereditary in practice. (Their descendants became Grand Dukes of Lithuania, and they used the influence this conferred to ensure their election as King of Poland.) Nevertheless, the szlachta elected a *Sejm* (parliament), which could veto laws and limit the King's ability to declare war.

The disintegration of Mongol power continued. In the 1440s, the Khanate of Crimea and the Khanate of Kazan had broken away, and after 1500, independence was declared by the Khanate of Astrakhan (on the lower Volga), the Khanate of Sibir (east of the Ural Mountains), and the Nogai Horde (on the steppe between the Sea of Azov and the Caspian Sea). The last remnants of the Golden Horde, having been driven southward toward the Caucasus, were finally defeated and absorbed by the expanding Ottoman Empire. As the Ottomans seized the northern shore of the Black Sea, however, they refrained from annexing the Crimean Tatars. Out of respect for the their Khan, who was a direct descendant of Genghis Khan, the Ottoman Sultan allowed the Crimea Tatars to remain independent under his protection. Indeed, the Crimean Khan, as an heir to the Golden Horde, continued to insist that Moscow was his tributary, and Moscow continued to pay tribute until 1699.

In the fifteenth century, individuals escaping from the agricultural societies of western Inner Eurasia, began to form autonomous communities on the model of traditional steppe nomads on the borderland (ukraina) between the forest and the steppe. The first Cossacks (*kazakh*, the same term used by independent Uzbek tribes north of the Syr Darya, meant "free man" and implied "freebooter") were probably renegade bands of Crimean Tatars who fled the Crimean Khan (just as the Kazakhs of Central Asia had fled the Uzbek Khan) and hired themselves out to Muscovite and Lithuanian princes as border patrols. They paid allegiance to no ruler, and they lived under their own laws. As the landowning elite of Eastern Europe increased its exploitation of the farming population, oppressed farmers fled to join the Cossacks. Romanians, Jews, Turks, and other nationalities joined these bands, but they were far outnumbered, over time, by Eastern Slavs. Ultimately the Cossacks became identified as Slavic-speaking believers in Eastern Orthodoxy.

Cossack communities were relatively egalitarian and elected their leaders. They were essentially military forces, modeled on the armies of the steppe nomads, who sold their services to Poland, Lithuania, and Moscow. When not in active service, Cossacks were farmers, growing grain, raising cattle, and keeping bees. In the tradition of steppe nomads, they were also traders and raiders. United into armies, they carried out raids against the Khanate of Crimea; in smaller bands, they plundered one another and preyed on Volga River merchants.

THE CREATION OF MUSCOVITE RUSSIA

Three rulers of Moscow, Ivan III (1462–1505), Vasilii III (1505–33), and Ivan IV (1533–1584) not only greatly expanded the Principality of Moscow, they transformed it from a conglomeration of cities and territories into a centralized, uniformly administered, imperial state.

Ivan III began the process by subordinating most of the Rurikovich princes; he annexed Iaroslavl in 1463, he bought Rostov in 1474, and, in 1485, he annexed all of Tver and half of Riazan. Ivan also conquered and annexed Novgorod. In 1471, after Novgorod had signed a treaty with King Kasimir of Poland-Lithuania, Ivan led an army to Novgorod and forced its leaders to nullify the treaty and pay a large fine. Seven years later, accusing Novgorod both of continued disloyalty and of fostering Roman Catholicism, Ivan again seized the city. This time he placed it under his direct rule, abolished all institutions of self-government, and, in a crowning symbolic act, removed the veche bell. Ivan took possession of Novgorod's northern territories and confiscated the properties of the city's great landowners. Ivan also expanded westward. In 1494, he forced Lithuania to sign a treaty recognizing him as "Sovereign of all the Rus," and in 1502, he defeated Lithuania and seized a one-third of its territory.

Ivan III reorganized Moscow's government. He began to centralize its administration, creating a rudimentary bureaucracy in which state secretaries (usually boiars) specialized in particular functions, such as registering land, supervising servitors, or maintaining court and tax records. To standardize the legal system of the emerging Muscovite state, Ivan promulgated the *Sudebnik* (law code) of 1497, the first code of laws since Iaroslav's *Russkaia Pravda*. It provided legal norms for theft, murder, land ownership, and slavery, but its main concern was to standardize legal procedures and fees, providing income for the government. Most justice continued to be resolved between individuals according to customary law. Ivan allowed the Rurikovich princes, who had been subordinated to Moscow, to keep their personal property in land and their high social status, but he took away their administrative powers. To replace them as administrators, Ivan appointed *namestniki* (governors) and their deputies, who were paid with a share of court fees and with kormlenie—food, services, and cash requisitioned from the local population.

Ivan created a single national army by consolidating, standardizing, and centralizing the disparate military forces of the former principalities of the northeast. As a part of this process, he made all landowners liable to military service, and he confiscated the lands of anyone who served a foreign ruler. In addition, Ivan made the pomestie, the conditional grant of land in exchange for service originated by his father Vasilii II, the standard form of land grant. Ivan began this practice in 1478 when he confiscated Novgorod's land and divided it among two thousand military servitors, and he also used pomestie estates to support soldiers stationed on the southern borderlands.

Moscow had been effectively free of Mongol rule for most of the century preceding his reign, but Ivan made a formal declaration of independence in 1462. It took the Mongol Khan almost twenty years to attempt the reconquest of Moscow, but, finally, in 1480, after making an alliance with Lithuania, he marched on Moscow. The Mongol and the Russian armies met by a tributary of the Oka River in the late summer, but neither side took the initiative. Just before winter, having given up hope that the Lithuanian army would join them, the Mongol army withdrew. As the ruler of a sovereign state, Ivan III established diplomatic contact with the Papacy, various Italian city states, the Holy Roman Empire, Sweden, Denmark, Poland, the Ottoman Empire, and the Khanates of Kazan, Crimea, Sibir, and Astrakhan.

Ivan also sought to elevate the position of Moscow's ruler. He increasingly referred to himself as "Tsar" or "Caesar," a title that was used to refer both to the Emperor of Constantinople and the Mongol Khan. Ivan adopted the double-headed eagle for his state seal, thereby visually associating Moscow with two empires; the seal imitated that of the Holy Roman Empire, while the eagle within it followed the Byzantine style. After his first wife died, Ivan married Sofia Paleologa, the niece of the last emperor of Byzantium. He then began to stage elaborate court rituals on the Byzantine model, including coronations, public processions, formal audiences with foreign dignitaries, and pilgrimages to holy sites.

Ivan made similar efforts to exalt his capital. He brought Italian architects to Moscow to construct a new and larger Kremlin and to build three magnificent churches within it. The centerpiece of the Kremlin was the Cathedral of the Dormition of the Virgin, designed to imitate the church of the same name in Vladimir built by Andrei Bogoliubskii in 1160. Just as Bogoliubskii had intended his church to signify Vladimir's precedence over Kiev, so Ivan's church construction asserted Moscow's claim to be capital of the Rus.

After Vasilii III succeeded Ivan III, he annexed the two remaining independent fragments of the northeast. In 1509, he subordinated the city of Pskov, and in 1520 he annexed the remaining segment of the principality of Riazan. He also continued to encroach on Lithuanian territory, seizing the city of Smolensk and the east bank of the Dnieper almost as far south as Kiev. Vasilii also pursued an active foreign policy. In 1514, he gained international recognition for Moscow's imperial pretensions when Maximillian, the Holy Roman Emperor, recognized him in a treaty as Tsar of all Rus. Vasilii established direct trade with the Ottoman Sultan, and he allied with the Khan of Astrakhan against the Khanates of Kazan and the Crimea.

Vasilii's great shortcoming, as far as the dynasty was concerned, was his failure to live long enough to be succeeded by an adult male. Vasilii produced no children with his first wife, and as he approached the age of fifty he asked the Church to grant him a divorce. His subsequent marriage to Elena Glinskaia produced two sons, but when he died in 1533, the elder, Ivan, was only three years old.

The fact that Ivan was an infant was, at first, of no particular consequence. His mother served as regent, and she proved to be an effective administrator. Elena continued the policy of centralizing the administration. She increased government revenues by ending monasteries' immunity from taxation, and in 1535, she established a standard currency for Muscovite Russia. In foreign affairs, she negotiated treaties with Kazan, Crimea, Poland, and Sweden, and she established fortified settlements in the south to protect from nomad and Cossack raids.

In 1538, however, Elena suddenly died, and for the next nine years the Moscow boiars fought among themselves, arresting, exiling, and murdering one another. The young Ivan, though not directly threatened, felt powerless and demeaned. The boiars made no attempt to prevent Ivan's accession to the throne when he turned sixteen, but in later years Ivan would feel that he had been ill-treated by them.

In January, 1547, Ivan was crowned Tsar in a magnificent ceremony orchestrated by the Metropolitan Makarii. Three weeks later, he married Anastasia Romanovna Zakharina, a young woman from an aristocratic Muscovite family. For the next thirteen years, Ivan was an effective ruler, continuing the policies of his ancestors and adding innovations of his own.

Ivan's first innovation was to summon general meetings of boiars, church leaders, lesser nobility, and important merchants. Thereafter such a meeting was known as a *zemskii sobor* ("assembly of the land"). They were not elective (generally they included whichever notable people happened to be in Moscow at the time), and they were not legislative institutions; Ivan used them more to express his opinion and ask for support than to solicit advice. Nevertheless, they are part of a European trend in which centralizing monarchs convened representative gatherings to enhance and project their power.

Ivan reformed Muscovy's legal system and administrative structure. In 1550, Ivan arranged for his grandfather's law code to be updated, clarified, and expanded. In the central government, he organized a more rational structure based on the *prikaz* (bureau). A prikaz was directed by a State Secretary and staffed by lesser secretaries and scribes; it dealt with a single administrative function, such as supervising the postal system, suppressing banditry, coordinating military forces, and registering pomestie estates. In provincial administration, Ivan created local regions (each called a *guba*) and allowed each to choose its own namestnik. He also changed the way provincial officials were paid. He abolished the kormlenie system and replaced it with regular salaries paid for by a new standardized system of taxation. The end of kormlenie did not decrease the burden on the population, however. Because a new layer of local officials had been created to collect taxes and administer civil law, the rate of taxation actually doubled.

Ivan also reformed the army. He standardized military obligations by making terms of service relative to the amount of land held by a servitor. Ivan created a new military formation, a standing army of foot soldiers armed with muskets, known as *streltsy* (singular, *strelets*, "shooter"). Russians had been using firearms since the 1300s, and Ivan III had created an artillery regiment, but the streltsy were the first regiments formed entirely of musketeers.

Ivan used his army to continue his ancestors' expansionist policies. In the west, he furthered the project of "gathering the lands of the Rus" by defeating the Livonian knights in 1558 and taking Polotsk from Lithuania in 1563. In the east, however, Ivan initiated a momentous new trend, the building of an empire. In 1552, he seized the city of Kazan, brought its Khanate to an end, and incorporated its territories into Muscovy. Ivan authorized the Stroganov family to begin the settlement of the headwaters of the Kama River, and the Stroganovs, using hired Cossack bands, expanded their holdings beyond the Ural Mountains and conquered the Khanate of Sibir. In 1556, Ivan annexed the Khanate of Astrakhan, thus gaining control over the entire Volga River, and he went on to subordinate the Nogai tribes on the steppes east of the Volga, and the Circassians in the territory north of the Caucasus.

As he expanded eastward, Ivan followed imperial rather than nation-building policies. It is true that he removed the Muslim population of the cities of Kazan and Astrakhan, replaced them with Russians, and built Orthodox churches. Nevertheless, the Mongol tribes were not forcibly converted from Islam, and their princes were welcomed into Moscow's ruling elite. Ivan himself, later in his reign, was to marry a Circassian princess. Similarly, the peoples of Siberia were allowed to follow their traditional beliefs and way of life, as long as they paid tribute and recognized the Muscovite Tsar as their overlord.

MUSCOVITE THEOCRACY

Although there are many similarities between the absolutist "new monarchies" of Western Europe and the new state of Muscovy, including centralization, militarization, increased taxation, and glorification of the ruler, there was an important difference. The power to which

Western European monarchs aspired was that of the pagan Roman Emperors. Hence, though asserting their divine right to rule, they conceived of their states in secular terms. In Russia, the model for the office of Tsar was the Christian Emperor, Constantine, and they did not distinguish between political and religious authority.

Moscow's rulers have been revealingly compared with the monarchs of medieval rather than modern Europe, and their style of government has been called "theocratic." That is, they believed that they carried out an important religious function and were essential to the church. The relationship of tsar to boiars was personal and not legalistic. The boiars were not motivated by the desire for aristocratic rights vis-a-vis the prince, but for a close personal relationship with him. They valued tradition, honor, and religion. They participated in court rituals that elevated the majesty of the prince, even though it meant showing public deference to the Tsar, because this served to elevate the boiars' own status in Muscovite society.[1]

After the Renaissance, the political status of royal women in the West was severely limited, but in Moscow, elite women played an important role in court life, as they had in medieval Europe. Ivan III, for example, consulted his mother before making such crucial decisions as who to marry and whether to declare independence of the Mongols. Ivan's wife, Maria, was active in diplomacy, and Ivan expected his daughter, Elena, to serve as his agent after her marriage to the Grand Duke of Lithuania. Elena Glinskaia's regency for Ivan IV has already been noted. Furthermore, Isolde Thyrêt has pointed out that the *terem* (a separate residence for women, to be discussed below) may have been separate from the buildings where men lived, but women were not cut off from the political world.[2] Royal women of Muscovy participated in ceremonies welcoming foreign dignitaries. They commissioned art projects, gave alms, and supported charities.

Thyrêt has further argued that Muscovite royal women used Orthodox Christian concepts to promote the myth of "the Tsaritsa's blessed womb," that is, the notion that the tsaritsa was "a receptacle and a transmitter of divine grace during the conception of the future ruler."[3] The Church promoted the notion that the Tsaritsa was an essential helpmate for her spouse. When Ivan IV and Anastasia were married, for example, Metropolitan Makarii instructed them that they were both shepherds of Christ's flock and emphasized the importance of partnership and mutual loyalty. Like Tsaritsas before her, Anastasia's sacred role was manifested in her participation in religious processions and pilgrimages.

RELIGION AND CULTURE

The Church continued to play an active role in promoting the power of Moscow, as it had from the very beginning of Moscow's rise. Metropolitan Makarii orchestrated and presided over the coronation of Ivan IV as Tsar, and in the homily delivered during the ceremony Makarii told Ivan that he was divinely ordained to be the protector of the Church. Makarii also encouraged Ivan to think of his wars of expansion as crusades against Roman Catholicism in the west and Islam in the east.

Church writers also developed an ideology that represented Moscow as the successor to the Roman Empire and its prince as an heir to Constantine. The notion was first expressed in "The Tale of the White Cowl" written by Archbishop Gennadii of Novgorod, during the reign of Ivan III. According to this (created) legend, if the infidels were ever to capture Constantinople, then the grace of the holy spirit would pass to Moscow, Moscow's Tsar would be elevated by God over all other rulers, and Moscow itself would become greater than the first two Romes. Then, in the reign of Vasilii III, Filofei, a monk, who had fled to Moscow from Constantinople after its fall, announced that Rome and Constantinople had fallen because they had turned away from the true teachings of the Church. He asserted that the

Grand Prince of Moscow was the only true Christian ruler in the world and now had the responsibility to rule all Orthodox Christians. Moscow, said Filofei, was the third Rome, and there would be no fourth.

Muscovite rulers, while claiming to rule by divine right, did not themselves explicitly adopt these concepts, probably because of the not very hidden subtext of their message. Gennadii wrote the legend of the White Cowl at the time that Ivan III was subordinating Novgorod, and the point of his story was to pressure Ivan to treat the Novgorod Archbishopric well. Filofei's doctrine of Moscow–Third Rome was equally self-serving. He held that a Christian ruler had no right to take land and wealth away from churches and monasteries. These two writers also must have directed their stories toward the leaders of the Eastern Church. If Moscow was the Third Rome, its religious community should be an independent realm rather than a mere province of the Byzantine Empire (which no longer existed, anyway), and its religious leader should be a patriarch rather than a metropolitan, equal in stature with the other patriarchs of the Orthodox Church (if not first among them).

Church ownership of land and immunity from taxes had become a major problem for church and state. In Ivan IV's day, the church may have owned one-third of all the populated land in Muscovy, much of it exempted from taxes and service obligations. This meant foregoing a huge amount of tax revenue, and Moscow's rulers, beginning with Ivan III, began to rescind charters of immunity for Church land. Vasilii III decreed that land could not be given to the Church in some regions without his permission. Ivan IV extended this law to all of Muscovy in 1551 and even forbade the Church to purchase land with its own money. The law was only enforced for a few years, however, and Ivan IV himself became its worst offender, piously giving large gifts of land to the church.

Within the church, two views of wealth existed. One school, the "possessors," considered the ownership of land as essential to the work of the Church in providing for the spiritual and social welfare of the people. The "nonpossessors," on the other hand, considered wealth to be a spiritual danger to the Church and called for monks to return to lives of poverty. In the sixteenth century, these two schools reached back in history and claimed as their spiritual forebears two figures from the reign of Ivan III. The possessors chose Iosif Volotskii, who had stood for discipline, organization, and the communal life of the monastery; the nonpossessors chose Nil Sorskii, who had advocated the search for spiritual life in isolated hermitages.

It is now believed that Iosif and Nil were not fundamentally opposed to one another; both were more concerned with the common struggle against heresy than with the question of land ownership. Where the two monks did in fact disagree, according to Dimitry Pospielovsky, was on the question of church-state relations. Nil Sorskii believed that the Church was superior to the state and should be independent of it, while Iosif Volotskii insisted that the Church should play an active role in secular government but that royal power should be supreme in both secular and ecclesiastical affairs.[4] Iosif's view on secular power and the possessors' view on church property triumphed within the church hierarchy, and Pospielovsky considers this to be a crucial step toward the political subordination of the church by the Russian state.

In the century from 1450 to 1550, the Muscovite Church faced serious questions of doctrine, liturgy, and practice. As sacred books had been copied and recopied over the centuries, variations had crept in. Since they explained the fall of Constantinople to the Turks as caused by incorrect beliefs, Russian church leaders felt that verifying and correcting their religious texts was critically important. They brought from Constantinople a learned monk, known as Maxim the Greek, to verify Slavonic translations from the Greek. Unfortunately for Maxim, he allowed himself to be embroiled in the dispute between the possessors and nonpossessors. Maxim was a moderate on the issue, advocating an end to the abuse of wealth and not total renunciation of possessions, but his opinions were not welcomed by the Church hierarchy; he was mistrusted as a foreigner, and he spent the rest of his life under house arrest in monasteries. He died in 1556 without completing the verification of Russian religious texts.

Just as the Grand Princes of Moscow built a homogenous state and military structure, so the Church felt it necessary to standardize liturgy, beliefs, and practices, and Ivan IV called church councils in 1547, 1549, and 1551 to do so. The Church Council of 1551 attempted to make Christian practices and moral standards uniform, to end abuses by church people, and to raise the influence of the local clergy over their parishioners. It repeated past prohibitions of pagan festivals and the use of witchcraft. These councils took it upon themselves to re-view cases of locally-venerated saints in order to determine those which deserved national status. Among the newly recognized saints were some Grand Princes of Moscow, including Aleksandr Nevskii and Dmitrii Donskoi, who were venerated not as miracle-workers but as warriors for holy Rus.

The religious life of Muscovite society was transformed and reoriented in this time pe-riod. In the fifteenth century, the ideal of Russian spirituality had been the ascetic, miracle-working monk living in an independent monastery. After 1500, according to Paul Bushkovitch, religious ideals began to change. Living a holy life and doing good deeds began to be perceived as more essential for earning sainthood than performing miracles. Models of spirituality were now found in the Church hierarchy rather than in monasteries, and bishops replaced monks as saints.[5]

The Church underwent a social transformation, as well, as sons of boiar families ceased to choose the Church for a career. In the sixteenth century, it was the lesser nobility, merchant families, and even slaves who filled the church's higher levels. Priests continued to be of the same social class as their communicants. Therefore, most parish priests were farmers, virtu-ally indistinguishable from the people they served except when they donned their vest-ments to perform church services. The fees they earned for blessing homes, performing weddings, or presiding over burials supplemented their income from farming.

ROLES AND STATUS OF WOMEN

It is not uncommon for women to be honored in the realm of ideals but oppressed in the real world. So it was in Muscovite Russia, where the actual status of women deteriorated even while Tsaritsas were being sacralized. In the reign of Ivan IV, women in wealthy families began to be segregated from men. Women's living quarters, called the terem, were often built separately from the house in which the adult men of the family lived. Even among the poorer classes who could not afford such arrangements, women ate separately from men.

Natalia Pushkareva has argued that "The laws of the Muscovite state, like those of most European nations of this time, intensified the inequality most women experienced in their lives, making them more dependent and more subordinate to their husbands and to other male relatives."[6] She points out that there was even a double-standard for the murder of a spouse. A women who killed her husband was now a "state killer," a new criminal category that applied to anyone who killed someone of a higher social class, and was subject to execu-tion by being buried alive. There was no penalty, however, for husbands who killed their wives. Moreover, in the new legal system, all judicial functions were carried out by formally appointed administrators, positions for which women were not eligible.

The institution of the pomestie also had a negative effect on women. The votchina, land given outright as private property, was inherited by a servitor's widow and passed to her children. The pomestie, however, reverted back to the state when the servitor died or re-tired, and the widow was left with nothing but an inadequate pension. Provisions were made to give a widow the use of land if her husband died while in service, but she lost it if she remarried.

ECONOMIC AND SOCIAL TRENDS

The economic recovery, which had begun after 1400, continued until 1560. By 1500, the population reached its pre-plague levels, and it continued to rise throughout the century. In Central Russia, the land became heavily settled, the three-field system became the norm, and slash-and-burn agriculture was now used only in the borderlands. The increase in the production of grain fed the expanding urban population and fueled a boom in manufacturing and trade.

Moscow led the way. In the early sixteenth century, Moscow's population was 100,000—four times the size of Novgorod, formerly the largest city in the region. It had also become the commercial center; it contained artisans with a wide variety of skills (one historian counted 210 different occupations), including carpenters, masons, coppersmiths, blacksmiths, armor makers, artists, jewelers, potters, weavers, leatherworkers, millers, and brickmakers. Other cities contributed to the national economy as well. Pskov was famous for iron and silver, Novgorod and Kazan for leather, and Mozhaisk for wool.

International trade thrived. Under Vasilii III, Moscow gained control of the Dnieper trade-route and came in direct contact with the Ottoman Empire, which now possessed the ports of Caffa and Tana on the northern Black Sea coast. Moscow traded grain, woollen cloth (from Europe), and luxury furs for silk, gems, spices, and dyes. Smolensk, also captured by Vasilii III, became a key trading center with Lithuania, Poland, and Germany. By conquering Kazan and Astrakhan, Ivan IV gained the entire Volga river trading system. The subjugation of the Nogai meant control of the trade route between the Black Sea and Central Asia. In addition, Russia began to trade directly with England. In 1533, an English merchant explorer, searching for a northeast passage to the Orient, made contact with a Russian community on the White Sea. England began to buy naval supplies—rope, timber, and tar—and Ivan IV allowed them to use the Volga River to trade with Central Asia.

There was a merchant class, but it was not allowed a monopoly on trade. Anyone from peasant to boiar was permitted to engage in commerce, and the Tsar himself was the single greatest merchant in the country. He claimed a monopoly on the sale of luxury goods such as sables, caviar, potash, and walrus tusks. The Tsar used leading merchants as agents for managing these monopolies and for collecting commercial taxes and fees.

One of the most lucrative of the Tsars monopolies was on liquor. Although distilling technology appears to have come to Russia from Western Europe in the first half of the sixteenth century, it did not play a significant role in Russian society until the reign of Ivan IV, who made the production and sale of liquor a state monopoly. While the brewing of beer and kvass was a normal part of the home economy, the production of spirits was forbidden to anyone not licensed by the Tsar. Ivan established taverns, which both regulated the sale of liquor and provided revenue for the government. Foreign travelers' reports soon gave Muscovy the reputation of a land of heavy drinkers.

The ranks of the Moscow boiars grew significantly in the period 1460 to 1560. Some of the increase occurred as Moscow added new territories and accepted the service of their princes, boiars, and great landowner. Some of it came as Vasilii III and Ivan IV promoted lesser servitors into the boiar duma in order to check the power of the oldest families. This increase in the number of boiars caused great anxiety among all the members of the landed elite who, like typical aristocrats, were extremely sensitive to issues of hierarchy, precedence, and honor. In response, they elaborated a system known as *mestnichestvo,* a ranking system based on the status of one's clan, one's seniority within the clan, and one's length of service to the Tsar. Mestnichestvo originated in a system for assigning seats at court ceremonies but was extended to civil and military appointments as well. No one could be asked to serve under a noble who ranked lower in the mestnichestvo hierarchy.

This system served the interests of both boiars and tsar. It served boiars by protecting the interests of the oldest families, and it reduced uncertainty by clarifying relationships. On the other hand, it elevated the status of the Tsar, who was the focal point of the system. Its major drawback was that it limited the ability of the Tsar to make promotions based on ability rather than rank. This drawback was mitigated to some extent in Ivan IV's military reforms, which suspended the application of mestnichestvo during war.

Lesser landholders also gained in rights and privileges during this period. When Ivan III first began to make pomestie grants, the recipient (called a *pomeshchik*) could possess the land only while in active service. When he retired, the land was given to another servitor. By the reign of Vasilii III, it had become customary for a son to take over the pomestie when his father died, and Ivan IV turned this custom into law. Thus the distinction between the votchina, land owned outright, and the pomestie began to erode. In the military reforms of 1556, when obligations were standardized and related to the size of a servitors holdings, the law made no distinction between a *votchinnik* (one who owned land outright) and a pomeshchik.

The rise of Muscovite Russia had disastrous effects on the agricultural population. The increase in government bureaucracy, army, and wars of expansion resulted in a dramatic increase in taxation. It has been estimated that taxes for peasants tripled in Vasilii III's reign, and more than doubled again between 1533 and 1561. This burden was somewhat lessened by yet another of Ivan IV's standardizing reforms. Ivan set the unit of tax collection, the "sokha," at 1,000 acres of good land, 1,350 of medium land or 1,600 acres of poor land. Surveyors worked with the peasants to determine the value of the land, and the result was a more fair and efficient system based on the ability to pay.

The pomestie system also affected the rural economy. The growth of cities created a national market for grain, and pomeshchiks increasingly required barshchina (labor) in place of obrok (in-kind or cash payments). The consequence of this was that they expanded the amount of land they claimed for their own fields, and peasant allotments shrank accordingly. To make matters worse for peasants, pomeshchiks, because they owned less land than boiars and other large landowners, tended to be more demanding of their tenants. As a result, there was continual incentive for peasants to move to the lands of a greater lord.

Pomeshchiks, therefore, pressured the government to limit peasant movement. After 1460, the Tsar began to accede to this demand by forbidding peasants in certain regions to move except during a two-week period in the fall, usually a week before and a week after St. George's day (November 26), and then only if taxes, debts, and an exit fee was paid. In Ivan III's Sudebnik of 1497, this law was extended to all of Muscovy. Landlords could deprive peasants of even this limited freedom to move by using force to keep them from leaving, by charging impossibly high exit fees, or even by being absent in the fall so that peasants could not give notice of their desire to move. Few peasants were able to overcome these obstacles, and most peasants who left estates were illegal runaways.

CONCLUSION

Between 1460 and 1560, Muscovite Russia became a large, wealthy, and powerful state. State, church, and social institutions and practices were standardized, the power and prestige of the ruler were enhanced, and the economy thrived. Ivan IV's predecessors had reunified the majority of the lands of the Rus, and Ivan had begun to build an empire in the east and had expanded westward to the shores of the Baltic Sea. This western adventure, however, was a turning point in Ivan's reign. Sweden and Poland felt threatened by Muscovite aggression and they determined to push Moscow away from the Baltic. The long war which ensued devastated the Russian economy, caused social unrest, and coincided with erratic and self-destructive behavior by the tsar. In 1560, the Rurikovich dynasty was on the verge of disaster.

NOTES

1. Nancy Shields Kollmann, *Kinship and Politics: The Making of the Muscovite Political System, 1345–1547* (Stanford, CA: Stanford University Press, 1987).
2. Isolde Thyrêt, *Between God and Tsar: Religious Symbolism and the Royal Women of Muscovite Russia* (DeKalb, IL: Northern Illinois University Press, 2001), Chap. 4.
3. Ibid., 22.
4. Dimitry V. Pospielovsky, *The Orthodox Church in the History of Russia* (Crestwood, NY: St. Vladimir's Seminary Press, 1998), 61.
5. Paul Bushkovitch, *Religion and Society in Russia: The Sixteenth and Seventeenth Centuries* (New York: Oxford University Press, 1992).
6. Natalia Pushkareva, *Women in Russian History: From the Tenth to the Twentieth Century*, Eve Levin, Trans. and Ed. (Armonk, NY: M. E. Sharpe, 1997), 112.

—————————— TEXT DOCUMENTS ——————————

The Sudebnik (Law Code) of 1497

Ivan III issued the first Russian law code since Kiev Rus. Some of its provisions are listed here.

- What seems to be the interest of the Grand Prince in compiling this code?
- How were suits between individuals adjudicated?
- What does this reveal about social structure, gender, the Muscovite economy, and the status of the peasantry?

3.   And the boiar and secretary are to take from the guilty party, whether plaintiff or defendant, out of a ruble case: the boiar two altyns, the secretary eight dengi. And if the case involves more than a ruble or less, the boiar shall take [fees] in the same proportion.

4.   And if a case is to be tried by judicial duel but the parties become reconciled without having stood in the dueling field, the boiar and the secretary are to take [fees] in the same proportion . . . but the okolnichii and secretary and the bailiffs shall be paid no judicial-duel fees.

10.   And if a thief be caught stealing in any way for the first time . . . and there has been no previous accusation of other theft made against him, then he shall be punished in the market place, flogged with the knout and made to pay plaintiff's damages, and the judge shall sell him [or] impose a fine upon him. And if the thief has no property with which to pay the sum at issue, then, after flogging him with the knout, they shall give him over to the plaintiff in slavery to make good plaintiff's loss, and the judge shall take nothing from him.

11.   And if a thief be caught a second time stealing, then he shall be executed and the sum at issue paid from his property, the remainder of his property going to the judge. And if he has no property sufficient for the satisfaction of the plaintiff's loss, he shall [nevertheless] not be given up to plaintiff [in slavery] to cover his damages, but shall be put to death.

42.   And if anyone presents a [slave's] manumission without report to the boiar and without the secretary's signature, or from the cities without report to the viceregent who has the status of a petty boiar with full-jurisdictional grant, then such manumission shall be invalid unless the (slave's) master shall have written it with his own hand, [in which case] the manumission is valid.

46.   And if a person buys something new, except a horse, not knowing the vendor, and if [the transaction] be known to two or three good men (who represent the community in court), and if [subsequently those objects] are seized from him [as stolen goods], those good men shall testify in accordance with the law that defendant bought the goods at the market in their presence, then the person in whose possession [those objects] were seized is without fault and need not kiss [the cross].

Source: Horace W. Dewey. *Muscovite Judicial Texts, 1488–1556.* Ann Arbor: University of Michigan Department of Slavic Languages and Literature, 1966. Reprinted by permission of University of Michigan Department of Slavic Languages and Literature.

52.   And if a woman, or small child, or an old person, or a sick person, or cripple, or priest, or monk, or nun shall bring suit against anyone or if any of these shall serve as a witness for anyone, then he is allowed to hire a substitute [for dueling]. And the litigants or witness must kiss [the cross] but the hired fighters must fight. Against these hired fighters the plaintiff or defendant [may hire] fighters [of his own, or], if he so desires, he may himself fight in the [dueling] field.

55.   And if a slave be captured by Tatar enemy troops and escapes from captivity, he shall be free and no longer the slave of his former master.

56.   And peasants may leave a canton [to go to another canton], or [go] from village to village, once a year, for a week before and a week after St. George's Day in the autumn [November 26]. For field living quarters they shall pay one ruble, for forest quarters a half-ruble. And whatsoever peasant shall live one year under a given master and then leave, he shall pay one-fourth of the living-quarters' value, or if he lives two years and leaves, he shall pay one-half; if he lives three years and leaves, he shall pay three-fourths of the living-quarters' value, and if he lives four years he shall pay the full amount of living-quarters' value.

60.   And if a person dies without a will and has no son, then all his personal property and lands [shall pass] to the daughter; and if he has no daughter, then his closest of kin shall take [it].

66.   By a full-slavery document [one becomes] a slave. By taking the position of a deputy or village steward, one becomes a slave whether with formal report [to higher authorities] or without it, along with one's wife and one's children, provided they live under the same master; and those children who shall have begun living under another master, or by themselves, shall not become slaves; and by being a city steward [one does not become] a slave. Whoever marries a female slave becomes himself a slave; a woman marrying a slave becomes herself a slave. Slaves may pass by dowry and by will.

The Domostroi

The Domostroi was a book of rules for managing a household. It included information and advice on etiquette, standards of personal morality, how to supervise servants, how to do household tasks, how to store and prepare food, how to brew beer, etc. Such books as these were very common throughout Europe among the gentry and wealthy townspeople. There is no standard, printed version of the book, and no single author. The head of a household (generally a man) would borrow the book, and copy it out, adding or subtracting information as he saw fit.

- What do these selections reveal about the status of women? About the terem and the problems it might create for men?
- What do they reveal about the lifestyle and values of wealthy townspeople in sixteenth-century Russia?

36.   Instruction to Women and Servants on Drunkenness. And on Secrets, Which You Should Never Keep. How You Should Not Listen to Servants' Lies or Calumnies without Correcting Them. How to Correct Them with Fear, and Your Wife Also. And How to Be a Guest and How to Manage Your Household in Every Way.

A woman should never under any circumstances drink alcohol—wine, mead, or beer—nor should she receive it as a present. Liquor should be kept in the cellar or the icehouse. A woman should drink weak beer or kvass, both at home and in public.

If women come visiting, therefore, do not give them alcohol. Nor should your own women and maids drink to the point of drunkenness, in public or at home.

A wife should not eat or drink without her husband's knowledge, nor conceal food or drink from him. Nor should she have secrets from her husband.

At the houses of her women friends, she should not ask for drink or food, or for scraps or tidbits without her husband's knowledge, nor should she allow such behavior in others. She should not keep a stranger in her house without her husband's knowledge. She should consult with her husband, not her manservant or maidservant.

A woman should guard herself from evil and should protect her male and female servants also. She should not gossip with her husband, telling him falsehoods. She should not hold grudges. If someone errs, she should tell her husband about it directly, without embellishment.

The husband and wife should never listen to gossip or believe a tale without direct evidence. A wife should not lightly inform upon her domestics to her husband. She should report, truthfully, only that which she cannot correct herself or a truly wicked deed. If a maid heeds neither scolding nor punishment, the mistress must not keep her, or she will commit some new evil. In these instances, the wife should discuss with her husband what kind of punishment to mete out.

When the mistress entertains guests and drinking is appropriate, she herself must not touch alcohol. A single adult man should bring the drink, the food, and all the utensils. He

Source: Reprinted from Carolyn Johnston Pouncy: *The Domostroi: Rules for Russian Households in the Time of Ivan the Terrible.* Copyright (c) 1994 by Cornell University. Used by permission of the publisher, Cornell University Press.

should be the only man present, whatever the time of day. Then any dishonor or ignorance can be laid to his account.

Men and women should not breakfast unless they are ill; eat and drink at appropriate times.

37.   How a Woman Should Care for Clothing.

Take care of the dresses, shifts, and kerchiefs you wear every day. Do not scatter your clothes about; do not let them smell musty; do not wrinkle them or drop them in dirt or water. Do not throw them down just anywhere. Gather them together, store them carefully, and guard them well. Teach your servants to do this too.

The master, the mistress, their children, and their servants should work in old clothes. When the work is done, they should change into clean everyday clothes and boots. But in good weather, on a holy day, to go out in public, to go to church or to visit, put on your best clothes. Throughout the day, guard yourself from mud and rain and snow. Do not spill drink on your clothes or spatter them with food or fat. Do not let your clothes get musty; do not sit in dust or moisture.

When you come back from a festival, from church, or from visiting, take off your best clothes, examine them, dry them, remove the wrinkles, brush them, and clean them most thoroughly. Put them away in a closet.

All old and everyday clothes (outer and inner robes, linen and boots) should be washed frequently. Old clothes should be patched and darned. Then they remain fit for others to see as well as pleasant for you. You can also give them to the poor for your salvation.

All clothes and cloths should be packed away and folded carefully. Put them somewhere in a chest or box. Always keep them under lock and key, so you need not fear scandal.

Stoglav Council of 1551

The Stoglav Council was the third of the church councils called by Ivan IV in order to standardize Church policies and doctrine. It was called the Stoglav (meaning one hundred chapters) because, when it answered the long list of questions given by Ivan IV and Metropolitan Makarii, its answers were organized into one hundred chapters.

- What does this reveal about perceptions of impropriety in the church?
- What does it suggest about the continuation of pagan practices?

Chapter 5, Question 8. Concerning monasteries and monks: And in the monasteries monks and priests take the vows for the salvation of their souls. But some take the vows for the sake of bodily comfort, so that they might constantly indulge in drunkenness and ride to

Source: "The Stoglav Council," in George Vernadsky, Ed., *A Source Book for Russian History from Early Times to 1917, Vol. 1: Early Times to the Late Seventeenth Century* (New Haven, Conn.: Yale University Press, 1972), 165–166, (c) Yale University Press. Reprinted by permission.

the [monastery] villages to take their leisure. Concerning archimandrites and abbots: Some archimandrites and abbots obtain their position through bribery, and know not the divine services and the refectory table and the brotherhood, and take their repose in their cells with guests. . . .

Chapter 26. Concerning schools of learning in all the towns: And in accordance with the tsar's advice we have jointly decreed that in the ruling city of Moscow and in all the towns these same archpriests and senior priests, together with all the priests and deacons, each in his own town, shall select, with the blessing of their bishop, worthy, pious priests and deacons and married sextons and pious men, with the fear of God in their hearts, who can be of use to others and who know their letters and reading and writing, and shall establish schools in the houses of these priests, deacons, and sextons, so that priests and deacons and all Orthodox Christians in each town would send them their children to learn reading and writing and church singing. . . .

Chapter 41, Question 24. [Concerning] the festivities [rusalia] on the eve of Saint John's and Christmas and the Epiphany: Men and women and girls gather at night for revelry, indecorous speech, devilish singing and dancing, and acts hateful to God; and youths are polluted and girls defiled. When the night comes to an end, then they go off to the river with great shouting, like devils, [and] wash themselves in the water; and when the bells begin to ring for matins they go to their houses and fall as if dead from the great clamor. . . .

Chapter 76. . . . And [as for the fact] that money belonging to the prelates is lent for interest and grain for compensation, and that likewise money belonging to the monasteries is lent for interest and grain for compensation, the divine Scriptures and sacred rules not only forbid this to bishops, presbyters, deacons, and all priests and monks but also prohibit ordinary men from taking interest and practicing usury. Thus henceforth, in accordance with the sacred rules, prelates and all monasteries shall lend money to the peasants in their villages without interest and grain without compensation, so that their peasants may live with them and so that their villages may not be empty.

Settlement in Siberia

After Ivan IV's conquest of Kazan, the Kama River was opened to Russian settlement. This is a patent, dated April 4, 1558, in which Ivan IV granted to Grigorii Stroganov financial, judicial, and trade privileges on uninhabited lands along the Kama River.

- What does this reveal about the methods of Russian territorial expansion?
- How would you characterize the powers that Grigorii Stroganov was given?
- What social and economic concerns in Russian society does this reflect?
- What effect will this have on Russian subjects? On native inhabitants of Siberia?

I, the Tsar and Grand Prince Ivan Vasilevich of all Russia, have been asked to grant to Grigorii Anikievich Stroganov . . . the uninhabited lands, black [coniferous] forests, wild rivers and lakes and uninhabited islands and marshlands . . . along . . . the Kama . . . 146 versts [97 miles]. . . . . If it is true, as Grigorii has stated in his petition . . . that these uninhabited lands have hitherto paid us no tribute and presently pay none, that the Perm people pay no taxes from this region nor do they pay any *iasak* [tribute in furs] from it to Kazan, nor have they done so in the past; and if this patent will present no hardship either to the Perm people or to travelers, then I . . . do grant this petition of Grigorii Anikievich Stroganov, and authorize him to build a small town . . . in a secure and well protected location, and emplace cannon and defense guns in that town, and I authorize him, at his own expense, to station cannoneers and gunners and gate guards there to protect the town against the Nogai people and other hordes. He may cut timber around that small town along the rivers and lakes and up to the headwaters, and plough arable lands, and establish farmsteads, and invite unregistered, non-tax-paying persons to settle in that small town. But Grigorii is neither to invite nor accept registered tax-payers from Perm or from other towns into our Empire, nor is he to accept lawbreakers or persons who have run off from boiars with their possessions. If tax-payers from other towns within our Empire should come to Grigorii with their wives and children, and the namestniki [administrators] or volosteli [supervisors] or the elected officials object to this, then Grigorii is to send such tax-payers and their wives and children back to the towns from which written objections have come. . . . Persons who come to this town from our Empire or from other lands with money or with goods who wish to purchase salt or fish or other things are free to sell their goods and to purchase other items without paying duty. Grigorii may accept persons who move from Perm to settle in his town, provided they are unregistered and have no tax obligations.

Wherever he may find salt deposits he is to build saltworks and evaporate salt. He may fish in the rivers and lakes without paying obrok [quitrent]. Grigorii is to report to our Treasury officials immediately if he should find silver, copper or lead ores, but he is not to mine these deposits for himself without our consent. He is not to intrude into the Perm bee-keeping and fishing concessions. I have granted him these patents for a period of 20 years

---

Source: Reprinted from Basil Dmytryshyn, E. A. P. Crownhart-Vaughan, and Thomas Vaughan, Eds. and Trans., *Russia's Conquest of Siberia, 1558–1700,* (Portland: Western Imprints, The Press of the Oregon Historical Society, 1985), 3–6, (c) 1985, Western Imprints, the Press of the Oregon Historical Society. Reprinted with permission.

. . . For the duration of this 20-year patent period, Grigorii is not obliged to pay dan to me . . . on behalf of any unregistered non-tax-paying persons who may come to his town or settlement, or to the farms near the town, or to the villages. He is likewise not obliged to perform postal or town service, nor pay either duty or obrok for his saltworks and fisheries in those places. . . . But if he takes out or sends out his salt and fish through other towns, he must pay all the taxes on the salt and fish, just as our taxes would be collected from other traders.

Our Perm namestniks and their tians [agents] will have no judicial authority over Grigorii Stroganov, nor over the farming or non-farming persons who may settle in his town and villages. . . . Grigorii has complete judicial authority over his settlers. If any person in another town has a complaint against Grigorii, such person is to secure an official warrant, on the basis of which both plaintiff and defendant will appear before our Treasury officials in Moscow by the Feast of the Annunciation in the same year.

When the fixed period has expired, Grigorii Stroganov will be required to bring to our Treasury in Moscow . . . whatever settlement our officials call for.

I also grant the following to Grigorii Anikievich Stroganov: for the duration of the 20-year privilege, Grigorii and his settlers are not obligated to provide transport, guides or provisions for any of our envoys who go through his town en route from Moscow to Siberia or from Siberia to Moscow, or for our envoys who go from Kazan to Perm or from Perm to Kazan. Merchants in the town should have bread, salt and other provisions available, and sell these to envoys and emissaries and travelers at the same price at which they would sell such things to one another. Travelers may hire whatever carts, sailing vessels or rowboats they wish, as well as porters, from whatever person asks the lowest price.

VISUAL DOCUMENTS

Figure 6-1 Coin with the Image of Ivan III
- Compare this with earlier coins in regard to the political functions coins can serve.
- What messages does this coin convey?

Source: de Chaudoir, *Obozrenie Russkikh deneg.* Part 2, Plate 4, Drawing 5.

Figure 6-2 Ivan IV
- In what style is Ivan painted? What message does this convey?

Source: National Museum of Denmark.

Figure 6-3 Cathedral of the Dormition
This Cathedral was commissioned by Ivan III. It is the centerpiece of the Kremlin.
• What was the significance of this building?
Source: Getty Images, Inc. Photodisc.

Figure 6-4 Muscovite Soldiers
This is a drawing of soldiers from the reign of Ivan IV.
• What kind of warfare are these soldiers equipped to fight?
• What does this suggest about Russia's geographical orientation?
• Where did these soldiers fit in Russia's social and political structure?
Source: Sigmund, Freiherr von Herberstein, *Rerum Moscoviticarum Commentarii,* 1571.

Figure 6-5 Clerks

This is a miniature from the Nikon Chronicle, which was written in the middle of the sixteenth century. It depicts government clerks taking dictation.

• How is this related to trends and developments in Russian government between 1460 and 1560?

Source: A. V. Artsikhovskii. *Drevnerusskie miniatiury kak istoricheskii istochnik.* Moscow: MGU, 1944. Figure 44.

Figure 6-6 Western Eurasia in 1560

By the reign of Ivan IV, Russia was on its way to becoming a multinational empire and the next hegemonic power in Inner Eurasia. It had conquered and incorporated the Mongol Khanates of Kazan and Astrakhan, on the Volga River, and the Khanate of Sibir, across the Ural Mountains. In the west, however, Lithuania and the Crimean Tatars resisted Muscovite expansion.

─────────────── **FOR FURTHER READING** ───────────────

(In addition to the books by Blum, Crummy, de Hartog, Fennell, Kollmann, Levin, Martin, Thyrêt, and Ostrowski from the previous chapter.)

Bushkovitch, Paul. *Religion and Society in Russia: The Sixteenth and Seventeenth Centuries.* New York: Oxford University Press, 1992.

Grey, Ian. *Ivan III and the Unification of Russia.* New York: Collier Books, 1964.

Khodarkovsky, Michael. *Russia's Steppe Frontier: The Making of a Colonial Empire, 1500–1800.* Bloomington, IN: Indiana University Press, 2001.

Platonov, S. F. *Ivan the Terrible.* Joseph L. Wieczynski, Ed. and Trans. With "In Search of Ivan the Terrible" by Richard Hellie. Gulf Breeze, FL: Academic International Press, 1974.

Skrynnikov, Ruslan G. *Ivan the Terrible.* Hugh F. Graham, Ed. and Trans. Gulf Breeze, FL: Academic International Press, 1981.

CHAPTER SEVEN

THE COLLAPSE AND RECOVERY OF MUSCOVY, 1560–1620

For two hundred years after the death of Ivan II, Moscow, under the leadership of shrewd, long-lived (and lucky) rulers, had steadily grown in wealth, power, and territory into a significant Eurasian power. Ivan IV at first seemed to be an able successor to the Muscovite tradition. Soon after 1560, however, the fabric of Russian society began to unravel. Not only did Ivan IV embroil his country in a costly and protracted war with Poland and Sweden, he also began to follow erratic and disruptive domestic policies that have made some historians question his sanity. He killed his eldest son, leaving only an incompetent and childless heir to his throne. In 1598, that heir, Fyodor, the last direct descendant of the Moscow branch of the Rurikovichi, died, and at the beginning of the new century Russia was engulfed in social rebellion, civil war, and foreign invasion. Just when it appeared likely that Russia would be partitioned by Sweden and Poland, Russian patriots from the northeast gathered an army and restored Russian unity and independence. It was not until the third decade of the seventeenth century that Russia was able to begin to recover.

EURASIAN CONTEXT

Russia was not alone. Most of the civilizations of Eurasia experienced turmoil and distress of one kind or another in this time period. The Ming Dynasty in China faced a series of crises from the middle of the sixteenth to the middle of the seventeenth centuries. The urban economy experienced severe inflation as it was flooded with silver from European

---

Turn to page 147 for a map showing key geographic locations and features for this time period.

merchants who had an insatiable demand for Chinese porcelain, tea, and silk. At the same time, the rural population suffered from crop failures, famines, and plagues. China faced increased pressure from yet another nomadic society on its northern borders, the Manchus. The economy could not bear the strain of the higher taxes needed for defense, and China was shaken by rebellions.

The Uzbek Khans continued to rule in Transoxiana throughout this period, but their civilization declined. The Khanates of Khorazm and Bukhara fought between themselves, even as they continually fended off invasions from Safavid Iran. European shipping in the Indian and Atlantic Oceans caused overland trade to decline, and trade along the old Silk Road, through Bukhara and Samarkand, remained stagnant. By the late sixteenth century, the Kazakhs occupied the steppe from the Yaik River to the Irtysh; they were divided into (from west to east) the Lesser, Middle, and Greater Hordes. In the early seventeenth century, the Kalmyks, a Mongol tribe who adhered to Tibetan Buddhism, caused turmoil on the Inner Eurasian steppe when they moved from what is now western Xinjiang to steppe north of the Caspian Sea.

The one success story in Eurasia was Iran, where Shah Abbas (1588–1629) brought the Safavid dynasty to the peak of its power, wealth, and territorial expansion. Abbas centralized and streamlined his government and army and increased the use of firearms. He conquered the Caucasus, driving out the Ottomans who had only recently seized the region. Abbas was an oppressive ruler there, deporting many Georgians and Armenians to Iran. Abbas also took Mesopotamia from the Ottoman Empire. He employed Armenian merchants to promote trade with Europe and particularly fostered the production of silk textiles and "Persian" (as Iran was known in Europe) carpets.

Following the death of Süleyman I in 1566, the Ottoman Empire experienced a half century of turmoil. The empire ceased to expand, taxation replaced plunder as a form of income, and revenues fell. The Ottoman Empire also suffered from inflation caused by the influx of New World silver. Emergency taxes levied to support the army caused social unrest, local revolts, and widespread banditry. The government was beset by intrigue, nepotism, and corruption, and interference by Janissary officers. Nevertheless, the Ottoman Empire remained a major power in the Middle East and in Southeast Europe.

In the second half of the sixteenth century, continental Europe experienced religious warfare and economic depression. France was convulsed by civil wars between Catholics and Protestants, and Protestant Netherlands fought a long war of independence from Catholic Spain. Spain and Portugal continued to dominate trade in the Atlantic, and the huge amount of silver Spain extracted from the New World caused inflation in Europe (as well as in India and China). Germany was particularly hard hit by inflation which drove up the price of grain, which benefitted aristocratic landowners but devastated the urban, commercial economy.

A major turning point in Polish and Lithuanian history occurred during the reign of Sigismund II (1548–1572) who had no heirs and wanted to unite Poland and Lithuania permanently before he died. The Lithuanian nobility opposed the terms that Sigismund offered, but Sigismund detached from Lithuania a large southwestern territory containing Volynia and Kiev and annexed it to Poland. Under the threat of having the remainder of their territory annexed as well, they agreed to unification. In the Union of Lublin (1569), a Lithuanian-Polish state was created. Each nation kept its own territory, laws, administration, and army, but they were jointly governed by an elected king and Sejm.

Polish and Lithuanian society began to change. Sigismund's death marked the beginning of the free election of the Polish King by the szlachta and the subsequent rise of the szlachta and decline of the monarchy. The polonization of Lithuania's wealthy elite intensified, and the use of the Polish language and confession of the Catholic faith became practically universal among Lithuanian aristocrats. Lithuanian landowners also followed the lead of the

Polish szlachta in establishing serfdom, permanently binding peasants to the estates on which they worked. Serfdom was made law in Poland in 1573 and in Lithuania in 1588. Thus the Union of Liublin was a victory for Poland; its institutions, language, and religion triumphed, and Lithuania lost its independence.

As a consequence, landowners in the territory of old Kiev Rus became increasingly alien from the Orthodox East Slav peasantry who were now their serfs. The situation was made worse in 1596 by the Union of Brest-Litovsk in which the Orthodox Church in Poland-Lithuania was subordinated to the Papacy. The new church, called the "Uniate Church" followed the Eastern Rites, but its bishops and priests were consecrated by and responsible to the Pope. The Eastern Orthodox believers in Poland-Lithuania now had to practice their religion in secret, and, alienated from their rulers, began to look to the Cossacks for liberation.

In northern Europe, Sweden continued to grow as a regional power. The primary goal of Swedish kings was to control the profitable East Baltic trade routes, which supplied Europe with grain, iron, timber, tar, hemp, and furs. This meant conflict with Poland and Russia, who shared the same goal. Erik XIV of Sweden (1560–1568), alarmed by Ivan IV's invasion of Livonia in 1558, used the Russian threat to convince the nobility in Esthonia to accept Swedish rule. John III (1568–1592), Erik XIV's successor, defeated Russian armies and forced Ivan IV to withdraw from Livonia in 1583. Then John entered into a plan with the Polish szlachta to unite Poland and Sweden under one king, John's son, Sigismund. John converted to Roman Catholicism and married a Polish princess, and their son was duly elected King Sigismund III of Poland (1587–1632). Then, when John died in 1592, Sigismund succeeded to the Swedish crown as well. Sigismund only ruled Sweden for seven years. Sigismund's uncle, Charles, representing the interests of the Lutheran clergy and the Swedish gentry, declared Sweden a Lutheran country. In 1599, Sigismund was forced to abandon the Swedish throne, and Charles IX (1599–1611) succeeded him. Charles soon came into conflict with Poland during Russia's Time of Troubles.

POLITICAL DEVELOPMENTS TO 1605

In 1560, when his first wife, Anastasia died, Ivan began to act in the erratic, irrational, and cruel ways that earned him the name "Ivan the Terrible." He began by breaking up the close group of advisers with whom he had planned the reforms of the first part of his reign. He arrested and imprisoned two of those former advisers, and he began to arrest and execute those he thought were critical of him. In 1564, Ivan suddenly moved to Alexandrov, a small town sixty miles from Moscow. He sent a letter to the Metropolitan denouncing the higher clergy and the boiars and declaring his intention to abdicate. A delegation of Moscow notables traveled to Alexandrov and begged him to remain on the throne. Ivan agreed, provided he was allowed a free hand in searching out and punishing traitors. The Moscow elite accepted.

Ivan then created an entirely new administrative system, called the *oprichnina* (meaning "set apart"). Special regions were carved out (within Russia) to be ruled by Ivan personally; the remainder of the territory of Muscovite Russia, called the *zemshchina*, Ivan left for the boiars to rule. The central administration, prikaz bureaucracy, and army would function normally, and the Moscow boiars were directed to refer only the most important questions to Ivan. Within the special regions, the oprichnina, Ivan erected an administration staffed without regard to mestnichestvo or family background and whose officials and soldiers, the oprichniks, would not be subject to the laws and procedures of the Muscovite state; they would obey the commands and act in the personal interest of the Tsar.

The oprichniks, numbering about six thousand at their height, began a reign of terror. Dressing all in black and carrying dogs' heads as symbols of their authority, they searched the houses of people they claimed to suspect of treason, arrested suspects, used torture to obtain confessions of guilt, and executed their victims. Oprichniks were also allowed to confiscate the property and lands of traitors. One of their worst excesses was the sack of Novgorod in 1570 in which at least twenty-two hundred people were tortured and executed. Overall, more than four thousand people across Russia died.

The oprichnina lasted seven years before Ivan ended it as suddenly as he had begun it. The precipitating factor seems to have been an attack on Moscow by Crimean Tatars in 1571. The Tatars defeated the oprichnik defenders and burned part of the city. In 1572, however, a similar attack was turned away by a zemshchina army. Soon after this, the oprichnina was dismantled and the territories it had administered were transferred back to the regular government. Some confiscated estates were given back to their former owners.

Some historians have explained away the madness of the oprichnina as political strategy, an attempt by Ivan IV to curtail the power of the boiars, but no pattern of persecution is, in fact, evident. Ivan appointed boiars, pomeshchiks, and ordinary townspeople to the oprichnina, and the oprichniks arrested and executed their victims without discriminating according to social class. Furthermore, by the end of his reign, Ivan had reestablished the boiar elite by reducing the Duma to fewer than twenty and by appointing men who came from prominent families or who had distinguished themselves in military or administrative service.

Even after he ended the oprichnina, Ivan continued to act in inexplicable ways. In 1575, he formally abdicated the throne and named Simeon Bekbulatovich, a Tatar prince, to replace him as Tsar. Bekbulatovich seems to have had no real power, and the bizarre arrangement ended in 1576 when he stepped down and Ivan resumed the title of Tsar.

Ivan's foreign policies were equally irrational. In 1558, he had seized Livonia and its Baltic Sea ports, and in 1563 his armies had taken the city of Polotsk from Lithuania. In 1566, however, when Lithuania accepted Russia's gains and sued for peace, Ivan refused. His continued aggression contributed to the union of Poland and Lithuania in 1569, which brought Polish forces into action against Russia and was followed by anti-Russian alliances between Poland and the Crimean Tatars and Poland and Sweden. The Crimean Tatars began a series of raids, including the 1571 attack in which they burned Moscow. Poland, Lithuania, and Sweden then combined to drive Russia out of Livonia. In treaties with Poland in 1582 and Sweden in 1583, Ivan gave up all his gains in the Baltic. His twenty-five-year war in the northwest ended in complete failure and at enormous cost in resources and human lives.

Ivan's most tragic act after the oprichnina occurred in 1581 when, in a fit of anger during a trivial family argument, he struck his elder son, Ivan, with an iron rod, killing him. This meant that when Ivan IV died he was succeeded by his remaining son, Fyodor I (1584–1598), an exception to the long tradition of able and assertive Muscovite Grand Princes. Fyodor suffered from poor health and extremely limited mental gifts. He left the work of governing Muscovy to his wife Irina Godunova and her brother, Boris Godunov.

The Godunovs were the descendants of a Mongol prince who had transferred his allegiance to Moscow in the fourteenth century. Their family was not particularly distinguished, until Boris married the daughter of one of Ivan IV's courtiers, and Irina married the tsarevich Fyodor. In 1580, the year of Irina's wedding, Boris was made a boiar. The position of the Godunovs was opposed by the most powerful boiar families, and in response the Godunovs used their influence over the Tsar to purge their enemies, most notably the Shuiskiis, and exile them from the capital. By 1588, Boris Godunov was perceived by many to be tsar in all but name. Irina Godunova, too, was actively involved in government. She attended receptions and granted pardons, and at court the boiars referred to her as "Great Sovereign."

Among the most significant achievements of Fyodor's reign was the elevation of the Russian Church to a patriarchate. The Russian Orthodox Church hierarchy had been acting independently of Constantinople and choosing its own Metropolitan since 1448, but the

Eastern Patriarchs had maintained the fiction that it was still a part of the Byzantine Church. In 1588, the Patriarch of Constantinople came to Moscow looking for financial support, and Boris Godunov convinced him to recognize the independence of the Russian Church. When the Patriarch acquiesced, Godunov chose Job (1588–1605) to be the first Patriarch of Moscow.

Godunov also supervised a successful military and foreign policy. He repelled a Crimean Tatar invasion in 1591 and forced the Crimean Khan to agree to a truce. He won a war with Sweden, in which he regained some of the coast of Finland that Ivan IV had briefly held. In the 1590s, he built new forts on the Volga, Don, and Terek rivers to contain the Crimean Tatars and to control the Cossacks.

Fyodor and Irina remained childless, so succession to the throne was uncertain. Fyodor had a half-brother, Dmitrii, who was Ivan IV's son by his seventh wife. The Orthodox Church recognizes and only allows three remarriages for a man; any subsequent relationships are not sanctified by the church, and any children of those relationships are illegitimate. Technically, therefore, Dmitrii could not claim any right of inheritance from his father, Ivan IV. In practical terms, however, Dmitrii was considered a possible claimant to the throne, and Godunov had exiled him (and his mother) to Uglich where, in 1591, Dmitrii died of a knife wound in the neck. His mother claimed the boy was murdered by agents of Godunov, but a commission headed by V. I. Shuisky concluded that the boy had suffered an epileptic attack while playing a game and had stabbed himself. As a result of Dmitrii's death, when Fyodor died in 1598, there were no living sons of Ivan IV, legitimate or otherwise, to succeed him.

When Fyodor died, Godunov briefly considered making Irina queen, but the boiars refused and forced her to enter a convent. Godunov then summoned a Zemskii Sobor, and, with the help of the Patriarch Job, arranged for his own election as tsar. Tsar Boris (1598–1605) then began a ruthless persecution of the boiar families he believed to be his enemies. He charged the Romanovs (related to Ivan IV's first wife Anastasia) with practicing sorcery and sent many of them into exile. The senior member of the Romanov family was forced to become a monk (he took the name Filaret) and was locked up in a monastery. In other aspects of his reign, however, Tsar Boris continued to be a competent ruler. He sent students to western Europe to be educated, he reformed the judicial system, and he began to negotiate for the reacquisition of Livonia.

Troubles were nevertheless approaching. Early frosts in 1601 and 1602 caused widespread crop failures. Famine followed, and peasants abandoned their farms looking for food. In 1603, a major slave rebellion broke out, and the army had to be called out to suppress it. Then, in 1604, a man calling himself Tsar Dmitrii appeared in the southwest at the head of a rebel army. He claimed to be Ivan IV's son Dmitrii, declaring that he had not been killed in 1591 but had gone into hiding.

In reality it appears that this man, known to history as "the First False Dmitrii," began life as Grishka Otrepev, a peasant on a Romanov estate. He had become a monk, was defrocked for some transgression, and then had fled to Poland. With Polish encouragement, the First False Dmitrii recruited pomeshchiks, Cossacks, and peasants from the south and marched toward Moscow. Tsar Boris fended off the pretender's army and kept Russia's crisis under control. After Boris died in 1605, however, the Time of Troubles began.

THE TIME OF TROUBLES

Ivan IV's oprichnina and his protracted wars over Livonia had caused a massive economic depression from which Russia had never fully recovered. The peasantry was immiserated. Their farms had been plundered by oprichniks and by Crimean Tatar raiders. Their taxes were steadily increased to pay for the war, and pomeshchiks, themselves in dire financial straits, continually raised their demands. Many peasants fled to the borderlands, and subsequent depopulation meant a greater tax burden for those who were left. Peasant flight also caused the government to decree "forbidden years" in which all movement of peasant households was proscribed. At least half of the years between 1581 and 1603 were forbidden years and so was every year from 1603 until the end of the Time of Troubles. This exacerbated peasant unrest.

The economic depression affected townspeople as well. Tver and Novgorod had been plundered by the oprichnina and the effects were devastating and long-lasting. Merchants and artisans everywhere were hurt by high taxes and by the decline in trade caused by the collapse of agriculture. Pomeshchiks, too, were in a miserable situation. Many had lost their land during the oprichnina, and when they were allowed to return to their estates they often found that their property had been ruined and the peasants driven off the land. Pomeshchiks were also bankrupted by constant military service in Russia's wars. By the end of the sixteenth century, the average pomeshchik spent a full 75 percent of his income on expenses related to military service. Some pomeshchiks ran off to be Cossacks and some became slaves of wealthier aristocrats. The boiars, though economically better provided for than the rest of the population, were nevertheless also unhappy. Ivan's reign had made them extremely insecure, and Boris Godunov's attack on the elite families of Moscow only made them feel more vulnerable.

When Boris Godunov died in 1605, having named his sixteen-year-old son, Fyodor, to succeed him, Godunov's old boiar enemies refused to recognize his son as Tsar. They arrested and killed Fyodor and his mother, and they deposed and exiled the Patriarch Job. Then, when the False Dmitrii took up the offensive again and led his army toward Moscow, the boiars welcomed him and accepted him as Tsar, no doubt hoping to use him as a puppet. Vasilii Shuiskii, the man who had once pronounced Dmitrii's death accidental, now changed his story and asserted that Dmitrii had not died, and the mother of the real Dmitrii officially recognized the False Dmitrii as her son. The clique of boiars now in control also released from exile the families whom Boris Godunov had persecuted, Filaret Romanov among them.

The First False Dmitrii soon alienated the boiars. While in Poland he had converted to Catholicism, and his entourage included many Poles and a number of Jesuit priests. In the spring of 1606, he married Marina Mnisech, a Polish Catholic aristocrat, and she was crowned Tsaritsa. This could not be borne by the anti-Catholic Russian boiars. Only nine days after the wedding, Vasilii Shuisky and his supporters broke into the Kremlin and murdered the False Dmitrii. They incited the populace against the False Dmitrii's entourage, and in the ensuing two weeks of mob violence, two thousand Poles were killed.

Vasilii Shuiskii was then proclaimed Tsar by his supporters and the Moscow crowd (no Zemskii Sobor was called). He reversed his story on the death of Dmitrii and had the real Dmitrii's bones dug up and brought to Moscow to prove it. Effective at seizing power, Shuiskii was ineffective at wielding it. He alienated the Romanovs by passing over Filaret Romanov and appointing a prelate named Germogen to succeed Job as Patriarch. He alienated the peasantry by extending the statute of limitations for the return of runaway peasants from five to fifteen years. (The law had little impact, since Shuiskii ruled little more that the city of Moscow.)

Meanwhile, a massive rebellion was growing in the south. Ivan Bolotnikov, an escaped slave turned Cossack, organized a heterogeneous army that included boiars, pomeshchiks, Cossacks, fugitive slaves, and peasants. This army advanced all the way to Moscow, when it was stopped, not by Shuiskii's forces, but by internal dissension. Bolotnikov had begun to call on slaves to murder their masters, and the poor to kill the rich. Alarmed, the boiars and pomeshchiks began to abandon the movement and join Shuiskii. The rebel army was repelled from Moscow in 1606 and defeated in 1607. Bolotnikov was killed, the nobles who

had continued to serve under him were exiled, and lower-class soldiers were executed or sold as slaves.

While the Bolotnikov Rebellion was being suppressed, a new pretender to the throne, a Second False Dmitrii, appeared in eastern Poland at the head of an army of Poles and Cossacks. By the spring of 1608, he reached Moscow, and, when he failed to capture the city, he took up residence in Tushino, a small town not far away. There the Second False Dmitrii set up a court and began to act as if he were Tsar. Marina Mnisech, the widow of the First False Dmitrii, recognized him as her husband, and the mother of the real Dmitrii recognized him as her son. The Romanov family also supported him, and the Second False Dmitrii appointed Filaret Romanov as Patriarch. There were now two Tsars of Russia, neither legitimate, with two separate courts. Neither had any control over the south.

This situation continued for the remainder of 1608. Then, in early 1609, Vasilii Shuiskii turned to Charles IX, King of Sweden, for help. Shuiskii renounced Russia's claims in Livonia and promised to support Sweden against Poland; in return, Charles IX sent a Swedish army to Moscow. With the Swedish help, Shuiskii began to clear the forces of the Second False Dmitrii out of the north.

This brought Poland into the fray. Sigismund III, fearful of Swedish expansion into northwest Russia and angry at the anti-Polish alliance between Shuiskii and Charles IX, invaded Russia in the fall of 1609. As the Russian-Swedish forces and the Polish army converged on Tushino in the spring of 1610, the Second False Dmitrii fled, leaving behind Filaret Romanov and his boiar allies. Filaret sent a delegation to Sigismund III in which he offered to accept Sigismund's son, Wladislaw, as Tsar of Russia provided he would convert to Russian Orthodoxy and respect boiar rights and privileges. Sigismund agreed to these terms.

Now the tide turned against Vasilii Shuiskii. His forces, even with Swedish reinforcements, were smaller than the Polish army, and they were pushed back to Moscow. In July, a group of boiars, including some Romanovs, staged a coup. They mobilized public opinion against Shuiskii, arrested him, forced him to become a monk, and confined him in the Kremlin. This boiar clique ruled Moscow as a provisional government without a tsar. In the meantime, the Second False Dmitrii had acquired Cossack and peasant reinforcements in the south and was marching back toward Moscow.

Now the leading boiar families, including both Romanovs and Shuiskiis, looking for some way to preserve their wealth and power, decided to overcome their differences and use Poland to their advantage. They admitted the Polish army into Moscow and summoned a zemskii sobor which elected Wladislaw Tsar of Russia. The population of Moscow swore allegiance to him, and the Polish army began to suppress rebellion, restore order, and defend against the Second False Dmitrii.

However, Sigismund III changed the situation by renouncing the treaty he had signed only a few months earlier. He now decided that he, himself, would become Tsar of Russia. He also announced that he would not convert to Eastern Orthodoxy. This alarmed the Moscow boiars, and they refused to accept him. Patriarch Germogen called on all Orthodox Russians to unite against the foreign invaders, and he forbade them to swear allegiance to a Roman Catholic. The Polish, now in control of Moscow, imprisoned Germogen in the Kremlin. They also arrested Filaret and sent him to Poland as a hostage.

In early 1611, Prokopii Liapunov, an aristocrat from Riazan, attempted to create a Russian patriotic army. He recruited pomeshchik officers and a rank and file made up of the same Cossacks and landless poor who had rallied behind Bolotnikov and the various pretenders to the throne. To gain their support, Liapunov promised land and freedom to all runaway peasants and fugitive slaves. This army successfully reached Moscow in the summer of 1611, but before it could engage the Poles, it collapsed. Liapunov made the mistake of bringing back the old order in the regions his army occupied and directing that peasants and slaves were to be returned to their former lords. Betrayed by its leader, the army revolted and murdered him. It then reorganized to support a new cause—yet another false Dmitrii, the third, the infant son of Marina Mniszek and the Second False Dmitrii.

The summer of 1611 was the nadir of Russia's fortunes. Moscow was in the hands of a Polish regiment. Sigismund, King of Poland had taken Smolensk and was at the head of an invading Polish army. The Swedish army occupied Novgorod, and Novgorod's population had accepted Charles IX as their king. Finally, an army of Cossacks, outlaws, and runaway slaves and peasants was on the outskirts of Moscow with their own candidate for the throne.

It was at this point that a movement arose among the propertied classes—landowners, merchants, and clergy—in the northern Volga region to restore the Muscovite state. Kuzma Minin, a Nizhnii-Novgorod merchant, took the lead in gathering donations to fund an army, and Prince Dmitrii Pozharskii volunteered to be its general. They decided to avoid the fate of Bolotnikov and Liapunov by resisting the temptation to appeal to the landless poor or to create a pretender to the throne. Instead they chose to build an army of patriotic pomeshchiks and to call a Zemskii Sobor that could find and legitimate a new Tsar. Conservative elements responded enthusiastically and by early 1612 the patriotic movement controlled the entire Volga region. Minin and Pozharskii set up a provisional government in Iaroslavl and invited boiars, clergy, and pomeshchiks from across Russia to join them.

Minin and Pozharskii's growing army cleared the Cossack bands from the north, either subordinating them or driving them away. They then negotiated a cease-fire with the Swedish troops who still occupied Novgorod, and in the autumn of 1612 they drove the Poles out of Moscow. As soon as they took possession of the capital, the patriotic forces called for elections to a zemskii sobor for the purpose of choosing a new Tsar. In January 1613, a zemskii sobor met in Moscow with delegates representing all the free classes in Russia, including boiars, pomeshchiks, clergy, townspeople, and free peasants.

This Zemskii Sobor chose sixteen-year-old Michael Romanov, nephew of Ivan IV's first wife Anastasia, first cousin of Tsar Fyodor, and son of Filaret Romanov, the boiar who had negotiated the turbulent times more successfully than any other Muscovite. Filaret's association with both the First and the Second False Dmitrii probably helped his standing with the Cossacks and the peasantry. Moreover, his imprisonment in Poland made Filaret a symbol of Polish Catholic persecution of Russia. Michael was crowned Tsar of Russia in July 1613.

Working closely together, the new Tsar, the boiars, and the zemskii sobor, which remained in session, mobilized all possible resources toward restoring order in the country and driving out the foreign occupiers. By 1614, the Cossack armies were finally brought under control and the anarchy in the south was suppressed. In 1617, Michael negotiated a treaty with Sweden in which, in exchange for the removal of Swedish troops from Novgorod, he ceded Russia's last Baltic possession, a strip of territory on the Gulf of Finland. Sigismund of Poland was more difficult to deal with. In 1618 Sigismund agreed to a cease-fire, but he did not withdraw from Smolensk, and he did not renounce his son Wladislaw's claim, based on the treaty of 1610, to be Tsar of Russia. The following year Sigismund finally released Filaret from captivity. On his return to Russia, Filaret was made patriarch. He was also given the title of "Great Sovereign" and was recognized as a co-ruler with his son.

THE RUSSIAN CHURCH

The unity of the Eastern Slavs had always been a major preoccupation of the Russian Orthodox Church, and never was its participation in the political life of the nation as important as during the Time of Troubles. Patriarch Germogen played a key role in rallying the Russian national forces against foreign invaders. It was his call for unity against Poland that led to his arrest, and his messages on that theme, smuggled from his prison cell, were used to inspire the patriotic forces. Furthermore, before dying in Polish captivity in 1612, Germogen had put his support behind the candidacy of Michael Romanov to be tsar.

The Russian church had other reasons to rally the propertied classes to restore traditional society. The Church remained the biggest single land owner in Russia, and it had been a core institution in the Russian state. Thus, its material interests coincided exactly with the patriotic movement. Nevertheless, changes had been occurring in the church's attitude toward its ownership of land. Church leaders realized that the extent of their land holdings was excessive, and in 1580 a church council forbade church officials to buy land or to give mortgages on land. In 1584 the Church acquiesced in a state law that ended all exemptions from taxation for church lands.

The Church hierarchy began asserting its authority over monasteries, subordinating abbots to bishops. Monks had been withdrawing from public affairs, and the general decline in respect for monasteries continued. Monks had lost their reputation for virtue in Russian society, and stories of monasteries as hotbeds of sin began to circulate. Church writers increasingly represented archbishops and not abbots as models of spirituality, and used this to enhance the power of the episcopate.

The Church hierarchy was also of the opinion that it was superior to secular authority. This trend reached its peak when Filaret became Patriarch and took the title of "Great Sovereign." He was the real ruler of Russia as long as he was alive, although this probably had more to do with the fact that he was the senior member of the Romanov family and the father of the Tsar than because he was patriarch of the church. Later in the seventeenth century when Patriarch Nikon tried to assume the title of "Great Sovereign" it was his undoing.

ROLES AND STATUS OF WOMEN

Women continued to be deprived of independence and power in their daily lives, even as the wives of princes were celebrated in church ideology. Isolde Thyrêt argues that the Romanovs used Anastasia to elevate themselves, and they chose the surname "Romanov" because they wanted to highlight their family connection with her. A myth of the pious Tsaritsa Anastasia was put forward, and a genealogy was constructed for her that traced her ancestry back to Caesar Augustus. She was incorporated into Russian folklore as the moral force that restrained Ivan the Terrible in the first part of his reign; it was only after her death that he began to behave terribly.

Nevertheless, despite this religious idealization of rulers' wives, the day-to-day lives of women were limited and subordinate to men. The terem, separate living quarters for women, continued among the wealthy classes. Fathers had absolute power over their children (both girls and boys) and could even sell them into slavery. Girls were often forced to marry as early as ten or eleven. Women could avoid unwanted marriages by refusing to participate in the wedding ceremony, but this was extremely rare.

Divorce was also a male prerogative; and men who sued for divorce usually claimed unfaithfulness. In the era of the terem, this could mean merely being seen in public without the company of a male relative. Few women asked for or were granted divorce. Divorced men were allowed to remarry, but divorced women were expected to remain single. This rule was generally disregarded, however, especially during and after the Time of Troubles when the state wanted the population to grow.

It was in the sixteenth century that Russia began to acquire the reputation as a land of wife-beaters. Foreign travelers reported that Russian women considered beatings from their husbands as signs of love, although there is no evidence that this is true. Russia was a society in which corporal punishment was common. Undoubtedly husbands beat their wives on occasion, and wives probably hit their husbands. Nevertheless, cruelty was not celebrated, and physical mistreatment was, in fact, grounds for divorce. Moreover, as in all societies, individual men did not act as badly as the law gave them the right to. Despite the social norms that put women under the authority of their husbands or fathers, private letters of the time give evidence of real love and respect between couples.

ECONOMIC AND SOCIAL TRENDS

The Time of Troubles was devastating for Russia. There were actually dozens of pretenders to the throne, each at the head of an armed band. In addition, leaderless mobs roamed the countryside. Peasants fled from the central regions where both fighting and taxation were highest, and between 1601 and 1620 the depopulation of the land was even worse than it had been after the oprichnina.

Taxes continued to rise. Ivan IV had attempted to tax farmers on the basis of their ability to pay. He created a unit of taxation called the *vyt*, the amount of land necessary to support a peasant household. Surveyors, taking into account the quality of the land, treated a vyt as forty acres of good, fifty acres of average, or sixty acres of poor land, plus four acres of pasture. In the 1560s, the tax on a vyt was 40 rubles, in the 1560s it was 150, and in 1620 it was over 500. Some of this increase was caused by inflation, but there was a real increase as well. To make matters worse, during the Time of Troubles the system of surveying and evaluating land value broke down, and taxes began to be assessed without regard to the quality of land or the ability to pay.

High taxes served to bind peasants more permanently to the estate on which they worked. The mir had broken down as a unit of tax collection, and the responsibility for collecting taxes fell to owners of the estates. If the peasants were unable to pay all their taxes, the landlord paid for them. Thus, according to the St. George's Day law, their debt to the landowner meant that he could forbid them to move away.

Another consequence of the Russian tax system was an increase in the amount of barshchina (labor service) that was required. Landlords were not taxed on their personal land, they were required only to collect taxes from the peasantry. Therefore, if a lord took land away from the peasants and forced the peasants to work on it as a labor obligation, his income rose and his tax obligation fell. In the early seventeenth century, it was not unusual for peasants to be required to work three days a week for their lord, and this suggests that they lost three-sevenths of their land to the lord.

Debt slavery, becoming known as kabala slavery, increased in this time period. The kabala slave became an unpaid laborer in exchange for a loan of money. Kabala slavery was not particularly onerous; it ended when the debt was paid or the master died, slave status was not inherited by children, and the master could not mistreat, give away, or sell his or her kabala slaves. A significant attraction of kabala slavery was the exemption of the slave from taxation.

A new social category appeared after the Time of Troubles, the *bobyl* or cottager. Bobyls owned only a cottage with no land other than a garden plot and earned their livings as paid agricultural laborers. In the 1620s, it is estimated that 40 percent of all peasant households in the central Moscow region had bobyl status, an indication, perhaps of the desire to escape the payment of taxes, from which a bobyl was exempt.

There were only three regions in Russia where life was relatively good for peasant farmers. One was the forest country of the far north, from the shores of the White Sea to the Ural

Mountains. There were very few nobles, only a few large monasteries, and many free, self-governing peasant communities. Peasant farmers supplemented their income by trapping fur-bearing animals, fishing, and making salt. The region also benefitted from Russia's trade with England which passed along the North Dvina from the port of Archangel on the White Sea.

The second region of relative prosperity was the land that was being opened up south of the Oka River. The government secured the land by building a line of forts and giving pomesties to the soldiers who defended them. The tsar then granted large tracts of land to monasteries, boiars, and other servitors, expecting them to bring in slaves or peasants to work the land. There was also plenty of black land where peasants could create free communes. The income from farms on the southeastern steppes was three or four times greater than farm income in the central region around Moscow.

The third region was east of the Ural Mountains on the Siberian steppe. The Stroganov family, who had become wealthy in the first part of Ivan IV's reign by colonizing the land east of the Kama River, took it upon themselves to expand east of the Ural Mountains. They hired a Cossack band led by Ermak Timofeievich, and in 1582 Ermak's forces defeated the Khan of Sibir. Ivan IV, pleased with this unexpected development, sent the Russian army to follow up on Ermak's success. His successors rapidly pushed Russia's eastward border eastward. The Russians built Tobolsk on the Tobol River in 1587, and forts on the Irtysh in 1594, the Ob in 1596, and the Yenesei in 1619. By 1620, peasant settlers had only begun to move to Siberia, but it must have seemed a paradise. No noble landholding was allowed in Siberia, and all peasant communities were therefore self-governing.

CONCLUSION

Between 1560 and 1620, Muscovite Russia expanded, collapsed, and was revived. The social system had been shaken to its foundations by civil wars and rebellions that had some of the characteristics of class warfare. However, when the dust had settled, the same social classes remained: a small elite of landowners, including noble servitors and church leaders, and a huge mass of poor agriculturalists whose labor supported the landowning classes. The old political structure had been revived, as well; a Tsar, claiming to rule by divine right, governed with the help of a narrow circle of boiar aristocrats. The task of Michael Romanov and his descendants was to built a political system that could, at best, reconcile or, at least, contain the social conflicts and contradictions that had fueled the Time of Troubles.

_____ TEXT DOCUMENTS _____

An English View of Muscovite Government

In 1588 Giles Fletcher was sent by Queen Elizabeth to represent England at the Muscovite court. After he returned to England, Fletcher wrote Of the Russe Commonwealth *in which he described the structure of Russia's government and church and the way of life of the Russians and their neighbors.*

- How does Fletcher depict the nature of Muscovite government?
- What does he mean by the word "tyranny?" How does he seem to think tyranny can be prevented?
- What light does this cast on the role of the tsaritsa in Muscovite political life?

The state and form of their government is plain tyrannical, as applying all to the benefit of the prince and that after a most open and barbarous manner. . . .

Concerning the principal points and matters of state wherein the sovereignty consists (as the making and annulling of public laws, the making of magistrates, power to make war or league with any foreign state, to execute or to pardon life, with the right of appeal in all matters both civil and criminal) they do so wholly and absolutely pertain to the Emperor and his counsel under him, as that he may be said to be both the sovereign commander and the executioner of all these. For as touching any law or public order of the realm, it is ever determined of before any public assembly or parliament be summoned. Where, besides his counsel, he has none other to consult with him of such matters as are concluded before hand but only a few bishops, abbots, and friars. . . .

Secondly, as touching the public offices and magistracies of the realm, there is none hereditary, neither any so great nor so little in that country, but the bestowing of it is done immediately by the Emperor himself. . . .

Thirdly, the like is to be said of the jurisdiction concerning matters judicial, specially such as concern life and death. Wherein there is none that hath any authority or public jurisdiction that is inherited or is held by charter but all at the appointment and pleasure of the Emperor. And the same practiced by the judges with such awe and restraint as they dare not determine upon any special matter but must refer the same wholly up to Moscow to the Emperor's counsel. . . .

Fourthly, for the sovereign appeal and giving of pardons in criminal matters to such as are convicted, it is wholly at the pleasure and grace of the Emperor. Wherein also the Empress that now is, being a woman of great clemency and moreover delighting to deal in public affairs of the realm (the rather to supply the defect of her husband) behaves herself after an absolute manner, giving out pardon (especially on her birthday and other solemn times) in her own name by open proclamation, without any mention at all of the Emperor.

Source: Giles Fletcher, *Of the Russe Commonwealth*, in *Russia at the Close of the Sixteenth Century* (London: The Hakluyt Society, 1856), 26–27, 28–29. Spelling and some terms and expressions have been modernized.

Letter from the First National Host

Prince Pozharskii, the leader of the Russian national army that brought the Time of Troubles to an end, sent copies of this letter to cities throughout the Russian heartland in June 1612.

- How does Pozharskii explain the origins of his movement?
- How does he express the idea of Russian national identity?
- What are the political implications of this appeal?

And in Nizhnii-Novgorod the gosti and the posad men and the elected deputy Kuzma Minin, concerned for the general good and unsparing of their possessions, began to provide the soldiers with monetary wages; and they repeatedly sent for me, Prince Dmitrii [Pozharskii], from Nizhnii [Novgorod], [urging] that I go to Nizhnii to take counsel with the land; and at their request I went to them in Nizhnii; and in Nizhnii boiars and voevody and stolniki and striapchie and dvoriane of high rank [Moscow dvoriane] and [other] dvoriane and deti boiarskie began to come to me from Viazma, Dorogobuzh, Smolensk, and various other towns; and I, praying for God's grace, began to confer with them all and with the elected deputy Kuzma Minin and the posad men, that we might all make common cause for the Muscovite state against the enemies and destroyers of the Christian faith, the Poles and Lithuanians, and not serve the rogue who is in Pskov [Sidorka] or Marina [Mniszek] and her son, and oppose them and those who would serve them, and choose a sovereign by all the land, whomever the merciful God may grant. And having so resolved, we pledged our souls to God on this, and gave monetary wages to all the soldiers without stint. . . .

. . . And we implore you, sirs, and tearfully beseech you, brothers of our own blood, Orthodox Christians, to have mercy on yourselves and on your souls, to . . . repudiate the rogue and Marina and her son, and to unite with us and with the entire land, lest the Poles and Lithuanians utterly destroy both you and us through our disunity. . . . And you, sirs . . . should send us two or three men from every rank to hold a common council of the land; and in response to this letter you should send us your written judgment, with your signatures, [as to] how we should stand up against our common enemies, the Poles and the Lithuanians, and how we are to live without a sovereign in these evil times; and we should choose a sovereign by all the land, whomever God in his righteous love of mankind may grant.

And if you, sirs, should fail to send us [your men] soon to take counsel, and fail to repudiate the rogue and Marina and her son, and fail to unite with us and with the entire land and to choose a sovereign for the Muscovite state by common counsel with us, then we shall have to part with you, with heartfelt tears; and we shall choose a sovereign by common counsel with the towns of the Littoral and of the Lower Volga [i.e. the middle and lower regions, from Kazan to Astrakhan] and beyond the Moscow River, whomever God may grant us, lest we be without a sovereign in these evil times, and lest the Muscovite state and all the towns of the Muscovite state be utterly ruined without a sovereign. . . .

Source: George Vernadsky, Ed. *A Source Book for Russian History from Early Times to 1917, Vol. 1: Early Times to the Late Seventeenth Century* (New Haven, CT.: Yale University Press, 1972), 207–208, (c) Yale University Press. Reprinted by permission.

The Life of Iuliana Osorina

Iuliana Osorina was born in the reign of Ivan IV and died in 1604. Her life was written by her son, Kallistrat Druzhina-Osorin. Previously biographies had written exclusively about saints, princes and princesses, and religious leaders; this is the first biography of an ordinary person to be written in Old Slavonic.

- What does it have in common with the life of St. Sergei, and how is it different?
- What does this reveal about new directions in Russian spirituality and religiosity?
- What does it reveal about gender roles and relations in early seventeenth-century Russia?

[Iuliana] was six years old when her mother died, and her grandmother took her to the territory of Murom . . . and her grandmother raised her in all piety and purity for six years. When the grandmother died, according to her wishes, Iuliana's aunt, Natalia . . . took her in. Since the blessed Iuliana from the earliest age had loved God and the Most-pure Mother of God, she was dutiful to her aunt and her aunt's daughters, she showed obedience and humility in all things, and she was diligent in prayer and fasting. And for this her aunt often scolded her and her cousins laughed at her, and they said, "Oh, insane one! Why in such early youth do you exhaust your flesh and ruin your pure beauty?" And beginning in the morning they urged her to eat and drink, but she did not surrender to their will. She accepted everything with gratitude and walked away in silence. She showed obedience to all people. And from her youth she was meek and silent, never obstinate or vain, and kept aloof from laughter and all games. Although she was often urged by the girls of her age to play games and sing secular songs, she did not join in with them, pretending she did not understand in order to hide her virtues. She applied herself with great diligence to spinning and sewing, and her candle burned all night. She did the sewing for all the orphans and infirm widows in the village, and she gave all kinds of help to the needy and the sick, so that everyone marveled at her wisdom and good behavior. And the fear of God was in her. . . .

When she turned sixteen, she was given in marriage to a virtuous and wealthy man named Georgii Osorin. And they were married in the village of her husband in the church of St. Lazarus by the priest who was in residence there. The priest taught them the law of God according to the rules of the Holy Fathers, and she listened to the teachings and instruction attentively, and lived up to them. Her father-in-law and mother-in-law, seeing her wisdom and goodness in all things, entrusted her, while they were still alive, with the care of all the household management. She meekly subordinated herself to them, never disobeyed them, contradicted them in nothing, honored them and carried out without refusal all that was asked of her, so that everyone who saw her marveled at her. Many people examined her with questions, and she gave a decorous and intelligent answer to every question, and everyone marveled at her wisdom and praised God. In the evenings she prayed much to God, doing one hundred genuflections and more, and, getting up early in the morning, she did the same thing together with her husband.

When her husband happened to be away in the tsar's service in Astrakhan for a year or two, and one time even for three, she spent all night without sleep praying or occupying

Source: Mikhail Osipovich Skripil, Ed. *Russkaia povest' XVII veka*. Leningrad: Gosudarstvennoe izdatel'stvo khudozhestvennoi literatury, 1954, 39–40, 40–41, 44–45, 46, 47. Translation by the author.

herself with needlework, the spinning wheel, or the embroidery hoop. Selling her needle-work, she gave the income to the unfortunate or for church construction. At night she gave many alms in secret from her father-in-law and mother-in-law and by day she managed the household. She took care of widows and orphans as if she were their real mother; with her own hands she washed them and fed them and gave them drink. She provided the servants with sufficient food and clothing and gave them tasks according to their strength, and she called no one disparaging names. She did not demand from servants water to wash her hands nor help untying her shoes, but did everything herself. And she instructed foolish ser-vants with meekness and humility, correcting them while blaming herself. She slandered no one. She placed all her hopes in God and in the Most-pure Mother of God. She called for the help of the great miracle-worker Nicholas and received help from him. . . .

[She gave birth to sons and daughters. Later in life she asked her husband to let her be-come a nun, but he refused. After he died, she did not become a nun but became even less worldly than before.]

Living as a widow for nine years, she did much good for everyone, she gave out much wealth in alms, she kept only what was necessary for household needs, doled out food as necessary, and all the time gave what was left over to those in need. She continued to live until the reign of Tsar Boris. At that time there was a cruel famine in the whole Russian land, when many, from need, ate foul animals and human flesh, and countless numbers of people died of hunger. And in her house there was an extreme shortage of food and all kinds of supplies, since the grain that was planted did not sprout, and horses and other livestock died. She begged her children and servants not to encroach on anyone else's property or to give in to thievery. She sold the remaining livestock and clothes and dishes and used the money to buy bread to feed the servants and to give sufficient charity. Even in poverty she did not stop giving her customary alms, not allowing anyone to beg in vain. When she came to the most extreme destitution, so that not a grain was left in her house, even then she was not dismayed but placed all her hope in God. . . .

[She died on January 2, 1604.] She committed her soul to the hands of God, whom she had loved since she was a child. Everyone saw around her head a golden circle just like the golden circles around the heads of saints in icons. Having washed her, they placed her in a shed, and in the night they saw a light in the shed like burning candles, and a strong fra-grance wafted from the shed. Then, having laid her in an oak coffin, they sent her to the ter-ritory of Murom and buried her four versts from the village of Lazarev at the Church of St. Lazarus, next to her husband on the January 10, 1604.

[After many years her coffin was uncovered and her body had not decomposed and the coffin was full of myrrh.] Many heard about this and came and anointed themselves with the myrrh and were cured of various illnesses. When all the myrrh had been given out, a dust like sand began to come forth near the coffin, and to this day people who suffer from various illnesses come and rub themselves with this sand and find relief. And we would not dare to write about this if there were no witnesses to prove it.

Law on the "Forbidden Years"

The first "forbidden year" was declared in 1581, and they became a standard practice during the Time of Troubles. This is one such declaration.

- How does this represent a change in the status of peasants from earlier times?
- What does it reveal about the nature of Muscovite government?
- What does it reveal about peasant labor, society, and gender roles?

9 March 1607

Any peasants who for 15 years before this date were recorded in the registers of the year [1592-3] are to be under those under whom they were registered; but if those peasants have departed to anyone else and in that matter there is a petition against those peasants, or against those who hold them, and those cases are not completed, or if any shall petition up to the 1st September this year [1607-8], those peasants are to be given up according to those registers with their wives and children and all their property to those under whom they were registered, up to Christmas of the year [1607-8] without dwelling payment; and if anyone shall not give them up by that date, then he shall be charged for acceptance and the dwelling payment in accordance with this statute; and if there was no petition for any peasants to date, and shall be none by 1st September, then those shall not be given up, but they shall be recorded in the registers to those under whom they now live and henceforth for fifteen years there shall be no cases relating to peasants and peasants shall not be exported [nor returned].

But if there be any who, henceforth, leaving a [lord], transfer to anyone else at all, and he to whom he comes accepts him contrary to this our statute to the Assembly, the peasant, having been seized from him, shall be transferred with all his goods whence he had fled; and for the tenement, if that peasant had built one, [the lord] shall pay what is judged, but he shall not take the tenement; and the Tsar shall demand from him [i.e. the landowner], because he accepted the peasant contrary to the stature, 10 rubles . . .

And if a peasant shall come to anyone to hire himself for work for summer or for winter or for the whole year, but not in families, and whoever hires him for not more than a year, he is not guilty for accepting him and no dwelling payment shall be exacted; because his lord knows where he lives.

But if a woman or widow or maid flees to some else's estate and marries, that peasant who takes to wife another's woman shall be given to him to whom the woman belongs with all his property and the children born of that runaway; and if that man has children of his first wife, there is no case against them, they are not to be given back with the stepmother; but if they are small, then let them go with their father until one passes 15 years old. . . .

And in the towns the royal representatives, military commanders and justices and clerks and every sort of department people are to enquire throughout their uezd or competence through the reeves and the hundred-men and the clergy whether there are not new arrivals anywhere, and when they tell him [that there are any], he is to take them and firmly question them; whose he is, where from, when he ran away and where and for how long he lived

Source: R. E. F. Smith, *The Enserfment of the Russian Peasantry* (Cambridge: Cambridge University Press, 1968), 104–107. Reprinted with the permission of Cambridge University Press.

and whether anyone did not incite him; and if he says someone incited him and produces evidence against him, this instigation is to be punished with the marketplace punishment [beaten with the knout] and a guarantee is to be taken from him so that he takes back that runaway to his lord; and a fine of 10 rubles is to be taken from him to the treasury; and from every one of those who accepted him [i.e. the runaway] and kept him more than 7 days in the village there are to be exacted 10 rubles to the treasury per tenement and per man on his own, and 3 rubles for accepting a woman and for a maid.

But if they accept someone's villein or peasant or woman in villages or volosts of the Tsar and Grand Prince or in black volosts or in Patriarchal and prelatic and monastic villages, then for accepting [them] exaction is to be made from the volost heads [or the stewards] and the reeve who was then administering that volost and accepted the arrival; and dwelling payments for the tenements are to be had from those villages and volosts, and in towns, from all artisan quarter people in accordance with this statute.

But if any royal representative or justice or clerk and other Department person shall not enquire about, search out and question about arrivals in his uezd and does not take the money for accepting them, and they report him in this, the money is to exacted from him twofold and he is to be thrown out from the matter and henceforward he is to have no part in any affair of the Sovereign.

Description of the Crimean Tatars

In this selection, Giles Fletcher describes the Crimean Tatars.

- What does this reveal about Tatar-Russian relations?
- Has anything changed in the lifestyle of the peoples of the Black Sea steppe since the era of the Scythians? What changes do you anticipate in the future?

. . . [T]here are brought yearly to Moscow, to be exchanged for other commodities, 30 or 40 thousand Tatar horses, which they call *cones*. The keep also great herds of cattle and flocks of black sheep, rather for the skins and milk (which they carry with them in great bottles) than for the use of the flesh, though they sometimes eat of it. Some use they have of rice, figs, and other fruits. They drink milk or warm blood, and for the most part mix them both together. They use sometimes as they travel to take their horse's blood from a vein and drink it warm as it comes from his body.

Towns they plant none, nor other standing buildings, but have walking houses . . . built upon wheels like a shepherd's cottage. These they draw with them wherever they go, driving their cattle with them. And when they come to their stage or standing place, they

---

Source: Giles Fletcher, *Of the Russe Commonwealth*, 92–93.

plant their cart houses very orderly in a rank, and so make the form of streets and of a large town. And this is the manner of the emperor himself, who has no other seat of his empire but an assembly place or town of wood that moves with him wherever he goes. . . .

They begin to move their houses and cattle in the springtime from the south part of their country toward the north parts. And so driving on till they have grazed all up to the farthest part northward, they return back again towards their south country (where they continue all the winter) by ten or twelve miles a stage; in the meanwhile the grass being sprung up again to serve for their cattle as they return. . . .

Of money they have no use at all, and therefore prefer brass and steel before other metals, specially bullate, which they use for swords, knives, and other necessaries. As for gold and silver they neglect it for the purpose (as they neglect all tillage of their ground) to be more free for their wandering kind of life, and to keep their country less subject to invasions. Which gives them great advantage against all their neighbors, ever invading and never being invaded.

Figure 7-1 Sixteenth-Century Rebellion

This miniature, depicting an uprising in Muscovy, comes from the *Life of Antonii Siiskii* (d. 1557).

- What does this suggest about social relations in Muscovite Russia?
- Why might the saint be depicted as encouraging the uprising?

Source. A. V. Artsikhovskii., *Drevnerusskie miniatiury kak istoricheskii istochnik* (Moscow: MGU, 1944). Figure 55.

Figure 7-2 A Street in Sixteenth-Century Moscow

This woodcut shows a lady's carriage.

- What does this reveal about gender relations in Muscovite Russia?
- What does it reveal about Moscow?

Source: Sixteenth-century woodcut.

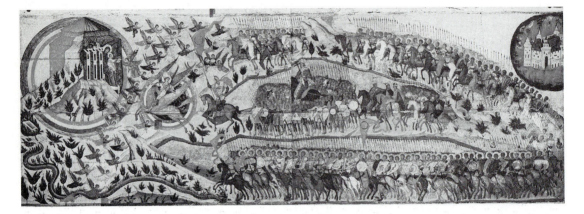

Figure 7-3 "The Church Militant"

This icon represents Ivan IV's conquest of Kazan. In the upper left, the Archangel Michael and Ivan IV lead the victorious Russian army back toward the Moscow (portrayed as the City of Heaven) while in the lower right Kazan (portrayed as Sodom) is in flames. Just below Ivan IV is Vladimir Monomakh, leading the main body of the army.
- What does this reveal about the political and religious ideology of the Musovite Tsar?
- About the connection between church and state? The relation of Moscow to Kiev Rus?
- What does this imply regarding Moscow's conception of its eastern neighbors?

Source: Tretiakov Gallery, Moscow.

Figure 7-4 Agriculture in Muscovy

This miniature comes from the *Life of St. Nicholas of Syria* written in the sixteenth century.
- What are the differences between this depiction and previous portrayals of Russian agriculture?
- What gender roles might be inferred from this? (What do women do? Not do?)
- What would have been the relationship of the agricultural workers to the monastery?

Source: Life of St. Nicholas of Syria. Facsimile edition, St Petersburg, 1882.

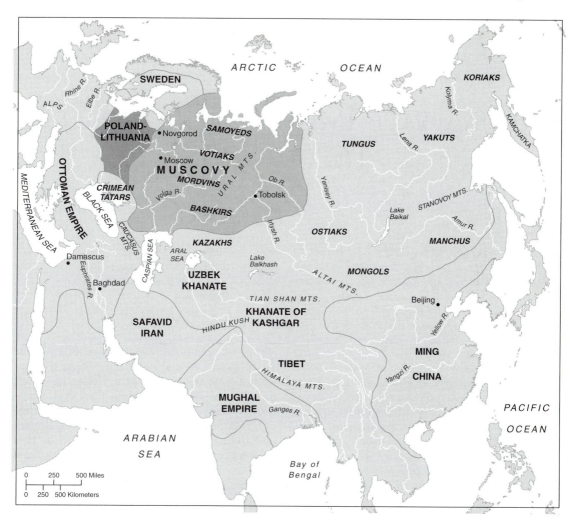

Figure 7-5 Eurasia, ca. 1600.
This map shows the multi-national nature of Muscovy and the neighboring peoples in the east who would soon be subject to Muscovite expansion. In the west, following the Union of Liulin of 1569, a united Poland and Lithuania presented an even more formidable threat.

_____ FOR FURTHER READING _____

(In addition to the books by Blum, Bushkovitch, Crummy, Khodarkovsky, Levin, Martin, Ostrowski, Platonov, Skrynnikov, and Thyrêt from the previous chapter.)

Dunning, Chester S. L. *Russia's First Civil War: The Time of Troubles and the Founding of the Romanov Dynasty.* University Park, PA: Pennsylvania State University Press, 2001.

Perrie, Maureen. *Pretenders and Popular Monarchism in Early Modern Russia: The False Tsars of the Time of Troubles.* Cambridge: Cambridge University Press, 1995.

CHAPTER EIGHT

MUSCOVITE IMPERIAL EXPANSION, 1620–1700

The crisis faced by Russia during the Time of Troubles was not lower-class rebellion in itself. That rebels were led by supposed heirs of Ivan IV shows that ordinary people did not consciously reject the political system. They behaved in ways typical of societies in which manual laborers have no social prestige or political role: They fled when they could, endured what they had to, and made suicidal attacks on their "betters" when life became unlivable. The real crisis for the Russian state was the conflict within the boiar elite. Rather than suppress lower-class rebellion, they used it for their own purposes, and it was this that had led to anarchy. It was only when the noble classes presented a united front that the Time of Troubles came to an end.

This lesson was taken to heart, and the landed elite willingly allowed the Romanovs to continue where Ivan IV had left off (before his descent into madness), building a centralized autocratic state and a regimented, professional army. Boiars acquiesced in this process because they were given the most prestigious positions in the administration and officer corps, and the pomeshchiks acquiesced because they were confirmed as a hereditary noble class and were given control over the tenants of their lands. Russian society continued to experience social turmoil in the form of popular rebellion, Cossack uprisings, and violent rejection of Church reforms. However, no new Time of Troubles erupted; in the later seventeenth century the privileged classes were conservative supporters of the state.

EURASIAN CONTEXT

Taking advantage of a rebellion against the Ming emperor in 1644, the Manchus, a formerly nomadic people on China's northeastern border, invaded and installed themselves as a new dynasty, the Qing (1644–1911). The Manchus had already established a centralized state on

---

Turn to page 168 for a map showing key geographic locations and features for this time period.

the Chinese model; their officials spoke Chinese and were well-grounded in the Confucian tradition, and they were generally accepted by the gentry class. The emperor Kanxi (1661–1722) expanded the empire by conquering Mongolia, Tibet, and Xinjiang, expanding westward almost as far as the Caspian Sea.

After Shah Abbas I of Iran died in 1629, he was succeeded by a series of incompetent and corrupt rulers. The extravagance of the court and the expense of a large standing army led to excessive taxation; trade declined, internal rivalries weakened the army, and at the end of the century the Shah's court was rife with greed, corruption, and incompetence. By 1700, the Safavid dynasty was on the verge of collapse.

The decline of the Ottoman Empire was halted in the middle of the seventeenth century by a series of prime ministers who made taxation more equitable, suppressed rebellions, forced peasants to return to the land, encouraged trade, and prosecuted corrupt officials. These conservative policies restored the regime and allowed the government to turn the tide against Iran and to reconquer Mesopotamia in 1638. These reforms, however, did not change the Ottoman Empire's military decline vis-a-vis Europe. After a series of defeats by the combined armies of Austria, Hungary, and Poland, the Ottoman Empire signed the Treaty of Karlowitz (1699) and withdrew entirely from Hungary and Galicia. The long withdrawal of Turkey from the Balkan Peninsula had begun.

The Safavid dynasty lost a large part of Armenia when the Ottoman Empire seized Mesopotamia, but Iran managed to retain the region around Yerevan; only in the mountains of Karabakh did a few Armenian princes preserve their independence. In the Caucasus, Safavid Shahs ended deportations of Georgians and ruled Georgia more leniently, and under their influence, Muslims of the Caucasus adopted the Shi'a tradition.

In the Thirty-Years War (1618–1848) in Europe, the Holy Roman Empire attempted to force the Protestant German states and Bohemia to reconvert to Catholicism, but Protestant forces prevailed. The war brought the age of religious wars to an end, and the Peace of Westphalia (1648) established the modern secular nation-state system. However, the war devastated Central Europe; crops were ruined, commerce was interrupted, and up to one-third of the population died from war, disease, or starvation. In the west, many farmers lost their land, while in the east they were bound to the land as serfs.

France, Sweden, and Prussia gained from the war. France, though Catholic, had joined the Protestant side for strategic reasons, and it replaced Spain as the dominant power in western Europe. Louis XIV (1643–1715) made himself the object of awe, envy, and emulation by monarchs across Europe. Modeling himself on the emperors of Rome, Louis shared power with no one and claimed to embody the state. He subordinated the aristocracy, enhanced the bureaucracy, and created a large and powerful army. Louis undertook magnificent building projects, most notably the palace at Versailles, and fostered a glittering life at his court. His aggressive wars of expansion, however, prompted a European-wide alliance against him, and his reign ended in failure and bankruptcy.

In Prussia, which emerged from the Thirty Years' War as the preeminent northern German state, Frederick William (1640–1688) established himself as an absolute monarch. In return for freedom from taxation and full control over the enserfed peasantry, the landed aristocracy allowed him the power to govern without interference. Frederick William built a large and efficient army and an obedient bureaucracy. His son, Frederick I (1688–1713) imitated Louis XIV's court and secured international recognition as King.

In Sweden royal absolutism triumphed without the need for bargains to be made between king and aristocracy, since the landed elite, who staffed the administration and led the army, actively supported their King's desire to advance Swedish influence. Gustaf II Adolf (1611–1632) created a standing army of conscripted peasant infantry led by a professional officer corps and supplied with the best muskets and cannon in Europe. His administration became a model of professionalism and efficiency. Gustaf fought successfully against Russia, Poland, Denmark, and Austria and made Sweden the hegemonic power in Northern Europe. Defending and expanding Gustaf's territorial gains became the chief occupation of his successors.

England began its rise to world power status in seventeenth century. Following a civil war at midcentury, Lord Protector Oliver Cromwell (1653–1658) built up the navy, fostered capitalism, and promoted trade with Asia and colonization of the New World. In 1688, the Protestant William III of Orange (King of Holland) was invited to replace Catholic James II, and he set England on a course of struggle with France for hegemony over the world's oceans. The English Parliament asserted its sovereignty as the representative of an aristocratic oligarchy that was united in its desire to promote their nation's commercial and naval power.

The Thirty Years' War meant the end of the Holy Roman Empire as a force in European international politics. Emperor, Leopold I (1658–1705), who was hereditary king of Austria, chose to build Austria into a centralized absolutist state on the model of France. Leopold retained control of Bohemia and joined in the wars against Louis XIV. He also organized the alliance that drove the Turks out of Hungary, and established himself as the king of Hungary after it was liberated.

In Polish history, the second half of the seventeenth century is known as "the ruin." Poland's troubles began with a rebellion by the Zaporozhian Cossacks (who lived on the Dnieper River south of Kiev). Poland, which regularly hired the Zaporozhian host as mercenaries, had registered the officer class as a privileged elite. When these registered Cossacks asked to be admitted as equal members of the szlachta in 1632, they were refused, and their subsequent rebellion was suppressed by the Polish Army in 1638. Ten years later, however, Bohdan Khmelnytskyi became the Cossacks' leader, and he attempted to separate Ukraine from Poland and make himself king. He appealed to the East Slavic population of Kiev, promising to liberate them from Polish Catholic rule and to restore the Orthodox Church. Although he became a hero to the people of Kiev, his forces were defeated by Poland in 1651, and he was forced to turn to Russia for aid. In 1654 Khmelnytskyi pledged allegiance to the Russian Tsar and the next year Russia defeated a Polish army sent against him.

To forestall a Russian invasion of Poland, Charles X of Sweden himself invaded, with stunning success: within weeks the Polish government surrendered and was forced to accept Swedish occupation. Russia took the opportunity to seize Lithuania. The Polish people—szlachta and peasantry alike—fought a grueling guerrilla war of resistance for the next five years, during which time King John, who had fled into exile, enlisted the support of Austria, Denmark, and Prussia. In 1660, the Swedes were finally driven out, and John was able to turn his attention to the task of driving Russian forces from Lithuania. Seven years later, Russia agreed to withdraw from Lithuania proper, but Ukraine was divided in two. Kiev and the east bank of the Dnieper River was annexed by Russia while Poland retained the west bank.

Despite victory, Poland never recovered its former greatness. The war was followed by famine and epidemics and the population fell from eleven to seven million. The government was bankrupted, and attempts to strengthen and centralize the administration of the Polish state failed. Not only was the power of the King limited, the sovereignty of the Szejm was curtailed as well. In 1652, the principle of *liberum veto* (free veto) was adopted. This meant that a single negative vote by a member of the Sejm could veto a law or even disband the session of the Szejm and declare all its previous decisions null and void. The szlachta clung to the liberum veto as a protection against the tyranny of the majority, but its real outcome was fragmentation and weakness.

In the early seventeenth century, the steppes of Inner Eurasia were thrown into turmoil when a new confederation of nomads invaded from the east. The Kalmyks were a Mongol people who had converted to Tibetan Buddhism, and who were perceived as mortal enemies by the Muslim Turk nomads of Inner Eurasia. In 1622, the Kalmyks first began to cross the Yaik (now Ural) River, and by the 1630s, they were in full control of the Caspian Steppe. As a result of their invasion, the Nogai Horde was broken up into separate bands that offered their services to the Crimean Tatars, the Kalmyks, Russia, and various nomadic peoples of the north Caucasus.

POLITICAL DEVELOPMENTS AND FOREIGN AFFAIRS

By 1620, the Russian government, under Tsar Michael (1613–1645) and his father, Filaret, Patriarch of the Orthodox Church, had driven out all foreign forces and suppressed rebellion throughout the land. A major concern of the new regime was to restore its finances, which it did through several emergency tax surcharges and by a steady and general increase in taxes. The bureaucracy was also expanded in ways that reveal the concerns of Russia's rulers. New prikazes were created to supervise the cavalry and the infantry, to organize and pay Cossack regiments, to recruit foreign soldiers, to collect taxes, to mint money, to suppress social unrest, to review petitions, and to govern Siberia. In 1632, Michael brought in Dutch experts to build a modern weapons factory in Tula.

Despite the attention he devoted to developing a professional army, Michael was concerned primarily with defense. The only major war he initiated was an attempt in 1732 to take Smolensk back from Poland. Michael failed in his territorial goal, but he did force the Polish king Wladislaw IV (1632–1648) gave up his claim to the Russian throne. The greatest military problem faced by Muscovy was pressure from nomads on the southern steppe. The Kalmyks did not prey only on their fellow nomads, they also burned and looted towns in Siberia and Russia. Raids by bands of Crimean Tatars also continued. Michael Khodarkovsky has estimated that in the first half of the seventeenth century between 150,000 and 200,000 Russians were captured, to be either ransomed or sold as slaves in the east.[1]

Michael pursued a two-prong strategy against the nomads. In 1635, he began a new line of fortifications running from Tambov in the west to Samara in the east, limiting large scale movement of nomads and encouraging Russian peasants to settle the land. Michael also armed the Don Cossacks and authorized them to raid the nomads. The Cossacks, however, preferred to raid the Ottoman trade caravans or Crimean Tatar settlements. In 1637 Don Cossacks seized the Turkish fortress at Azov, and, in 1641, realizing that they could not defend it without help, offered it to Russia. Unwilling to fight both Ottoman Turks and Crimean Tatars, Michael declined the offer, and the Cossacks withdrew.

Michael died in 1645 and was succeeded by his son Aleksei (1645–1676). Aleksei was faced by continual social unrest throughout his reign. In 1648, he had to mollify a Moscow mob which rioted against high taxes, killing an official and burning boiar houses. In 1662, Russian cities were swept by "Copper Riots" in which poor people protested the devaluation of copper currency and the increase of taxes on salt (a government monopoly). Aleksei brutally suppressed the rebels; hundreds of rioters were tortured and killed, and hundreds more were exiled to Siberia. Only five years later, class war burst out again, when peasants flocked to the support of a rebellious Cossack, Stenka Razin. Razin began as a pirate leader on the Caspian sea, but by 1669, he had a forces large enough to seize Astrakhan and Tsaritisyn on the Volga River. Razin called on peasants to rise against their landlords, and he announced his intention of marching on Moscow and killing boiars, nobles, and great landowners. Aleksei mounted a major military offensive, and in 1671, the Cossack army was defeated, Razin was captured, and he and thousands of his supporters were executed.

Aleksei worked at building the machinery of autocracy. He reduced the collective power of the boiars by expanding size of the boiar duma and by promoting lesser-ranking nobles to boiar status. He enhanced the power of the Tsar by creating a more obedient bureaucracy; he created new prikazes, enlarged prikaz staffs, and made procedures in all branches of government more regular and impersonal. This did not mean that the government became any less aristocratic; Aleksei based his power on a close alliance with the landed elite. The boiar duma had little influence on policy, but boiars still enjoyed a monopoly on the highest positions in the state and army. Aleksei's closest advisers were boiars, and boiars headed the prikazes.

Aleksei also added a new (lower) stratum to the ruling class by granting hereditary nobility to the pomeshchiks. The pomeshchiks had been clamoring for this status as a result of Michael's and Aleksei's military reforms which had created a modern, professional cavalry paid salaries and not supported with grants of land. Pomeshchiks feared being put into these units and losing their land and peasant labor which was a mark of noble status. Aleksei gave the what they wanted in the Ulozhenie (law code) of 1649. The Ulozhenie incarnated Aleksei's policy of alliance with the landed elite to rule the landless. It made all social estates (noble, merchant, peasant, etc.) hereditary, and it codified serfdom as the law of the land. Peasants permanently lost the right to move (without permission) from the estate on which they were born, and no statute of limitations was set on the return of runaway serfs. Landless artisans and workers in cities and towns were also forbidden to move without permission. In addition, the Ulozhenie also provided harsh penalties for those who threatened the political, religious, or social order of Muscovy.

Aleksei followed a more aggressive foreign policy than his father. He took advantage of Bohdan Khmelnytskyi's rebellion against Poland to annex part of the Ukraine. In 1653 when Khmelnytskyi had asked for Russia's protection, a specially summoned Zemskii Sobor recommended support for the rebellious Cossack leader. In 1654, in the Union of Pereyaslavl, Khmelnytskyi swore allegiance to Russia, expecting the Tsar to reciprocate with a promise to respect the rights and liberties of the Cossacks. This did not occur, for Aleksei treated Ukraine and the Cossacks as subjects to whom he owed no obligations. Aleksei considered himself to be regaining old Rus lands, of which he was the rightful heir, while many Ukrainians looked on him as an imperialist invader.

Incorporating Ukraine into Russia meant conflict with Poland, and after a thirteen-year war, Russia had achieved at least its minimum goals. According to the terms of the 1667 Treaty of Andrusovo, Poland surrendered all Ukraine east of the Dnieper River, the city of Kiev, and the territory that Poland had seized during the Time of Troubles, including the city of Smolensk. The west bank of the Dnieper remained a part of Poland.

Concurrent with his successes in the west, Aleksei continued Russian expansion eastward. Michael had built a fort at Yakutsk on the Lena River in 1632, and in 1639, Russian explorers first reached the Pacific Ocean. Under Aleksei, Tobolsk became the center of administration for Siberia. Okhotsk, on the Pacific Ocean, was founded in 1649, and on the border of China, Nerchinsk was founded in 1659 and Albazin in 1665.

In Aleksei's reign, Tobolsk became the center of administration for Siberia. As Russia had expanded across Siberia, it signed treaties with the native hunter-gatherers in the forests in which the natives promised to pay "tribute" in the form of furs and in exchange the Russian Tsar paid an annual stipend to his "tributaries" and provided them with metal tools, woolen cloth, and other manufactured products. From the point of view of Russia, the natives had been subordinate; to the natives, it probably looked more like trade. The forests did not support a large population; in the seventeenth century there were probably about 100,000 Russians and 200,000 natives in all Siberia.

On the southern steppe, Aleksei continued to build the line of fortifications that Michael had begun to control the southern nomads. After he accepted Ukraine as a protectorate, Aleksei's relations with the Khanate of Crimea deteriorated, and he decided to ally with the Kalmyks, accept their presence on the Caspian steppe, and use them as a counterweight to the Crimean Tatars. In 1655, the Kalmyks signed a treaty with Russia, but each side saw it differently. Aleksei thought the Kalmyks had become a subordinate whose military forces were at his disposal, while the Kalmyks thought of themselves as an equal ally. This alliance with the Kalmyks caused unrest among the Bashkirs, whose lands were encroached upon by Kalmyk herders. As a result, there was a Bashkir uprising against Moscow in 1662 to 1664.

Aleksei died in 1676 and was succeeded by his eldest son, Fyodor III (1676–1682), a young man (he was only fourteen when he acceded to the throne) whose health was poor and who allowed the government to be run by relatives and courtiers. The most notable reform of Fyodor's reign was the abolition of mestnichestvo in 1682, which further enhanced the power of the Tsar; henceforth, family connections were less important than the favor of the Tsar in determining social prestige. In foreign affairs, the first direct military confrontation between Russia and the Ottoman Empire began in 1677 when Turkey tried to annex Ukraine and laid seige to Kiev. The Russian army arrived before it fell, and in the end Ottoman forces withdrew. To secure peace, however, Fyodor, was forced to give up claims to the southern Dnieper and to promise to pay annual tribute to the Crimean Khan. (The Khan, an heir of Genghis Khan, continued to insist that he was still Moscow's overlord.)

By his first wife, Maria Miloslavskaia, Aleksei had had two sons, Fyodor and Ivan, and four daughters, one named Sofia. By his second wife, Natalia Naryshkina, Aleksei had another son named Peter. When Fyodor died in 1682, the Naryshkins, with the support of the Patriarch Ioakim, managed to bypass Ivan and have his younger half-brother, Peter, declared Tsar. The Milosolavskiis, however, led by Sofia and supported by the streltsy, struck back. They seized the Kremlin, killed leading members of the Naryshkin family, and installed Sofia as regent with Ivan and Peter as co-Tsars.

In the west, Sofia (1682–1689) integrated Ukraine with Russia economically by eliminating customs duties and restrictions on trade between them. She was responsible for signing a permanent peace treaty with Poland that recognized the terms of the treaty of Andrusovo of 1667. She launched two military campaigns against the Crimean Tatars, but they both failed.

In the east, she resolved a border dispute with China. In the middle of the century, Russians had begun to move into the Amur River valley to trade with the native people of the region. Aleksei and Fyodor had built forts and trading posts on the Amur river. China considered this territory to be under its dominion, and demanded that the Russians withdraw to Lake Baikal. Protracted negotiations ensued. Sofia resolved the question in 1689 by signing the Treaty of Nerchinsk in which Russia agreed to dismantle its forts on the Amur while China accepted the Amur River as the border between the two countries and allowed Russian merchants to carry on trade in the region.

While Sofia was regent, Ivan V lived under her supervision at the court, while Peter I lived with his mother in the village of Preobrazhenskoe three miles from Moscow. Ivan V played the role of Tsar in the traditional court and church rituals, while Peter was left to his own devices. Peter's principal passion was for the military, and he was allowed to create two "play" regiments, the Preobrazhenskii and Semenovskii. Though commanded by a child, they were composed of real adult soldiers. In 1689, Peter married, and the issue of Sofia's regency came to a head. The Miloslavskii and Naryshkin clans moved against one another, and this time the streltsy, apparently unhappy with Sofia's military failures, supported Natalia Naryshkina and her son Peter. Sofia was required to leave public life and live in a monastery, while Ivan continued to fulfill the court duties of Tsar until his death in 1696.

Natalia was Russia's effective ruler until she died in 1694. Peter's only notable activity, aside from continued attention to his regiments, was to lead fellow notables in what he called the "Most Drunken Synod of Fools and Jesters," a parody of church and court ceremony at which drunkenness was a requirement. Peter was a devout Orthodox believer and a regular churchgoer, and he considered his "Drunken Synod" to be harmless fun. His sense of humor, however, was very offensive to some Russians.

After he took on the full duties of Tsar in 1694, Peter devoted all his energies to the military. He wanted Russia to become a naval power, so he began the construction of a fleet and took action to gain ports on the Black and Baltic Seas. He used the Preobrazhenskii and Semenovskii guards regiments to seize the port of Azov from the Crimean Tatars in 1696. To gain a port on the Baltic, Peter began a major reorganization and enlargement of the army in preparation for war with Sweden.

Peter traveled to Western Europe in 1697 with two goals in mind: to organize a Christian crusade against the Ottoman Empire and to bring the latest European navigation and shipbuilding knowledge back to Russia. In 1698, his visit was cut short when Peter received word that the Moscow streltsy had rebelled in favor of Sofia. The coup failed, and Peter personally took charge of the punishment of the conspirators, which involved gruesome torture ending in execution. The streltsy were disbanded. Sofia had not instigated the plot, but she would have been its beneficiary; she was forced to become a nun and was confined in a convent once again.

Back in Russia, Peter now began to put into effect his plan to gain territory on the Baltic coast. In 1699 he joined in an alliance with Denmark and Poland against Sweden. The war began disastrously. Even before Russia began to fight, Charles XII of Sweden defeated Denmark and forced it to withdraw from the alliance. Then, in October 1700 when Peter led an army of 35,000 soldiers to lay siege to the fortress at Narva, Charles XII counter-attacked. Though only one quarter the size of Russian forces, the Swedish army won a devastating victory. Charles then led his army south to deal with Poland.

RELIGION AND CULTURE

The rise of secular society in western Europe is most often associated with the Renaissance, the revival of the humanism and rationalism of the classical world, but it was also a product of the Reformation. Protestants denied that monks and nuns were uniquely holy (i.e., that it was better to withdraw from the world than participate in it), they emphasized the need of individuals to read and reason about the Bible, and they transformed organized worship by denying the miracle of the sacrament of holy communion and by emphasizing the sermon, a reasoned application of the scriptures to the problems of everyday life.

Russia experienced neither Renaissance nor Reformation, but Russian religious culture had been independently moving in the direction of secularism. Over time, monks ceased to represent the highest form of spirituality, and legends of miracles became less important that stories of good deeds as a qualification for saintliness. These trends continued to accelerate in the seventeenth century.

An informal group of churchmen known as the Zealots of Piety coalesced in the 1640s. They hoped to promote morality among the people by raising the moral stature of the parish clergy and by suppressing pagan festivals and public drunkenness. They were lead by Stefan Vonifatev, priest of the Annunciation Cathedral, the church attended by the royal family, and their ideas were influential upon the Tsar. Aleksei outlawed trade on Sundays and religious holidays and forbade pagan practices at Christmas, Easter, and midsummer. Under the influence of the Zealots of Piety, the sermon became a key part of Russian church services.

The annexation of Kiev reinforced these secularizing trends. The creation of the Uniate Church in 1596 had caused a powerful Orthodox revival as churchmen criticized Uniate theology. Yet even as they argued over points of doctrine, Orthodox writers were influenced by Catholic practices (which were, themselves, a reaction to the Protestant Reformation). That is, they emphasized sermons and the solution of practical moral problems and deemphasized monasticism and miracles. Kiev also introduced secular learning into Russia. The Kiev Academy, modeled on the western European grammar school (which emphasize the study of Greek and Latin), had been founded in 1632.

The greatest of the sermon-writers and religious thinkers was Simeon Polotskii, a Russian who was born in Polotsk, under Polish rule, and was educated at the Kiev Academy. Polotskii was brought to Moscow by Aleksei to be court poet, to set up a school for government secretaries, and to educate the Tsar's children—daughters as well as sons. His students formed various schools in Moscow based on the model of the Kiev Academy, including the Moscow Slavic-Greek-Latin Academy in 1685. Though religious himself and never giving up the idea that faith was necessary for morality, Polotskii also defended learning and philosophy as sources of Christian morality. Paul Bushkovitch argues that he paved the way for secular rationalism in Russia.[2] Polotskii was not unique. A number of Russian boiars owned libraries with books in Latin and Western European languages.

The schism in the Russian Church also served to advance secularism. The schism had its origins in Aleksei's dream of incorporating the Balkan Peninsula and Constantinople into his empire. One empire and one church implied one common religious service. However, over the centuries since Russia had adopted the religion of the Byzantine Empire, the liturgical and ceremonial practices in the Byzantine and Russian Churches had each undergone a natural evolution; they were no longer identical. Supposing that the divergence had occurred because errors had crept into Russian texts, Aleksei asked the Metropolitan of Kiev to send scholars to Moscow to bring the Russian texts into conformity with the Greek originals. In fact, however, the scholars did not attempt to find the original texts; they simply translated the current Greek liturgy into Russian.

The project was aggressively advanced by Patriarch Nikon, appointed by Aleksei in 1652. Nikon gave his full support to the translation project, and he also changed ceremonial practices to match Greek usage. He directed that the sign of the cross should be made with three fingers instead of two and required that "hallelujah" be said three times instead of twice. He changed "our father" to "our God" in the Lord's prayer and the spelling of Jesus from Isus to Iisus in all sacred writings. Though trivial to modern sensibility, these changes upset many Russian churchmen, of whom the Archpriest Avvakum is the most famous. They mistrusted the translation project from the outset because they thought that the Kiev Church had been tainted by Polish Catholicism and the Greek Church corrupted by apostasy. They also believed that such things as the sign of the cross or the spelling of Jesus' name had sacramental power and that the changes in them would bring damnation on all who accepted them.

When Nikon became Patriarch he had asked for and been granted the right to use the title "Great Sovereign," which the Patriarch Filaret had used. Therefore, in 1654, when Aleksei led his army against Poland, Nikon felt that he was left with authority to govern in the name of the Tsar. He interfered in the government, and he used his power to persecute those who opposed his liturgical and ceremonial reforms. He excommunicated them, arrested them, and brutalized them.

When Aleksei returned from the war, he was alarmed at Nikon's intransigence and cruelty and attempted to rein him in. Nikon responded by retiring to the Voskresenskii Monastery, apparently hoping that the Tsar would beg him to return. Instead, Aleksei requested that Nikon resign, which Nikon refused to do. After a stand-off lasting eight years,

Aleksei summoned a church council headed by the Patriarchs of Antioch and Alexandria. The council met in 1666 to 1667 and resolved the Church's two main controversies: Nikon was removed from office, and the liturgical reforms were approved.

Aleksei, a far more conciliatory man than Nikon, gave the adherents of the old rituals every opportunity to compromise. He told them that they could use the old books and old practices as long as they did not denounce the new ones. The Old Ritualists, also know as Old Believers, refused. They were therefore excommunicated and prosecuted as heretics. In 1682, Avvakum was burned at the stake.

Resistance to the new forms of worship was widespread and troops were used to put down rebellions. Resistance also took the form of martyrdom; perhaps as many as twenty-thousand people killed themselves, gathering inside churches, setting them on fire, and dying in the flames. Georg Michels has argued that these protests were not, in fact, about change in liturgy but were a "war against the church" by monasteries and communities who resisted the centralization and autocratic policies of the Church hierarchy. Whatever the cause, Old Ritualist communities have continued in Russia until the present day. (Their condemnation as heretics was rescinded in 1971.) The schism furthered secularization of the Church by driving out its most uncompromising and least secular supporters, and Nikon's confrontation with the Aleksei revealed the declining power of the patriarch.

Roles and Status of Women

The lives of women changed very little over the course of the seventeenth century. As always, women in the family of the Tsar were able to exercise considerable influence. Michael and Aleksei required oaths of obedience not just to themselves but to the entire royal family. Maria Miloslavskaia, Aleksei's first wife, was known for her generosity toward the poor, and the fact that Old Believers appealed to her during the schism suggest that they considered her to be influential as well as devout. Isolde Thyrêt uses the case of Sofia's regency to argue that the terem could provide women both independence and power. Sofia had received an excellent education while living in the terem, and she used the rituals and myths of the terem to assert her authority. She oversaw charitable activities, commissioned religious buildings and art, and presented herself as a champion of orthodoxy. It was a woman, Natalia Naryshkina, mother of Peter I, who organized the coup against Sofia, and Natalia was effectively the ruler of Russia until her death in 1694.

As far as ordinary women were concerned, the Ulozhenie confirmed their subordinate legal status. Women who killed their husbands were to be buried alive, while the law provided no penalty for a man who killed his wife. The Ulozhenie did not permit women to testify against their husbands. It did recognize crimes against a woman's honor, such as rape, insult, or slander, but they were treated as crimes against her family. Women's honor was respected only because it had monetary value to men, and it was the father or husband who received the fine for offenses against it. Women could inherit neither a votchina nor a pomestie, on the grounds that the land was necessary to support a male servitor of the Tsar. On the other hand, a law of 1676 gave women full rights to buy and sell other forms of land without seeking the approval of their husbands.

Economic and Social Trends

The consolidation and centralization of the autocracy did nothing to diminish the wealth and only marginally affected the social prestige of the boiars. The end of mestnichestvo meant that family background was less important than service to the Tsar in determining social rank, but boiars had always served the Tsar, and they continued to be given the highest positions in the government and the military. Of Russia's total population of approximately 12,000,000 in 1700 there were no more than 1,000 adult males of boiar rank.

The pomeshchiks gained hereditary nobility in the Ulozhenie of 1649, and by the end of the century they come even closer to outright possession of their estates. Pomeshchiks were able to bequeath or sell a pomestie like any other piece of property; tsars began to sell land as votchina and to allow some servitors to convert their pomestie to a votchina. Tsars also continued to give land to servitors, 1.3 million acres between 1682 and 1711 alone. In 1700, there were probably around 15,000 pomeshchiks.

Over the course of the seventeenth century, Russia experienced a military transformation similar to the one that had been going on in Western Europe since the end of the Middle Ages. In feudal Europe, as in Muscovy, war had been the occupation of the landed nobility who trained themselves, provided their own equipment, and were rather haphazardly organized. With the development of reliable and effective muskets and cannon, a new kind of army emerged. It was composed of commoners who were paid salaries, supplied with weapons, and trained by professional officers. The new-style army was highly organized and bureaucratized.

Russia experienced this revolution at it most intense in the middle of the seventeenth century. In the 1630s, there were approximately 34,500 soldiers but by the 1680s this had grown to more than 200,000, two-thirds of them carrying firearms and serving in Western-style units. Unlike western Europe, however, Russia obtained its infantry by conscription rather than hiring mercenaries. The pomeshchik cavalry virtually disappeared and traditional Cossack regiments were broken up. Both pomeshchiks and Cossacks were assigned to the new-style cavalry units. By the end of the century, the streltsy had become obsolete and were used mainly as a militia to maintain domestic law and order.

The Russian economy expanded and diversified in the seventeenth century. Contact with western Europe increased. The Nemetskaia Sloboda ("German" or foreign quarter) had been destroyed in the Time of Troubles, but Aleksei reestablished it in 1652 to accommodate the growing numbers of European merchants and artisans in Moscow. In addition to the usual luxury goods, Russia imported increasing amounts of military equipment and everyday supplies, such as dyes, paper, pins and needles, and sugar. And in addition to the usual exports of furs, pitch, cordage, and masts, Russia exported increasing amounts of grain. Iron, salt, and grain were major factors in internal trade, and a native armaments industry had been established in Tula by 1630. Moscow was by far the largest city in Russia with more than 27,000 households. Although there were probably about 250 towns in Russia, only fifteen contained more than 500 households, the largest being Pskov, Novgorod, Kazan, Astrakhan, and Archangel. The major trade routes were the Volga, the Dnieper, and the Northern Dvina Rivers. Because Sweden controlled the Baltic coast, Russia's main port for trade with Europe was Archangel.

Social stratification in Russia's urban population was formalized in the seventeenth century. The wealthiest merchants were known as *gosti,* and they were exempted from taxes and fees and from oversight by the town *voevoda* (sheriff). They were permitted to travel abroad, and they were used by the Tsar to supervise trade and to collect customs duty and sales taxes. The remainder of the urban, tax-paying community was known as the *posad,* and it was divided into three categories based on wealth and status: The highest included the largest merchants and bankers, the second was made up of smaller merchants and artisans, and the third was made up of unskilled labor. All the taxpaying population was forbidden to move without permission. There were probably around 200,000 townspeople in Russia in 1700.

In the seventeenth century, perhaps as much as 10 percent of the population were slaves, most of them kabala slaves. One of the attractions to becoming a slave was that slaves paid no taxes, and this gave rise to a new form of "free slavery." In this relationship the "slave" would work for no wages other than the food and shelter usually given a slave but was free to leave the master at any time. Because of its ever-increasing need for income, the government began to transform slaves into serfs. It took the first step in 1680 when all slaves who lived in their own households had to pay taxes just like peasants. Slaves came under the protection of the law in 1669 when intentional murder of a slave became a capital offense.

Peasants continued to make up about 90 percent of the population. The Ulozhenie of 1649 completed their enserfment, and whereas previous limitation on movement had only applied to the head of the household, the Ulozhenie bound all family members to the land. Peasants lost property rights, and all their possessions were considered to belong to the landlord. They were put under the judicial authority of the lord, they could be moved from one estate to another, and they could be converted into domestic servants. Peasants living on state land lost their freedom as well; the mir was made collectively responsible for tax payments, and no family could leave unless it found another to take its place.

In the seventeenth century, taxation based on the ability to pay was abandoned. In 1645, a new census of all homesteads ignored the amount and quality of land possessed by a household, and instead a flat tax was levied on each homestead. This decreased the number of bobyls (cottagers), since there was no longer an incentive not to own land. It also tended to keep multigenerational families together. Married children were better off living with their parents and avoiding the tax they would be charged if they started a separate household.

CONCLUSION

The humiliating destruction of Russian forces at the Battle of Narva in 1700 did not demoralize Peter I. He later said that the defeat was good for him because it made him work even harder at mobilizing Russia's resources for war. Peter dedicated the remainder of his reign to making Russia one of the Great Powers of Europe.

NOTES

1. Michael Khodarkovsky, *Russia's Steppe Frontier: The Making of a Colonial Empire* (Bloomington, IN: Indiana University Press, 2002), 223.
2. Paul Bushkovitch, *Religion and Society in Russia: The Sixteenth and Seventeenth Centuries* (New York: Oxford University Press, 1992), 171–172.

The Ulozhenie (Law Code) of 1649

The Ulozhenie of 1649 is best known for permanently binding peasants to the land. In most respects, however, it was a restatement and reorganization of existing Muscovite law. This selection comes from Chapter 22, "Crimes Which Deserve the Death Penalty, and Crimes Which Don't."

- What does this reveal about life in Muscovy?
- What does it suggest about patriarchal anxieties? Religious attitudes?

1. If any son or daughter kills his father or mother: for patricide or matricide, punish them also with death, without the slightest mercy.

3. If a father or mother kills a son or daughter: imprison them . . . After having sat in prison for a year, they shall go to God's church, and in God's church they shall declare aloud that sin of theirs to all the people. Do not punish a father or mother with death for (killing) a son or daughter.

4. If someone, a son or a daughter, forgetting Christian law, proceeds to utter coarse speeches to a father or mother, or out of impudence strikes a father or mother . . . beat such forgetters of Christian law with the knout . . .

5. If any son or daughter plunder[s] a father's or mother's movable property by force; . . . or a son or daughter does not proceed to respect and feed a father and mother in their old age, does not proceed to support them materially in any way . . . inflict a severe punishment on such children for such deeds of theirs, beat them mercilessly with the knout, and command them to attend to their father and mother in all obedience without any back-talk. . . .

6. If any son or daughter proceed[s] to petition for a trial against a father or mother: do not grant them a trial in any matter against a father or mother. Beat them with the knout for such a petition and return them to the father and mother.

8. If someone's slave contemplates killing that person whom he serves; or, desiring to kill him, draws a weapon against him: cut off his hand . . .

9. If someone's slave kills that person whom he serves: punish him himself with death as well, without the slightest mercy.

13. Concerning insurgents who instigate civil disorder among the people, and plot evil-doings against many people by their own felonious design: punish such insurgents with death . . .

14. If a wife kills her husband, or feeds him poison, and that is established conclusively: punish her for that, bury her alive in the ground and punish her with that punishment without any mercy, even if the children of the killed [husband], or any other close relatives of his,

Source: Richard Hellie, *The Muscovite Law Code (Ulozhenie) of 1649. Part 1: Text and Translation.* Irvine, CA: Charles Schlacks, Jr., 1988, 220–223. Reprinted with permission of Charles Schlacks, Jr., Publisher.

do not desire that she be executed. Do not show her the slightest mercy, and keep her in the ground until that time when she dies.

15. If a woman is sentenced to the death penalty and she is pregnant at that time: do not punish that woman with death until she gives birth, and execute her at the time when she has given birth. Until that time, keep her in prison, or in the custody of reliable bailiffs, so that she will not depart.

24. If a Muslim by any means whatsoever, by force or by deceit, compels a Russian [to convert] to his Islamic faith, and he circumcises that Russian according to his Islamic faith; and that is established conclusively: punish that Muslim after investigation, burn him with fire without any mercy. Concerning the Russian whom he converted to Islam: send that Russian to the patriarch, or to another high ecclesiastical figure, and order him to compile a decree according to the canons of the Holy Apostles and the Holy Fathers.

25. If someone of the male gender, or the female gender, having forgotten the wrath of God and Christian law, proceeds to procure adult women and mature girls for fornication, and that is established conclusively: inflict a severe punishment on them for such a lawless and vile business, beat them with the knout.

26. If a woman proceeds to live in fornication and vileness, and in fornication begets children with someone; and she herself, or someone else at her command, destroys those children, and that is established conclusively: punish with death without any mercy such lawless women and that person who destroyed her children at her order so that others looking on will not commit such a lawless and vile deed and will refrain from fornication.

Will of Panteleimon Solovtsov, 1627

This will was written by a well-to-do Russian who lived through the Time of Troubles and died in the reign of Michael.

- How is the property divided, and what does this signify?
- What does this reveal about seventeenth-century Russian society, particularly class and gender relations?

In the name of the most holy and lifegiving, single, indivisible Trinity of the Father and Son and Holy Ghost. Lo I, God's oft-sinning and unworthy, useless slave Panteleimon Misur Solovtsov, and for my great lawlessness am I a slave to sin, most of all to fornication, do

Source: H. W. Dewey and A. M. Kleimola, Eds. *Russian Private Law: XIV–XVII Centuries.* Ann Arbor: Department of Slavic Languages and Literatures, 1973, 231–234. Reprinted with permission of the University of Michigan Department of Slavic Languages and Literatures.

write this, my will, being of sound mind and reason . . . and I entrust my sinful soul to (i.e. I designate as my executors and administrators) my wife Stefanida and my son Ondrei.

I am to give thirty *altyns* to Ostafei Kuvginov in Moscow, and my son Ondrei is to pay that money, and I am not to be left in debt, and my soul is not to suffer harm by that.

And I bless my son Ondrei with God's mercy [and give him] the icon of the Almighty Savior on the throne in power, with [triptych] side panels, on the right side the icon of the Immaculate Mother of God, on the left side the icon of St. John the Baptist, and those icons are studded with jewels . . .

And I bless my wife Stefanida [and give her] the icon of the Immaculate Mother of God of Kazan, in a folding frame (and) encased in silver, with side panels, [with] the Kazan wonder-workers Gurei and Varsonofei on the panels, encased in silver.

[He describes seven more icons, and names as recipients his daughter-in-law, his grand-daughter, his brother, his sister-in-law, the wife of one of his nephews, and his priest.] And all those [remaining] icons [I give to] my wife Stefanida and my son Ondrei and to my daughter-in-law and to my granddaughter Uliana.

And I bless my servants. [I give] to my son Ondrei the hereditary peasants Mishka, Petrusha's son, and Mishka's father, the German war prisoner, with wife and children—with daughter Nastka and with son Zakharko. And whatever slaves [are listed] in contracts of servitude in Ondrei's name, all those [go] to my son Ondrei; and whatever slaves [are listed] in contracts of servitude in my name, they are all to be given freedom. And the slave woman, Ulianka, Osip's daughter, was awarded to [my] son Ondrei by Osip Priklonskoi and Fedor Mostinin of the court of arbitration, and my will does not concern that female slave of Ondrei's, with her sons Ivashko and little Ivashko; and the slave woman Varka, Pavel's daughter, who lived with me during my life, [and] married my son Ondrei's manservant, the indentured slave Tomilko Sidorov, by her own wish, and my will does not concern that slave woman of Ondrei's, Varka. . . . .

And for the forty-day prayers [after my death] five rubles in cash shall be given to the Savior's cathedral, and shall be written in the book of daily prayers for the dead; . . . [He goes on to apportion more money among six churches, six monasteries, and five individual priests and monks.]

And with whomever of my clan I have had violent quarrels, with uncles, with brothers, and with nephews and their wives, or with any outside (i.e. non-familial) persons, they should have mercy [and] forgive me and bless my sinful soul and absolve [it] now and forevermore, and may God forgive them, my lords, and bless [them] in everything now and forevermore: I, the sinful one, am guilty before them in all matters; and likewise whomever of my slaves . . . who served me, their husbands and wives and widows and children, I shall have offended in any way by giving vent to my bile, by beating [them], whether or not they were wrong, and having [given offense] to their wives and widows by force, [and] by de-flowering the virgins, and in my sinfulness I put others to death–I sinned in all matters and am guilty before them: forgive me, the sinful one, and bless and absolve my sinful soul now and forevermore . . .

A Southern Slav's View of Russia in the 1660s

Juraj Krizanic (known in Russian as Iurii Krizhanich, 1617–1682) was a Croatian Catholic Priest who went to Moscow to promote the union of the Russian Orthodox and the Roman Catholic churches. He was exiled to Siberia from 1661 until 1676 when he was allowed to leave. While in Siberia he wrote an account of Russian society from which these excerpts are taken.

- What does this reveal about trends in Russian society?
- What does it suggest about trading patterns and Russia's relations with its neighbors?

A reply to the barking of foreigners. . . . All those who write anything about the Russians, or any other Slavic people, seem to write foolish, caustic tales rather than the truth. They exaggerate our defects, imperfections, and innate failings and make them seem ten times greater than they actually are; and where there are no evils at all, they invent them and lie. And they write shameful lying tales about us too.

You [foreigners] scorn our temperate, modest way of life, and consider this to be mere coarseness, barbarism, and slovenliness. But as for your own excesses and luxury and effeminate life, you regard this as if it all came from heaven, and as if there were nothing wrong with it. But if we indulged in your excesses and concern for the body and softness, if we sunk ourselves into feather beds, if we slept until noon, and if we ate viands with a thousand different sauces, then you would scorn us prodigiously for being immoderate and dissipated.

Another of our grievous misfortunes is that other peoples, Greeks, Italians, Germans, Tatars, involve us in [the affairs of] their countries, involve us in their quarrels, and sow disharmony in our midst. And we in our foolishness allow them to lead us astray, and we fight for others, and make foreign wars our own, and come to hate each other, and fight [each other] to the death, and brother drives out brother without any need or reason. We trust the foreigners in everything, and keep friendship and faith with them; but we are ashamed of ourselves and of our own people, and turn away from them.

That which the Greeks call xenomania, and we call the foreign craze [chuzhebesie], is a senseless love for foreign things and peoples: an unwarranted, senseless trust in foreigners. This deadly sickness (or infectious disease) has infected our entire nation. It brings untold harm and shame, from which our entire nation (on either side of the Danube) has suffered and continues to suffer as a result of the foreign craze. That is, we trust foreigners too much and make friends and intermarry with them; and we let them do what they please in our land. Truly all the evils we endure flow from that source: that we mix too much with foreigners and trust them too much.

Under the guise of commerce, the foreigners reduce us to extreme impoverishment. . . . here in Russia (except for the tsar's treasury) one cannot see or hear of any riches anywhere; instead there is wretched, empty-handed poverty everywhere. All the wealth of this realm and all the fat and sweetness of this land are carried away by foreign tradesmen or thieves, or are consumed by them as we look on passively.

Source: "Krizanic on Russia in the 1660s." In George Vernadsky, Ed., *A Source Book for Russian History from Early Times to 1917, Vol. 1: Early Times to the Late Seventeenth Century* (New Haven: Yale University Press, 1972), 251–253. (c) Yale University Press. Reprinted by permission.

Under the pretext of being experts and of serving us, [foreigners] likewise draw out all our possessions: for they work as doctors, own mines, [and] make glass, weapons, powder, and other things. And these experts will never teach our own natives, so that they may continue to reap all the profit themselves.

And what is the situation here in Russia? Foreign tradesmen, Germans, Greeks, and Bukharan, rake in all the wealth and products of this realm for themselves. Everywhere they own warehouses and act as tax farmers and engage in various trades and transactions. They travel freely throughout the land and buy our goods at the lowest prices; while they bring in to us many useless [but] expensive wares: beads, precious stones, and Venetian glass. . . . And finally, being sly, they cheat our tradesmen out of large sums of money.

At the present time this glorious realm suffers from two great and exceeding national evils or injuries, at the hands of two peoples, the Crimean [Tatars] and the Germans. Somehow they have both subjected Russia to their power and make us pay tribute and extortions, the Crimeans by force, the Germans by cunning And they have reduced our sovereign, the most powerful and glorious tsar, to such a state that he sits between them in such a fashion as if he were a collector of revenues for them. All the best that this land produces goes in part to the Crimea, in part to the German land. And the greed of these peoples knows no bounds; as a result this realm has perforce turned into a savage tyranny, and into a merciless, inhuman extortion. Which of these two evils causes greater harm to the sovereign tsar and to the entire nation, I cannot judge. But this I do avow: that the injury caused by the Germans is more shameful and disgraceful than that caused by the Crimeans.

Russian Relations with Tatars and Kalmyks

Adam Olearius was a member of two delegations sent in 1633 and 1629 by the Duke of Holstein to travel through Russia to Persia to negotiate trade relations. The following excerpt comes from his account of his journey.

- What is the relationship between Russians and Tatars and between Tatars and Kalmyks?
- How is the relation between nomad sedentary societies in Eurasia changing?
- What economic trends are evident?

The Nogai capital, Astrakhan, was taken by storm on August 1, 1554. The Tatars were expelled and the Russians occupied the city.

. . . Seen from without, on the Volga (which here is 2,260 feet wide), the city makes a fine appearance, owing to its many towers and church steeples; but within, [one sees that] it consists chiefly of wooden structures. It is well looked after by a strong garrison equipped with many (they say 500) metal guns. Among these there are several full-size and half-size siege guns, which we ourselves saw. It is said that there now are nine regiments here, each consisting of 500 soldiers. They are commanded by two voevodas, a diak, and several captains, and are ever on the alert to keep the Tatars in check. In the city, not only the Russians but also the Persians and the Indians each have their own market. Since the Bukharans [of Central Asia], the Crimean and Nogai Tatars, and the Armenians (a Christian people) also carry on a great traffic with all sorts. of goods, the city is said annually to bring His Tsarist Majesty a large sum, as much as 1200 rubles, in duties alone.

The native Tatars—partly Nogai and partly Crimean—are not permitted to settle inside the city, but only in designated places outside. They may close off their settlements with nothing more than a fence. It should be added that wherever they reside they do not construct fortified towns or villages, but live in tents. These are round in shape, commonly with a diameter of ten feet. They are woven of reeds or rushes, and resemble our chicken coops. They are covered above with felt, in the center of which is an aperture through which smoke may escape; attached there is another piece of felt to shut out the wind. When their fires of dry reeds and dried cow dung have burned out and the smoke has left, they lower the felt and shut the aperture. The whole hut is [already] surrounded by felt or reeds so that when the weather is cold the wife and children may sit around the coals and ashes and be warmed by the heat, which is preserved for a considerable time.

In the summer they have no definite place of residence but move whenever they need to find good, fresh pastures for the cattle. Then they set their dwellings on tall wagons, which they always have near them, and move on, with the wives, children, and household equipment loaded onto cows, oxen, horses, and camels. . . . In the winter they divide into several hordes . . . , or companies, go to Astrakhan, and settle closely enough that in case of need they can assist one another. For they are often attacked and plundered by their permanent enemies, the Kalmyks, who are scattered not only from here to Saratov (in this area they are called Bulgarian Tatars), but also beyond the Yaik [Ural River]. The Kalmyks make their raids when the waters have frozen, and it is easy to cross everywhere. So that the Tatars may better defend themselves against their enemies at these times the Russian arsenal lends them firearms and other military equipment, which they must return at the beginning of the summer. They are not permitted to have any other weapons.

It is true that they pay no tribute to the Grand Prince, but when he wishes to put them into the field against a foe, they must appear. They are glad enough to do so, in the hope of plunder, which they, like the Dagestan Tatars, view as the surest source of prosperity. They can swiftly collect several thousand men, and are very brave in attacking the enemy. They are permitted to have their own princes, headmen, and judges but in order to diminish the likelihood of rebellion, some of the princes' relatives, by turns, must always be kept as hostages in the Astrakhan fortress.

. . . The Tatars sustain themselves by raising cattle, fishing, and catching birds. Their horned cattle, like Polish cattle, are large and strong, and their sheep, like the Persian, have big, thick tails of pure fat, which may weigh 20 to 30 pounds. The sheep also have drooping, spaniel-like ears and crooked noses. Their horses are unimpressive looking, but strong and of great endurance. They also have camels, most of which have two humps, but some only one. . .

Their common food is fish, dried in the sun, which they use in place of bread. They bake cakes of ground rice and wheat in vegetable oil or honey. They eat camel's meat and horse meat, as well as other kinds, and drink water and milk, especially mare's milk, which they prize as a tasty and healthful drink. Thus, when the ambassadors once rode out to see their hordes and camels, we were offered some of this milk poured out of a leather bag.

The Tatars are Moslems of the Turkish [Sunni] rather than the Persian [Shiite] rite. Some of them have adopted the Russian religion and allowed themselves to be baptized.

Figure 8-1 "Christ Carrying the Cross"

This icon was painted toward the end of the seventeenth century.

- Compare this icon with earlier examples.
- What are the continuities? The innovations?
- What does this imply about Russian civilization?

Source: Tretiakov Gallery, Moscow.

Figure 8-2 Coin from the Reign of Aleksei

- Compare this with previous representations of Tsars.
- What does this reveal about Aleksei's conception of himself and of the Russian state?

Source: de Chaudoir, *Obozrenie Russkikh deneg*. Part 2, plate 8, drawing 1.

Figure 8-3 Russian Recreation in the Seventeenth Century
This engraving was used to illustrate Adam Olearius's book about his travels in Muscovy.
• What does it add to your understanding of Russia in the seventeenth century?
Source: Adam Olearius, *Voyages*, Leyden, 1718.

Figure 8-4 Kalmyks
This is an engraving of three Kalmyks made by a traveler in Central Asia in the second half of the seventeenth century.
• What does this drawing reveal about Central Asian people and society in the seventeenth century?
• What does it reveal about European ethnographers?
Source: A. Kircher, *China Monumentis Illustrata.* Amsterdam: n.p., 1667.

Figure 8-5 Russia in 1689

By the beginning of the reign of Peter the Great, Muscovite Russia had expanded to the Dnieper River in the west and the Pacific Ocean in the east. In her last year as regent, Peter's older sister, Sofia, sent a delegation to China that negotiated a common border at Nerchinsk.

_____ FOR FURTHER READING _____

(In addition to the books by Blum, Khodarkovsky, Levin, and Thyrêt from the previous chapter.)

Dukes, Paul. *The Making of Russian Absolutism, 1613–1801.* London: Longman, 1982.

Fuhrmann, Joseph T. *Tsar Alexis, His Reign and His Russia.* Gulf Breeze, FL: Academic International Press, 1981.

Hartley, Janet M. *A Social History of the Russian Empire, 1650–1825.* New York: Longman, 1999.

Hellie, Richard. *Enserfment and Military Change in Muscovy.* Chicago: University of Chicago Press, 1971.

_____. *The Economy and Material Culture of Russia, 1600–1725.* Chicago: University of Chicago Press, 1999.

Hughes, Lindsey. *Sophia, Regent of Russia, 1657–1704.* New Haven: Yale University Press, 1990.

Kivelson, Valerie A. *Autocracy in the Provinces: The Muscovite Gentry and Political Culture in the Seventeenth Century.* Stanford: Stanford University Press, 1996.

Longworth, Philip. *Alexis, Tsar of All the Russias.* New York: F. Watts, 1984.

Lupinin, Nickolas. *Religious Revolt in the XVIIth Century: The Schism of the Russian Church.* Princeton: Kingston Press, 1984.

Meyendorff, Paul. *Russia, Ritual, and Reform: The Liturgical Reforms of Nikon in the Seventeenth Century.* Crestwood, NY: St. Vladimir's Seminary Press, 1991.

Michels, Georg Bernhard. *At War with the Church: Religious Dissent in Seventeenth-century Russia.* Stanford: Stanford University Press, 1999.

Moon, David. *The Russian Peasantry, 1600–1930: The World the Peasants Made.* New York: Longman, 1999.

Stevens, Carol Belkin. *Soldiers on the Steppe: Army Reform and Social Change in Early Modern Russia.* DeKalb, IL: Northern Illinois University Press, 1995.

CHAPTER NINE

RUSSIA BECOMES A EUROPEAN "GREAT POWER," 1700–1750

Over the course of the sixteenth and seventeenth centuries, as Russia grew in size and strength, its borders moving steadily westward, it increasingly attracted the attention of western Europeans. Russia looked exotic to them: men wore long robes and grew beards, aristocratic women were kept in seclusion, and church architecture was unlike anything in the West. Not surprisingly, western observers cast Russia as the "other"—the opposite, that is, of their own culture. Russia was portrayed as uncultured and barbarous, a nation of slaves ruled by a tyrant, "Asiatic" rather than European.

Peter I wanted Europe to accept Russia as an equal, and to this end, he changed both Russia's physical appearance and its international posture. Peter forced Russians to look and act like western Europeans, no matter how offensive this was to traditional values. Male aristocrats were made to shave their faces and wear German styles; elite women were required to appear in public wearing western-style low-cut dresses, and to dance at balls with men to whom they were not related. Peter brought in western architects to make his new capital, St. Petersburg, look like a western European city, and he changed the structure of the Russian government to make it conform to western models. Peter I also forced Europeans to respect Russia by mobilizing a huge army organized on western lines and by defeating Sweden, the formerly hegemonic power in northern Europe. By the end of Peter's reign, Russia was sending permanent ambassadors to the major courts of Europe for the first time.

What was most striking about Peter I was his impatience and willfulness. The changes he ordered were so sudden and so extreme that it seems as if he delighted in the unsentimental

Turn to page 192 for a map showing key geographic locations and features for this time period.

rejection of traditional values, but Peter did not lead Russia in unprecedented directions. He was a violent catalyst who only accelerated trends that had begun long before: the enhancement of the monarch, centralization of the state bureaucracy, development of a modern army, simplification and regimentation of society, subordination of aristocracy and church to state, and secularization of Russian society and culture.

EURASIAN CONTEXT

The year 1700 can be used as a convenient point to mark the beginning of a new era in Eurasian history, an era in which the center of gravity moved from East to West. The great land empires of Eurasia still surpassed the combined countries of the European peninsula in population, wealth, standing armies, and sophistication of civilization (except in regard to military technology), but Europeans were developing institutions that would one day make it possible for them to dominate the globe politically and economically.

The period 1700 to 1750 began a new stage in the global economy. The first two hundred years of European expansion had involved trade in luxury goods and the transfer of silver from the west to Asia. As European ships grew in size and number, and trade networks expanded, mass consumption consumer goods such as cotton cloth from India and sugar and tobacco from the Americas began to dominate international trade. Across Europe there was a rise of urbanization, consumerism, and economic prosperity. This economic boom, however, had a dark side; it was based on unfree labor. Just as the rise of a consumer lifestyle among the aristocratic elite of eastern Europe was based on their unlimited power to exploit the serf population, so the consuming classes of western Europe were indirectly fed and clothed by the labor of African slaves. In the first half of the eighteenth century, about fifty thousand slaves a year were shipped to the New World where they worked on plantations producing staples for the European market.

Louis XIV of France lived until 1715, and, even though his expansive ambitions were thwarted by a European-wide alliance against him, France remained the wealthiest and most powerful nation in Europe. After 1688, however England began to compete with France both as a political model and a military power. If France was the envy of monarchs across Europe, England was the envy of Europe's aristocratic elites. After the death of the last Stewart monarch (Anne, 1702–1714), parliament decisively asserted its sovereignty. The English monarch remained a powerful executive, but the making of law, formulation of policy, and control over finances was in the hands of a parliament that represented the aristocratic oligarchy. At the turn of the eighteenth century, England built a coalition that prevented French hegemony over Europe and made "balance of power" a central concept in European international relations. France and England both developed powerful navies and established competing colonies in North America and the Caribbean, and competing trading posts in India.

In eastern Europe, Prussia continued its rise. King Frederick William I (1713–1740) doubled the size of the Prussian army and made it the best trained in Europe. Prussia became a militarist state, in which the government and the economy were subordinated to the interests of the army. By the middle of the century, one of every twenty-eight subjects was a soldier and one of every seven nobles was an officer. Frederick William I was reluctant to use his army, but his son, Frederick II "the Great"(1740–1786), was not, and, upon gaining the throne, he immediately began to use it to expand his realm.

After the Holy Roman Empire lost its authority and coherence, the challenge faced by the Habsburgs was to unite their Austrian and central European possessions into a successful state. The greatest test came when the young Maria Theresa (1740–1780) acceded to the throne, and Frederick II invaded the Austrian possession of Silesia. The resulting War of the Austrian Succession became a struggle of two alliance systems: France, Spain, and Prussia on one side, and Austria, Great Britain, and Russia on the other. In the end, Prussia won Silesia and established itself as the dominant German state, but Austria survived the war otherwise intact and proved that it was a viable state. It was a milestone for Russia, too, since the imperial title of Russia's monarch was recognized in the treaty that ended the war.

With the death of Charles XII in battle, in 1718, the Swedish "Age of Greatness" came to an end. Charles XII had no son, and the Diet elected his sister, Ulrika, to succeed him. When she abdicated in favor of her husband, Frederick (1520–1551), the Swedish nobility took the opportunity to assert its authority and limit the power of the king. They constructed a parliamentary government very similar to the English system. The Diet chose a policy of peace, and ended the Great Northern War, signing the Peace of Nystad (1721) with Russia, giving Peter I the outlet on the Baltic he had been fighting for. From then until midcentury, Sweden initiated no wars, but lost more Finnish territory near St. Petersburg to Russian aggression in 1741 to 1743.

The decline of Poland continued in the eighteenth century. Russia and France repeatedly used bribery and intimidation to influence elections to the Polish throne, and the kings they installed were mistrusted by the Sejm and were not permitted to initiate much needed reforms. The Sejm, for its part, accepted Russian and French money, and jealously preserved the liberum veto. During the reigns of Augustus II (1697–1733) and Augustus III (1733–1763)—both backed by Russia—fifteen of thirty-three sessions of the Sejm were dissolved by the liberum veto. In the reign of Augustus III, the Sejm came to no decisions and passed no laws at all.

In the first half of the eighteenth century, the Ottoman Empire held its own against Persia, but in a war against Austria and Russia (1736–1739), it was decisively defeated by the Russian army. Alarmed that Russia might annex the Balkan Peninsula, Austria withdrew from the war, and France intervened to bring the war to an end. Russia was denied any significant territorial gains. The Ottoman ruling elite, recognizing the need to modernize its army, began a series of reforms similar to those of Peter I of Russia. The Sultan hired French military experts to modernize their army, exchanged ambassadors with the nations of Europe, and encouraged the study of western science, history, and geography and the imitation of western fashion.

The Safavid Dynasty in Iran, weakened by a collapsing economy, was brought to an end in 1723 by an invading Afghan army. Russia and Turkey planned to divide Iran between themselves, but before this could occur, Nadir Shah (1736–1747), a Turk from eastern Iran, forged an alliance with remnants of the Safavids and restored the Persian empire. Russia immediately switched sides and allied with Iran against Turkey. Nadir Shah then defeated the Turks and drove them out of western Iran and the Caucasus. He added Afghanistan, Bukhara and Khiva to his empire, but in 1747, he was assassinated and Iran again descended into anarchy.

In China the prosperity of the Qing dynasty continued under the emperors Kangxi (1661–1722) and Qianlong (1736–1796). By the middle of the eighteenth century China had expanded to the furthest extent in its history: it included Mongolia, Tibet, and Central Asia as far as Lake Balkhash. Korea, Indo-China and Burma were tributary states. China was enormously wealthy and was far more powerful than any of its neighbors, but it had turned conservative. Although the Chinese had invented gunpowder and projectile devices, leadership in weapons technology was taken up by Europe, and China began to buy cannons and firearms from the West.

POLITICAL DEVELOPMENTS AND FOREIGN AFFAIRS

Among the many superficial differences that distinguished Russia from western Europe was its calendar. Russians celebrated New Year's Day on September 1, and they numbered years from the creation rather than the birth of Christ. On December 20 in the Russian year 7208 (1699 in western Europe), Peter decreed that the upcoming January 1 would be New Year's Day of the year 1700.[1] This was only the beginning of a series of decrees intended to "westernize" Russia. On January 4, 1700, Peter outlawed traditional clothing for noblemen and ordered that they wear Hungarian and German styles. In December of that year, the same law was applied to women. In addition, men were required to shave their beards and women to dress their hair according to western fashion. Peter repealed the Muscovite law against the use of tobacco and began to smoke a pipe himself.

Perhaps the most significant change political change Peter made was in the role of the Russian monarch. As Richard Wortman has pointed out, past Tsars of Russia had legitimized their rule by legitimate descent and by divine right, whereas Peter presented himself as ruler by right of conquest. Peter no longer participated in court ceremonies (such as the blessing of the waters at Epiphany), which represented the Tsar as sacred and priestly. Instead Peter's ceremonial entrances into the capital during celebrations took the form of triumphal military processions in which he played the role of victorious general. According to Wortman these were intended to be symbolic conquests of Russia itself.[2]

This new attitude was encapsulated in Peter's characterization of himself as "the first servant of the state." In other words, the supreme justification of his right to rule was not his role as protector of the Orthodox Church and people but his role as promoter of the secular wealth and power of the state. His new conception of the Russian ruler was also revealed in Peter's decision, in 1721 to use the title of *imperator.* There was no need for this term, if all he meant was to call himself an emperor, since *tsar* already conveyed that idea adequately. Tsar, however, was a term associated with the Byzantine Empire, and imperator is Latin for "victorious general," one of the titles used by the emperors of pagan Rome. Peter, therefore, was replacing the Christian emperor Constantine with the Pagan Emperor Augustus as the model for the Russian ruler, thereby replacing the idea of symphony between church and state with the notion of the absolute supremacy of the state. The Senate bestowed the Latin title pater patriae (father of the fatherland) on Peter, just as the Roman Senate had done for Augustus. Peter compared himself with the pagan gods Hercules and Mars.[3]

Peter I completely restructured the government on western models. He no longer referred to the Boiar Duma, and he established a Privy Council, staffed with his closest friends and associates, as the highest policy-making body. He originally created the Senate to administer the government when he was away from the capital; it later became a permanent body of nine members in charge of the government bureaucracy. A Procurator-General, directly responsible to the tsar, represented Peter in the Senate.

In 1720 Peter began to replace the unsystematic prikaz bureaucracy with a ministerial system of "colleges," based on the Swedish model. There were eleven colleges: war, admiralty, foreign affairs, tax collection, supervision of funds, expenditure of funds, mines, manufacturing, commerce, justice, and estates (which adjudicated land disputes among the landed nobility). In theory each college had eleven members (a president, vice-president, foreign adviser, four counselors, four assessors), and they were supposed to arrive at decisions by majority vote. In reality, they were rarely fully staffed. To oversee the bureaucracy Peter instituted a network of *fiskaly* to prevent abuses of power and misappropriation of funds or bribery. They were put under the control of the Procurator-General and were essentially spies for the tsar.

Peter reorganized local government, as well. In 1719, he divided Russia into fifty uniformly administered provinces. Each province (*guberniia*—a Latin term) was directed by a *voevoda* or military governor, and was subdivided into counties (*uezd*), headed by commissars. Town government was similarly standardized in 1721 to 1722. A magistrate and one to four commissioners (singular, *burgomistr*) were chosen by the townspeople. They were responsible for administration, tax collection, and enforcement of law and order. Peter's reform required that town magistrates set up hospitals, correction houses, and schools, but no funding was provided, and this provision went unimplemented.

Peter also standardized the army. He eliminated the streltsy, the pomeshchik cavalry, and all mercenary and irregular forces except for Tatar and Kalmyk cavalry regiments. Solders were conscripted on the basis of one soldier for every twenty households. They constituted a full-time, standing army; when not on campaign or in training, they lived in garrisons or were quartered in the homes of peasants or towndwellers. Officers came from the nobility, who were universally required to serve either in the civil administration or in the military. Peter directed that they begin their military careers as privates and earn officer rank on merit. Both officers and soldiers served for life. A military manual of 1716 defined the divisions and ranks of the army, listed the duties of the ranks, set down the principles of military discipline and justice, and described military drill and tactics. While western European governments still relied on mercenary soldiers of greater or lesser reliability, Peter I created Europe's first mass, conscripted, standing army; one with a high level of training and morale.

Peter the Great involved Russia in military conflict in virtually every year of his reign. Undeterred by his defeat by Sweden at the Battle of Narva in 1700, Peter quickly raised another army and marched back to the Baltic coast. In 1702, with Charles XII occupied in Poland, Peter was able to seize the Neva River and the land where it flows into the Baltic Sea. As a sign of his intention to stay, in 1703 he began the construction of a city, St. Petersburg, on the banks of the Neva. (In 1712 he made it the capital of Russia.) Peter also continued to build and transform his military forces. He raised taxes, declared a nation-wide conscription, and vastly expanded Russia's munitions industry. He even melted Church bells to forge canon to make up for those lost in the Battle of Narva.

By 1709, Charles XII, still occupying Poland, allied with the Zaporozhian Cossacks and prepared to invade Russia from the south. The armies of Charles XII and Peter I met at Poltava, and this time Sweden was defeated, thanks largely to Russia's superior firepower in the form of newly forged mobile cannon. Charles, now without an army, fled to Ottoman territory (in what is now Moldova), and tried to convince the Turks to ally with him against Russia. In the meantime, Peter seized Finland, Livonia, and Poland, where he restored Augustus II as king.

In 1711, Turkey entered the war on the side of Sweden, and Peter had to march south again. This time Peter was outnumbered and surrounded by Turkish forces, and he had to sue for peace, promising to give up Azov, pull his troops out of Poland, and permit Charles XII to return to Sweden. Nevertheless, Sweden's hegemony in the north was over. After Charles XII died in 1718 in a futile attempt to restore his military fortunes, the Swedish Diet decided to seek peace. In the Treaty of Nystad of 1721, Russia received Estonia, Livonia, Ingria, and the Vyborg district of Finland. In return, Russia withdrew its army from the rest of Finland, promised not to interfere in Swedish politics, and paid Sweden one and a half million rubles.

The Great Northern War (1699–1721) occupied most of Peter's reign and achieved one of the principal goals of his reign, recognition as a major European power. In other military and diplomatic efforts, Peter was less successful. In 1716 to 1717 he sent two military expeditions to Khiva and Kokand, but both were destroyed. A Russian embassy to China in 1719 gained little. In 1723, Persia ceded the western and southern shores of the Caspian to Russia in return for military aid against Turkey, but Russia's possession of the territory was brief.

Peter's personal life was both unconventional and tragic. A marriage had been arranged between him and Evodkhiia Lopukhina in 1689, but Peter did not find her congenial and in 1698 he forced her to retire to a convent. Before their separation, Evdokiia had given birth to a son, Aleksei, who grew up apart from Peter, opposed his father's reforms, and fled to Austria. Suspected of conspiring with Peter's enemies, Aleksei was tricked into returning to Russia where he was tried to treason and condemned to death. (Aleksei died in prison before he could be executed.) In the meantime, Peter had fallen in love with a Lithuanian woman of peasant origin who had been the mistress of his closest associate, Aleksandr Menshikov. They were married in 1712, and Catherine was crowned Empress in 1724.

In 1723, Peter had decreed that the emperor of Russia (like those of Rome) should choose his own successor, but he failed to do so before he died. After his death, the old aristocratic families supported Peter Alekseevich (Peter's grandson), but the men who had been in Peter's closest circle, led by Menshikov and backed by the guards regiments, confirmed Peter's wife, the Empress Catherine, as his successor. Catherine I (1725–1727) was not an active ruler; Menshikov created a Supreme Privy Council that ran the government.

Catherine did not name a successor, either, and when she died in 1727, Menshikov was willing for Peter Alekseevich, who was twelve, to become Emperor. To maintain his influence at court, Menshikov arranged a marriage between Peter II and his own daughter, but before the marriage could occur, the aristocratic faction, led by the Golitsyns and Dolgorukiis, managed to have Menshikov arrested and exiled to Siberia. They took control of the Supreme Privy Council and moved the capital back to Moscow. They arranged for Peter II to marry a Dolgorukaia princess, but Peter died of smallpox in early 1730 on the day of the planned wedding.

The Supreme Privy Council then turned to Anna (widowed duchess of Cortland), a daughter of Peter the Great's half-brother Ivan V. To guarantee their continued hold on power, they made Anna (1730–1740) sign a promise not to declare war, grant titles or estates, raise taxes, or spend money without approval by the Privy Council. Anna initially agreed to these terms, but when she arrived in Moscow, a different alliance of nobles, seeking to replace the Golitsyns and Dolgorukiis at the center of the court, encouraged her to tear up the agreement and send the Golitysns and Dolgorukiis into exile. Anna then abolished the Supreme Privy Council and created a governing cabinet made up of her supporters. In her reign, the capital was moved back to St. Petersburg.

Anna was childless, and on her deathbed she declared her grand-nephew Ivan (a great-grandson of Ivan V) her successor and named her favorite, Count Ernst Biron, regent for the infant Tsar Ivan IV (1741). Anna had been accused of surrounding herself with Germans, and, shortly after she died, an aristocratic faction used this to rally the guards regiments against the "German-controlled" court. Ivan VI, his mother, and several German ministers were arrested, and the throne was given to Elizabeth, a daughter of Peter I and Catherine I. The Empress Elizabeth (1741–1762), like Anna, left the government in the hands of aristocratic courtiers. She eliminated the Cabinet and made the Senate, once again, the central executive organ of the state.

In foreign affairs, Russia's influence in Europe continued to increase under Peter I's successors. By 1756, Russia's army was the largest in Europe. In international diplomacy, Russia found that its interests generally coincided with those of Austria, since they were both the enemies of Turkey and Sweden. Since France was allied with Turkey and Sweden (and the enemy of Austria), Russia also found itself an enemy of France. For most of the eighteenth century, Russia maintained good relations with Great Britain, mostly because of their economic ties. The British had become Russia's biggest trading partner by 1730s, buying two-fifths of its total exports.

In the War of the Polish Succession, 1733 to 1735, Austria and Russia competed with France for the right to place their candidate on the Polish throne. Russia and Austria won, and their choice, Augustus III (1733–1763), was made king. In the course of that war, Russia shocked western Europe by marching an army of ten thousand to banks of the Rhine River. In 1736 to 1739, Russia and Austria fought Turkey, and Russia won its first significant victories against the Ottoman Empire. Russia gained little, however. The Austrian army was defeated, thereby losing bargaining power, and France stepped in as a mediator. Russia was forced to settle only for the return of Azov (which had to remain unfortified) and a section of the Black Sea steppe. In 1743, Russia seized another strip of Finland from Sweden. Russia also entered the War of the Austrian succession (1740–1748) on the side of Austria and against Prussia. Russia's involvement did not affect the outcome, but it confirmed Russia's Great Power status and gained international recognition of the imperial title of Russia's ruler.

Russia's expansion eastward continued to the Pacific Ocean and beyond to North America. In 1728, Vitus Bering, a Danish explorer hired by Peter I, discovered the strait that now bears his name as well as the Kamchatka Peninsula. From 1733 to 1743, a "Great Northern Expedition" charted the western end of Asia and eastern end of North America and claimed what is now Alaska as Russian territory. China, also an expansive power, attempted to extend its northern border, and in 1727 the Treaty of Kiakhta set the Argun river as the boundary between the two empires.

Domestic politics did not fare as well under Peter's successors. His plans for a standardized and rationalized government failed. At the center, the colleges had never been fully functional, and his reorganization of the provinces had never gone fully into effect. The failure of central institutions to oversee provincial offices allowed widespread corruption and dereliction of duty. At the uezd level, there was virtually no government at all. Bands of outlaws looted villages and robbed travelers with impunity. Large landlords provided their own law and order, and frequently preyed on their weaker neighbors. Over time, the central administration gradually managed to stabilize the countryside. It reduced taxation and conscription, and restored the Muscovite system of provincial rule in which governors had wide discretionary powers. By the middle of the eighteenth century, the number of bureaucrats in central and provincial service had doubled, and the Russian countryside, though still seriously undergoverned, was at least stabilized.

RELIGION AND CULTURE

The secularization of society and culture increased significantly as a result of Peter's reforms. Secularization does not mean atheism or opposition to church-going; it means that the church is subordinate to the state, that activity in the world is more highly valued than withdrawal from it, and that salvation is a private and not a public matter. Secular European governments encouraged church attendance, since their leaders believed that Christianity fostered morality and obedience to authority. What distinguishes a secular state from a theocracy is the refusal of the secular state to subordinate its own interests to morality or to allow clerics to influence state policy, and this was precisely Peter I's attitude toward the church. He was a devout Christian, but he wanted to use the church rather than be used by it.

The principal obstacle to the control of the state by the church was the office of Patriarch. Adrian, whom Peter I's mother had chosen to be patriarch in 1690, is a case in point. When he assumed his office, Adrian repeated Nikon's claim of papal supremacy, quoting from the gospels in support of his position. Adrian was also close to the conservatives who attempted to remove Peter and restore Sofia in 1698. After Adrian died in 1700, Peter knew that any Russian prelate would resist the subordination of the church, so he decided not to appoint a patriarch at all. Instead he appointed an unknown Ukrainian cleric to be exarch (a term usually indicating a Patriarch's emissary) and placed him charge of a committee of bishops to govern the church.

Even this new exarch turned out to be too conservative, however, and Peter found a more compatible spirit in Feofan Prokopovich, another Ukrainian, whom he put in charge of reorganizing the Russian church. Prokopovich opposed the Byzantine notion of symphony between church and state and defended the idea that the monarch was the head of both church and state. In 1716, Prokopovich required all Russian bishops to swear an oath of obedience and loyalty to the Tsar and promise not to interfere in the government. When Peter established the collegial bureaucracy, Prokopovich created a College for Church affairs, to be headed by Russia's senior metropolitan and with a board composed of archbishops, heads of monasteries, and archpriests. At the first meeting, however, the college protested, arguing that the body had to be at least equal in power to the Senate and could take orders from no official but the Tsar. Peter agreed, and allowed a Holy Synod to be created. It was composed of twelve clerics selected by the Church hierarchy (subject to the Tsar's approval) presided over by a chief procurator who reported directly to the tsar.

Church rules, the "Spiritual Regulations," written by Prokopovich, explicitly recognized the subordination of the Church to the Tsar, glorified autocracy, and represented the Church not as the mystical body of Christ but as a community of individuals working together to defend themselves from their enemies. Priests were required to report to the police any treasonous or seditious ideas they heard during confession. They were instructed to teach their congregations to fear God and the Tsar and to obey their betters, and they were required to read state commands and pronouncements in church. Monks were no longer allowed to write in the privacy of their cells, and what they wrote (in public) was subject to censorship. On the other hand, the state did not meddle in theology; indeed, the coercive power of the state was put at the disposal of the church in order to support orthodoxy and suppress dissent.

Peter promoted the secularization of Russian culture in several ways. In 1703, he began the publication of the first Russian newspaper, *Vedomosti* (Gazette), to keep government officials abreast of national and international news. In 1710, the Old Church Slavonic alphabet was revised to create a modern script for secular writings. Peter created a publishing industry to spread western European knowledge and ideas. He favored scientific and technical works, but a significant number of books dealt with history, law, and etiquette. Classical mythology, previously unknown in Russia, became very popular. Although most of the books published in Russia in the first half of the eighteenth century were translations from other European languages, a Russian literary prose nevertheless developed, since a new vocabulary was necessary to express European social and political concepts.

Poetry was the genre in which modern Russian literature first appeared, and the first of the modern poets was Antiokh Kantemir, a Moldavian noble who served in the Russian administration. In addition to translating several Latin and French classics, Kantemir also wrote original poetry and satires of life in the capital. Vasilii Trediakovskii contributed to the development of literary Russian with both poetry and theoretical works on poetry and grammar. His *Theoptia*, based on Alexander Pope's *Essay on Man*, promoted deism and the scientific outlook.

Mikhail Lomonosov, son of a poor state peasant, who managed to be admitted to the Moscow Slavonic-Latin Academy and later studied in Germany, became not only a notable poet but an important scientist, courtier and administrator. He studied mining, metallurgy, and glassmaking, and made original contributions to chemistry, electricity, and physics. His poetry and prose contributed further to the development of literary Russian, and, in 1747, Lomonosov was the first Russian to be made a full member of the Russian Academy of Sciences. (Peter the Great had established the Academy in 1724, but for the first two decades of its existence it was staffed entirely by foreigners.)

Peter also fostered secular education. He made education a duty of the nobility, and required all noble sons to become literate and numerate before they could get married. Most elementary education for the nobility was given at home, but Peter also established a multitude of schools. In 1701, he opened the School of Mathematics and Navigation with British teachers, and graduates of the school then opened similar schools in Novgorod, Narva, and Revel. In 1715, Peter founded a Naval Academy and in 1716 a School of Mines. He also experimented with national primary education. All military garrisons had schools attached to teach basic literacy and arithmetic to soldiers' children. All monasteries and dioceses were directed to set up similar schools, but in 1722, the Church withdrew its support and the schools closed.

The only significant educational initiative made by Peter's immediate successors was the creation of a cadet school for the nobility in 1731 by Empress Anna. This school circumvented Peter's decree that all nobles had to begin their military service as privates and earn higher rank by service; graduates were immediately commissioned as officers. The cadet academy was so successful that similar schools were soon opened in other cities.

ROLES AND STATUS OF WOMEN

Peter the Great ended the seclusion of women and brought them into public gatherings and activities. In 1718, he announced the beginning of "assemblies," meetings at which men and women could meet and socialize. In 1725, he required the elites in Russia's major cities to attend evening balls, and he required elite women to wear western-style clothing, dance with any man who asked, and to stay until dawn. He also decreed that women of marriageable age should be allowed to stroll in public, attend street dances, and attend gatherings with mixed company. Peter ended the tradition of marriages between strangers and required that both parties know one another before the wedding. He outlawed forced marriage, requiring parents to swear that they had not made their children marry against their will.

Lindsey Hughes points out that Peter's reforms should not be thought of as "liberating." The new behavior required of women did not make them freer; it was, instead, "a female version of service to the state."[4] Life became more difficult as noblewomen had to negotiate between two moral codes: their traditional Orthodox upbringing and their emperor's new demands. Maintaining a residence in St. Petersburg, another requirement of the aristocratic elite, was a burden to many women. Furthermore, after Peter's reforms it was more difficult for women to become nuns.

The gender roles of peasant women were hardly affected by Peter's reforms. Peter intended his law against forced marriage to apply to the peasantry, but he issued another law requiring serf women to be married before the age of twenty. For Peter, state interests were always paramount, and he thought Russia needed the maximum growth of the tax-paying, conscript-providing population. In the eighteenth century, the average marriage age for girls fell to between twelve and fourteen years old.

SOCIAL AND ECONOMIC TRENDS

Peter the Great's reforms made Russian society even more hierarchical, rigidly defined, simplified, and subordinated to the needs of the state than had the Ulozhenie of 1649. In 1722, in imitation of a recently enacted Prussian standardization of ranks, Peter issued a "Table of Ranks" to clarify the order of precedence among the wealthy elite. The Table of Ranks created three parallel hierarchies: civil administration, army, and navy. (For example, the highest level included, respectively, chancellor, general-field marshal, and general-admiral, while level fourteen, the entry level, included collegiate registrar, ensign, and midshipman.) At each level, the military ranks had precedence over the civilian.

Peter's reform eliminated traditional distinctions among boiars, lesser aristocrats, and pomeshchiks, and created a single noble class. Peter called it the *shliakhestvo* (from the Polish szlachta), but by the end of the eighteenth century it was known as the *dvorianstvo* (based on the term for court servitors in the early Muscovite period). This new class was defined by common privileges, the most distinctive of which was exemption from the poll tax, and by a common obligation to serve the Tsar.

The Table of Ranks gave a superficial appearance of social equality and mobility. All nobles were required to enter government service in the lower ranks and to earn a position in the hierarchy. Additionally, a non-noble soldier or clerk appointed to even the lowest rank on the Table of Ranks attained personal nobility for his lifetime; one who rose to level eight in the military hierarchy (level six in the civil list) was granted noble status that was inherited by his children. In fact, however, there was little social mobility; those of noble background were promoted rapidly while those of non-noble origins gained promotion only with great difficulty. Eighty-five percent of the officer corps were from noble families.

Peter gave the pomeshchik class what it had long desired: in 1714, the distinction between votchina and pomestie was finally eliminated in law as well as practice, and pomeshchiks became absolute owners of their estates. Moreover, pomeshchiks were brought into a homogenous and cohesive noble elite that officially recognized no social distinction other than service to the state. Unofficially, however, the highest aristocracy received special favor, and the old boiar families continued to be appointed to the highest levels of civil and military administration. In fact, the Table of Ranks was welcomed by the nobility as a necessary replacement for mestnichestvo in defining and clarifying precedence and hierarchy.

Empress Anna served the nobility by limiting some of Peter's requirements. In 1731, she created a military academy so that nobles could enter the service as officers. In 1736, she set a time limit of twenty-five years on required service. (This only applied to the nobility; lifetime service continued for conscripted soldiers). Anna also decreed that one son in every noble family could be exempted from service in order to supervise the family's estates.

Peter instituted a new classification of town dwellers. At the top were two guilds. The first was made up of wealthy merchants and members of the professions (such as doctors). They were subject to the poll tax and conscription, but they were able to buy exemption from conscription for 100 rubles (at a time when the poll tax was 1 ruble 25 kopecks). The second guild was composed of artisans and lesser merchants. At the bottom, with no rights or privileges whatsoever, were hired laborers. A posad assembly included all people registered as towndwellers. Even the poorest were allowed to attend, but they were not always allowed to vote. The posad assembly functioned similarly to the mir: Its principal tasks were to allocate taxes and choose conscripts. Invariably it conscripted either the most undesirable elements or the poorest and least influential. After the reform of 1721 to 1722, the posad was also given the power to choose their magistrate.

The greatest simplification of social class was imposed on the non-noble population. Peter's poll tax laws of 1722 to 1724 created one general class of non-noble manual laborers. All adult males in this class paid the poll tax and were subject to conscription for both the army and for government construction projects. The only difference was the level of taxation: Towndwellers paid the highest poll tax, state peasants paid somewhat less, serfs on noble estates paid the least (so their lords could demand higher rents and dues). The poll-tax population was also forbidden to move or travel without permission of their town, mir, or landlord, and a state registration and passport system was implemented. Debt slavery continued through the eighteenth century, but it became increasingly uncommon.

Peasants made up 90 percent of the overall population and 95 percent of the poll-tax paying population in reign of Peter. Fifty-five percent of the peasantry were serfs, the remainder were state, church, and court peasants. As in the past, state peasants were more numerous on the periphery of Russia; serfs were most common in the center. The mir gained in importance in the eighteenth century, but only to the benefit of government and landlords, not the peasantry. The mir was given the responsibility for collecting taxes and choosing conscripts. As in the towns, those who were considered "lazy" or "troublemakers" were generally conscripted, as were sons from families powerless to protect them. On estates that required obrok (payments in cash or produce), landlords allowed the mir broad autonomy in determining what crops to plant and how to schedule labor. (Because Russian agriculture was based on crop rotation and on a strip-farming system, it was essential that labor be coordinated.)

In regard to the economy, as in every other aspect of Russian life, Peter I was a radical interventionist. For the construction of St. Petersburg twenty-thousand peasants were conscripted each year from 1702 to 1715. Taxation increased by 500 percent between 1680 to 1725. Besides the poll tax, which continually rose, Peter taxed beards (of merchants who refused to shave; nobles had no choice but to shave), bathhouses, beehives, hats, boots, watermelons, and more. The government also made money off its monopolies on legal paper, salt, oak coffins, and vodka. In fact, taxes were more than the economy could bear: payments were frequently in arrears, in both town and countryside, because the people simply lacked the money to pay them.

The burdens Peter imposed did not prevent Russia from experiencing the fastest population growth in Europe (which was, itself, experiencing unusually rapid growth). Russia grew from 9 million in 1678 to 18.2 million in 1744. Between 1719 and 1762 European Russia grew 33.8 percent and Siberia grew by 77 percent. St. Petersburg was an uninhabited swamp when it was founded in 1703, but by 1750 it had a population of almost 75,000.

In agriculture, Peter was less interested in producing for export than avoiding the need to import. He promoted the planting of fruit orchards, tobacco, and grapes. He hired Italians to establish a silk industry near Moscow. He also imported sheep from Silesia and Spain to improve native lines, and he regulated forests to prevent deforestation and to preserve bees (in order to harvest wax and honey). Peter tried to introduce scythes to replace the use of sickles, which he considered inefficient, but although Russian peasants accepted scythes for cutting hay, they refused to use them for harvesting grain.

Peter sponsored a huge increase in manufacturing by building state-owned factories and also by supporting private entrepreneurship, which he did by paying subsidies, imposing protective tariffs, and excusing all merchants who owned factories from the obligation to quarter soldiers in their homes. In Peter's reign, 180 large-scale enterprises were established, including forty ironworks, fifteen foundries of other metals, twenty-four textile mills, and numerous leather, glass, and gunpowder works. In 1700, Russia imported most of its iron; by 1725, it was exporting iron to Europe.

Peter wanted St. Petersburg and the Baltic ports to replace Archangel as Russia's principal trade outlet with the West. He began the construction of a canal that would connect the headwaters of the Volga with St. Petersburg, and it was completed in 1732. Trade with Central Asia passed principally through Astrakhan until 1744 when Orenburg became Russia's trade center in the East. During Peter's reign, Russia sent a trade caravan to China every two years.

The increase in manufacturing meant an increase in the need for industrial workers, a major problem in a country in which labor was not free to move and in which 90 percent of the population were peasants. One source of workers was to conscript people who were not productive, that is, beggars in the towns, vagabonds on the roads, and criminals. Another method was to assign state peasants to a manufacturer. In this option, a merchant was allowed to purchase a village of state peasants; he could then require a proportion of the adult males to work in the factory. Factory workers were extremely unhappy: They were regimented, treated brutally, and paid little or nothing. They were not paid for the time they spent traveling to and from the factory in which they worked (which could take many days, or even weeks). Accustomed to the life of agricultural labor, peasants found factory discipline and working indoors to be torture.

PEOPLES OF THE EMPIRE

In the Volga region and on the Central Asian Steppe, Russian continued its efforts to subordinate the nomads. The Bashkirs and the Volga Tatars had long since accepted Russian authority. They had lost political autonomy and lived under Russian administration, and they had given up raiding and earned their living instead by selling livestock in Russian markets. Many raised hay instead of moving their herds to new pastures, and some had become sedentary farmers. However, they had not assimilated into Russian society. They attempted, as much as possible, to maintain their traditional way of life, and they resented the increased regimentation, as well as the collection of taxes by Russian authorities. In the first half of the eighteenth century, there were three major Tatar uprisings and six major Bashkir uprisings. Each uprising was suppressed and was followed by attempts to isolate clan elites from the people and turn the people into state peasants.

The Cossacks, the empire's Slavic, Christian nomads, faced the same pressures. In 1707, the Don Cossacks staged an uprising against the Russian government. They resented the expansion of the Russian state and Russia's attempt to turn their free society into a regimented and professional army. Kondraty Bulavin, a local Don Cossack chief, began the revolt, and attempted to ally with Kalmyks, Nogais, and Crimean Tatars. Their goal was not to conquer Russia or overthrow its government, but to maintain the independence and traditional nomadic lifestyle of the southern steppe. The uprising was suppressed, and the Don Cossacks continued to lose their freedom.

The Kazakhs (in Central Asia) and Kalmyks (in the northern Caucasian steppe) also resisted incorporation into the Empire. The Russian government had built fortification lines between the Don and Volga Rivers in the late seventeenth century, and this allowed them to control the Kalmyks by restricting their ability to take their herds north to summer pastures. The same technique was applied to the Kazakhs. A fortress was built at Orenburg on the upper Yaik River in 1744 to be the center of another defensive line.

As Russia's military power grew and that of the nomads declined, Russia's sense of imperial mission began to change. Russia no longer had to defend itself against nomad raids and did not need to play one group of nomads against another. Instead, Russia saw itself as the provider of law and order to savage peoples. The government began to punish those who engaged in raids and to offer trade opportunities so the nomads could earn their livings peacefully. This was the purpose of Orenburg which anchored a line of fortifications that separated the Kazakhs in the south, the Bashkirs in north, and the Kalmyks in west. Orenburg soon became the largest market on the Steppe. Nomads traded horses and sheep there, and it also became the center of trade with the Khanates of Central Asia. Furthermore, it provided protection for sedentary agriculturalists and encouraged the settlement of Russian peasants.

Conclusion

By the middle of the eighteenth century, Peter's plans had been realized. Russia was recognized as an empire and a European Great Power, and its army was one of the most formidable in Europe. In Russia, the initial conservative reluctance to change had been overcome, and the nobility enthusiastically adopted the culture and fashions of Europe. The population continued to grow and the economy to expand. Yet even greater achievements were in store for Russia in the second half of the century.

Notes

1. Ironically, Peter did not quite succeed in bringing Russia up-to-date. In 1700, two calendars were in use in Europe, and Peter chose the Julian calendar which lagged eleven days behind the Gregorian calendar. Ultimately western Europe made the Gregorian calendar standard, while Russia clung to the Julian calendar. Russia's calendar fell behind Europe's by one day every century, so that by the twentieth century it was thirteen years behind Europe. David Christian, *A History of Russia, Central Asia and Mongolia, Volume I, Inner Eurasia from Prehistory to the Mongol Empire* (Oxford: Blackwell, 1998).
2. Richard S. Wortman, *Scenarios of Power: Myth and Ceremony in Russian Monarchy*, vol. 1 (Princeton, N.J.: Princeton University Press, 1995), 44.
3. Wortman, *Scenarios of Power*.
4. Lindsey Hughes, *Russia in the Age of Peter the Great* (New Haven: Yale University Press, 1998), 201.

TEXT DOCUMENTS

Duties of Parish Priests

Feofan Prokopovich (1681–1636) was an Orthodox cleric from Ukraine who became one of Peter the Great's closest advisers and who was put in charge of restructuring the Orthodox Church. He wrote the Spiritual Regulations, *a sort of constitution for the Church, from which this excerpt is taken.*

- What does this reveal about Prokopovich's (and Peter the Great's) attitude toward the relation of church and state?
- How sensitive is this to the religious duties of priests? How respectful of religious concerns is it?
- What effects might this have on relations between priests and the community they serve?

11. If someone in confession informs his spiritual father of some illegality that has not been committed, but that he yet intends to commit, especially treason or mutiny against the Sovereign or against the state, or evil designs upon the honor or well-being of the Sovereign and upon His Majesty's family, and in informing of such a great intended evil, he reveals himself as not repenting but considers himself in the right, does not lay aside his intention, and does not confess it as though it were a sin, but rather, so that with his confessor's assent or silence he might become confirmed in his intention—what can be concluded therefrom is this: When the spiritual father, in God's name, enjoins him to abandon completely his evil intention, and he, silently, as though undecided or justifying himself, does not appear to have changed his mind, then the confessor must not only not honor as valid the forgiveness and remission of the confessed sins, for it is not a regular confession if someone does not repent of all his transgressions, but he must expeditiously report concerning them, where it is fitting, pursuant to His Imperial Majesty's personal ukase, promulgated on the twenty-eighth day of April of the present year, 1722, which was published in printed form with reference to these misdeeds, in accordance with which it is ordered to bring such malefactors to designated places, exercising the greatest speed, even as the result of statements concerning His Imperial Majesty's high honor and damaging to the state. Wherefore a confessor, in compliance with the provisions of that personal ukase of His Imperial Majesty, must immediately report, to whom it is appropriate, such a person who thus displays in confession his evil and unrepentant intention. However, in that report, the salient points of what has transpired in confession shall not be disclosed, since in accordance with that ukase, it is prohibited to interrogate such malefactors, who appear in connection with making the afore-mentioned damaging statements, anywhere except in the Privy Chancery or in the Preobrazhensky Central Administrative Office. But in that report shall only be stated secretly that such a person, indicating therein his name and rank, harbors evil ideas and

Source: Alexander V. Muller, Trans. and Ed., *The Spiritual Regulation of Peter the Great* (Seattle: University of Washington Press, 1972), 60–63. Reprinted by permission of University of Washington Press.

impenitent intent against the Sovereign or against the rest of what was referred to above, from which he desires that there be great harm: Therefore he must be apprehended and placed under arrest without delay. And whereas, by that same personal ukase of His Imperial Majesty, it is ordered to send the informers also, under surety furnished by guarantors, or if there are no guarantors, under escort in honorable arrest, to the aforementioned Privy Chancery or the Preobrazhensky Central Administrative Office for proper arraignment of those malefactors, accordingly a priest who has reported that matter, after giving surety for himself, shall proceed, upon being dispatched, to the prescribed place without postponement or evasion. And there, where investigation is made into such misdeeds, he shall report specifically, without any concealment or indecision, everything that was heard regarding that evil intention. For, by this report, the confessor does not disclose a genuine confession and does not transgress the canons, but rather fulfills the Lord's reaching, spoken thus: "If thy brother sin against thee, go and show him his fault, between thee and him alone. If he listen to thee, thou hast won thy brother," etc. "If he refuses to listen, tell it to the church." [Matt. 18: 15, 16, 17.]

12. Not only must priests inform of an evil that seeks to be put into action, but also of a scandal that has already been perpetrated against the people. For example: when someone, having imagined it somewhere in some way or having hypocritically contrived it, spreads the news of a false miracle and the ordinary, undiscriminating people accept it as real. Later, if such a fabricator discloses that to be a fantasy of his in confession, but does not display repentance for it and does not promise to make it known publicly (so that the ignorant may not accept that lie as real), that lie, being accepted as real through ignorance, will be added to the number of genuine miracles and in time will for everyone become firmly established in memory and renown. Therefore a confessor must inform of that, where it is fitting, without delay, so that such a falsehood may be halted and the people, beguiled by that lie, might not sin through ignorance and accept that lie as real. For, by use of such false miracles, not only is contumely of one kind or another perpetrated, but God's commandment, "You shall not take the name of the Lord, your God, in vain," is violated. Those who recount such miracles use God's name in a lie, so that it is not glorified by them, but is taken in vain. And upon the piety of Orthodox believers descends censure from those of other faiths. Accordingly it is most necessary to halt such illegal and impious activity; and confessors, as was mentioned herein, must inform of such cases without concealment and immediately.

First Issue of *Vedomosti (Gazette)*

Peter the Great established Russia's first newspaper in order to keep his government informed of events in Russia and the world. This is the first issue of Vedomosti, *dated January 2, 1703.*

- What does this newspaper indicate about Peter's interests and goals?
- What does it reveal about his idea of Russia's relations with the world?
- Why do you think he included reports from Sweden regarding their war with Russia?

In Moscow today 400 cannon and small and large brass mortars were cast. The cannons were made to fire shot of 24, 18, and 12 pounds. The small mortars were made for bombs of 36 pounds and 18 pounds. The large mortars were made for bombs of 360, 108, and 72 pounds and less. And there are still many large and middle-size forms prepared for the casting of cannons and mortars. In addition, more than 720 tons of brass is now in the canon-yard ready for new casting.

By his majesty's command, the number of schools in Moscow has been increased and forty-five people are studying philosophy and have already completed dialectics. In the mathematics and navigation school more than 300 people are studying and are diligently applying themselves to the study of science.

In Moscow between November 24 and December 24, 386 people of the male and female sex were born.

From Persia [Iran] it is reported: The Tsar of India sent a gift of elephants and many other things to our sovereign. It arrived in Astrakhan from the city of Shemakha after an uneventful voyage.

From Kazan it is reported: A lot of petroleum and copper ore has been discovered on the Soka River. It is expected that the copper smelted from the ore will produce a considerable income for the Muscovite state.

From Siberia it is reported: In the Chinese government Jesuits have become really disliked for their intrigues and several of them have been executed.

From Olonets it is reported: Priest Ivan Okulov, of the town of Olonets, gathered a thousand hunters, went to the Swedish border and destroyed Swedish border outposts. At these outposts they killed a large number of soldiers and took many cavalry banners, drums, swords, and horses. They also seized provisions and belongings which [Okulov] gave to his men. The remaining belongings and food supplies that could not be taken away were all burned. The Soloskii farmstead was burned, and many farmsteads near Soloskii, and a thousand peasant houses as well. And, according to the captives that were taken at the outposts mentioned above, 50 Swedish cavalrymen and 400 infantry were killed, 50 cavalrymen and 100 infantry ran away, and only two of the priest's forces only two soldiers were injured.

Source: S. S. Dmitriev and M. V. Nechkina, *Khrestomatiia po istorii SSSR, Vol 2, 1682–1856* (Moscow: Gosudarstvennoe Uchebno-Pedagicheskoe Izdatel'stvo Ministerstva Prosveshcheniia RSFSR, 1953), 115–116. Translated by author.

From Lvov it is reported: December 14. Cossack forces under Colonel Samus are multiplying daily. They have annihilated the commander and his troops in Nemigorod and have seized the city, and now Samus intends to take Belaia Tserkov. He expects that after taking the town he will unite his forces with Palei, and they announce that when they unite they will be a host of 12,000 men all together. The Litovsk royal hetman is going to his host in Brest-Litovsk. According to the testimony of secretary Orukho, part of the Swedish army is in Kazimer and part is in Sandemir, and it is reported that they are going through Great Poland toward Prussia. . . .

From Nien in Ingria: [A Swedish report.] October 16. We are living here in a poor situation since Moscow is behaving very badly here, and therefore many people are going away from here out of fear to Vyborg and Finland, taking the best goods with them.

The Fortress Oreshek, 40 versts from here, is high and protected by a deep moat, and it is now under a fierce siege by a Muscovite army. Twenty shots are returned for every four fired at them, and more than 1500 bombs have been thrown, but as of this time, they have caused little damage and they will find it very difficult to take the fortress.

From Narva: [Also a Swedish report.] October 13. On September 26, a Muscovite force of 10,000 men arrived on this side of the Neva River at Notenburg between the Russian and Ingrian borders and stopped there and began to dig trenches 500 paces from the fortress on this side of the river. Our [the Swedish] army with general Kroniort stands on the other side of the river across from Notenburg with sufficient infantry, cavalry, and canon balls to deny the passage of the river to the Russian army, which they would like to cross. They [the Russians] intend to bombard the fortress at Notenburg with cannons, but since it is made of stone and there are good troops within it and 400 more men have now been sent there, there is no reason for apprehension.

From Amsterdam: November 10. From the city of Archangel it is reported that on September 20 his Majesty the Tsar has dispatched troops in various ships to the White Sea, sent them further from there, and summoned the ships back again to Archangel [with more troops], and now 15,000 soldiers are gathered there, and 600 men are working on the new fortress on the banks of the Dvina every day.

Peter I's Assemblies

The following is a description of an "Assembly" in Moscow, taken from the diary of a German officer in the Russian Army dated February 18, 1722.

- How has the status of women changed from the Muscovite period?
- Can you see any continuities with the past?
- Can you see any other social changes or continuities?

I will briefly relate here what sort of thing these assemblies were and the rules that were followed at them. They were organized in the manner of the Petersburg assemblies which, by the express will of the emperor, were held every winter.

First, the hosting of these assemblies was divided among all the high society families without observing any particular order or precedence. The local commandant asks either his majesty the emperor (when he happens to be here) to name the host of the next meeting, or the members of high society, themselves, determine when and where it will be convenient to hold the next assembly, and then, before the gathering disperses, it is announced to the guests where the next assembly will be. In Petersburg the chief of police usually does this. Everyone has the right to come to the assembly.

Second, the host does not have to formally receive or introduce anyone in the room, with the exception of the emperor himself.

Third, in the room where they are dancing (if there is room, or else as close to it as possible) there must be prepared: a table with pipes, tobacco, and wooden torches (which are used here instead of bits of paper to light the pipes) and a few more tables for games of chess and checkers. Playing cards are not desired and they are not put out.

Fourth, the host, hostess, or one of the family begins the dancing, after which, depending on the place, one or two pairs can dance the minuet, the Anglaise or the Polonaise as they desire. However, in the minuet the rule is observed that not just anyone can dance. When a gentleman or a lady who, having danced the minuet, dances it again, they must dance with a different partner, choosing whomever they like. One pair or several pairs may dance. After the minuet, if the dancers want to dance the Anglaise or the Polonaise, then they announce it and the gentlemen who want to take part in the dance choose ladies. Ladies do not choose gentlemen, considering it, as a rule, to worst impropriety.

Fifth, all have the right to do as they like, i.e., may either dance or smoke tobacco, or play checkers, or converse, or look at the others; and in the same way each may ask for wine, beer, vodka, tea, coffee, and they always receive what they ask for. But the host is not obligated, and in fact is not allowed, to press the guests to drink or eat but can only say what refreshments there are and then grant them complete freedom.

Sixth and last, these gatherings, begin at about five o'clock, last no later than ten, and then all must disperse to their homes.

What I least like in these assemblies is that they smoke tobacco and play checkers in the same room where the ladies are and where the dancing takes place. The stink and the

Source: Dmitriev, *Khrestomatiia po istorii SSSR, Vol 2, 1682–1856,* 121. Translated by the author.

tapping noise is inappropriate where there are ladies and where music is played. The second thing I dislike is that the ladies always sit apart from the men, so that they not only cannot converse, they are almost completely unable to say a word. When they do not dance, they all sit like they are dumb and only look at one another.

Native Uprisings

This is a report from Anadyrsk in far eastern Siberia. It was written by Captain Peter Tatarinov to the Commandant of Yakutsk, Colonel Iakov Ageevich.

- What does this reveal about Russian relations with the peoples of Siberia?
- What does it reveal about the nature of the Russian occupation of Siberia?

On December 2, 1714, two tribes of iasak [tribute-paying] Iukagirs, the Chiuvans and the Khodyns, were en route from Oliutorsk ostrog [stockade] with the Great Sovereign's Treasury. At Talovsk Pass near Anadyrsk ostrog they rebelled and stole the entire Treasury of the Great Sovereign and killed the prikashchik Afanasii Petrov [and many others]. . . . Some of the servitors escaped . . . These men are in Aklansk ostrog under siege. The Iukagirs have surrounded the ostrog. They do not have any powder or shot. The Iukagirs attack these Aklansk men, and life is very hard. They do not know when and where they might be killed, nor how they might escape to the Anadyrsk or Oliutorsk ostrogs.

The Iukagirs have stolen from them all the transport reindeer as well as the ones intended to be slaughtered for food which had been acquired from the reindeer Koriaks and from the Kamchadals. The Iukagirs have driven off all these reindeer and now they boast that they will seize Anadyrsk ostrog as well and kill all the government reindeer and also kill all the servitors. We must reinforce the [loyal] Oliutors who have remained near the ostrog to guard the Great Sovereign's Treasury.

Ivan Pavlov, who lived in Anadyrsk, passed through Argish on his way home and before he reached his home he discovered the bodies of the many servitors. He returned to Vasilii Kolesov and his men to report the massacre. The Iukagir Sopina and his men heard about the killing and returned to Argish. Vasilii Kolesov and Ivan Eniseiskii and the servitors who were with them, all traveling light, together hastened on to Aklansk, On the way the Iukagir bandits caught up with them and stabbed the piatidesiatnik Nikifor Martianov. Vasilii Kolesov and his men ran day and night to escape them. Three days later, traveling by rein-

---

Source: Reprinted from Basil Dmytryshyn, E. A. P. Crownhart-Vaughan, and Thomas Vaughan, Eds. and Trans., *Russian Penetration of the North Pacific Ocean, 1700–1799* (Portland: Oregon Historical Society Press, 1986), 54–58. (c) 1988, The Oregon Historical Society. Reprinted with permission.

deer, they managed to reach Aklansk ostrog. It was the evening of December 5. The next morning 20 Iukagir murderers pursued them to Aklansk carrying shields and muskets. Each man had two muskets and a bow and arrows.

They told Vasilii Kolesov and Ivan Eniseiskii that they had killed the prikashchik Afanasii Petrov because he had brought on them so many abuses and taxes, and such ruination and despoliation. The Iukagirs had killed all the servitors with him, but promised to return the Great Sovereign's Treasury. They said they would bring it to the Koriaks at Akiansk so it could be sent on to Anadyrsk ostrog. These same Iukagirs have threatened to kill Vasilii Kolesov and Ivan Eniseiskii and all the rest of the servitors in Akiansk ostrog, and will not under any circumstances permit them to come out. They have also vowed they will kill the servitors and the reindeer in Anadyrsk ostrog and will take the ostrog itself.

On December 17 Vasilii Lavrinov and his comrades reached Anadyrsk ostrog and reported to me that they had left Anadyrsk ostrog and at night reached the reindeer herd. A herder, one of the reindeer Koriaks, was standing near the iurts. When he approached the nearest iurt a Koriak woman came out and said to Vasilii, "The Iukagirs attacked Vasilii [Kolesov] in great numbers. They drove off the reindeer herd and tied up the men and stripped them of all their clothes." . . .

At present there are only 40 servitors left in Anadyrsk, a very small number indeed, and this includes 18 men who are old and sick. There is such a shortage of men that there is no one to send from Anadyrsk to Aklansk to help with the warehouse supplies of the Great Sovereign, or to go on an expedition against those outlaw Iukagirs, or to act as replacements for the men who are guarding the Great Sovereign's warehouses. Because of this shortage of manpower in Anadyrsk at present as well as in the future, there will be a very dangerous situation because of those outlaw Iukagirs.

As of December 19 we have not received any information in Anadyrsk from Aklansk because the Iukagirs have blockaded the entire road. In the future I will report to you whatever word I receive about any action these Iukagirs may take, or about any news from Aklansk concerning the servitors and the Great Sovereign's Treasury.

Figure 9-1 Coin from the Reign of Peter I
- Compare this image with earlier depictions of Russian rulers.
- How is this different? What does the difference mean?

Source: de Chaudoir, Obozrenie Russkikhdeneg. Part 2 plate II, drawing 2.

Figure 9-2 The First "Winter Palace"

The first Winter Palace was built before 1711, when this engraving was made. It was later torn down and replaced with the more magnificent Winter Palace in the reign of Elizabeth.
- Compare this builder with earlier examples of Russian architecture.
- What does the change of style mean?

Source: Eighteenth-century engraving.

Figure 9-3 Vedomosti

The text of *Vedomosti* (*Gazette*), Russia's first newspaper, appears above. This is a copy of the first page of one of the first issues. The story refers to German and British politics, but the illustration is of St. Petersburg.

• What government interests are revealed by the appearance of this paper?

Source: Library of Congress.

Figure 9-4 Nerchinsk

This is an early eighteenth-century engraving of the city of Nerchinsk on what was then the border with China.

• What does this image reveal about the nature of Russian expansion?

Source: Evert Ysbrandszoon Ides, *Three years travels from Moscow over-land to China: thro' Great Ustign, Siriania, Permia, Sibir, Daour, Great Tartary, & to Peking* (London, W. Freeman, 1706).

Figure 9-5 North Central Europe in 1725

In his reign, Peter the Great had acquired an outlet on the Black Sea. Peter's expansion at the expense of Persia did not survive him, and Poland and the Crimean Tatars (under the protection of the Ottoman Empire) remained powerful.

FOR FURTHER READING

(In addition to the books by Blum, Dukes, Hartley, Khodarkovsky, and Moon from the previous chapter.)

Anderson, M. S. *Peter the Great*, 2nd ed. New York: Longman, 2000.

Bushkovitch, Paul. *Peter the Great: The Struggle for Power, 1671–1725*. Cambridge: Cambridge University Press, 2001.

Cracraft, James. *The Church Reform of Peter the Great*. Stanford, CA: Stanford University Press, 1971.

_____. *The Revolution of Peter the Great*. Cambridge, MA: Harvard University Press, 2003.

Hughes, Lindsey. *Russia in the Age of Peter the Great*. New Haven: Yale University Press, 1998.

Kahan, Arcadius. *The Plow, the Hammer, and the Knout: An Economic History of Eighteenth-Century Russia*. Chicago: University of Chicago Press, 1985.

LeDonne, John P. *Absolutism and Ruling Class: The Formation of the Russian Political Order, 1700–1825*. New York: Oxford University Press, 1991.

Wortman, Richard S. *Scenarios of Power: Myth and Ceremony in Russian Monarchy*. Vol. 1. Princeton, NJ: Princeton University Press, 1995.

CHAPTER TEN

RUSSIA IN THE AGE OF ENLIGHTENMENT, 1750–1815

Peter the Great's desire to make Russia a European great power was enthusiastically adopted by his successors. The height of Russia's identification with Europe came during the reign of Catherine II (1762–1796), whose explicit goal was to realize Enlightenment values. (Peter himself had anticipated many of the features of the Enlightenment; he had a thoroughly secular outlook, he believed in the value of science and technology, and he thought that society could be improved by the imposition of rational laws and institutions.) During Catherine's reign, Russia won two major victories over the Ottoman Empire and annexed half of Poland. Her grandson, Alexander I (1801–1825) led a coalition that defeated Napoleon and thwarted his bid to rule all Europe. Even in his wildest dreams, Peter I could hardly have imagined that little more than a century after the Battle of Poltava a Russian Tsar would march into Paris at the head of a victorious army.

EURASIAN CONTEXT

The dominant outlook of Europe's wealthy and educated elite in the second half of the eighteenth century was known as the Enlightenment. Enlightenment thinkers were committed to secularism, humanism, individualism, and rationalism. A few were outright atheists, more were Deists (believing in a creator god who made a material universe that operated according to fixed laws of nature), and many retained their faith in Christianity, but they all be-

Turn to page 217 for a map showing key geographic locations and features for this time period.

lieved that religion was a matter of individual choice, the state should not regulate belief, and clerics should not be involved in government and education. Adherents to the Enlightenment held that human beings are naturally good and that evil is caused by faulty upbringing and bad government; they opposed torture and cruel punishment; and they believed that human beings have natural rights to life, liberty, and property. They opposed slavery. Enlightenment thinkers had supreme confidence in the ability of reasonable people to create institutions—schools, courts, prisons—that would make the society progressively better. The Enlightenment was neither democratic nor populist. "Enlightened despotism," the absolute rule of a just, rational, and humane monarch, was fully consistent with Enlightenment ideals, and some considered it to be the ideal form of government.

Monarchs across Europe implemented Enlightenment ideals. In Austria, Maria Theresa (1740–1780) and Joseph II (1780–1790) centralized their bureaucracy, diminished the power of the nobility, standardized the administration across their multinational realm, promoted education, and secured greater control over taxation. Joseph II codified the law, practiced religious toleration, and improved conditions for the peasantry. Frederick II the Great of Prussia (1740–1786) reformed Prussia's judiciary, expanded the state education system, fostered science and the arts, and permitted freedom of conscience and greater religious toleration for Catholics. In Sweden, Gustaf III (1771–1792) attempted to revive royal absolutism. He promoted the arts and sciences and represented himself as an enlightened monarch. In 1789, a Diet representing all classes did give him the executive power that he wanted, but the three lower estates served their own interests, as well, by abolishing most of the privileges of the nobility.

The most striking exception to the principles of Enlightened monarchy was in the homeland of Enlightenment theorizing, France. There the incompetent and tradition-bound Louis XVI (1774–1793) did nothing but alienate his people. The French Revolution (1789–1799), which brought an end first to his reign and then to his life, manifested both Enlightenment and democratic, populist values, but Napoleon Bonaparte (1799–1814), who took advantage of the revolution to seize power, epitomized enlightened despotism. He created a standard, nationwide educational system, codified the law, confirmed individual liberty and equality, and asserted the supremacy of the secular state.

In global politics, this was the era of the decisive struggle between Great Britain and France for world supremacy. In the Seven-Years' War (1756–1763) Great Britain won Canada (thereby controlling all of North America east of the Mississippi), obtained most of the West Indies, and eliminated French political influence from India (in preparation for British colonization). In the War of the American Revolution (1776–1783), France assured the independence of England's former colonies, the United States of America, but England successfully resisted French efforts to regain the territories it had previously lost. In the Napoleonic Wars (1773–1815), the British navy again proved its mastery of the seas and added still more territories to its overseas empire.

Poland was weakened by factionalism and corruption in the Sejm and by mistrust between the king and the Sejm; in consequence it was unable to defend against its expansive neighbors. In 1772, in the context of the first Russo-Turkish War (discussed below), Frederick II of Prussia convinced Austria and Russia that they should annex parts of Poland; Austria took Galicia, Prussia took Eastern Pomerania, and Russia took eastern Lithuania. In 1791, the Polish aristocracy, anxious to rejuvenate their state, undertook a fundamental reform and wrote a new constitution based on Enlightenment principles. In addition, to create a stronger executive and military they established a hereditary constitutional monarchy, and to create a stronger legislature they abolished the liberum veto and adopted the principle of majority rule. Russia feared the consequences of a strong Poland, and in 1792, Russian agents instigated a conservative insurrection, which was then used as a pretext for a

Russian invasion. Prussia invaded as well, and in 1793, Prussia annexed western Poland and Russia annexed more of Lithuania and most of Ukraine. In 1794, Polish patriots staged a national uprising, but this only provided an excuse for Austria, Prussia, and Russia to invade once again and partition Poland for the third and final time. Austria took southern Poland, Prussia took central Poland, and Russia took the remainder of Lithuania. The Polish state ceased to exist and was erased from the map of Europe.

At the other end of Eurasia, the Qing Dynasty in China was at the height of its wealth and power. Eurasian demand for Chinese luxury goods remained strong, and the government regulated foreign trade by limiting foreign merchants to two cities, Kashgar in far Western Xinjiang, to deal with Central Asia, and Canton on the South China Sea, to deal with Europeans. Some long-term problems were evident, however, including rapid population growth, deforestation, and depletion of the soil. In the middle of the century, the Emperor Qianlong (1736–1796) began a series of expensive wars to pacify nomads in Xinjiang and Tibet. Depletion of the treasury mean the decay of public works, which, in turn, contributed to flooding, famine, and social unrest.

In Iran, after Nadir Shah's murder in 1747, his empire soon disintegrated. This provided the opportunity for border regions to assert their independence. The Caucasus, including Georgia and Azerbaijan, broke free from Iranian rule only to be absorbed by the Russian empire, Georgia willingly and Azerbaijan unwillingly. Afghanistan, however, not only became independent under the leadership of Ahmad Khan (1747–1773), a former Iranian general, it also expanded into an empire that briefly included eastern Iran and northwestern India. In Central Asia, the Khanates of Khiva, Bukhara, and Kokand, engaged in border disputes among themselves, but maintained their independence.

The Ottoman Empire remained the dominant power in Southwest Eurasia, but its role in Europe underwent a dramatic reversal. In the reign of Catherine the Great, Russia soundly defeated the Turks in two major wars and could have drastically rolled back Ottoman rule in the Balkans. This was prevented by European powers who began to fear Russia more than Turkey and supported the status quo in the Balkans. In the meantime, Ottoman Sultans continued to westernize their empire. Selim III (1789–1807) reorganized the government, founded engineering academies, modernized the navy, imported French military technology, and hired French officers to create a new Ottoman army on Western lines. Conservative forces opposed these reforms, and in 1807, the Janissaries, the traditional elite corps of the Ottoman army, revolted. They deposed Selim, repealed his reforms, and replaced him with a puppet.

POLITICAL DEVELOPMENTS AND FOREIGN AFFAIRS

Elizabeth (1740–1762) continued to leave government in the hands of her favorites, but she was active in the realm of culture. She founded the Russian Academy of Arts and the University of Moscow—Russia's first university—sponsored architecture, including rebuilding the Winter Palace on a more magnificent scale. She also maintained a lavish court that showcased the most current western fashions. In Elizabeth's reign, Russia allied with Austria and France against Prussia in the Seven Years' War (1756–1763). Russia's success against the famous Prussian army of Frederick the Great frightened its allies, however, and they began to withdraw from the war. In early 1762, when Russian forces had the Prussian army on the run and were on the outskirts of Berlin, Elizabeth died and was succeeded by Peter III.

Elizabeth had no desire to marry, but to avoid palace intrigue, she sought to establish a clear line of succession. In 1742, she had brought her fourteen-year-old nephew, Peter, Prince of Holstein-Gottorp and a grandson of Peter the Great, to Russia to be her heir. Elizabeth also chose a wife for the future emperor, Sophie, Princess of Anhalt Zerbst, a small German principality. Sophie, was renamed Catherine when she converted to Russian Orthodoxy; she was expected to produce a son to further extend the line of succession. Intensely aware of the need to ingratiate herself with Elizabeth and the Russian court, Catherine quickly learned Russian and conscientiously observed the rituals of Russian Orthodoxy. According to her own (self-serving) account, when Peter proved to be incapable of consummating their marriage, Catherine, anxious to produce the baby that Elizabeth required, began a series of affairs.

Peter III (1762) quickly alienated the Russian court. He had not developed any interest in or respect for Russian culture or religion. He retained Lutheran sympathies even after converting to Orthodoxy, and he was more interested in his native principality of Holstein-Gottorp than in Russia. Moreover, he admired Prussia and idolized Frederick the Great. Indeed, Peter's first act was to announce an end to hostilities with Prussia, withdraw the Russian army from Berlin, and request an alliance with Frederick, Russia's former enemy. Peter then prepared to send Russian troops to fight Denmark on behalf of Holstein. Peter ordered all icons (except those depicting Christ) to be removed from Russian churches, and he required Orthodox priests to dress in vestments similar to those worn by Lutheran pastors. He also announced plans to disband the guards regiments.

All these actions served to alienate the Russian nobility, in particular the guards (who had been instrumental in all the reign changes in Russia since Peter the Great). His final, fatal mistake, however, was to alienate and frighten his wife, Catherine. After the disastrous beginning to Peter's reign, she must have realized that there would be plots against him, and that in the event of a palace coup, she would share his fate. Catherine had an additional reason to fear Peter: He hated her, suspecting (probably wrongly) that her son, Paul, was not his child. Peter did not mention Paul as his heir in his accession decree, and several months later, Peter threatened to arrest and imprison Catherine.

Implying that she was acting on behalf of her son, Paul, Catherine organized a palace coup against her husband, secretly gaining the support of Church officials, the chief of police of St. Petersburg, and Count Nikita Panin. Catherine's lover, Grigorii Orlov, who was an officer in the Guards, brought his fellow officers into the conspiracy, and, in late June, the Guards arrested Peter and pledged their allegiance to Catherine. Catherine did not declare herself to be regent for her son, instead, she announced that she was ascending the throne as Empress Catherine II.

Catherine II (1762–1796) had been an avid reader of French literature and social thought, and she ascended the throne intending to be an Enlightened ruler. She began a correspondence with Voltaire, Diderot, and other intellectual leaders of the Enlightenment, and she instituted a series of reforms that epitomized Enlightened despotism. Like Peter I, Catherine reformed virtually every aspect of Russian society.

Catherine's first project was to transform the Senate from an institution that convened as a single deliberative body into one with six specialized departments. Next, she secularized Church property: All income-producing land was transferred to the state. Peasants on those lands, now called "economic" peasants, became virtually indistinguishable from state peasants. No longer independently wealthy, the church now had to make do on an annual subsidy of only one-third its former income. (Only one church leader, Metropolitan Arsenii, was brave enough to protest this aloud, and he spent the rest of his life in solitary confinement.)

Next, Catherine began to plan a major codification and reform of Russia's laws, which had not been undertaken since the Ulozhenie of 1649. In 1766, she summoned a Legislative Assembly, and she wrote a Nakaz (Instruction), which set down the principles she wished them to follow. In it, Catherine made references to a variety of progressive thinkers, including Cesare Beccaria, who opposed torture and advocated quick, consistent, and mild punishment of crime, and Adam Smith, who opposed government interference in the economy and proposed that the material possessions of citizens was a better measure of a nation's wealth than the gold in its treasury. The greatest contribution to the Nakaz came from Montesquieu, who advocated civil rights and the rule of law, held that large states need absolute monarchs, and believed that the best defense of liberty was an independent and wealthy aristocracy.

The Legislative Assembly met in 1767; it included representatives from the administration, nobility, industrialists, merchants, state peasants, Cossacks, and non-Slavic peoples (such as Bashkirs and Tatars). More than one-third were nobles, while merchants made up the second largest category. The Church was allowed only one delegate (out of 564) and serfs none at all. Though it met for more than a year and held over two hundred committee meetings, the Legislative Assembly failed to write a single law. Instead the delegates used the Assembly as a forum in which to express their grievances. In 1768, using the first Russo-Turkish war as an excuse, Catherine disbanded the Legislative Assembly, and the laws of Russia remained uncodified. Nevertheless, the exercise was not a complete waste of time. The petitions, memorials, and grievances presented by the delegates taught Catherine a great deal about conditions in Russia and contributed to her subsequent reforms.

Catherine's reform program was interrupted first by the war with Turkey (1768–1774) and then by the Pugachev Rebellion (1773–1775), the most widespread and destructive popular uprising up to that time. The Pugachev Rebellion was not a single movement, but a Cossack war against Russian rule that inspired many (uncoordinated) local uprisings and disorders. It began among the Yaik Cossacks who were then being incorporated into the Russian empire and who resented being reduced from free farmers to state peasants and being subjected to regular military discipline and regimentation.

In 1773, the Yaik Cossacks killed a Russian general who had been sent to investigate their grievances. At this point Emelian Pugachev, a Don Cossack, arrived on the scene. Pugachev passed himself off as Peter III, who had been transformed in folk legend into a friend of the people removed from power by corrupt boiars. Pugachev brought into his movement neighboring nomads, such as the Tatars and Bashkirs, who were also being incorporated into the empire. His initial goal was to take the strategic fortress at Orenburg and declare independence of Russia. When their attack failed in 1773, Pugachev changed his plans and began to march up the Volga River towards Moscow. The Russian army met them in Kazan in 1774 and pushed them back.

As Pugachev fled back down the Volga, he sent out proclamations in the name of Peter III announcing an end to serfdom, taxation, and conscription and calling on serfs to kill nobles and take their estates. Rebellion sprang up all across Russia, as the most oppressed segments of the population—peasants assigned to factories and mines, Old Believers, and serfs—rose up. It has been estimated that as many as 10 percent of the Russian nobility were murdered. In the province of Moscow, alone, 1,572 nobles, 1,037 officials, and 237 clergy were killed. Predictably, however, popular brutality evoked even more brutal reprisals by the government. Pugachev killed perhaps 3,000 people, while the Russian army killed 10,000. In the end, Pugachev himself was captured, brought to the capital in a cage, and executed.

The Pugachev rebellion convinced Catherine of the need to reform provincial administration. In 1775, she created 41 (later increased to 50) provinces (guberniia), each containing 300,000 males (the Russian census counted only men) divided into 10 counties (uezd) of 30,000 males each. Provincial and local government was decentralized and was subject to checks and balances; judicial, administrative, and tax functions were kept separate. Catherine also added 27,000 new administrative staff positions in the provinces (thus tripling the number of administrators).

In foreign affairs, immediately after deposing her husband, Catherine canceled his order to send troops to Denmark in support of Holstein's claim on Saxony. She did not, however, reverse his decision to withdraw from the Seven-Year's War. Catherine found that Russia and Prussia had interests in common, and in 1764, she signed a defensive alliance with Frederick the Great. In 1768, Turkey, seeking to regain territory lost to Russia during the reign of Anna, used Russian intervention in Polish politics as a pretext for war. Catherine welcomed the war, and her forces won a resounding victory. The Russian navy destroyed the Turkish fleet at the Battle of Chesme in 1770, and the Russian army pushed Turkish forces south of the Danube River. At this point, Europe began to fear Russia more than Turkey. France pressed Turkey to resist, and Prussia and Austria intervened to restrain their ally. The Treaty of Kuchuk Kainarji (1774) preserved Ottoman possession of the Balkan Peninsula, although it did give greater autonomy to Wallachia and Moldavia. Russia was given only the port of Azov, a small strip of territory on the Black Sea coast west of Crimea, and the right of commercial navigation on the Black Sea. The biggest loser was the Khanate of Crimea, which was given its "independence," another term for losing Turkey's protection. Poland also lost as a consequence of the war; the First Partition of Poland was intended to compensate Russia for its exclusion from the Balkan peninsula.

Soon after the war was over, Catherine took as her lover Grigorii Potemkin, one of the heroes of the war, and put him in charge of Russia's military forces. Together, Catherine and Potemkin began a plan, known as the "Greek Project," to revive Tsar Aleksei's old dream of driving the Turks out of the Balkans, and creating a Slavic, Christian nation with its capital in Constantinople. When tsarevich Paul's second son (Catherine's grandson) was born in 1779, Catherine named him Konstantin to prepare him to rule this new kingdom.

In 1783, Russia conquered the Khanate of Crimea and incorporated it into the Russian Empire. The Ottoman Sultan, angry at the annexation and hoping to avenge his past losses, prepared for war. He forged an alliance with Sweden, secured a promise of support from Great Britain and Prussia, and in 1787 declared war on Russia. When the French Revolution began in 1789, however, England and Prussia were suddenly preoccupied with western European politics and were unable to help Turkey. Russia won a series of victories in 1789 and 1790 that forced the Sultan to sue for peace. The Treaty of Jassy (1792) affirmed Kuchuk Kainarji, recognized Russia's annexation of the Crimea, and ceded to Russia the Black Sea coast between the Bug and the Dniester Rivers. The Balkans remained in Turkish hands, however, and Catherine's "Greek Project" remained a dream.

Catherine's territorial gains in Europe were impressive. As a result of the Turkish wars, Russia now controlled all the Black Sea coast from the Caucasus Mountains to the Dniester. As a result of the three partitions of Poland, Russia had added all of Ukraine, Belarus, and Lithuania to its empire. Catherine justified her participation in the partitions as liberating the Orthodox Slavs from foreign oppression and restoring Russian rule in the lands of old Kiev Rus. She did not acknowledge that in the intervening eight centuries Ukraine and Belarus had become distinctive nations nor that the homelands of Lithuania, Latvia, and Estonia had never been Russian territories at all.

Catherine had been shocked by the French Revolution and the execution of Louis XVI, but, preoccupied with her wars with Turkey and Sweden, and the partitions of Poland, she had not joined Prussia and Austria in their attempt to restore the Bourbons. In 1796, Catherine finally resolved to send troops to France, but she died before they were sent.

Paul (1796–1801) had not been raised by his mother, Catherine, but by the Empress Elizabeth, and he and his mother were not close. Catherine prevented Paul from having any role in the government, and he lived away from the capital on an estate at Gatchina. Catherine provided Paul an enlightenment education, but he rejected it in favor of militarism and traditional notions of autocracy. Paul became emperor at the age of forty-two, having had no experience other than managing his small estate and drilling his private regiment.

One of Paul's first acts was to release his mother's political prisoners. He did this out of spite for his mother not out of principle; in fact, he himself established something of a police state sentencing twelve thousand political opponents without trial. Paul also reversed Catherine's habit of fostering civilian culture and values at the court. He appointed officers to government posts, he reformed the army on the Prussian model, and he spent a large part of his day personally reviewing military drills.

Paul revived Peter the Great's concept of a service state. He reinstituted mandatory service for all nobles, he repealed their right to petition the Emperor directly, and he even restored corporal punishment of the nobility. To reduce the possibility of military interference in future successions to the throne, Paul decreed in 1797 that the Russian throne would be inherited through the oldest male child.

Paul began his reign by pursuing peace. He canceled Catherine's decision to send troops to intervene in France, and he worked for closer relations with Sweden. A year later, Paul helped organize a coalition against France that included Austria, Great Britain, and Turkey. By 1800, however, the erratic Paul reversed his policy again. Feeling slighted by Great Britain and attracted to Napoleon, Paul broke with the coalition and allied with France. At Napoleon's suggestion, Paul sent an army of twenty thousand Don Cossacks to invade India.

In 1801, Paul was deposed and murdered by former officials of Catherine the Great who opposed Paul's autocratic, anti-noble, and pro-French policies. The English ambassador, concerned by Paul's anti-British actions, was also involved in the plot. Alexander, Paul's eldest son and heir to the throne, did not participate in the plot, but he was informed of it and did nothing to prevent it, and he must have known that his father would die.

Alexander I (1801–1825) had been taken from his parents by his grandmother, Catherine the Great, to be raised and educated, and he had been given an Enlightenment education. However, he also spent a considerable amount of time with his father in Gatchina, where he was exposed to the militaristic atmosphere of his father's court. His first actions were intended to satisfy the nobility. He granted amnesty to Paul's political prisoners and reaffirmed the noble rights that had been granted by Catherine's Charter of 1785. Yet he also distanced himself from the conspirators who had brought him to the throne; those who did not retire were assigned to posts away from St. Petersburg.

Alexander began his reign with a series of government reforms. He began to formulate policy with an unofficial committee of intimate associates, and he created a Council of State to review and refine legislation that he wished to enact. Alexander replaced Peter the Great's colleges with ministries of foreign affairs, war, navy, finance, commerce, education, interior, justice, each headed by an single minister, not a board. The Senate, formerly the highest organ of the administration, was turned into a supreme court, and its former administrative role was taken over by a council made up of the heads of the ministries. In 1811, he created a Ministry of Police.

Alexander's legal reforms were less successful than his structural reforms. He formed a commission to codify the law, but it made little progress. He toyed with the idea of eliminating serfdom, but his only achievement in the first decade of his reign was to allow serfs to buy their freedom from landlords. He intended to end the sale of peasants without land, but all he did was to prevent advertising of such sales. Alexander's principal adviser, Mikhail Speranskii drew up a detailed plan to transform Russia into a constitutional monarchy with a separation of powers, equal civil rights for all classes, and an indirectly elected legislature. However, Speranskii may never have revealed to Alexander the full extent of his plan, and, in any event, aristocratic hostility toward the Francophile Speranskii forced him from office in 1812. The Russian autocracy remained unlimited.

Alexander began his reign by taking a pro-British position in foreign affairs. He immediately recalled the Cossacks from their expedition to India, and in 1804 he joined Great Britain, Prussia, and Austria in the Third Coalition against France. At the Battle of Austerlitz in 1805, however, Austria surrendered, Prussia withdrew from the coalition, and Russia, not wanting to fight France alone, retreated. Yet a fourth anti-French coalition was created among Russia, Prussia, and Great Britain in 1806, but later in the year, Prussia was defeated at the Battle of Jena and Russia lost the Battle of Friedland. France subordinated Prussia, but Russia was too powerful to defeat or dismember, and Napoleon settled for a Franco-Russian alliance, signed at Tilsit in 1807, in which Russia accepted Napoleon's hegemony in Europe and supported his continued struggle against Great Britain.

This alliance lasted from 1807 to 1812, and it had mixed consequences for Russia. Russia was hurt by Napoleon's Continental System which attempted to undermine Great Britain by denying it European markets. This cost Russia its best trading partner. Furthermore, French interference in Poland was worrisome to Alexander. Napoleon created a new Polish state, the Grand Duchy of Warsaw from the territories Austria and Prussia had taken in the Partitions of Poland. This encouraged Polish nationalism and the hope that the territory Russia had annexed might also be restored. On the other hand, alliance with France gave Russia the opportunity to gain territory in both the north and the south. Sweden was an enemy of France and therefore fair game for Russian aggression. In 1808 to 1809, Russia defeated Sweden and annexed Finland. In a war with Turkey from 1806 to 1812, Russia won Bessarabia.

By the end of 1810, however, Russia was regularly violating the Continental System, and Napoleon made plans to punish it. In June 1812, Napoleon invaded Russia with an army of 500,000, seeking a smashing victory that would force Alexander to surrender. Russian generals, however, followed an unpopular but effective policy of retreat, drawing the French army into the Russian heartland where its supply lines were overextended and its forces depleted. In September, when Russian forces finally engaged with the French at Borodino, not far from Moscow, the battle was fought to a draw, but the French suffered more casualties.

Nevertheless, Napoleon's army was still superior, and Kutuzov, Russia's commanding general, continued to retreat, allowing Napoleon to enter Moscow. Napoleon stayed there for a month (during which time a large part of the city burned), hoping that Alexander would surrender. In October, realizing that no surrender was forthcoming, and concerned about the coming of winter, Napoleon withdrew from Moscow. As he retreated, his army was harassed by the Russian regular army and by guerrilla forces. By the middle of December, the French army had practically disappeared, and Napoleon fled west with only a small bodyguard.

Alexander then went on the offensive, renewing the alliance with Austria, Prussia, and Great Britain. Napoleon quickly assembled another army of 250,000 and won his first engagement with the allied armies in August 1813. At Dresden in October, however, Napoleon was at last defeated and driven out of Germany. In early 1814, Russian troops led the invasion of France and entered and occupied Paris. When his generals refused to continue fighting, Napoleon abdicated and accepted exile on the island of Elba. Russia withdrew from France, and the victorious powers gathered in Vienna to plan the future of Europe. Napoleon's brief one-hundred-day attempt to regain his empire was only a postscript that did not change the course of events. England defeated Napoleon at the final Battle of Waterloo, but it was Russia that came out of the war in a position to dominate continental Europe. In 1815, a Russian army paraded down the Champs Elysees, and a Russian was appointed to govern Paris.

Religion and Culture

By the end of the eighteenth century, the Church hierarchy had less impact on the political and cultural affairs of Russia's elite than ever. Its administration was subordinated to the state, it had lost property and wealth, and its seminaries followed a curriculum (taught in Latin) that reflected state needs more than church interests. Fewer Russians were attracted to the spiritual life, and over the course of the century the number of monasteries and convents had declined by two-thirds, and the number of monks and nuns by more than one-half. The number of parish priests increased, but not in proportion to the general population. The priesthood became a hereditary profession as priests managed to prevent anyone other than their sons from attending seminaries. Seminaries did not produce only priests, however. Many seminary graduates could not (or preferred not to) find openings in the church and entered the civil service or became teachers instead.

Outside the formal church hierarchy and the seminary system, monks at Optina Pustyn independently revived the hesychast tradition of quiet contemplation and communion with God through continual prayer. Educated Russians, however, increasingly turned from the church to freemasonry, a highly abstract and rationalized religion that professed belief in a creator God and individual immortality but observed its own unique set of secret rituals. Freemasons accepted Christian ethics and engaged in charitable work, especially education and publishing. Masonic lodges provided an opportunity for the educated elite to socialize and converse on social issues free from the self-censorship that servants of the state were required to observe in public discourse. Almost all of Russia's scholars and authors were Masons, and it was very popular among government leaders, military officers, and the highest aristocracy.

Elizabeth continued Peter's project of translating and publishing western books, but Catherine took it to a new level. She created a Society for the Translation of Foreign Books and gave it a budget of five thousand rubles a year to hire translators. By the end of her reign almost nine thousand books from the Western tradition were published, including Greek and Latin classics, French Enlightenment authors (including Voltaire's complete works), and English literature. In 1783, to further encourage publishing, Catherine allowed private individuals from any social estate to own printing presses. Paradoxically, this meant the beginning of censorship, which had been unnecessary as long as the state had a monopoly on publication. Catherine put local police chiefs in charge of reviewing privately published books to ensure that they were not offensive to the monarch, the Orthodox Church, or public morals.

The first to run afoul of the censorship laws was Aleksandr Radishchev, a noble who had been educated at the St. Petersburg Corps of Pages and the University of Leipzig. After rising through the civil service, Radishchev retired to his estate where he wrote *A Journey from St. Petersburg to Moscow*, a celebration of Enlightenment values and a biting criticism of social injustice, serfdom, government corruption, and autocracy. After gaining approval from the police by submitting an innocuous manuscript, Radishchev published his book on his own press. He was arrested, found guilty of disrespect to the Empress and sedition against government, and sentenced to death. His death sentence was commuted to exile to Siberia, and he was pardoned by Paul in 1796.

Nikolai Novikov, a publisher of textbooks and editor of literary and satirical journals, also suffered for his free-thinking. He broke no censorship law, but he was a freemason and his publication of masonic literature frightened Catherine. In 1792, she had him arrested and imprisoned him without a trial. Novikov was also released by Paul.

In mainstream high culture, Aleksandr Sumarokov was the first noble to make literature his career. A prolific, if mediocre poet, he is remembered as Russia's first dramatist, as well. Gavriil Derzhavin, son of a poor provincial pomeshchik who became a high-ranking civil servant, was Russia's most accomplished poet of the eighteenth century. Derzhavin is particularly famous for his religious and philosophical odes. Denis Fonvizin, of the Moscow nobility was the best comic dramatist of the eighteenth century. His "The Minor," a satire of the provincial gentry, is thoroughly Russian (not an imitation of western situations) and is still performed in Russia today.

Nikolai Karamzin wrote a thoroughly fluent Russian prose that prepared the way for the standard literary Russian of the nineteenth century. Karamzin began his career as a liberal cosmopolitan and first earned fame with *Letters of a Russian Traveler* published in the 1790s after a journey through Europe. After Alexander I appointed him court historiographer, Karamzin turned conservative. Although Karamzin felt that the westernization of Russia was a progressive development, he was one of the first to criticize Peter I for cutting Russia off from its moral roots and sacred traditions.

In addition to literature, Catherine also patronized the arts. She sponsored court theater and music, and her building of palaces, government buildings, and mansions for her favorites popularized neoclassical architecture and English-style landscape architecture. Catherine spent huge sums of money acquiring works by Renaissance masters, as well as contemporary European artists, and she made the Russian court collection one of the most distinguished in Europe. Catherine also fostered native Russian art by commissioning many portraits and sculptures of herself and her courtiers.

Education continued to advance in the second half of the eighteenth century. In 1755, Empress Elizabeth founded the University of Moscow and two high schools to prepare students for it. Catherine II established a Commission for Popular Schools in 1782 and a teachers' college in St. Petersburg in 1783. The first class of hundred teachers graduated in 1786, and that same year Catherine issued a Statute on National Schools which called for a major school in the capital of each province, and minor schools in the principal town of each district. Minor schools provided the first two years, and major schools last two years of elementary education. The curriculum included religion, foreign languages, philosophy, natural science, mathematics, history, and geography. The schools were publicly funded; teachers were hired by the state, books were provided free of charge, and tuition was free and open to children of all classes.

Alexander I expanded Catherine's system in 1802 when he created the Ministry of Education. He instituted a four-level system by adding primary schools at the parish level, expanding the curriculum of the district and provincial schools, and creating a university system at the top. Universities already existed in Moscow, Dorpat, and Vilna; Alexander established new ones in Kharkov, Kazan, and St. Petersburg. At the lower levels, education continued to be provided at no charge, and at the university level, scholarships were given to needy students. In 1811, in order to create a more cultured bureaucratic elite, Alexander established a school for aristocrats at Tsarskoe Selo, which offered courses in fine arts, history, Latin, French, German, and Russian.

ROLES AND STATUS OF WOMEN

Catherine the Great wrote no feminist tracts, yet her policies—and the very example of her life—played a significant role in awakening elite women to the idea that they could play roles other than wife and mother. In the second year of her reign, Catherine established the first schools in Russia specifically to educate women, the Smolnyi Institute for daughters of poor nobles and the Novodevichii Institute for non-noble girls. The schools taught drawing, dancing, music, sewing, and etiquette, but also Russian, foreign languages, arithmetic, history, geography, and law. Moreover, the nationwide school system that Catherine created later in her reign was open to children of both sexes. Since the Russian public was not as liberal as Catherine, only a small fraction of students were girls.

Catherine was also a literary model for women. She sponsored several satirical journals, to which she herself contributed articles under the name "Granny." Catherine wrote essays, plays, operas, memoirs, and children's stories. Seventy women began to publish their writing in Catherine's reign, and female novelists, though far from advocating the equality of the sexes, brought a new attitude toward women, treating them as individuals, not mere appendages of men, and stressing the importance of friendship as well as love between husband and wife.

Russian women were still constrained by tradition, however. Marriages were still arranged and sometimes forced, producing, on occasion, both suicide and the murder of spouses. Divorce was far more common in Russia than in West, and it most often benefitted men, because it allowed a man to keep his wife's dowry. Grounds for divorce in the Orthodox Church included adultery, desertion, impotence, and incurable disease. The nobility always sought divorce through the church; in cities, couples often simply renounced their marriage in front of witnesses. Among the peasantry, divorce was handled by the mir, which could both dissolve marriages and allow remarriage. Children generally opposed their mother's remarriage, since their stepfather would gain a share of the family property.

On the other hand, in this period, as in all others, there is evidence of affection and mutual respect between husbands and wives. Veneration of mothers continued to be a central value of Russian society, and, as the multigenerational family became the norm, the numbers of families headed by widowed mothers increased. In cities one in five families was headed by a woman; in the country it may have been more. In the mir, women who headed families had equal rights with men in the village assembly.

ECONOMIC AND SOCIAL TRENDS

To facilitate trade, internal tolls were abolished (1753) and transportation was improved. The modern science of road construction was in its infancy, and Russia, like all European nations, depended on rivers and canals to transport goods. Peter I had connected the Volga to the Neva by canal, and his successors connected the Dnieper with the Western Dvina. Over the course of the century, the number of people involved in river transportation grew from 60,000 to 200,000.

The conquest of Crimea permitted the introduction of agriculture on the Black Sea steppe for the first time, and this greatly stimulated the Russian economy. Catherine encouraged the movement of peasants to the region and also invited colonists, most of them German, to emigrate from Europe. In the last two decades of eighteenth century, grain production almost doubled, and wheat shipped from the newly built port of Odessa on the Crimean Peninsula helped feed the rapidly growing cities of western Europe. In addition, the numbers of cattle, horses, and sheep increased, as did the production of hides, tallow, butter, and meat.

Industrial production also grew. In 1800, Russia led the world in the production of pig iron. The textile industry expanded and diversified, and the steady growth of the publishing industry stimulated the building of paper mills. Production of rope and shipbuilding products more than doubled. Over the course of Catherine's reign, exports and imports both tripled, but exports were twice as large as imports, giving Russia a healthy trade surplus.

From the beginning of the Muscovite state, Russian rulers depended upon the support and cooperation of an aristocratic elite. Peter the Great had made this relationship one of obligation and coercion. Catherine attempted to create a symbiosis of autocracy and aristocracy based on mutual respect and self-interest, and she largely succeeded; by the end of her reign, service in military and government was thought of not as a burden but as a privilege and honor.

In his only popular act, "Manifesto on the Freedom of the Nobility" in 1762, Peter III had released the nobility from compulsory service to the state. In 1785, Catherine issued a Charter of the Nobility that clarified the rights and privileges of the nobility and attempted to give them a collective identity as Russia's governing elite. This charter confirmed the nobility's freedom from the obligation to serve, exempted them from the poll tax and obligation to quarter troops in their homes, and declared them not subject to corporal punishment. Nobles were recognized as full owners of their estates, including mineral and timber rights, and their exclusive right to own serfs was confirmed. Finally, nobles could not be deprived of wealth, rank, or estate without trial by a jury of their peers.

The Charter also provided for an elected Marshall of the Nobility and noble assemblies at both the Provincial and District levels. The assemblies kept official records, maintained a registry of nobles, and adjudicated claims of nobility. They also served as agencies for collecting donations for social welfare, local schools, and war efforts. Any noble who owned an estate in the district could attend the assembly, but the right to vote and be elected was restricted to those who had achieved at least the fourteenth (the entry level) rank in the Table of Ranks.

The nobility was encouraged to engage in industry and commerce in two ways: by being freed from the service requirement and by being given the exclusive right to own serfs (the major source of industrial labor). By 1814, nobles owned 64 percent of mines, 78 percent of wool textile mills, 60 percent paper mills, 66 percent of crystal and glass factories, and 80 percent of potash production. In 1765, nobles were given the government's former monopoly on distilling.

Although it was an hereditary estate, the nobility was not a closed caste. The Table of Ranks continued to permit exceptional individuals to earn nobility although this was quite rare. The monarch could also grant noble titles to individuals, usually to extremely successful merchants and industrialists. In addition, intermarriage was permitted, and many merchants secured nobility for their descendants by marrying their daughters to noblemen. (Marriage of merchant sons to noblewomen was rare.) Nevertheless, the nobility was a very small elite, making up only 2 percent of the Russian population. It was also highly stratified. In 1797, 1.5 percent of the nobility owned more than one thousand serfs, while 83.5 percent owned fewer than hundred. Most were too poor to acquire an education or to enter government service without financial aid from the government, and some were virtually indistinguishable from their own peasants.

In 1785, Catherine attempted to create the same sort of collective identity for towndwellers as she had for the nobility. Her Town Charter recognized six categories of towndwellers: 1. landowners living in the towns; 2. merchants (subdivided into three guilds based on wealth); 3. artisans registered in craft guilds; 4. foreigners and merchants from other towns; 5. "eminent citizens," which included the very wealthy (bankers, ship owners, and wholesale traders) and artists, university graduates, university faculty, and city administrators; and 6. other residents who did not have the wealth or skill to fit in other categories. Rights were not equal across the urban community. "Eminent citizens" and the first two merchant guilds were not subject to the poll tax (they were taxed on their capital, instead) and were exempt from corporal punishment. Merchants were allowed to buy the right not to be drafted into the military, and they could not be drafted as laborers. All registered city residents had the right of trial by a jury of their peers.

The charter also granted self-government to the towns. An assembly of all citizens elected a town duma of six members (one from each category). All registered citizens could attend the assembly, which elected the duma, but only those with an income of over fifty rubles a year or property worth more than one thousand rubles were allowed to vote and be elected. The duma was given authority to enforce law and order, promote trade, provide for social welfare, and manage public building.

Catherine did nothing, however, to address one of the towndwellers' major concerns: competition from peasant artisans and traders. Peasants often made up the largest proportion of the town population, but because they were classified as peasants they were not registered nor did they pay taxes. Catherine permitted this situation to continue not because of sympathy for the peasants, but because it was in the interests of the nobility. Nobles could train their serfs as artisans (or simply allow them to practice traditional crafts) or set them up in business as merchants. Because they paid no taxes, peasants could undercut the prices of town merchants and artisans, and the profits they earned were taken by their lord through obrok levies.

Early in her reign, Catherine talked about emancipating of the serfs, but nothing ever came of it. She drafted a Charter for State Peasants on the lines of her Charters for the Nobility and Towndwellers, but it was never implemented. Ultimately, Catherine's highest priority was to foster the nobility, and the nobility's principal concern was to preserve serfdom. Catherine's reforms regarding the peasantry were minor. She gave governors the authority to confiscate the property of landlords who were excessively cruel. She decreed that no serf who had been freed could be enserfed again, that serfs could not be assigned to factories against their will, that abandoned orphans were to be raised as free towndwellers, and that any serf who enrolled in a university could not be sent back to his or her estate.

The mir remained the basic unit of peasant society. The *skhod* (village assembly) was composed of all heads of households. It was predominantly male, but widows who headed extended families were allowed to attend, and husbands could also send wives as proxies. The skhod elected village elders and officials and appointed constables and clerks. It judged family and interfamily disputes, and punished immoral behavior and minor violations of the law. It also apportioned taxes, chose conscripts, and supervised periodic redistribution of the land. The skhod provided for social welfare by arranging for soldiers' wives, orphans, illegitimate children, and the disabled to live with families who were subsidized by the commune.

Like all of Russian society, villages were stratified, and the wealthiest families generally ruled the commune. Sometimes they served in leadership positions themselves, sometimes they sponsored poor clients. They generally dominated the skhod simply by intimidating poor families. Furthermore, since the surest way win support for a proposal was to ply the voters with vodka, the wealthy had a natural advantage.

If the mir belonged to a landlord, the lord was able to intervene at will. The lord had to approve the choice of overseer (and sometimes hired his own from outside the mir) and could veto the skhod's choice of elders and officials. In addition, landlords attempted to prevent the skhod from conscripting artisans and men with families. Beyond this, the lord could force peasants to marry, move them from one estate to another, convert them into household servants, train them as artisans, and determine their obrok and barshchina obligations with no limitation (except what the village elders could negotiate). Lords could not execute serfs, but they could order floggings that they knew would result in death. Punishable offenses included drunkenness, laziness, absence from church, and theft. Lords also had the right to send serfs they deemed "unruly" to Siberia. (This was not as severe as it might seem. In Siberia serfs became state peasants and were given state grants to set up households.)

PEOPLES OF THE EMPIRE

Many more ethnic groups were added to the Russian empire in the second half of the eighteenth century. In 1719, Russians made up 69 percent of the population of the empire, in 1782 only 48 percent. The partitions of Poland added Lithuanians, Balts, Belarusians, and Ukrainians, many of them members of the Catholic or Uniate Churches. Jews made up as much as 10 percent of the population of the Polish territories. Catherine showed greater tolerance for Jews than her predecessors, but she retained the tradition of keeping them out of Russia proper. In 1791, she confirmed a "Pale of Settlement" that restricted Jews to Belarus, Ukraine, New Russia, and the western borderlands annexed from Poland and Turkey.

Alexander I annexed the Grand Duchy of Finland in 1809. At the Congress of Vienna in 1815, he acquired the Grand Duchy of Warsaw, which meant that Russia now owned all the territory that had been Poland before the reign of Catherine II. Alexander also oversaw Russia's expansion into the southern Caucasus. Georgia joined the Empire willingly. As a Christian nation, it preferred Russian rule to rule by Muslim Iranians or Turks, and in 1801, after decades of negotiation, Georgia's king abdicated and allowed his realm to be administratively absorbed into the Russian empire. Armenia and Azerbaijan were annexed from Turkey and Iran, respectively. However, the southern border was drawn without respect for national unity, and Azerbaijanis and Armenians in the Russian Empire were separated from the majority of their ethnic compatriots. Furthermore, although Russia incorporated the south Caucasus into its empire, the Muslim tribes (Circassians, Kabardians, Chechens, etc.) of the northern Caucasus region remained independent.

By the early nineteenth century, all the nomadic peoples east of the Volga River, with the exception of the Kazakh Great Horde in Central Asia, were subordinated to Russia and incorporated into imperial administration. Nomadic peoples such as the Bashkirs, Tatars, and Kazakhs, did not completely abandon their nomadic lifestyle and they did not give up their ethnic identity. Their movements were restricted, however, by the increasing numbers of peasant communities who began to turn the steppe pastures into tilled fields. This forced many nomads to become farmers themselves, growing hay to feed their herds instead of moving them to new pastures. In some regions, the nomads became a minority group. In Ufa province, for example, the Bashkir population fell from more than three quarters of the total in 1762 to less than a half in 1844. By the end of the eighteenth century, Russian immigrants made up 70 percent of the population of Siberia.

Only a few ethnic groups chose to emigrate rather than join the empire. Most Crimean Tatars who had lived on the Black Sea steppe emigrated to the Ottoman Empire; only a small community remained in the Crimean peninsula. In 1771, the Kalmyks made a disastrous attempt to migrate back to their original homeland in China. Of the 150,000 who began the exodus, more than 100,000 died en route, and those who made it were incorporated into the Chinese empire. About 11,000 Kalmyk households remained in the Volga region. They lost their status as an autonomous people, and they became increasingly sedentary.

Catherine the Great and Alexander I, in the spirit of Enlightened cosmopolitanism, fostered the vision of Russia as a tolerant, multiethnic empire. Catherine, in particular, deemphasized Orthodoxy and represented the Russian Empire as engaged in a broad project of spreading Enlightened civilization. Russia's rulers generally favored education in the Russian language and the building of Orthodox churches, but neither was an absolute requirement. As long as a people accepted subordination to the Emperor, the language they spoke and the religion they professed was negotiable. When a non-Russian nation was incorporated into the empire, its noble elite was granted the rights and privileges of membership in the Russian nobility. The only exception was that non-Christian nobles were not allowed to own Christian serfs (but were free to own serfs of other religions).

Catherine had ended the practice of forced conversion of the nomads. In fact, she thought that Islam could be used as a "civilizing" force in Central Asia, and she encouraged the construction of mosques and missionary activity by pro-Russian Muslim clerics. When Alexander I annexed Azerbaijan, Armenia, and Georgia, he made no attempt to convert the populations. When he gained the Grand Duchy of Poland (1815) and the Grand Duchy of Finland (1809), he did not incorporate them into the empire at all, but ruled them as autonomous provinces. Poles and Finns were allowed to keep their traditional rights and institutions.

CONCLUSION

In 1815, Russia appeared to be on the verge of dominating Europe. It was the largest European country in both territory and population. Over the course of the previous century, its prosperity had steadily increased, and it had won every war it fought. In 1814, the Russian army had defeated the previously invincible Napoleon, occupied Paris, and been welcomed by Europe as a liberator. Yet only forty years later, Russia would suffer a humiliating defeat on its own soil at the hands of France, England, and Sardinia, and its self-confidence would be shaken. The next chapter will examine how this came about.

_____ TEXT DOCUMENTS _____

Petitions to Catherine the Great

Throughout her reign, Catherine encouraged the population (except for serfs) to petition her regarding their grievances and concerns. Nobles were allowed to petition her directly; Townspeople could petition through the governor of their province. Below are three petitions, the first was submitted during the Legislative Assembly of 1767; the second and third were submitted later in her reign.

PETITION FROM TATAR NOBLES IN KAZAN PROVINCE, 1767

- What tell us about ethnic relations in the Russian empire?
- What does it reveal Russian social and religious policies in the borderlands?

12. We the under-signed believe that nothing is more offensive to a person, regardless of his faith and rank, than to suffer disrespect and insults toward his religion. This makes one extremely agitated and provokes unnecessary words of abuse. But it often happens that people of various ranks say extremely contemptuous things about our religion and our prophet (also during our religious worship), and this is a great affront for us. Therefore, we request a law that anyone who curses our religion be held legally accountable (in a manner that the commission for the preparation of a new law code sees fit.) [We further ask] that we Tatars and nobles not be forced to convert to Orthodoxy, but that only those who so wish (in accordance with petitions that they file themselves in government offices) be baptized. . . .

15. If any of our people are voluntarily baptized into the faith of the Greek confession, they should be ordered to move to settlements with Russians and converts the very same year in which the conversion takes place; meanwhile they are to remain in the poll-tax under our name, but for less than a quarter share. We ask that, under no circumstances, are converts to be permitted to sell their houses, garden plots, and hayland to Russians or people of other ranks, but are to sell only to us Tatars; they must sell either to unconverted kinsmen or other Tatars. For this it could be ordered that households and garden plots in our settlements (according to square meters), as well as haylands near these settlements in Kazan, be evaluated in terms of hay yield (in accordance with the Law Code of 1649 and other decrees) so that, when the converted people resettle, they will be satisfied with the compensation and raise no disputes. Also, without a special personal order from Her Imperial Majesty, no churches should be built in our suburbs and thereby put pressure upon us. And if anyone constructs a church in our settlements without a decree of Her Imperial Majesty, could not a decree be issued against this while the law code is still in preparation?

_____

Source: *From Supplication to Revolution: A Documentary Social History of Imperial Russia* by Gregory L. Freeze, copyright 1988 by Oxford University Press, Inc. Used by permission of Oxford University Press, Inc.

PETITION FROM BELARUSIAN JEWS, 1784

- What must have been said in the "imperial manifesto" that is referred to in this petition?
- What does this reveal about Catherine's social policy and the changing nature of the Russian Empire?

1. Some [Belarusian Jews] who live in towns engage in trade and, especially, in the distillation of spirits, beer and mead, which they sell wholesale and retail. This privilege was also extended to them when Belarus joined the Russian Empire [in the partitions]. Hence everyone active in this business used all their resources to construct buildings suitable for distillation and pursuit of this trade in the cities. After the Belarusian region joined the Russian Empire, the Jews in some towns constructed more of these in the same fashion and at great expense. The imperial monarchical decree [on Jews] emboldens them to request tearfully some monarchical mercy.

2. According to an ancient custom, when the squires built a new village, they summoned the Jews to reside there and gave them certain privileges for several years and the permanent liberty to distill spirits, brew beer and mead, and sell these drinks. On this basis, the Jews built houses and distillation plants at considerable expense. The squires, at their own volition, farmed out the inns to Jews, with the freedom to distill and sell liquor. As a result, the head of the household and his family employed other poor [people] and paid their taxes. A new decree of Her Imperial Majesty on 3 May 1783, reserved [this right] of the squires to their hamlets and villages. But a decree of the governor-general of Belarus has now forbidden the squires to farm out distillation in their villages to Jews, even if the squires want to do this. As a result, the poor Jews who built houses in small villages and promoted both this trade and distillation have been deprived of these and left completely impoverished. But until all the Jewish people are totally ruined, the Jewish merchants suffer restraints equally with the poor rural Jews, since their law obliges them to assist all who share their religious faith. They therefore request an imperial decree authorizing the squire, if he wishes, to farm out distillation to Jews in rural areas.

3. Although, with Her Imperial Majesty's permission, Jews may be elected as officials (per the imperial statute on provincial administration), Jews are allotted fewer votes than other people and hence no Jew can ever attain office. Consequently, Jews have no one to defend them in courts and find themselves in a desperate situation—given their fear and ignorance of Russian—in case of misfortune, even if innocent. To consummate all the good already bestowed, Jews dare to petition that an equal number of electors be required from Jews as from others (or, at least, that in matters involving Jews and non-Jews, a representative from the Jewish community hold equal rights with non-Jews, be present to accompany Jews in court, and attend the interrogation of Jews. But cases involving only Jews (except for promissory notes and debts) should be handled solely in Jewish courts, because Jews assume obligations among themselves, make agreements and conclude all kinds of deals in the Jewish language and in accordance with Jewish rites and law (which are not known to others). Moreover, those who transgress their laws and order should be judged in Jewish courts. Similarly, preserve intact all their customs and holidays in the spirit of their faith, as is mercifully assured in the imperial manifesto. . . .

Source: *From Supplication to Revolution: A Documentary Social History of Imperial Russia* by Gregory L. Freeze, copyright 1988 by Oxford University Press, Inc. Used by permission of Oxford University Press, Inc.

PETITION FROM A RUSSIAN NOBLEWOMAN, 1768

- What does this reveal about women's rights and gender relations in Russia in the late eighteenth century?
- What does it reveal about master-serf relations?

This petition comes from Aleksandra Ivanovna Krotkaia, the wife of Life-Guards Captain Vasilii Fedorovich Karamyshev, and the daughter of Ivan Krotkii, and addresses the following points:

1. In 1762 I was given in marriage by my father, court councillor Ivan Egorovich Krotkii, to the husband named above.

2. Prior to our wedding, my husband did not have the slightest affection and love for me (as became apparent from his subsequent behavior), but his sole aim in marrying me was to exercise his rights as my husband and to enjoy the landed estate which my father deigned to grant me. That is exactly what happened: after we married, he not only did not leave his mistress (his serf girl Daria Moiseeva, who had been such prior to our marriage), but with no shame or sense of decency, and to vex and humiliate me, he treated her like his legal wife. And all the time he constantly subjected me to every conceivable mistreatment.

3. No matter how insulting such behavior may have been, I tried to conceal my feelings from my husband, and always sought to perform the duties of love and respect that are required of me by law. I continued to hope that, by being patient and by submitting completely to his will and wishes, even if I could not elicit mutual love toward me (in accordance with our marital union), then at least I could make him feel pity for my condition. But all this only made him even more brutal and unfeeling. Thus, in spite of everything, he subjected me to even greater mistreatment: he was not content to have the serf girl occupy my place as his legal wife, but to satisfy his wild lust and passion, went to my estate [where he] forcibly took wives from husbands and daughters from fathers (including underage girls) and raped them. I can prove all this with incontrovertible evidence.

4. For the four harrowing years that I lived with him, the words simply do not exist to describe all the vexation and disappointment that I experienced at my husband's hands. So that my patience is now fully exhausted. No matter how much I wished to remain patient, I could see that I lack the strength to restrain his gross misconduct and therefore—under the pretext of visiting my mother—had to leave my husband.

So may Your Imperial Majesty have the Most Holy Governing Synod accept my petition with regard to the adultery committed by my husband with his serf girl Daria Moiseeva and with others, and for the unendurable maltreatment. And order that I the undersigned be separated from him and be permitted to live a peaceful secure life until the end of my days on my estate. My husband is presently now at his village in Moscow District, in the village of Nikolskoe.

A Serf's Memoirs

Aleksandr Nikitenko began his life as a serf, but managed to acquire an education, his free-dom, and a professional career. He wrote a memoir describing his background and youth.

- What does this reveal about the nature of Russian society?
- The possibilities for social mobility among peasants? The limitations on that mobility?
- Stratification in peasant communities?
- Changes in Russian courtship patterns?
- Attitudes of the educated toward the peasantry?

. . . When father, Vasilii Mikhailovich Nikitenko, was eleven or twelve, one of Count Sheremetev's agents arrived in Alekseyevka to select boys for the count's choir. Father had a fine soprano voice, so he was sent to Moscow to join it. . . .

The Sheremetev choir ran a school where, besides studying music, young choirboys learned to read and write. Father displayed an unusual talent for everything he was taught. In his free time he read a great deal and acquired all sorts of knowledge, far above his station in life. He even learned French.

His intelligence, kindness, and talent, as well as his lively and pleasant manner, endeared him to everyone. Soon he became the most popular youngster among his choir mates, and even came to the attention of Count Sheremetev. . . .

In the meantime, my father's voice had changed. He was already seventeen, and, in keeping with custom in the count's administration, he was sent to one of the count's estates to do clerical work. The post was in Father's native village. His abilities and conduct were considered so outstanding that despite his youth, he was assigned the important position of chief clerk of Alekseyevka. . . .

[The village was governed by officials appointed by the count, officials elected by the commune, and the commune assembly. Nevertheless,] all administrative power was actually concentrated in the hands of the count's agent or steward, but the power behind the community's mainspring and direction lay in the hands of the wealthy serfs, the so-called meshchane. They were mostly involved in trade, and many possessed considerable capital—anywhere from one thousand to two hundred thousand or more rubles.

Their main trade was in grain, tallow, and skins. As for their ways, nothing good could be said about them. . . . Inflated by their wealth, these Little Russians [Ukrainians] had contempt for those below them, that is, for people who had less than they. The meshchane swindled like crazy and owed their prosperity to crooked deals. . . .

Real Little Russians, their customs and ways, were to be found almost exclusively in hamlets outside Alekseyevka. There you could meet temperaments of true Homeric simplicity, good-hearted, honest folk, displaying that selfless hospitality for which Little Russians have always been famous. Thievery, deception, and Muscovite audacity and swindling were unheard of among them. . . .

Source: Aleksandr Nikitenko, *Up From Serfdom: My Childhood and Youth in Russia, 1804–1824.* (New Haven: Yale University Press, 2001), 6–14. (c) Yale University Press. Reprinted by permission.

The meshchane hurt [the] peasants by employing various devices, like trying to subject them to their authority, seizing small plots of productive land and woods, or by foisting on them community burdens that the meshchane were unwilling to bear. All this was done with impunity. The count's agents thought only of how they could enrich themselves. As for the elected representatives of the people or the commune assembly, they came from those same meshchane, who had at their disposal the elections as well as the votes in the commune assembly. . . .

This was the kind of society to which Father was first summoned to live and work. He arrived in Alekseyevka in 1800 or 1801, when he had just turned eighteen. From the meshchane he received a cold welcome. . . .

Suspecting Father of being a secret agent of the count, the rich meshchane were very upset at first. Their gloom vanished quickly when they saw they were dealing with a hot-headed, inexperienced youth who would be easy to handle. They calculated that it was only necessary to let his fervor build up a little more and wait patiently for the appropriate moment to strike.

In the beginning the local aristocrats still hoped to curb the unwelcome reformer by employing other tactics—peaceful ones. They wanted to marry him off to one of their kin and, by involving him in family matters, make him more compliant. But Father defied them all. Indeed, he rushed into marriage, but to someone of his choice.

Here's how it happened. One evening he was crossing the bridge . . . a crowd of women surged forth from the village to meet them. And in the crowd was an attractive, modest-looking young woman who caught my father's eye. From a friend he learned her name and that she was the daughter of a tailor of humble means who made sheepskin coats. . . .

Three days later he told his parents that he wanted to marry her. Grandmother Nikitenko was horrified when she learned that her son's intended wife was not the daughter of a rich meshchane but of a poor, obscure tailor.

Father was an important figure in the sloboda; first, because of his administrative position, and second, for his many talents. His Moscow education made him a real gentleman. All this gave his mother grounds to count on a far better marriage for her son. For a daughter-in-law she had hoped to have the daughter of some wealthy member of the sloboda's upper crust. To keep the young man from an unequal marriage she tried everything–she argued, pleaded, exhorted. All in vain. The romantic meeting, the girl's beauty, and her very poverty compelled the young man to stand firm. . . .

The elderly parents of my future mother were struck dumb when they learned why such an important guest as the chief clerk—my future father—had come to see them. "How can it be," exclaimed the old woman, "that our Katya would become your wife? What kind of match would that be? We are poor and simple folk, and you are an educated fellow, a gentleman, and a handsome one to boot, Katya has nothing, honest to goodness, only some skirts, slips, a few kerchiefs."

My father burst into some exalted prose. Naturally, the old woman didn't understand a word of it. But in the end they decided to summon Katya and ask if she would agree to marry the chief clerk, Vasilii Mikhailovich Nikitenko. Bewildered, trembling and blushing, Katya replied that she would do whatever her parents wished. About three weeks later the wedding took place, to the secret displeasure of the bridegroom's mother, and to the astonishment of Alekseyevka's upper crust, who from then on hated the renegade and became more determined in their intentions to ruin him.

Radishchev, *A Journey from St. Petersburg to Moscow*

In 1790, a nobleman, Aleksandr Radishchev, published A Journey from St. Peters-burg to Moscow *on his privately owned printing press. The copy he had submitted for approval by the censors did not contain, among other things, the following excerpt. When its true contents were discovered, Radishchev was arrested and exiled to Siberia by Catherine the Great.*

- To what intellectual traditions does Radishchev appeal?
- What is Radishchev's purpose in this selection? How does he make his case?

Having brought our beloved fatherland step by step to the flourishing condition in which it how finds itself, we see that science, art, and manufacturing have been brought to the high-est degree of perfection that humans are capable of, in our land we see human reason freely spreading its wings and unerringly ascending everywhere to greatness and that it has now become the trustworthy guarantor of public law. Under [reason's] sovereign protection, our hearts are free to rise up in prayers to the almighty creator. We can say with inexpressible joy that our fatherland is an abode that is pleasing to the divine being, since its construction is not based on prejudice and superstition, but on our inner feelings of the mercy of the father of all. We do not know the enmities that have so often separated people because of their be-liefs, we also do not know the compulsion to believe. Having been born in this freedom, we truly respect one another as brothers that belong to one family and have one father, God.

The torch of science, hovering over our legislation, now distinguishes it from the legisla-tion of many other countries. The balance of powers and the equality of property destroy the root of civil discord. Moderation in punishment creates respect for the laws of the supreme power which are respected like the commands of tender parents to their offspring and pre-vents even guileless evildoing. Clarity in the laws pertaining to the acquisition and protec-tion of property prevents family quarrels from arising. The boundary that separates one citizen and his property from another is deep, clear to everyone, and respected as sacred by everyone. Private injuries are rare among us and are amicably reconciled. Public education is concerned with making us gentle, making us peace-loving citizens, but above all, making us human beings.

Enjoying domestic tranquility, have no foreign enemies, having brought society to the highest bliss of accord, is it possible that we could be so alien from humanitarian feeling, so alien from the impulse of pity, so alien from the tenderness of noble hearts, so alien from brotherly love, that we can allow in our sight a never-ending reproach to us, a disgrace to our furthest posterity, that a whole third of our fellows, our equal fellow citizens, our beloved brothers in nature, are in the heavy bonds of slavery and bondage? . . .

Oh, our beloved fellow citizens! Oh, true sons of the fatherland! Look about and under-stand your delusions. Servants of the eternal divinity, pursuing the benefit of society and the happiness of humanity, of one mind with us, have explained to you in their teachings in the

Source: A. N. Radishchev, *Puteshestvie iz Peterburga v Moskvu. Polnoe sobranie sochinenii* (Moscow-Leningrad: Izdatel'stvo Akademii Nauk SSSR, 1938), 311–312, 313, 314–315, 320–321. Translated by the author.

name of the most merciful God in whom they believe, how contrary it is to his wisdom and love to rule capriciously over your neighbor. They have tried with arguments taken from nature and from our hearts to prove to you your cruelty, injustice, and sinfulness. Even now their voice, solemn in the temples of the living god, cries loudly, "Think about your errors, soften your heard-heartedness, break the fetters of your brothers, open the prison of servitude, and let those who are just like you taste the sweetness of community life, for which they have been destined by the All-Merciful just as you have. . . ."

In school, when you were young, they taught you the foundations of natural law and civil law. Natural law showed you that human beings, hypothetically outside of society, were given the same constitution by nature, and therefore had the same rights, and were consequently equal to one another, and no one should rule another. Civil law showed you people who had exchanged unlimited freedom for the peaceful enjoyment of that freedom. But if you all have set limits on your freedom, and obey the law, since all are equal from birth in natural law, they must also be equally limited. . . . All this is familiar to you, you have imbibed these laws with your mother's milk. It is only the prejudice of the moment, only greed (please don't be offended by my words), only greed blinds us and makes us become like madmen in darkness.

But who among us wears the fetters, who feels the weight of slavery? The farmer! The person who feeds our leanness and satisfies our hunger, the one who gives us our health and prolongs our life, all the while himself not having the right to dispose of what he makes or what he produces. But who has the best right to a field if not the one who tills it? . . . At the beginning of social life, he who was able to cultivate a field had the right to possess it, and, having cultivated it had the exclusive right to its fruits. But how far we have diverged from the original social constitution regarding property! With us, the one who has that very natural right is not only completely denied it, but while working in someone else's field, he sees that his own subsistence is dependant on the power of another. . . .

Do you not know, beloved fellow citizens, what ruin is in store for us and in what danger we find ourselves? All the callous feelings of the slaves, that are not softened by a nod toward the blessing of freedom, will get stronger and will intensify their inner feelings. A stream that is stopped in its flow, becomes stronger as the obstruction to it becomes stronger. Having burst through the dam, nothing can stop its outpouring. It is the same with our brothers who we are keeping in chains. They are awaiting for the right opportunity. The bell rings. And all the destruction of bestial atrocity pours out instantly. Around us we will see sword and poison. Death and fire will be our due for our harshness and inhumanity. And the longer it takes us and the more stubborn we are about releasing their bonds, the more implacable they will be in their revenge. . . .

This is what stands before us, this is what we must expect. Ruin and grief are steadily approaching, danger is hovering over our heads. Time has already raised its scythe, it waits for an hour of opportunity, and the first flatterer or lover of humanity who arises to awaken the unfortunates will hasten the scythe's stroke. Beware!

Figure 10-1 Coins from the Reigns of Catherine II and Alexander I

- Compare these images with one another and with coins that have previously appeared.
- How are the two monarchs represented?

Source: de Chaudoir, *Obozrenie Russkikh deneg.* Part 2, plate 38, drawing 4 and plate 47, drawing 3.

Figure 10-2 Cathedral of the Virgin of Kazan

The Kazan Cathedral in St. Petersburg was planned by Paul and completed in the reign of Alexander I.

- Compare this with previous images of Russian churches.
- What is the difference? What does this reveal?

Source: Dorling Kindersley Media Library

Figure 10-3 An Officer and a Soldier

This is an engraving from a book about the uniforms of the Russian army published during the reign of Catherine II. This is titled "Officer and Enlisted Man, 1756–62."

- Compare this with earlier images of Russian soldiers.
- What does this reveal about the changing nature of the Russian military?
- Of trends in Russian society?

Source: Unknown eighteenth-century artist.

Figure 10-4 Peoples of the Empire

These engravings made by a German ethnographer were published in a book titled *Description of All the Peoples of the Russian Empire*, which was commissioned by Catherine the Great in the late-eighteenth century.

- What do they reveal about the diversity of the empire?
- What does this project (i.e., publishing the book in which these illustrations appear) reveal about Russia's imperial attitudes?

Source: Johann Gottlieb Georgi, *Beschreibung aller nationen des Russischer Reiches*, St. Petersburg, 1776.

Figure 10-5 Western Russia in 1815

Less than a century after the death of Peter the Great, Russia had absorbed its immediate western and southern neighbors and now shared borders with Iran, the Ottoman Empire, Austria-Hungary, and Prussia. In the Partitions of Poland, Catherine the Great had seized all of the former Lithuania and the northern Black Sea steppe. Alexander I gained the former Poland (the Grand Duchy of Warsaw), Finland, and Georgia.

FOR FURTHER READING

(In addition to the books by Blum, Hartley, Kahan, Khodarkovsky, LeDonne, Moon, and Wortman from the previous chapter.)

Dixon, Simon. *Catherine the Great*. New York: Longman, 2001.

Hartley, Janet M. *Alexander I*. New York : Longman, 1994.

de Madariaga, Isabel. *Catherine the Great: A Short History*. New Haven, CT: Yale University Press, 1990.

_____ *Russia in the Age of Catherine the Great*. New Haven, Conn.: Yale University Press, 1981.

Saunders, David. *Russia in the Age of Reaction and Reform, 1801–1881*. London: Longman, 1992.

CHAPTER ELEVEN

RUSSIA IN THE AGE
OF CONSERVATISM, 1815–1856

Between 1815 and 1855, Russia's rulers managed to achieve what all the ruling elites of Europe of the day aspired to: the preservation of their traditional prerogatives while resisting demands for increased participation in government. Nevertheless, the educational and cultural policies of Catherine the Great and Alexander I had produced a writing and reading public that thought independently and, despite censorship, was beyond the control of the rulers. In high culture, the first half of the nineteenth century was Russia's Golden Age of poetry. It was also a period in which independent social critics were not isolated, as Radishchev had been, but were numerous enough to form a dynamic subculture, the "intelligentsia." Like Peter the Great, Tsars Alexander I (1801–1825) and Nicholas I (1825–1855) continued to reform Russian society (or at least to plan reforms), but unlike their great ancestor, they were no longer radical activists in the vanguard of Russian society. They were now reluctant reformers who wanted only to renovate the monarchy; the most radical ideas for reform now came from the intelligentsia and even from the bureaucracy.

EURASIAN CONTEXT

By the end of the Napoleonic Wars in 1815, Europe's collective devotion to the principles of the Enlightenment had been exhausted. Many Enlightenment ideas did in fact live on among the middle classes: faith that science could understand and master the world, the lib-

Turn to page 243 for a map showing key geographic locations and features for this time period.

eral conception of individual liberties, the contract theory of government, and laissez-faire economics. These ideas, however, were considered passé, and in art, philosophy, and political thought, there was a strong reaction against the outlook of the Enlightenment. Romantic poets and artists rejected the rationalist, classical, and urbane tone of the eighteenth century and celebrated genius, intuition, and passion. Romantics sought communion with nature and became interested in folk culture. In philosophy, idealists rejected empiricism and the conception of the universe as a machine, and they proposed that reality is ultimately spiritual and that the universe is a living and evolving organism.

In politics, conservatives created a philosophy to counter Locke's contract theory of government. Nostalgic for a hierarchical, Christian society, in which people knew their place, conservatives used history to argue that society did not originate in a contract but in accident, that the logic of history is superior to individual reason, and that tradition embodies the wisdom of the ages. Christianity also experienced a revival. To many, the personal God of the Old Testament and the promise of salvation of the New, was more spiritually satisfying than the abstract propositions of Deism. Christianity was also promoted by conservative theorists and by the ruling elites because they believed it contributed to social stability.

The most important ideologies to arise from the French Revolution were the closely entwined ideas of democracy, popular sovereignty, nationalism, and socialism. In 1793, after King Louis XVI was executed and the monarchy abolished, the leaders of the revolutionary French state needed a new source of legitimacy for their government and a new inspiration for patriotism. This they found in the idea of popular sovereignty: that the French nation was the repository of sovereign power. This contradicted the liberal notion that only property owners had a stake in the government, and it entailed universal manhood suffrage. At the same time, it suggested that there was a higher public good than merely the protection of individual liberties and property rights. Rejecting Enlightenment cosmopolitanism, they proposed that the French nation was an historically evolving entity, unique from other nations, and deserving the ultimate loyalty of all French people. This idea worked. Frenchmen enthusiastically responded to the summons to arms, and French patriotism contributed to the initial invincibility of Napoleon's armies. After 1815, radical democrats used the idea of popular sovereignty to advocate universal manhood suffrage. Socialists used the same notion to argue that the well-being of the entire people was more important than the property rights of the few. Nationalists used the idea that humanity is divided into nations to seek national consolidation (in the case of Germans and Italians who were fragmented by political divisions) or independence (in the case of Poles, Hungarians, and the southern Slavs who were ruled by foreigners).

The main task of the Congress of Vienna (1815) that ended the Napoleonic Wars was to restore the traditional ruling dynasties who had been deposed by Napoleon and to establish a balance of power to prevent the rise of another hegemonic. The Congress redrew boundary lines and transferred territory to the major victors, Russia, Austria, and Prussia. The Kingdom of Poland was reconstituted (from the partitions taken earlier by Austria and Prussia) and was given to Alexander I. The Congress also allowed France to remain a great power; Britain wanted France as a balance to Russia, while Russia wanted it to balance Prussia and Austria. The Congress also declared a "Concert of Europe": a plan for periodic congresses to negotiate international conflicts to avoid war and preserve the status quo.

Factory production had been increasing in England since the middle of the eighteenth century, but after 1815, the effects on society became so far-reaching that Europeans became aware that an economic revolution–the Industrial Revolution–was under way. Factory production of textiles led to the development of coal mining, the forging of steel, and railroad construction. Cities became larger, dirtier, more unhealthy, and more dangerous. The middle class grew in wealth and power, and the working class grew in numbers and misery. Furthermore, the development of steel and machine technology produced ever more deadly weapons of war that allowed European military forces to overcome the numerical superiority of the armies in the non-European world.

At the same time that Europe was experiencing unprecedented growth in wealth and power, the great land Empires of Eurasia were in decline. After 1800, China experienced a classic dynastic downturn. The population continued to rise, tax collectors became corrupt, and landowners were more exploitative; the bureaucracy was overworked and understaffed, and the army was demoralized. In addition, China's long tradition of positive trade balances finally came to an end when the English found a product that the Chinese would buy: opium. Opium addiction became rampant in the army and bureaucracy, and sale of the drug turned England's trade deficit into a surplus. When the Chinese government outlawed the sale of opium and confiscated British opium stocks in 1840, England used this violation of free trade principles as the pretext for war. England's military technology so far outmatched China's that it defeated China in only a few months of fighting. England forced China to open its ports and markets to English commerce (including, of course, the sale of opium).

The Ottoman Empire had chosen the wrong side in the Napoleonic Wars. The Congress of Vienna forced it to grant virtual independence to Serbia and to cede Bessarabia to Russia. Then, in the decades after 1815, the Ottoman Empire lost more territory: Greece won independence, and the governor of Egypt asserted his autonomy from the Sultan. These military setbacks prompted westernizing reforms by Sultan Mahmud II (after he destroyed the Janissaries in 1826). Mahmud then established western-style schools, limited the power of the Muslim clergy, and established printing presses for books and newspapers. In 1845, Mahmud's son and successor Abdul Mejid introduced the Tanzimat, the reorganization of the empire on western lines.

Dynastic civil war weakened Iran and made possible encroachment by England and Russia. England wanted to subordinate Iran politically in order to protect its access to India, while Russia, who shared a border with Iran, wanted to encroach on its territory. In 1828, Russia seized Iran's Caucasian territories and forced the Shah to accept Russian diplomatic and commercial agents. At the same time, Qajar shahs accepted English subsidies, and followed a pro-British foreign policy. The shahs brought in English officers to help reorganize their armies on western lines, and they began to send students to study in Europe.

Anglo-Russian rivalry in Central and Southwest Asia, known as "the Great Game," also affected Afghanistan. Russia supported an attempt by Iran to annex western Afghanistan, while the British, who saw this as a threat to India, sent aid to the Afghans. In1838 England used bribery and military intimidation to install a puppet ruler. Nevertheless, both Russia and England failed. Afghanistan repulsed the Russian-backed Iranian attack, and the British army was destroyed by hostile Afghan tribes as it withdrew to India in 1842.

POLITICAL DEVELOPMENTS AND FOREIGN AFFAIRS

Beginning in 1812 with Napoleon's invasion of Russia, Alexander I (1801–1825) had become increasingly religious; he read the New Testament for the first time, organized the Russian Bible Society, and surrounded himself with an eclectic group of evangelical and mystical Christians. His religious mood only intensified after his victory over Napoleon. In foreign affairs, Alexander proposed a "Holy Alliance" that would base international relations on Christian love rather than self-interest. (Most European governments signed the alliance, but it had no effect on their behavior.) At home, Alexander promoted his religious agenda through public education. In 1817, he transformed the Ministry of Education into the Ministry of Education and Spiritual Affairs, and he appointed as its minister Aleksandr Golitsyn, head of both the Holy Synod and the Russian Bible Society. Golitsyn supervised two campaigns to purge the Universities of Kazan and St. Petersburg of professors who did not teach in the spirit of Christianity. Alexander outlawed secret societies in 1822, largely because of his desire to stamp out freemasonry.

On the other hand, Alexander I did not entirely abandon his commitment to enlightened reform. When the Congress of Vienna created the Kingdom of Poland and made Alexander its hereditary king, he chose to rule it as a constitutional monarch. He was personally involved in writing its constitution which provided for an elected parliament, civil liberties including freedom of the press and of religion, and the right of habeas corpus. It also appears that Alexander seriously considered granting a constitution for Russia. In 1816, he commissioned Nicholas Novosiltsev to draw up a Constitutional Charter of Russian Empire on lines similar to the Polish constitution. The final draft (1819) provided for civil liberty and rule of law, and it organized the empire on federal principles, granting considerable autonomy to the provinces and providing for elected assemblies at regional and federal levels. The Charter was filed away, however, and was never put into effect.

Alexander continued to contemplate emancipation of the serfs, and, in what might have been a pilot program for the rest of the empire, he abolished serfdom in Estonia (1816), Courland (1817), and Livonia (1819). His program of emancipation was seriously flawed because the serfs were freed without land; they became the paid laborers of their former landlords. Though free, their standard of living deteriorated seriously, and they were deeply dissatisfied. Between 1816 and 1820, the Baltic provinces experienced sixty-six rebellions so serious that troops had to be sent to suppress them.

Alexander also undertook a major reform of the way in which the Russian army was conscripted and funded. During the Napoleonic Wars, Russia's standing army had more than doubled from under 400,000 to more than 1,000,000. A standing army of that size was too expensive to maintain but too dangerous to demobilize. To release perhaps half a million young military veterans, many of them former serfs, back into society could have been an invitation to rebellion. Alexander's solution was to begin to cease the conscription of serfs and to create "military colonies" among the state peasants instead. A military colony was a reconstituted village of state peasants to which an army regiment was attached. Each family housed one soldier, and, in exchange for food and shelter, he would work on the farm when not on active service. All the young men born in the colony, peasants' as well as soldiers' sons (except for the oldest son in every peasant family) would become soldiers. Once fully implemented, there would be no further need for conscription. The military colony system was also an experiment in Enlightenment social engineering: New villages were built on rational principles, including standard house designs and geometrical layout of village streets. Villages were also intended to be provided with medical services and schools.

Though an ingenious idea, the military colonies failed in practice. Although they no longer had to pay the poll tax, peasants were actually worse off: They lost a higher proportion of their income supporting the troops than they would have paid in taxes. They also resented the excessive regimentation of their lives. The man in charge of the military colonies, Aleksei Arakcheev (Alexander's principal adviser after 1815), was the most narrow-minded sort of military disciplinarian. Arakcheev insisted that peasants as well as soldiers should wear uniforms and be subject to military discipline—including set times for waking up, working in the fields, and going to bed at night. There were many local uprisings and at least two major rebellions, and the system was abandoned after 1831.

In foreign affairs, Alexander was more tolerant of constitutional government than his Great Power colleagues, but he willingly adhered to the "Concert of Europe," and he supported the policy of protecting monarchies against liberal rebels. The most notable interventions were in Italy and Spain 1822. The Greek nationalist rebellion against the Ottoman Empire presented a rather different situation, since it was not an internal liberal reform movement, but a struggle of national liberation of Orthodox Christians from Muslim rule. Although Alexander was extremely sympathetic to the Greek cause, he accepted the Concert's decision not to intervene.

When Alexander I died suddenly in 1825, a succession crisis ensued. Alexander's next older brother, Konstantin, Viceroy of Poland, had married a Polish Catholic, and Alexander felt this disqualified him for the Russian throne. Konstantin accepted his brother's judgement, and in 1823, Alexander wrote a decree making their younger brother Nicholas next in line. Alexander neglected, however, to submit the decree to be approved and published by the Senate. The announcement in 1825 that *Nicholas* would succeed to the throne therefore came as a shock to Russian society. The only law on concession anyone knew about (Paul's decree on inheritance) would have made Konstantin tsar. Indeed, Nicholas initially pledged allegiance to Konstantin, awaiting his older brother's formal renunciation of the throne. When, after weeks of waiting, Konstantin made no official announcement, Nicholas finally declared that he would require an oath of loyalty sworn to himself on December 14, 1825.

This extended period of uncertainty provided an opportunity for disaffected army officers to attempt a liberal revolution. The "Decembrists," as the rebels were known, represented a broad segment of Russian educated society, which had been disillusioned by Alexander's failure to live up to Enlightenment principles. After 1815, a number of secret societies had formed, united by their opposition to serfdom and autocracy. Some hoped for a constitutional monarchy with a parliament elected by property-owners, others had more visionary plans for a democratic republic combining socialism and capitalism. Army officers with ties to these secret societies, chose December 14, the day Nicholas had set for the oath of allegiance, as the time to act. They assembled three thousand soldiers in Senate Square in St. Petersburg and demanded a constitutional monarchy. The rest of the army, however, did not rally to their cause, and, although it was rumored that some high-ranking officials would have willingly served in a new government had the Decembrists succeeded, the government remained loyal to Nicholas. The new tsar waited for a few hours, then summoned loyal troops who easily suppressed the rebellion.

A government investigation, headed by Nicholas himself, identified 289 individuals as participants in the rebellion; almost all of them army officers. Five were executed, thirty-one were imprisoned, and the remainder were exiled to Siberia. Later revolutionary opponents of the Russian autocracy would look back upon the Decembrists as their precursors; they were the first activists to demand a systematic restructuring of Russian society on idealistic principles. On the other hand, they also have much in common with the guards officers responsible for many of the regime changes of the eighteenth century. The Decembrists were elitists; they did not promote a popular rebellion, and their goal was a coup d'etat rather than a revolution. Nevertheless, whether social revolutionaries or elite conspirators, this was the last attempt of aristocratic military officers to change the regime. Future rebels would come from other segments of the population.

Nicholas I (1825–1855) was nineteen years younger than Alexander, and unlike Alexander he had not been raised by Catherine the Great and so had not been exposed to Enlightenment ideas. On the contrary, his mother raised him to revere his militaristic father, Paul, and while a teenager Nicholas had served in the Russian army. He had taken part in the triumphal march into Paris in 1814, and he came to the throne believing that Russia's greatness was founded on its military forces.

In Nicholas's reign, the rift between educated society and the court widened. Nicholas was jealous of his autocratic prerogatives and refused, on principle, to pay attention to social opinion or to consider the possibility of representative institutions. He opposed liberal revolution abroad and repressed independent, critical thought at home. To many people across Europe and Russia, Nicholas stood for reactionary, autocratic despotism.

In reality, however, Nicholas was no less a reformer than Alexander had been. He immediately set up a commission to review all of Alexander's plans for reform. He continued to consider the emancipation of the serfs, appointing a number of ad hoc committees to propose solutions to the problem. Although Nicholas did not free the serfs, he did make a tentative start at regulating serf-lord relations. The government began to draw up inventories of peasant obligations and to codify contractual obligations between lords and their serfs. He decreed that landless nobles could not buy serfs apart from land, and he limited the kinds of punishments that lords could mete out. In 1847 he made it possible for serfs to buy their freedom (if their lord went bankrupt), and in1848 he provided that serfs could buy unpopulated land (if their lord approved).

Nicholas also made significant improvements in the rights and status of state peasants: he confirmed their legal rights to own property, to make legally binding contracts, to be educated, and to become civil servants. In 1837, he established a Ministry of State Properties to administer state peasants. It built village schools, provided insurance against fire and crop failure, supplied medical care, and promoted modern farming methods. Self-government for state peasants was confirmed, and they were given title to their land.

Nicholas preferred to rule though personal agents rather than the professional civil service. He relied heavily on secret ad hoc committees for developing policy, and he expanded His Majesty's Own Chancery, an institution originally intended to manage the Tsar's household, into his personal agency for implementing policy. He divided the Chancery into six departments: a Civil Service Inspectorate, a department to supervise legal reform; a secret police (the "Third Section") to manage censorship, uncover subversion, and prevent revolution; and departments to supervise charitable institutions, state peasants, and Caucasian affairs. In 1837, Nicholas abolished the position of Governor-General and placed provincial governors under the authority of the Minister of Interior. He made town government more representative of all classes (though property qualifications remained in force.)

In 1826 Nicholas put Mikhail Speranskii in charge of reviewing and compiling the laws of the empire, and a complete collection of Russian law was published in 1835. It was not a real codification, since it did not lay down general legal principles, standards, and norms (aside from affirming the absolute sovereignty of the tsar). Instead, the compilers sorted through existing Russian law and resolved contradictions by choosing the most recently promulgated law. The Law Code of 1835 remained in effect, with supplements, until the Revolution of 1917. Speranskii's final accomplishment was to establish an Imperial School of Jurisprudence to educate the next generation of legal experts.

Nicholas I followed a very cautious foreign policy. He loved his army so much that he was reluctant actually to use it. His first war was defensive, a reaction to Iran's invasion of Georgia. The Russian counterattack easily retook Georgia and Russian armies proceeded toward the capital of Iran. In 1828, the Shah sued for peace, paid an indemnity, and ceded some Armenian territory. Nicholas was rather more aggressive toward the Ottoman Empire. Although he stood for stability and traditional authority in Christian Europe, he did not apply these principles to the possessions of the Ottoman Empire; in 1827, he provided military aid to the Greek independence movement. Greek successes against the Turkish navy resulted in a Turkish declaration of war against Russia which Russia won. The Treaty of Adrianople (1829) ceded Russia the mouth of the Danube River, gave Russia the right of commercial navigation of the Turkish straits, and provided for increased autonomy for the Balkan provinces of Moldavia and Wallachia, under a temporary Russian protectorate.

The next year, Nicholas had every intention of intervening in the Revolution of 1830 in France, but his plans to do so were stopped by opposition from Austria and Prussia and by a rebellion in Poland. Polish university students were inspired by the revolution in France to take to the streets demanding independence. The students were soon joined by the Polish army, and by November, the rebellion was national in scope. In 1831, the Polish Sejm formally declared popular sovereignty and renounced allegiance to Nicholas I. A major war ensued, which Russia ultimately won. Nicholas then dissolved the Kingdom of Poland and absorbed its territories into the Russian Empire.

In 1832, Russia intervened in Ottoman imperial politics again, this time on the side of the Sultan. Muhammad Ali, an Albanian general and the governor of Egypt, had declared his independence of the Ottoman Empire. He defeated an army sent to discipline him, counterattacked, and captured Damascus. Nicholas I put Russian forces at the disposal of the Sultan, who was able to defend Constantinople and drive Muhammad Ali back into Egypt. As compensation for this aid, the Sultan signed the Treaty of Unkiar Skelessi (1833), which announced an alliance of the two empires in "perpetual friendship, peace, and mutual assistance" and declared that Russia had a special relationship with Turkey, which included the right to protect Orthodox Christians living in the Ottoman Empire.

This situation alarmed the other great powers of Europe. In 1839, when another war broke out between the Sultan and Muhammad Ali, Great Britain, France, Austria, and Prussia joined Russia in intervening on behalf of the Ottoman Empire. At the London Straits Convention in 1841, they all applied the terms of Unkiar Skelessi to themselves; all of them claimed a "special relationship" with Turkey.

During the Revolution of 1848, Nicholas I attempted to preserve the status quo in Europe. He pressed Austria and Prussia not to yield to the revolutionary demands of their peoples, and he sent Russian troops to suppress revolution in Hungary. In 1850, when Prussia was on the verge of accepting leadership of the German Confederation, Nicholas firmly supported Austria's decision to intervene and prevent it.

Nicholas also acted to protect his own country from the revolutionary contagion. He restricted the publication of news from western Europe, and he forbade Russians to travel abroad. He instituted stricter and more systematic censorship of printed material and imposed tighter controls over the universities. In 1849, university enrollments were cut by two-thirds, and the curriculum was changed to emphasize technical subjects over the liberal arts. One of the most notorious of Nicholas's reactions to the Revolutions of 1848 was his treatment of the Petrashevskii Circle, a group of intellectuals who met regularly to discuss western ideas. In 1849, the police arrested the circle and many of their acquaintances. Fifty-one people were exiled and twenty-one, including the writer Fyodor Dostoyevsky, were sentenced to death. Only at the last moment were they informed that their sentences had been commuted to imprisonment.

The last event of Nicholas's reign, the Crimean War, arose out of a clash of geopolitical ambitions. Napoleon III, a nephew of Napoleon Bonaparte, who had become Emperor of France following the Revolution of 1848, wanted to renew France's alliance with the Ottoman Empire and to reestablish France as the preeminent power on the continent. England, whose imperial designs on the continent of Asia made Russia its natural enemy, was intent on stopping Russian expansion wherever possible. Russia, for its part, was interested both in annexing more Ottoman territory and in supporting national independence movements among the southern Slavs. The precipitating factor, however, was Nicholas' insistence of the right to intervene on behalf of Orthodox Christians in the Ottoman Empire. When he invaded and occupied Moldavia and Wallachia to force the Sultan to recognize his claim, the Sultan, with British and French encouragement, declared war.

Nicholas did not vigorously prosecute the war. His navy defeated the Turkish fleet but did not advance on Constantinople. Nicholas withdrew Russian troops from Moldavia and Wallachia, and he offered to negotiate. Britain and France, however, wanted war, and in

1854, their combined navies destroyed the Russian Black Sea fleet and landed troops on the Crimean Peninsula. Anglo-French forces won three major battles and laid siege to Sevastopol. In 1855, while this siege was underway, Nicholas I died of pneumonia.

RELIGION AND CULTURE

The Russian educational system continued to expand through the first half of the nineteenth century. Alexander I's educational reforms were fully implemented, and by the end of his reign Russia had 6 universities, 3 lyceums, 57 high schools, and 511 district schools. Expansion of education continued under Nicholas I. There had been 62,000 students in public schools by end of eighteenth century, by the 1830s, there were about 250,000, and by midcentury there were more than 400,000. In addition, private schools flourished, and parochial schools and seminaries continued to supply professionals as well as priests. Most doctors and lawyers, as well as a large number of civil servants, graduated from seminaries.

Admiral Shishkov, Minister of Education in the 1820s, believed that education should be limited to the propertied classes, and that it was harmful for ordinary people to be educated. He needn't have worried, for in the reign of Nicholas I, only 1 out of every 142 people in the empire actually received an education. Nicholas, himself, would have preferred to restrict high school and university education to the nobility, but such a policy could not be implemented; Russia's need for educated professionals and civil servants was too great. However, in 1827 Nicholas did decree that serfs could not attend high schools or universities.

Nicholas I adopted the outlook of romantic, conservative nationalism, and he closely monitored the faculty and curricula of schools and universities, expecting schools to propagate Orthodoxy and Slavic nationalism. He raised the printing budget of the Holy Synod from 2,000 rubles in 1825 to 500,000 rubles by 1850. In 1835, Nicholas established two professorships in Slavonic studies.

The ground for Russian nationalism had been prepared by a number of Russian intellectuals. Nikolai Karamzin, who had gained fame as a liberal during the reign of Catherine, had turned conservative after Alexander I appointed him court historiographer. In his brilliantly written twelve-volume *History of the Russian State,* published between1818 and 1826, Karamzin celebrated the Russian autocracy; he argued that the Russian state was perfect and should not be changed. In 1819 Prince Petr Viazemskii coined the term *narodnost* (nationality or national character) to refer to Russian ethnicity. Sergei Uvarov, Deputy Minister of Education, used this concept in 1832 as the basis for a state ideology that attempted to harness the appeals of nationalism. Uvarov said that "Official Nationality" combined Orthodoxy, autocracy, and narodnost. The Church, he said, was an essential part of Russian life, the autocrat, whose authority came from God, was the central, essential element in the state, and Russians were a unique people with a special role to play in the world. Nicholas I made this ideology his own, and promoted Uvarov to Minister of Education.

One of the effects of Russia's successful educational system was the appearance of a reading public and an intellectual culture independent of state control. In the eighteenth century, most poets were connected with the court, and most publications were sponsored by the state. In the nineteenth century, the press had become independent. The publication of literary works increased three-fold between 1800 and 1840. Between 1801 and 1854, a total of 373 journals of literature and literary criticism were founded. Most were of very short duration, but in any given year, at least fifty such journals were in operation.

The 1820s and 1830s are known as the golden age of Russian poetry. Aleksandr Pushkin, who descended from an old boiar family and included in his ancestry an African slave who had been adopted by Peter the Great, is generally considered to be Russia's greatest poet.

Not only was Pushkin a master of poetic form and diction, he also wrote short stories, plays, and operas. His most famous work, *Evgenii Onegin,* was a novel in verse that satirized the westernized Russian dandy and created a heroine, Tatiana, who exemplified natural, unspoiled Russianness. His realistic description of Russian society prepared the way for the Russian realistic novel later in the century. Pushkin was politically progressive and ran afoul of the authorities more than once; he was killed in a duel 1837.

Nikolai Gogol, who came from Ukrainian Cossack gentry stock, was educated at a provincial grammar school, exerted an influence on Russian literature second only to Pushkin. He wrote prose—plays, short stories, and a novel—all of which combined realistic descriptions of Russian life with social satire and elements of surrealism. Gogol's most famous work was a novel (he called it a "poem in prose"), *Dead Souls* (1842), in which a swindler travels around Russia buying dead peasants from noble landlords in order to use them as collateral for mortgages. Because of his realistic writing and satirical outlook, many of Gogol's contemporaries thought him to be a bitter critic of the old regime, but they were wrong. Gogol was a fervent nationalist and devout Orthodox Christian.

Mikhail Lermontov, Russia's second-greatest poet, came from the provincial nobility, the son of an army captain. He earned fame with the poem "Prisoner of the Caucasus" written in the romantic style of Byron. A progressive, Lermontov was exiled to the Caucasus for writing a poem that blamed Pushkin's death on court aristocrats. His novel, *A Hero of Our Time* (1840), combined realistic descriptions with a liberal critique of Russian society. Lermontov, like Pushkin, died in a duel.

The direction of Russian literature and intellectual life was also shaped by a literary critic, Vissarion Belinskii, son of a doctor from Penza province. Belinskii attended the University of Moscow but was expelled, a common fate of critical thinkers, in 1832. He then earned his living by writing criticism for literary journals. Belinskii began his career reflecting the romantic idealism and nationalism of the time, but by the 1840s he had become a realist and an advocate of increased westernization in the spirit of Peter the Great. Belinskii was influential in many ways. He recognized and celebrated the genius of Pushkin, Gogol, Lermontov, Fyodor Dostoyevsky, and Ivan Turgenev, and helped create their literary reputations. He believed that literature should be evaluated by its social as well as by its artistic significance and that Russian literature should objectively describe Russian society. Finally, Belinskii showed how criticism of literary works could obliquely criticize Russian society in a way that avoid censorship.

Belinskii was a leader in the first generation of the Russian intelligentsia, that segment of Russia's educated elite that thought independently and critically of the autocratic regime. A critical, anti-autocratic counterculture thrived in Russia's high schools and universities, and most students were affected by its idealism. Many graduates went on to professional careers and repressed their idealism, but some chose not to compromise with the regime by working for the government or returning to their estates as landlords. Instead, they lived in cities where they could maintain contact with other like-minded intellectuals.

Romanticism and idealism created a serious intellectual challenge for Russian thinkers. In the age of the Enlightenment, with its cosmopolitan view of a common human nature and its confidence in reason and science, it was natural to think that Russia, through education and institutional reform, could easily share in western progress. This was not self-evident to the Romantics, however; they conceived of nations as unique, organic entities, each with its own genius and special destiny. Russian thinkers, therefore, became preoccupied with the nature of the Russian nation. Petr Chaadaev, an officer who was already alienated from the Russian autocracy in the early 1820s, was the first to struggle with this question, and his answer was depressing. In several "Philosophical Letters," Chaadaev argued that there *was* no Russian genius; Russia had no real history, no authentic culture, and had nothing to contribute to world history. Chaadaev implied that the history of Russia was no more than the history of the autocratic state. In 1836, the government declared Chaadaev insane.

In pursuit of the same question, however, a group of noble intellectuals centered in Moscow, known as the Slavophiles, did manage to discover a Russian nation. Aleksei Khomiakov, the originator of this variety of Russian nationalism, thought he had found the Russian soul in pre-Petrine Muscovy, and he concluded that the Russian nation was congruent with the Russian Orthodox Church. He opposed the secularism, individualism, and materialism of the West (and of Peter the Great), and celebrated what he called the *sobornost* or "organic community" of Muscovite Russia where people had been united by faith and love, valued things of the spirit, and cooperated rather than competed with one another. Khomiakov, in typical romantic fashion, idealized the peasantry, considering them to embody the Christian virtues of humility and brotherhood. Khomiakov was joined by Ivan Kireevskii and Konstantin Aksakov who helped elaborate these themes in print and in unpublished manuscripts.

Given Nicholas I's use of "Official Nationality" as a legitimizing ideology, one might assume that he would welcome Slavophile ideas. This was not the case, however. The Slavophile idea that it was Peter the Great who had put Russian on the wrong path was unacceptable to Nicholas. Moreover, the Slavophiles were critical of the government, opposed to serfdom, and in favor of freedom of speech and of conscience. Most importantly, however, nationalism implies that the ultimately source of values and legitimacy arises from the people not the government, and it is therefore incompatible with the logic of an imperial monarchy. Despite their apparent Russian patriotism, the Slavophiles were very much a part of the intelligentsia sub-culture. They were no less subject to censorship and repression than other critics of the regime.

The term "westernizer" was applied to those among the Russian intelligentsia who applauded Peter's reforms and wanted Russia to continue the Enlightenment project of education, institutional reform, and constitutional government. Vissarion Belinskii was considered a westernizer, as was Aleksandr Herzen. As a youth, Herzen had idolized the Decembrists for their heroic self-sacrifice, and the severe punishments imposed on them permanently alienated Herzen from the government of Nicholas I. In 1829, he enrolled at the University of Moscow where he joined a circle that studied Saint-Simon's program of socialism, radical democracy, and brotherly love. The study circle was arrested in 1834, and after a year in prison, Herzen was exiled to the provinces, where he was employed as a civil servant. The Tsar pardoned him in 1839, but in 1840 he was exiled once again for criticizing the local police chief in a private letter (opened by the authorities). In 1842, Herzen again returned to Moscow, where he debated with the Slavophiles, defending Peter the Great's project and advocating radical democracy and atheism. Herzen also advocated women's independence from control by men. Realizing that he could not freely express his ideas in Russia, Herzen emigrated to France in 1847.

ROLES AND STATUS OF WOMEN

Women were active participants in the literary and intellectual trends of the day. Poetry and prose by women writers was published regularly in Russian literary journals. However, as in Europe in general, there was a strong prejudice against women as serious artists, and their works were devalued by literary critics. Perhaps the most widely read woman writer was Nadezhda Durova, a young noblewoman who had run away from home, disguised herself as a man, and enlisted in a cavalry regiment. She fought in the Napoleon Wars and earned the St. George Cross for bravery. Her memoir, *Cavalry Maiden* (1836), was a best-seller.

Women also participated in the intellectual life of Russia by holding regular salons at which the educated and cultured elite socialized and shared ideas. Zinaida Volkonskaia hosted a salon on Monday afternoons that attracted the leading poets, artists, and intellectuals. She was particularly famous for free-thinking, and she even held a reception in honor of the Decembrists' wives who joined their husbands in exile. In 1829, Volkonskaia emigrated to Italy. Avdotia Elagina held salons on Tuesday, and she, also, had ties with the Decembrists. Rather more conservative were the salons of Ekaterina Karamzina, the widow of Nicholas Karamzin. Karamzina held parties where "Russian only" was spoken (most educated Russians spoke French).

Of the Decembrists who were arrested and punished, twenty-three were married, and Nicholas I offered their wives the opportunity to keep their titles and estates if they divorced their husbands. Twelve accepted, but eleven chose to join their husbands in exile. These Decembrist wives created a community in Chita, Siberia (the location of a major prison for political criminals). They not only provided emotional and material support for their husbands while they served their sentences, they also contributed to community life by establishing libraries and clinics and sponsoring lectures and concerts. They remained in Chita and continued to care for subsequent political prisoners and exiles who were regularly sent there through the reign of Nicholas I.

The idea of the equality of men and women had only begun to be entertained among a few progressive members of the intelligentsia. It did not exist at all in other spheres of Russian society. When Russian law was codified in 1836, it had this to say about women: "The woman must obey her husband, reside with him in love, respect, and unlimited obedience, and offer him every pleasantness and affection as the ruler of the household."

ECONOMIC AND SOCIAL TRENDS

The Russian economy stagnated somewhat after 1815. Russian production techniques did not keep pace with those of England. Handicraft production changed little. Exports of Russian pig iron declined in the face of competition from English wrought iron and steel. Russian transportation developed slowly. Hard-surface road construction had begun in France and England in the eighteenth century, while the first hard-surfaced road in Russia, connecting Moscow and St. Petersburg was only begun in 1817 and was not completed until 1834. By 1840, England had fifteen hundred miles of railroad track, while Russia had less than twenty miles. The first railroad the railroad connecting Moscow and St. Petersburg was not completed until 1851.

On the other hand, Russian wheat exports to Western Europe continued to increase. By 1850, thirty-six million bushels were exported, approximately 3.5 percent of the total grain crop. The textile industry continued to thrive, and for the first time, Russian textile mills began to process cotton. In 1802, the first sugar beet processing plant was built in Russia, and sugar production quickly became a major industry. Because of Russia's great size and lack of roads, transportation was a major obstacle to the distribution of goods. Most consumer goods were produced locally; cities were able to support factories while the provincial towns and villages were supplied by artisans in small workshops.

Part of the reason for the lack of railroads was Nicholas I's belief that railroads would bring revolution to Russia. Despite an underlying fear of the social changes brought by the industrial revolution, Egor Kankrin, Minister of Finance (1823–1844), nevertheless fostered

Russian industry by imposing protective tariffs. The Ministry of Finance also built schools for commerce, engineering and forestry. By 1850, more than 40 percent of the cities in European Russia were industrial, up from 4 percent only a century earlier.

Historians have tended to overemphasize Russia's comparative backwardness in relation to Western Europe, and it has been common to blame this on serfdom. While it is true that Russia had lagged behind Europe in terms of prosperity since the Mongol era, the explanation is best found in Russia's cold climate, relatively poor soil, and low population density. It is also the case that Russia did not experience the agricultural revolution (use of nitrogen-fixing cover crops, mechanization, scientific livestock breeding, and production of cash crops for the market) that was an essential prerequisite to the industrial revolution. It must be remembered, however, that one of the ways the agricultural revolution prepared for the industrial revolution was by creating a class of impoverished landless wage laborers (available to work in the new factories) through the process of enclosure and dispossession of small farmers.

In the southern black-earth districts, some nobles did organize their estates to produce wheat for the market, and there were a number of "improving" landlords who attempted to organize production efficiently and to use labor-saving equipment (which their peasants frequently sabotaged). Overall, however, the peasant commune controlled production, and the commune was most interested in self-sufficient, subsistence agriculture, not production for the market. In addition, community farming made it impossible for individual farmers to experiment with new techniques. Periodic land redistribution prevented the appearance of a landless rural working class.

The fact that an agricultural revolution did not occur in Russia may have meant slower industrial growth, but it meant less misery for the agricultural population in Russia than in Britain, for example. Western observers noted that Russian peasants were much better off than Scottish or Irish peasants, and their living conditions were certainly better than the dispossessed agriculturalists living in industrial cities. Historian Jerome Blum reports that in the Kaluga district in the first half of the nineteenth century the wealthiest peasants tilled an average of fifty-two acres and owned an average of eight horses, four cows, nineteen sheep, and four pigs. In the same region, the poorest peasant households owned almost six acres of land, two horses, two cows, seven sheep, and two pigs. By contrast, in Ireland before the great famine of the 1840s, it was not unusual for a family to subsist on potatoes grown on a quarter-acre of land.

Furthermore, there is no evidence that the institution of serfdom stood in the way of industrialization. Though peasants and serfs were bound to their commune or landlord, they were, in fact, a mobile workforce whenever it suited those who controlled them. In the central and northern regions of Russia where soil and climate were relatively unfavorable for agriculture, many landlords charged obrok (cash rent) rather than barshchina (labor services) and allowed their peasants freedom to travel to work elsewhere to earn the money. In the 1840s, 25 to 30 percent of male serfs lived permanently away from their commune and simply sent in their obrok payments. Many more engaged in seasonal labor. These serfs worked in Russia's factories and mines, served as laborers and cab drivers in the cities. Sometimes the males of a commune would work together as an economic unit (known as an artel), typically in construction and carpentry. In addition, 300,000 migrant laborers traveled south every year to help harvest the wheat crop.

Despite the relative material well-being of Russian peasants, however, there was widespread discontent, particularly among the serfs. Nicholas I had attempted to regulate what lords could demand of their serfs, but the power of the landlord was still virtually unlimited. One of the most onerous burdens that could be imposed on serfs was to be made a household servant. There was no limit on what sorts of occupations a lord could impose upon his household serfs. Many were maids, cooks, butlers, carriage drivers, gardeners, kitchen staff, and other domestic servants. In addition, in extremely wealthy noble households serfs could be required to become tailors, teachers, singers, and musicians.

Work as a household serf was the most demeaning and demoralizing kind of labor. Such serfs had no time for themselves, their work was extremely boring, and they lived in complete poverty. It is true they were fed and clothed by their lord, but they had no opportunity to earn an income of their own. Household serfs constituted a burden on the peasant commune as well, since they remained on the tax rolls, and therefore their share of the taxes were paid by the members of the commune who engaged in agriculture. The problem got worse as the century wore on. In the 1830s, approximately 4 percent of all serfs were household serfs; the proportion had risen to almost 7 percent by 1858. The Russian nobility had three to five times more servants than the nobles in Europe as a whole.

Over the course of the eighteenth century, the periodic redistribution of land became standard practice in central Russia. That is, every ten to twenty years, the skhod would reevaluate household size and re-divide the land based on the number of able-bodied workers in each household. This created another source of dissatisfaction for peasants. It was in the interests of the heads of households to maintain multigenerational families, in which sons and their wives remained in their parents' household. Households could not be broken up without permission by the skhod, and the skhod was made up of heads of households. In Russia only 10 percent of Russian men in their thirties were the heads of households.

PEOPLES OF THE EMPIRE

Russian imperial expansion continued in the first half of the nineteenth century. Russian explorers crossed the Bering Strait, and began to make claims on North America. The Russian-American Company was founded in 1799 and took control over the coast and islands of what is now the State of Alaska. Russians then moved south, building Fort Ross near San Francisco in 1812. In 1815 Russia established contact with Hawaii and began to build a Russian Orthodox Church there. The young United States of America, which also had interests on the Pacific Coast of North America, opposed Russian expansion, and in 1824, Alexander I agreed to limit his North American claims to Alaska. In 1841, Nicholas I sold Fort Ross to the United States.

Russia finally brought the last of the Kazakh federations, the Great Horde, under its authority. The Great Horde was under increasing pressure from the expansive Khanate of Kokand, and its leaders thought that living under Russian rule would be the lesser of two evils. Some Kazakhs continued to resist incorporation into the Russian Empire, but by 1848, Russia controlled Central Asia as far south as the Syr Darya River. Russian settlers continued to move into the region, and the Russian military continued to put pressure on the Khanates of Central Asia. However, an army sent to conquer the Khanate of Khiva in 1839 was destroyed.

The Caucasus continued to present problems. The idea of nationalism had spread among the nobility of Georgia, only recently incorporated into the Empire, and they rebelled (unsuccessfully) against Russian rule. In the Northern Caucasus, which had never been completely conquered, militant Islam inspired the local peoples to continue to resist Russian rule. The Chechens, led by a charismatic chief, Shamil, and the Circassians maintained their independence through the middle of the nineteenth century.

In the south and east, Russia continued its tradition of toleration for the religions and traditions of the indigenous peoples. In the west, however, Nicholas I aggressively promoted the Russification of the population. After the Polish rebellion of 1830 to 1831, Nicholas dissolved the Kingdom of Poland, abrogated its constitution, abolished the Sejm, disbanded the Polish Army, and closed the University of Warsaw. The Polish provinces were then absorbed into the administrative system of the Russian Empire.

At about the same time, Ukrainian intellectuals, under the influence of romantic nationalism, began to study the language, history, and folklore of the peasantry. Nicholas I, however, refused to accept any ethnic distinctions in the western provinces. He made Russian the language of local administration and of higher education, and he required that history textbooks treat Ukraine, Belarus, and Lithuania as historically a part of Russia. In1839, he outlawed the Uniate church (except in territory that was ethnically Polish), and he set up an Orthodox eparchy in Poland.

Nicholas also closed the University of Vilno and attempted to suppress Ukrainian nationalism. He suspected the Kirillo-Methodian Society, an organization for the study of history and folklore, of subversive intentions, and he suppressed it in 1847. Ten activists were arrested, including the Ukrainian poet, Taras Shevchenko.

Nicholas also attempted to assimilate the Jewish population, whom the law code of 1835 referred to as "aliens." He abolished their organs of self-government, pressured them to send their children to state schools, and conscripted Jewish boys at the age of twelve (instead of the standard age of twenty). Jews, however, resisted assimilation as successfully as the other ethnicities of the western empire.

Conclusion

In 1848, the conservative restoration of Europe following the Napoleonic Wars, came to an end, as revolutions struck every capital in Europe except for London and St. Petersburg. Social changes associated with economic growth, industrialization, and urbanization forced political reforms upon Europe's ruling elites. Nicholas I postponed reform until his death in 1855 during the Crimean War. It was left to his son, Alexander II, to undertake the further modernization of Russian social and political institutions.

_____ TEXT DOCUMENTS _____

Haxthausen on the Commune and the Tsar

August von Haxthausen was a German expert in agriculture who traveled in Russia during the reign of Nicholas I to study Russian rural life. In 1847, he published a record of his journey, Studies in the Interior of Russia, *which profoundly influenced the way educated Russians thought about the peasantry.*

- What parts of this description are realistic? What parts appear to be fantasy?
- How does this work as a justification of autocracy (and compare this with past justifications)?
- What might socialists find attractive in this?

Throughout Russia proper there . . . has developed . . . a rural organization in which the principle of communal property [of the ancient Slavs] has been fully retained. The forests and pasture land always remain undivided; the plowlands and meadows are apportioned to the various families in the commune, who, however, do not own the land but have only the right to use it temporarily. Formerly the lots may have been redistributed annually among the married couples of the community, each receiving a share equal to all the others in terms of quality. Today, however, in order to avoid expenses and great inconveniences the land is reapportioned after a certain number of years. If, for example, a father should die and leave six sons who are not of age, the widow generally continues to manage the farm until her sons marry. Then, however, they do not divide among themselves the plot which their father had cultivated; instead this land reverts to the commune, and all six sons receive a share equal to that held by the other members of the community. All together they might hold five to six times the amount of land which their father had held. If the six sons should marry when their father is still alive, then he claims for each one of them an equal allotment of the communal land. Since the sons continue to live in the same household with their father, he does not have to worry about establishing them. On the contrary, a marriage is fortunate for the family. Even if she has no dowry, the arrival of a daughter-in-law means an additional share of the communal property. The marriage and establishment of his daughters is thus the least of a Russian peasant's worries. . . .

The mother's command over the daughters is just as absolute as the father's authority over all his children. The same respect and obedience are shown to the communal authorities, the *starets* and the white heads and above all to their common father, the tsar. A Russian has one and the same word for addressing his natural father, the *starets*, his master, the emperor, and finally, God, namely, "father . . . little father" *(batushka).* Similarly he calls every fellow Russian "brother" *(brat),* whether he knows him or not!

Source: August von Haxthausen, *Studies on the Interior of Russia,* edited and with an introduction by S. Frederick Starr, translated by Eleanore L. M. Schmidt (Chicago: University of Chicago Press, 1972), 278–284. (c) University of Chicago Press. Reprinted with permission.

The common Russian (muzhik) knows absolutely no servile fear, but only a childlike fear or awe in the presence of his tsar, whom he loves with a devoted tenderness. He enters the military reluctantly, but once a soldier he harbors no resentment or ill will, serving the tsar with the greatest loyalty and devotion. The famous Russian word *prikazano* (it is ordered) has a magical effect on him. It goes without saying that whatever the tsar commands must be done. The Russian would never resist or defy the tsar's order; indeed, the impossibility of its execution would never occur to him. Even in the case of mere police proscriptions, the Russian does not say "it is forbidden" *(zapreshcheno)* but rather "it is not ordered" *(ni prikazano or nevoleno)*. The profound reverence shown the tsar is evidenced above all in the Russian's attitude toward everything regarded as belonging to the monarch. He has the greatest respect for the *kazennye,* the state lands or the tsar's property. A Russian proverb says: "The *kazennye* do not die are not consumed by fire and do not drown in water."

There is almost no case of persons responsible for collecting taxes ever having been attacked or robbed, even though they travel long distances alone and often carry considerable sums of money. In northern Russia, in the province of Vologda, where the customs are untainted and the inhabitants very honest, the tax collector, upon arriving in a village, knocks on every window and cries "kassa." Everyone brings him his tax for the year and drops it into a sack. Knowing he will never be cheated, the collector does not bother to check the amount. When night falls, he enters the first good house and places the sack of money under the icon of the saint. He then looks for lodging and sleeps without a care, confident that the next morning he will find everything just as he had left it!

. . . The patriarchal ruler, the tsar, appears to be absolutely essential to the existence and perpetuation of the nation. Consequently, we never find popular insurrections which challenge the authority of the government or the tsar as such. Rather, uprisings are directed against individuals and usually for so-called legitimate reasons: for and against the false Dmitrii, for Pugachev, who posed as the banished Peter III, and lastly in 1825 for a similar reason. The people always obeyed the government which ruled over them, even the Mongols. To be sure, they frequently complain about alleged injustices, but, after verbally expressing their grievances, they cease complaining and everyone is content.

The Autobiography of Aleksandra Kobiakova

Aleksandra Kobiakova (1823–1892) was a novelist who was born into the merchant class. She published her first novel in 1858 and her second in 1860, and in the same year the leading liberal journal of the day published her autobiography. The events related in this selection occurred during the reign of Nicholas I.

- What does this reveal about gender relations in early nineteenth-century Russia?
- How are betrothal practices changing? What attitudes remain the same?
- What does it reveal about the merchant class?

All the members of my family lived under one roof and belonged to the third merchants' guild. We lived in a two-storied stone house; there was a candle factory on the premises, and next to the store belonging to my grandfather's brother was a wine cellar. We had no shop assistants. The old men clung to the old ways. They had beards and wore Russian kaftans, drank neither wine nor tea, and loved to read the Scriptures. They considered coarse language and swearing sinful. Around town they had a reputation for honesty but were not considered wealthy. They never quarreled, but neither did they show much affection for each other, probably because of their upbringing rather than lack of love or mutual understanding.

My grandmother was typical of women raised in that harsh environment, which gives them a strong will and erases their soft feminine traits. Grandmother was naturally intelligent and, in different conditions and under different circumstances, she would have become a remarkable person, but all her strength was spent in vain or was pitifully misdirected.

Many people found her difficult, the more so since at home her despotic will was obeyed absolutely by everyone, even by grandfather himself. She led a simple and most austere life. She saw sin lurking everywhere and in everything—in short haircuts, rouge, singing—all were sins and crimes. My mother was a cheerful woman by nature who enjoyed life's pleasures and had been pampered by her father like an aristocratic young lady. Her temperament clashed with my grandmother's in particular. Grandmother's older daughter-in-law was much more to her liking, and Grandmother loved her best.

My mother found no joy, diversion, or sympathy within her family and ascribed all her afflictions to the mores of the merchant class. She believed that no woman could find happiness in that estate and that is why she wanted to see me marry a government official, someone she thought would be a more educated person.

I was fifteen years old when I started seeing a young man from a local townsman's family. He intended to study medicine after graduating from the Gymnasium. Because of my sheltered home life I felt predisposed to like the future doctor at our very first meeting. He seemed to me the only ideal a fifteen-year-old girl, whose imagination was aroused by reading romantic novels, could dream about.

Source: Toby W. Clyman and Judith Vowles, *Russia Through Women's Eyes: Autobiographies from Tsarist Russia* (New Haven, CT: Yale University Press, 1996), 60–74. (c) Yale University Press. Reprinted with permission.

The young man did not hide his interest in me and tried to please me in every way. He brought me books, and I was by no means indifferent to his generosity. Mother came to love him like a son and he, unconstrained by our social conventions, flatly declared that he hoped to become her son-in-law when he graduated. I returned his feelings and considered him my betrothed. He was four years older than I. My attachment to him was far from passionate, nevertheless it was strong and deep, and it was strengthened by the persecution to which my family subjected me because of our friendship. And it would probably have been short-lived had their opposition not aroused my defiant nature, which saw a challenge in every obstacle. Daily quarrels at home added fuel to my budding emotions, and I proudly endured them for the sake of my beloved dream. My mother was so simple and naive that she really believed that K. might someday be her son-in-law. My father disliked him and avoided his company, although he never said anything to me about it. Kos—tsyn left for Moscow to study at the Medical Surgical Academy; we wrote often. A year later he came back to Kostroma for the summer vacation and was as affectionate and attentive as before. All kinds of rumors were circulating about us in town. My relatives were in an uproar, but we remained true to our vows and comforted each other with dreams of our beautiful future together. His love for me was beyond reproach, and I felt it deserved to be fully reciprocated. . . .

I turned seventeen. One of the garrison officers, a worthy man, proposed to me. All my relatives hounded me with their advice, practically forcing me to marry him. I spent the next few weeks in that inner struggle that torments the heart when one of life's fateful questions rises before you and your answer is dictated by another's mind and will. Filled with doubt and indecision, I wrote to Kos—tsyn. He responded with a letter to my father in which he swore that he would shoot himself if they forced me to marry someone else. Father summoned me and we both spoke our minds. I told him that I thought it despicable to go back on my word. He said that he didn't want to impose his will upon me any longer and that I could decide my own fate.

From that time on I was entirely free to reject any suitor; my family left me in peace. But then the vacation came and, with it, the man for whom I had endured so many scenes, family arguments, and sleepless nights. And, just imagine! Not even the shadow of my former friend remained. He blatantly ridiculed my family's simple ways and argued with my mother. He quarreled with me and went out of his way to contradict me as rudely as possible. His outbursts were wild and senseless. For example, he would say that if he became an army doctor he would lock up his wife to prevent other officers from looking at her, and if she made the slightest attempt to gain her freedom, he would send her back to her parents. In short, he showed me the kind of husband he would be—a tyrant who preached passive obedience to his wife and denied her any will of her own or even a semblance of female dignity. At first his attitude enraged me, but then I became frightened. Inwardly I cried, but outwardly I argued and fought with him. I showed him the short pieces I'd written in his absence and listened to his moralizing: "Woman is created not for the pen but for the needle and oven prongs." I read him some verses I had jotted down and was reprimanded for passing off someone else's work as my own. I could bear it no longer. . . . I was amazed at the change in his character, once so gentle and kind, but now rude and captious. A woman outraged has only one recourse—revenge and contempt. So I, in turn, started tormenting him with my feminine whims and contrariness.

[She ultimately broke off the engagement with him.]

Muraviev on East Asia

In 1847, Count Nikolai Muraviev was appointed governor-general of Eastern Siberia. He wrote the following memorandum, "The Views of Count Nikolai N. Muravev Regarding the Necessity for Russia to control the Amur River," in 1849 to 1850.

- What does this reveal about the mentality of imperialism?
- Who was Russia's greatest rival? What was the nature of their competition?

Russia must occupy the mouth of the Amur River and that part of Sakhalin Island which lies opposite, as well as the left bank of the Amur River, for the following reasons:

I. Concern for the eastern frontier of the empire.

Rumors have for quite some time circulated through Siberia concerning the intentions of the English to occupy the mouth of the Amur River and Sakhalin Island. God forbid they should become entrenched there before we do! In order to establish more thorough and complete control over trade with China, the English undoubtedly need to control both the mouth of the Amur and the navigation on that river. If the Amur were not the only river flowing from Siberia to the Pacific Ocean, we might not have any objection to their intentions, but navigation via the Amur is the only suitable route to the east. This is a century-old dream of Siberians of all classes; it may be instinctive, but it is no less well grounded.

Upon review of all circumstances known to me, I can state that whoever controls the mouth of the Amur will also control Siberia, at least as far as Baikal, and that control will be firm. It is enough to control the mouth of this river and navigation on it for Siberia, which is increasing in population and flourishing in agriculture and industry, to remain an unalterable tributary and subject of the power which holds the key to it.

II. Strengthening and securing possession of the Kamchatka Peninsula.

Only when we have the left bank of the Amur and the navigation rights on it can we establish communication with Kamchatka, and thus be in a position to establish Russia's firm control over this peninsula. The reason is that the route via Yakutsk and Okhotsk or Aian offers no means of supplying Kamchatka with sufficient military capacity, nor to provide it with proper population, which in and of itself, under the protection of fortresses, would comprise the strength of this distant oblast and furnish local land and naval forces with their necessary provisions. With the establishment of steam navigation on the Amur, Kamchatka could be provisioned from Nerchinsk with people and all necessities in no more than two weeks. The Amur River flows from our frontiers to the island of Sakhalin for more than 2,000 versts, and according to all available information, is navigable for its entire length.

III. Support for our trade with China.

The decrease in the Kiakhta trade already indicates that the intentions of the English in China cannot be beneficial to us. During the first years after their war [Opium War, 1839-42],

Source: Reprinted from Basil Dmytryshyn, E. A. P. Crownhart-Vaughan, Thomas Vaughan, Eds. and Trans. *The Russian American Colonies* (Portland, OR: Oregon Historical Society Press, 1989), 482–484. © 1989, The Oregon Historical Society. Reprinted with permission.

we did not realize this, because the Chinese, motivated by their enmity toward the English, preferred to turn to us as their reliable and gracious neighbors. But time and material benefits mitigate the outburst of animosity and moderate a flame of friendship which does not represent substantial benefits. I believe that the only way to promote our trade with China is to change it from local to widespread, so that by sailing on the Amur we could supply the products of our manufacture to all the northeastern provinces of China, which are more distant from present activities of the English, and consequently, from their competition which is dangerous to our trade.

IV. Maintaining our influence in China.

The English war and peace in China have laid the foundation for the transformation of that populous empire under the influence of the English. But during the lifetime of the late Chinese Emperor, we still hoped he would personally announce that since he had been insulted by them, he could not be favorably disposed toward them and consequently would not allow the spread of English influence in his empire.

Now, with the ascension of his 18-year-old son, one can be certain that the English will hasten to turn this event to their advantage with their usual natural entrepreneurial spirit, speed and persistence, so as to gain control not only of trade, but also of China's politics. I cannot judge whether we can prevent this, when five of China's ports have been not only accessible to the English, but have actually almost become English cities.

I believe it would be prudent for us to have better security along the frontiers with China, to the extent of our domestic needs, so the English will not gain full control there, and thus we must control the Amur. I also think that we must capitalize on current developments in China so we can reveal our plans to them, based on the general benefits to both empires; to wit, that no one but Russia and China should control navigation on the Amur, and that the mouth of that river should be protected, and of course, not by the Chinese.

Russian Policy in Regard to Indigenous Peoples

The following regulations governing the natives of Siberia were promulgated on July 22, 1822.

- What do these regulations reveal about Russian attitudes toward the indigenous peoples of Siberia?
- Their attitudes toward religion? toward nomads? (How has this changed from the past?)
- How progressive were these laws? What might the long-run consequences be?

1. All native tribes inhabiting Siberia, which until now have officially been called the *iasak-paying people,* are henceforth, on the basis of their diverse levels of education and their current way of life, divided into three basic categories. The first includes the settled peoples, that is those who live in settlements and towns; the second encompasses nomads who live in specific regions but who annually move from one place to another; and the third includes migratory peoples or hunters who are constantly on the move along the rivers and overland.

12. Settled natives who profess Christian faith are not distinguished in any way from Russians. Those among them who profess paganism or Islam are known as settled natives of different faith to differentiate them from the rest.

13. All other settled natives have the same rights and obligations as the corresponding Russian classes. They are governed in accordance with general laws and regulations. . . .

17. All natives of different faiths who live in their own settlements . . . and are engaged in their own agriculture are included in the category of [Russian] state peasants.

18. These natives of different faiths are subject to the same taxes and obligations [as are Russian state peasants], but they are freed from military service.

19. Those among the natives of different faiths who are known as cossacks remain in the cossack group, and they are governed by a special cossack code.

20. Properties, which the natives of different faiths currently have, belong to them in accordance with their ancient rights. Those among them who have an insufficient amount of land should receive parcels from the nearby empty lands, as provided by regulations governing state peasants. . . .

24. Nomadic natives comprise a special category, similar to peasants, but are subject to a different form of administration.

25. These natives enjoy their ancient rights. They should be informed that, with the expansion of agriculture, they will not be included against their will in the category of peasants, and that, without their own request, they will not be assigned to any other category.

27. The distribution of [designated] properties is to be apportioned by the nomads themselves in accordance with the fair share rule or their other customs. . . .

29. Nomadic natives have full freedom to engage in agriculture, livestock herding, and other local enterprises, based on water or land that [Russian authorities] have allocated to them. . . .

Source: Basil Dmytryshyn, *Imperial Russia: A Source Book, 1700–1917* (Gulf Stream, FL: Academic International Press, 2001), 230–233. Copyright Academic International Press, Gulf Stream, FL. Reprinted with permission.

34. Nomadic natives are administered by their own tribal leaders who comprise their local administration.

35. All nomads are administered in accordance with local laws and customs of their tribes.

36. In all criminal cases, all nomads are to be tried in Russian courts in accordance with the prevailing state laws.

37. Criminal cases pertaining to the indigenous natives are: sedition, premeditated murder, theft and violence, counterfeiting, and , in general appropriation of Treasury and public property. . . .

42. All nomads are freed from military service.

VISUAL DOCUMENTS

Figure 11-1 "The Appearance of Christ to the People"

Aleksandr Ivanov (1806–1858) considered this to be his most important painting; he worked on it for two decades (1837–1858). It depicts John the Baptist and people waiting to be baptized, with Jesus in the background.

- Compare this painting with representations of Christ you have seen in previous chapters.
- What ideas do you think Ivanov intended to convey?

Source: Tretiakov Gallery, Moscow.

Figure 11-2 "Harvesting: Summer"
This is the work of Aleksei Gavrilovich Venetsianov (1780–1847). Venetsianov is most famous for his natural portrayal of peasant life and nature, themes that were popular in the Romantic movement across Europe.
- Compare this with previous works of art. What are the similarities? Differences?
- What is revealed about peasant life?
Source: Tretiakov Gallery, Moscow.

Figure 11-3 Russia's First Train

The first railroad track in Russia was opened in 1837, and this engraving was made the following year.
- What would this have meant to Russians?
- What significance did railroads have for Russian society and the economy?

Source: Nineteenth-century engraving.

Figure 11-4 "Parade on Tsarina's Meadow"

This is a detail from a painting by Grigorii Chernetsov (1802–1865), completed in 1831.
- What does this painting reveal about Russian society?
- What does it reveal about Russian attitudes toward its empire?

Source: Pushkin Museum, St. Petersburg.

Figure 11-5 Eurasia in 1856

By the end of the Crimean War, Russia had lost prestige and a small amount of territory at the mouth of the Danube. In the east, Russia's border with China remained the same, but in Central Asia, the Kazakhs were absorbed into the empire.

_____ FOR FURTHER READING _____

(In addition to the books by Blum, Hartley, Moon, Saunders, and Wortman from the previous chapter.)

Lincoln, W. Bruce. *Nicholas I.* Bloomington, IN: Indiana University Press, 1978.

Kahan, Arcadius. *Russian Economic History: The Nineteenth Century.* Roger Weiss, Ed. Chicago: University of Chicago Press, 1989.

Christian, David. *Living Water: Vodka and Russian Society on the Eve of Emancipation.* Oxford: Oxford University Press, 1990.

Engel, Barbara Alpern. *Mothers and Daughters: Women of the Intelligentsia in Nineteenth Century Russia.* Cambridge: Cambridge University Press, 1983.

Riasanovsky, Nicholas V. *A Parting of Ways: Government and the Educated Public in Russia, 1801–1855.* Oxford: Clarendon Press, 1976.

Hoch, Steven L. *Serfdom and Social Control in Russia: Petrovskoe, a Village in Tambov.* Chicago: University of Chicago Press, 1986.

Lincoln, W. Bruce. *In the Vanguard of Reform: Russia's Enlightened Bureaucrats, 1825–1861.* DeKalb, IL: Northern Illinois University Press, 1982

APPENDIX A

TIMELINE

North-Central Eurasia/Russia	Eastern Europe	Western Europe	Central Asia	Middle East	East Asia
Humans, having originated in Africa more than 1,000,000 years ago, populate Eurasia by 35,000 B.C.E.					
				10,000 B.C.E. Neolithic Revolution (domestication of plants and animals) begins.	
			After 7000 B.C.E. the Jeitun begin to practice agriculture.		
After 6000 B.C.E. "Linear Pottery" culture appears on the steppe north of the Black Sea.					
				3500 B.C.E. Origins of Sumerian civilization.	3500 B.C.E. Yangshao culture develops.
			2500 B.C.E. Horses are domesticated in Central Asia		
				2000–1600 B.C.E. Babylonian Empire. 1450–1200 Hittite Empire.	1600–1027 B.C.E. Shang dynasty.
After 1000 B.C.E. Scythians rule the Eurasian steppe.					1111–770 Western Zhou Dynasty.

North-Central Eurasia/Russia	Eastern Europe	Western Europe	Central Asia	Middle East	East Asia
		800 B.C.E. The beginnings of classical Greek civilization.			
After 700 B.C.E. Greeks establish colonies on the northern Black Sea coast.				745–612 Assyrian Empire.	770–476 B.C.E. "Spring and Autumn Period"
After 200 B.C.E. the Scythian Empire disintegrates.		500–400 B.C.E. Golden Age of Greece. 509–31 B.C.E. Rise of Roman civilization and the Roman Empire.	200 B.C.E.–200 C.E. The Silk Road connects China with the Roman Empire.	558–330 B.C.E. Achaemenid Dynasty. 323–83 B.C.E. Seleucid Dynasty.	475–221 B.C.E. Warring States Period.
200 B.C.E.–200 C.E. Sarmations occupy the Black Sea steppe.		31 B.C.E.–180 C.E. Pax Romana, height of the Roman Empire.		247 B.C.E.–224 C.E. Parthian Dynasty.	221–206 B.C.E. Qin Dynasty. 206 B.C.E.–220 C.E. Han Dynasty.
200–370 Goths displace Sarmations.		391 Theodosius makes Christianity the official religion of the Roman Empire. 476 Last Emperor in Rome is deposed.		224–ca. 650 Sasanian Dynasty.	220–581 "Six Dynasties" period.
550–620 Avar Confederation.	500 Slavs first appear in the historical record. 527–65, Justinian Emperor in Constantinople.	590–604 Papacy of Gregory I.	552–630 Turk Empire. 683–734 Second Turk Empire.	622 Muhammad flees Mecca for Medina. 661–752 Umayyad Dynasty.	618–907 Tang Dynasty.
620–965 Khazar Empire.	750–950 Era of Viking raids and invasions.		750 Arabs complete their conquest of Central Asia.	752 Abbasid Dynasty seizes power from the Umayyads everywhere but Spain.	

North-Central Eurasia/Russia	Eastern Europe	Western Europe	Central Asia	Middle East	East Asia
862 East Slavs invite Rurik to rule them. (Legend.) 965 Sviatoslav defeats the Khazars; their empire dissolves.	966 Poland's first king, Mieszko I (d. 992), converts to Christianity, accepts a crown from the Pope.	800–814 Reign of Charlemagne.	875 Samanid Dynasty asserts independence of Transoxiana from the Abassid Empire.	819–999 Samanids rule Iran.	960–1279 Song Dynasty.
988 Vladimir converts Rus to Christianity. 1019–54 Iaroslav the Wise, Grand Prince of Kiev. 1050 Kipchaks move into the Black Sea steppe.		1054 Schism between the eastern and western Christian Church. 1066 Norman conquest of England. 1095 First Crusade.	After 999, Seljuk Turk federation forms.	1044 Seljuk Turks conquer Iran. 1055 Seljuk Turks take Baghdad.	
1240 Mongol armies sack Kiev. 1242 Alexander Nevskii defeats Teutonic Knights. 1276–1303 Daniil is first prince of Moscow.	1241 Batu Khan defeats Poland and Hungary, but chooses not to invade Europe. 1251 King Mindaugas of Lithuania converts to Roman Catholicism.		1219–25 Mongols conquer Central Asia.	1260 After conquering all of Iran and the Middle East, the Mongol armies are stopped on the border of Syria. 1299 Osman founds Ottoman dynasty.	1227 Genghis Khan completes conquest of northern China. 1260 Mongol Kubilai Khan founds Yuan Dynasty. 1279 Southern Song Dynasty brought to an end by Mongol conquest.
1318 Iurii Dolgorukii of Moscow becomes Grand Prince of Vladimir. 1327 Ivan I conquers Tver. Black Death appears on the Black Sea coast in 1346; it hits Moscow in 1351.	By 1360 Lithuania has annexed most of the former Kiev Rus. 1385 Lithuania and Poland are dynastically unitedwhen Jagiello, Grand Duke of Lithuania, marries Jadwiga, Queen of Poland.	Hundred Years' War between France and England (1337–1453) Black Death appears in Italy in 1347.	1369 Timur (Tamerlane) consolidates rule over all Central Asia.	1392 Timur adds Iran, Mesopotamia, and the Caucasus to his empire.	1330s The Black Death appears in southern China 1368 Chinese rebels overthrow Mongol rule and establish the Ming Dynasty.

North-Central Eurasia/Russia	Eastern Europe	Western Europe	Central Asia	Middle East	East Asia
1380 Dmitrii Donskoi, Grand Prince of Moscow, defeats Mongol army at the Battle of Kulikovo.	1389 Ottoman Turks defeat Serbian army in the Battle of Kosovo.				
1420s Khanate of Crimea declares independence of Golden Horde. 1445 Khanate of Kazan declares independence of Golden Horde. 1478 Ivan III subordinates Novgorod. 1480 Ivan III declares independence of Mongol rule.	1439 Council of Florence. Eastern Church (temporarily) recognizes primacy of the Pope.	1453 Ottoman Turks seize Constantinople, Eastern Roman Empire comes to an end. 1488 Portuguese discover the Cape of Good Hope.		1453 Ottoman Turks seize Constantinople; they rule all Anatolia and the Balkan Peninsula.	1405–1433 Ming Emperor sends trading and exploration fleets to southern Eurasia and eastern Africa.
1552 Ivan IV conquers and annexes Kazan.	Gustaf I Vasa (1523–1560) makes Sweden the dominant power in the Baltic. 1529 First Ottoman siege of Vienna.	1500–1550 High Renaissance in Italy, beginning of Northern Renaissance. 1517 Martin Luther begins the Protestant Reformation.	1501–10 Uzbeks conquer Central Asia. Shaybanid Dynasty rules until 1598.	1502 Isma'il I founds Safavid Dynasty in Iran. 1520–66 Reign of Süleyman I "the Magnificent."	
1564–72 Ivan IV institutes the Oprichnina. 1588 Russian Orthodox Church becomes independent; Job is elected first Patriarch. 1598 Fyodor, last direct descendant of Rurik dies.	1569 Union of Lublin unites Lithuania and Poland into one state. 1596 Uniate Church is created in Lithuania.	1588 English defeat Spanish Armada.	By 1600 Kazakhs occupy steppe from the Yaik River to the Irtysh. After 1600, Kalmyks move from western Xinjiang to Caspian steppe.	Shah Abbas (1588–1629) brings the Safavid Dynasty to its peak of power.	

North-Central Eurasia/Russia	Eastern Europe	Western Europe	Central Asia	Middle East	East Asia
1598 Boris Godunov is elected Tsar. 1598–1613 Time of Troubles. 1613 Michael Romanov is elected Tsar. 1639 Russian explorers first reach the Pacific Ocean. 1648 Tsar Aleksei's Ulozhenie (law code) makes serfdom the law of the land in Russia. 1654 In the Union of Pereyaslavl Moscow claims right to rule Ukraine. 1682 Ivan IV and Peter I are named co-Tsars. 1689 Russia signs treaty of Nerchinsk with China. 1694 Peter I takes on full duties of Tsar.	1648–1667 "The Deluge" in Poland.	1618–1648 Thirty Years' War. 1642–1648 English Civil War. 1643–1715 Reign of Louis XIV of France. 1688 Glorious Revolution in England.	1622 Kalmyks cross 1638 Ottomans the Yaik River and occupy the Caucasian steppe.	1638 Ottomans retake Baghdad from Savafid rule. 1699 Treaty of Karlowitz; Ottomans withdraw from Hungary and Galicia.	1603 Tokugawa Shogunate is established in Japan. 1644 Ming Dynasty collapses; Manchus conquer China, establish Qing Dynasty. Qing emperor Kangxi (1661–1722) expands empire by conquering Mongolia, Tibet, and Xinjiang.
1700 Peter I adopts Julian calendar. 1703 St. Petersburg is founded. 1700–1721 Great Northern War between Russia and Sweden. 1725 Death of Peter I. 1725–27 Catherine I. 1727–30 Peter II.	Peace of Nystadt (1721) signals the decline of Sweden as a great power.	1713–40 Reign of King Frederick William I of Prussia who makes his army the best trained in Europe.	1700 Khanate of Kokand is founded. By the end of his reign, Nadir Shah (of Iran) has conquered most of Central Asia.	1723 Safavid Dynasty in Iran comes to an end. 1736–47 Nadir Shah, a Turk, reunifies Iran under his rule.	

North-Central Eurasia/Russia	Eastern Europe	Western Europe	Central Asia	Middle East	East Asia
1730–40 Anna. 1740–41 Ivan VI. 1741–62 Elizabeth. 1762 Peter III. 1762–1796 Catherine II, "the Great." 1768–74 First Turkish War. 1773–75 Pugachev Rebellion. 1787–92 Second Russo-Turkish War. 1796–1801 Paul.	1772, 1793, 1795 Partitions of Poland.	1740–86 Frederick II "the Great" of Prussia. 1756–63 Seven-Years' War. 1789–1799 French Revolution.	Under Ahmad Khan (1747–1773), Afghanistan breaks free from Iran. After death of Nadir Shah in 1747, Khanates of Khiva, Bukhara, and Kokand establish independence from Iran.	1789–1807 Reign of Ottoman Sultan Selim III. 1798 Napoleon invades Egypt.	1736–96 Reign of the Emperor Qianlong in China. 1755 China conquers . Mongolia
1801–25 Alexander I. 1801 Georgia is absorbed into the Russian Empire. 1802 Ministry of Education is created. 1812 Napoleon invades Russia. 1814 Alexander I and Russian army enter Paris. 1825–55 Nicholas I. 1825 Decembrist rebellion. 1854–56 Crimean War.	1809 Russia annexes Finland. 1815 Grand Duchy of Poland is given to Russia at the Congress of Vienna. 1831 Nicholas I dissolves the Grand Duchy of Poland and incorporates its territory into the Russian Empire.	1793–1815 Wars of the French Revolution. 1799–1815 Napoleon rules France. 1815 Battle of Waterloo. 1815 Congress of Vienna. 1830 Revolution in France. 1831 Greece wins independence from Ottoman Empire. 1848 All major capitals (except for London and Moscow) experience popular revolutions 1837–1901 Reign of Queen Victoria of Great Britain.	1820s. The last of the independent Kazakh federations is brought under Russian control.	1804–1848 Muhammad Ali rules Egypt. 1826 Sultan Mahmoud II destroys - Janissaries, begins western reforms. 1839–76 Tanzimat: Reforms in the Ottoman Empire.	1839–42 England defeats China in the Opium War. 1842 Treaty of Nanjing opens China to trade; cedes Hong Kong to Great Britain. 1853 U.S. Commodore Perry demands that Japan open to western contacts.

APPENDIX B

GUIDE TO TRANSLITERATION AND PRONUNCIATION OF THE RUSSIAN ALPHABET

As explained in the Preface, all Russian names appear in the form given in the 26th edition of the *Library of Congress Subject Headings* (2003), and all geographical terms are spelled as they appear in primary entry of *The Columbia Gazetteer of the World* (1998). All other names and terms will be transliterated from Russian according to the following modification of the Library of Congress transliteration system.

Russian Alphabet	Library of Congress	Used in Exploring Russia's Past	Pronunciation
Аа	Aa	Aa	<u>fa</u>ther
Бб	Bb	Bb	<u>b</u>all
Вв	Vv	Vv	<u>v</u>ery
Гг	Gg	Gg	<u>g</u>ood
Дд	Dd	Dd	<u>d</u>og
Ее	Ee	Ee	<u>y</u>et
Ёё	Ëë	Ee	<u>y</u>olk
Жж	Zh zh	Zh zh	a<u>z</u>ure
Зз	Zz	Zz	<u>z</u>one
Ии	Ii	Ii	<u>e</u>ven
й	i	i	<u>e</u>ven
Кк	Kk	Kk	<u>k</u>itten
Лл	Ll	Ll	<u>l</u>ong
Мм	Mm	Mm	<u>m</u>an

Нн	Nn	Nn	<u>n</u>o
Оо	Oo	Oo	b<u>oa</u>rd
Пп	Pp	Pp	<u>p</u>in
Рр	Rr	Rr	trilled "r" as in Spanish
Сс	Ss	Ss	<u>s</u>ing
Тт	Tt	Tt	<u>t</u>op
Уу	Uu	Uu	f<u>oo</u>l
Фф	Ff	Ff	<u>f</u>ool
Хх	Kh kh	Kh kh	as in German "bu<u>ch</u>"
Цц	TS ts	Ts ts	hi<u>ts</u>
Чч	Ch ch	Ch ch	<u>ch</u>eese
Шш	Sh sh	Sh sh	<u>sh</u>ot
Щщ	Shch shch	Shch shch	fre<u>sh ch</u>eese
Ъ	"	(omitted)	no sound
Ь	'	(omitted)	no sound
Ээ	Ée	Ee	g<u>e</u>t
Юю	I͡U i͡u	Iu iu	<u>you</u>
Яя	I͡A i͡a	Ia ia	<u>ya</u>rd

APPENDIX C

DYNASTIC SUCCESSION FROM KIEV RUS TO THE RUSSIAN EMPIRE

Only individuals who ruled (or who were parents of later rulers) are presented here. The dates refer to their reigns.

THE RURIKOVICHI

Grand Princes of Kiev

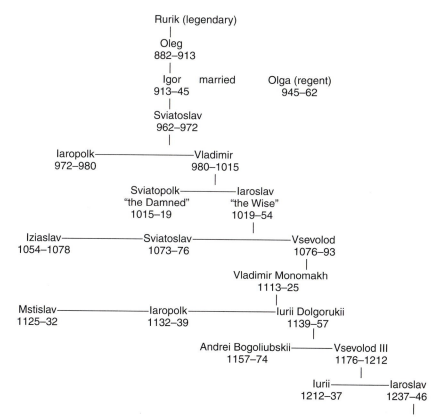

Rurik (legendary)

Oleg
882–913

Igor   married   Olga (regent)
913–45   945–62

Sviatoslav
962–972

Iaropolk————————————Vladimir
972–980   980–1015

Sviatopolk————————Iaroslav
"the Damned"   "the Wise"
1015–19   1019–54

Iziaslav——————Sviatoslav——————————Vsevolod
1054–1078   1073–76   1076–93

Vladimir Monomakh
1113–25

Mstislav——————————Iaropolk——————————Iurii Dolgorukii
1125–32   1132–39   1139–57

Andrei Bogoliubskii————————Vsevolod III
1157–74   1176–1212

Iurii————————Iaroslav
1212–37   1237–46

253

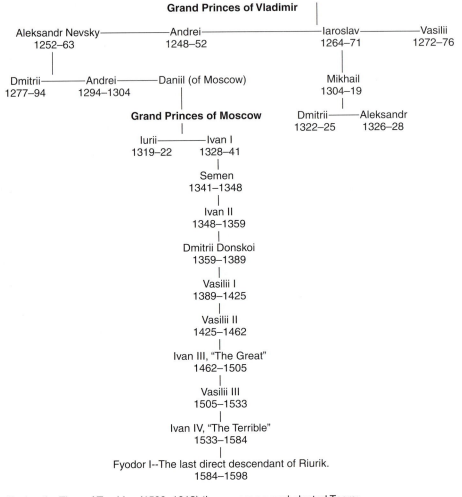

Grand Princes of Vladimir

Aleksandr Nevsky————————Andrei————————————————Iaroslav————————Vasilii
1252–63   1248–52   1264–71   1272–76

Dmitrii————Andrei————Daniil (of Moscow)   Mikhail
1277–94   1294–1304   1304–19

Grand Princes of Moscow   Dmitrii————Aleksandr
                                                        1322–25   1326–28

Iurii————————Ivan I
1319–22   1328–41

Semen
1341–1348

Ivan II
1348–1359

Dmitrii Donskoi
1359–1389

Vasilii I
1389–1425

Vasilii II
1425–1462

Ivan III, "The Great"
1462–1505

Vasilii III
1505–1533

Ivan IV, "The Terrible"
1533–1584

Fyodor I--The last direct descendant of Riurik.
1584–1598

During the Time of Troubles (1598–1613) there were several elected Tsars:
Boris Godunov, 1598–1605

Fyodor II (Godunov), 1605
Dmitrii II (The First "False Dmitrii"), 1605–6
Vasilii IV (Shuiskii), 1606–10

 The Time of Troubles was brought to an end with the election of Michael Romanov to be Tsar by a Zemskii Sobor in 1613.

THE ROMANOVS

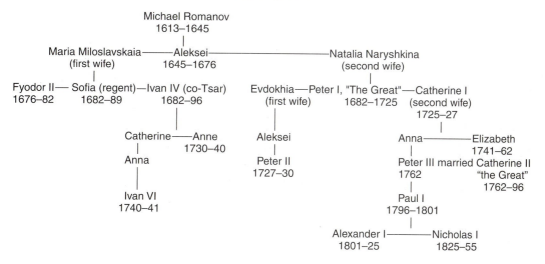

GLOSSARY

Barshchina   (баршина). Labor obligations owed by serfs to their landlord.

Black land/black people.   In Kiev Rus and the early centuries of Muscovy, "black land" referred to land that was not owned by a private (noble) landowner. Farmers, known as "black people," treated the land as their private property.

Black clergy/white clergy.   In the Russian Orthodox Church, parish priests, known as the "white clergy" must be married; they are not eligible for appointment to positions in the Church hierarchy. Monks, bishops, archbishops, and other church officials, known as the "black clergy" are celibate.

Bobyl   (бобыль). Rural residents in the pre-Petrine era who owned only a cottage with no land other than a garden plot and earned their livings as paid agricultural laborers.

Boiar   (боярь). The term boiar had been used in Kiev Rus to refer to the wealthiest elite, and this usage continued in the Northeast. The Moscow boiars were the ruling class until the end of the Muscovite period.

Commune/mir   The *mir*, also known as the commune, refers to the self-governing peasant village. Although the mir was typically stratified by wealth, the peasant community consistently presented a united front against the outside world of government officials and merchants. One of the remarkable features of the Russian mir was its practice of periodically redistributing land based on the number of able-bodied workers in each household.

Cossack   (The term comes from *kazakh,* a Turkic word meaning "free man" and implying "free-booter.") The first Cossacks (in the fifteenth century) were probably renegade bands of Crimean Tatars who fled the Crimean Khan and hired themselves out to Muscovite and Lithuanian princes as border guards. They paid allegiance to no ruler and they lived under their own laws. They were joined by peasants fleeing oppressive conditions in Russia and Poland-Lithuania, and ultimately the Cossacks became identified as Slavic-speaking believers in Eastern Orthodoxy. Cossack communities were relatively egalitarian and elected their leaders. When not in active service as mercenaries, Cossacks were farmers, growing grain, raising cattle, and keeping bees. They were also traders and raiders.

Druzhina   (дружина). At the beginning of the Viking invasion of Kiev Rus, the band of followers of Viking leaders who levied tribute on East Slavic cities was referred to as the druzhina. The druzhina, by accepting members of the Slavic wealthy elite, served as the principal institution by which the Slavs and Vikings merged into one society.

Dvorianstvo   (дворянство). Peter the Great consolidated the various privileged strata of Russian society into a single noble class with common rights and obligations (most often referred to as the gentry). The most distinctive obligations were to become educated and to serve the state in the military or in the government; the most distinctive privileges were exemptions from the poll tax and from corporal punishment.

Guberniia   (губерния). When Peter I divided Russia into provinces, he chose the Latin term guberniia to name them.

Gymnasium   Gymnasia were secondary, college-preparatory schools, which emphasized Greek and Latin, and were the preserve of the nobility. (Compare with **realschule**.)

Iarlyk   (ярлік) In the period of Mongol overlordship of the Rus, a *iarlyk* was an official document that granted a right or exemption to a person or institution. When capitalized, the Iarlyk refers to the patent given to the Grand Prince of Vladimir that confirmed the fact that the Khan recognized that individual as the legitimate head of the Rurikovichi and senior prince of the Rus.

Inner Eurasia   Refers to the subregion of northern Eurasia bounded in the west by the Carpathian Mountains and the Pripet Marshes and bounded in the south by the Black Sea, the Caucasus Mountains, the Caspian Sea, and the series of complex mountain ranges that extend eastward to the Pacific Ocean.

Intelligentsia   A segment of Russia's educated elite in the imperial period that thought independently and critically of the government. The intelligentsia was typified by its idealism and selflessness, and its tendency to adopt the most progressive and radical trends from western Europe. The intelligentsia provided the members of Russia's revolutionary parties, from *Zemlia i Volia* to the Bolsheviks, but it also included educated people, especially writers and journalists, and professionals not employed by the government.

Kabala slavery   One became a kabala slave by accepting a loan of money and working as an unpaid laborer until the debt was paid. Kabala slavery was not particularly onerous; it ended when the debt was paid or the master died, slave status was not inherited by children, and the master could not mistreat, give away, or sell his or her kabala slaves.

Legislative assembly   A legislative assembly, summoned by Catherine the Great to codify Russia's laws, met in 1767. It included representatives from the administration, nobility, industrialists, merchants, state peasants, Cossacks, and non-Slavic peoples. Though it met for more than a year and held over two hundred committee meetings, the legislative assembly failed to write a single law. Instead, the delegates used the assembly as a forum in which to express their grievances.

Mestnichestvo   (местничество) In Muscovite society, *mestnichestvo* was a ranking system for the aristocracy that assigned rank in a hierarchy based on the status of one's clan, one's seniority within the clan, and one's length of service to the Tsar. Mestnichestvo originated in a system for assigning seats at court ceremonies but was extended to civil and military appointments as well. No one could be asked to serve under a noble who ranked lower in the mestnichestvo hierarchy. Mestnichestvo was abolished in 1682.

Mir   See Commune/mir.

Nakaz   (наказ) When Catherine the Great summoned the Legislative Assembly she wrote a nakaz (instruction) which set down the principles she wished them to follow in codifying Russian law. Catherine was strongly influenced by the ideas of the Enlightenment thinkers, particularly Montesquieu. (See **Legislative assembly**.)

Non-possessors   (See **Possessors/Non-possessors**.)

Obrok   (оброк) Cash obligations owed by serfs to their landlord.

Old ritualists/old believers   refers to that segment of the Russian Church that refused to accept the reforms of the Patriarch Nikon in the 1650s. Despite aggressive persecution and discrimination, Old Ritualist communities have survived in Russia until the present day. (See **Schism in the Russian Church**.)

Oprichnina/zemshchina   (опричнина/земшина) Between 1564 and 1572, Ivan IV created two administrative systems within the Muscovite state. Special regions (the *oprichnina*, meaning "set apart") were to be ruled by Ivan personally; the remainder of the territory of Muscovite Russia, called the zemshchina, was left for the boiars to rule. Within the oprichnina, Ivan's agents, oprichniks, were not subject to the laws and procedures of the Muscovite state. The oprichniks, numbering about six thousand at their height, began a reign of terror—murdering, torturing, and confiscating land. In 1572, Ivan eliminated the oprichnina and brought the terror to an end

Panslavs   Adapted many of the ideas of the Slavophiles to the materialism and Realpolitik of the second half of the nineteenth century. They used the notion of Slavic racial unity to justify their demand that Russia should liberate the Southern Slavs from Ottoman rule. (See **Slavophiles**.)

Pomestie/pomeshchik (поместве/помещик) A *pomestie* was a piece of land that was granted by the Grand Prince (later the Tsar) of Moscow in exchange for service. When Ivan III first began to make pomestie grants, the recipient (called a *pomeshchik*) could possess the land only while in active service, and when he retired, the land was given to another servitor. As time went on, however, it became customary for a son to inherit his father's pomestie. Finally, in 1714 the legal distinction between the pomestie and votchina was eliminated, and pomesties became private property. (See **votchina/votchinnik.**)

Posadnik (посадник) In Kiev Rus, the *posadnik* was a governor who handled the day-to-day administration of the city on behalf of the prince.

Possessors/non-possessors In the sixteenth century, there were two schools of thought within the Russian Orthodox Church regarding the possession of wealth. "Possessors," considered the ownership of land as essential to the work of the church in providing for the spiritual and social welfare of the people. "Nonpossessors," on the other hand, considered wealth to be a spiritual danger to the church and called for monks to return to lives of poverty.

Prikaz (приказ) The basic institution of the Muscovite central government was the *prikaz* (bureau). A prikaz was directed by a state secretary and staffed by lesser secretaries and scribes; it dealt with a single administrative function, such as supervising the postal system, suppressing banditry, coordinating military forces, and registering pomestie estates.

Raznochintsy (разночины) Raznochintsy, "people of various ranks. This referred to people who didn't fit into the officially recognized categories of Russian society. In the reign of Peter I, it referred mostly to retired soldiers and lower-ranking officials who had not advanced far enough in the **Table of Ranks** to have earned noble status. After 1818, *raznochintsy* also referred to the children of those who had achieved personal noble status. By the middle of the century, it was used to refer to anyone who had gained an education and earned a living through mental labor but was not of noble blood.

Realschules These were high schools on the German model, which taught modern science, math, and technical subjects, and which were favored by the more practical non-noble classes. (Compare with **gymnasium**).

Rurikovichi (Рюриковичи) The Primary Chronicle tells that in 862 the Slavic tribes invited the "Varangian Rus" to rule over them and provide law and order. Three brothers, the eldest of whom was Rurik, agreed to rule the Slavs. All subsequent ruling princes in Kiev Rus and Muscovy (the *Rurikovichi* or descendents of Rurik) traced their ancestry back to Rurik. The line of Rurikovichi came to an end in 1598, when Ivan IV's last son, Fyodor died without an heir.

Schism in the Russian Church In the 1650s, the Russian Patriarch Nikon introduced changes in the traditional liturgy and ritual of the church (the spelling of Jesus' name, method of making the sign of the cross, etc.) in order to make Russian practice consistent with that of the Greek church. A significant segment of the Russian Church refused to accept these changes, causing a schism in the church. Tens of thousands were killed or committed suicide in the government's attempt to suppress the schismatics. (See **Old Ritualists/Old Believers.**)

Serfs A serf was a peasant, bound to the land, and living under the jurisdiction of a gentry landowner. Although limitation of peasant movement had begun in the fifteenth century, the binding peasants to the land was codified in 1649. Serfdom was ended by the Emancipation of 1861. Although serfs were not considered slaves (the property of landowners), there were no limits on the labor demands that the landowner could exact, and serfs lived under their landlord's legal jurisdiction.

Skhod (сход) The skhod, or village assembly, was composed of all heads of households in the peasant community. The skhod elected village elders and officials and appointed constables and clerks. It judged family and interfamily disputes, and punished immoral behavior and minor violations of the law. It also apportioned taxes, chose conscripts, supervised periodic redistribution of the land, and provided for social welfare.

Slavophiles Refers to Russian intellectuals in the first half of the nineteenth century who, under the influence of the European Romantic movement, attempted to discover true soul of the Russian nation. They found this in the Russian Orthodox Church and the culture of pre-Petrine Muscovy. Slavophiles opposed the secularism, individualism, and materialism of the West (and of Peter the Great), and celebrated the *sobornost* or "organic community" of Muscovite Russia where people had been united by faith and love, valued things of the spirit, and cooperated rather than competed with one another. (Compare with **Westernizers.**)

Sobor (собор) In the Russian Orthodox Church, a Sobor, an elected assembly representing the church hierarchy as well as local parishes, is the highest church authority. It elects the Patriarch, when the office becomes open, and it speaks with final authority on questions of faith.

Starozhiltsy (старожилыцы) In the early Muscovite period, landowners began to attempt to limit the traditional freedom of agriculturalists to move. The first to be denied the right to move were starozhiltsy or "long-time residents."

State peasant After Russian peasants were bound to the land in 1649, those peasants who lived on land that was not owned by private landowners or the royal family were known as state peasants. Like **serfs,** they were bound to the land and could not move without permission, but unlike serfs, state peasants were self-governing and owed no obligations to private landlords.

Strigolniki (стригольники) The *Strigolniki* made up a movement in the Russian Orthodox Church in the fourteenth century that accused the clergy of greed, objected to the practice of offering prayers in exchange for money, and protested against the practice of bishops charging a fee to ordain priests. They were suppressed by the Church and had disappeared by the middle of the fifteenth century.

Sudebnik (судебник) **of 1497** Ivan III's Sudebnik of 1497 was the first code of laws for the Rus since Iaroslav's Russkaia Pravda. It provided legal norms for theft, murder, land ownership, and slavery, but its main concern was to standardize legal procedures and fees, providing income for the government. Most justice continued to be resolved between individuals according to customary law.

Table of Ranks In 1722, in imitation of a recently enacted Prussian standardization of ranks, Peter issued a "Table of Ranks" to clarify the order of precedence among the wealthy elite. The Table of Ranks created three parallel hierarchies: civil administration, army, and navy. (For example, the highest level included, respectively, chancellor, general-field marshal, and general-admiral, while level fourteen, the entry level, included collegiate registrar, ensign, and midshipman.) At each level, the military ranks had precedence over the civilian.

Taiga The ecological zone just south of the **tundra.** It consists primarily of evergreen conifers but with some stands of birch and alder and occasional swamps and peat bogs. The taiga is home to a variety of small fur-bearing animals (including sable, squirrel, marten, and fox) and to elk, bear, muskrat, and wolf. The soils of the taiga are thin, acidic, and not conducive to agriculture.

Terem (терем) In the reign of Ivan IV, women in wealthy families began to be segregated from men. Women's living quarters, called the terem, were often built separately from the house in which the adult men of the family lived. Even among the poorer classes who could not afford such arrangements, women ate separately from men. This practice was brought to an end by Peter the Great.

Tundra The northernmost ecological region of Eurasia. It is a cold, flat land lying along the Arctic coast. The extreme cold (summer temperatures are rarely higher than 40° F, winter temperatures rarely higher than −25° F) and low rainfall (an average of 15 inches a year) permits only a very simple food web. Vegetation is sparse and predominantly composed of mosses, lichens, grasses, and low shrubs. Lemmings, hares, ptarmigan, migratory geese, and reindeer live off the vegetation, and they, in turn, are preyed upon by foxes, wolves, and snowy owls.

Tysatskii (тысяцкнй) In Kiev, the tysatskii, or military commander, headed the citizens' militia. Over time this position came to serve as a spokesperson for the common people.

Uezd (уезд) *Guberniias* (provinces) were divided into *uezds*. The U.S. equivalent would be a county.

Ulozhenie (уложение) **of 1649** The Ulozhenie (law code) of 1649 was promulgated by Tsar Aleksei. It incarnated Aleksei's policy of alliance with the landed elite to rule the landless, making all social estates (noble, merchant, peasant, etc.) hereditary, and by binding peasants to the land. Landless artisans and workers in cities and towns were also forbidden to move without permission.

Veche   (вече) In Kiev Rus, each principal city had an assembly of all free males called a veche. Little is known about the veche; it is mentioned in the *Chronicles* only during times of crisis when townspeople protested policies of or demanded action by the prince, but it appears that the veche could represent the political will of the people. On occasion the veche refused to accept the appointment of a particular prince.

Volost   (волость) The most fundamental division of political administration was the volost. The US equivalent would be a township.

Zemshchina   (See **Oprichnina/Zemshchina.**)

Votchina/votchinnik   (вотчина/вотчинник) A *votchina* was a piece of land that the owner owned outright and which could be sold and bequeathed. In the beginning, possession of a votchina entailed no obligation to serve the ruler. This right was gradually rescinded as the Grand Prince of Moscow increased in power, and in 1556 Ivan IV made the obligations of votchinniks and pomeshchiks equal. (See **pomestie/pomeshchik.**)

Westernizers   A trend within the nineteenth century intelligentsia who approved of the reforms of Peter the Great and wanted Russia to continue the Enlightenment project of education, institutional reform, and constitutional government. (Compare with **Slavophiles.**)

White clergy   (see **Black clergy/white clergy**).

Zemskii sobor   (земский собор) A zemskii sobor, "assembly of the land," was a general meeting of boiars, church leaders, lesser nobility and important merchants called by the Muscovite Tsar. In the beginning they were not elective (generally they included whichever notable people happened to be in Moscow at the time), and they were not legislative institutions; Ivan IV, who first called them, used them more to express his opinion and ask for support than to solicit advice. Aleksei (1645– 76) was the last Tsar to summon a zemskii sobor.

Zemstsvo   (земство) As a part of the Great Reforms of the 1860s, *zemstvos* were created to provide for limited local self-government. They were established at both the county and provincial level and were given the responsibility for general economic development and social welfare. Zemstvo boards maintained roads and bridges, built prisons, hospitals, and schools, and promoted industry, commerce, and agriculture.

INDEX